MAP OF THE DOMINIONS of the House of GORKHA

Scale of Miles

0   50   100   150   200

From Hamilton's 'Account of Nepal' 1816

GORKHA

THE STORY OF THE GURKHAS OF NEPAL

1. *The Annapurna Range from the North*

GORKHA

THE STORY OF THE GURKHAS OF NEPAL

———— ❄ ————

Lieutenant-General
SIR FRANCIS TUKER
K.C.I.E., C.B., D.S.O., O.B.E.

CONSTABLE & COMPANY LIMITED
10 ORANGE STREET · LONDON · WC2

LONDON
PUBLISHED BY
Constable and Company Ltd
10–12 ORANGE STREET W.C.2

·

CANADA
Longmans, Green and Company
TORONTO

·

SOUTH *and* EAST AFRICA
Longmans, Green and Company Ltd
CAPETOWN   NAIROBI

·

AUSTRALIA
Walter Standish and Sons
SYDNEY

First published 1957

PRINTED   IN GREAT BRITAIN BY ROBERT MACLEHOSE AND CO. LTD
THE UNIVERSITY PRESS GLASGOW

FOREWORD

GORKHA is a village in the Himalaya. Humble as it is, it is the home of the Gurkha people.

The history of every nation is moulded by some predominant feature, the sea, the stark desert, its position on a rich trade route or vital military approach, and so on. The history of the Gurkhas has been moulded by the excluding mountains which have through the ages cradled this people, and by the fever-raddled barrier of the low-lying, swampy, forested Terai.

I speak of the 'history of the Gurkhas' rather than of 'the history of Nepal' where the Gurkhas live, because the two, as this short account will show, have only become synonymous during the past two hundred years. This work is therefore devoted in the main to the years from A.D. 1742 when the Gurkhas first emerged into history. Before that time they were an unknown clan dotted about the alpine village of Gorkha, within an obscure tribe lying *to the West* of what was then known to the Hon'ble East India Company, to the Moghul Emperors at Delhi, and to its neighbour, the Nawab Vizier of Oudh, as Nepal. Here was a lush green valley four thousand feet up in the Himalaya mountains, peopled by a Mongoloid race of Newars, part Buddhist and part Hindu, with a civilisation and culture of their own stretching far back through the centuries into the twilight where history and legend strive to prevail.

Nepal, as the British left her in 1947, was the independent kingdom of the Gurkhas, a slab of land five hundred and twenty miles long by some hundred broad, from Sikkim to the Kali River, its boundary with Kumaon. It marches with Tibet along the highest of the eternal snows and with India along the lower mountains, the toes of the Grand Himalaya, with the Terai cut out of India from below Darjeeling to the Gandak River, as a foothold on the plains. She was an ally of Great Britain, an often proven comrade on the battlefields of the world and a sure support in every crisis. Her people have shown a veneration for the British Crown, and a selfless devotion to the British cause which can hardly be matched by any one race to another in the whole history of the world. Yet never have their King and their people been more than allies of the British: always they have been a sovereign and independent people so far as the British have been concerned. Why they should have thus treated us is something of a mystery. Why a Gurkha soldier should speak of the

British Crown as 'Our King' or 'Our Queen' is not easy for most others to understand. This book will attempt an explanation and will at least recount how history brought the two races together and how each served the other: and it will tell who the Gurkhas really are and by what means they came to reign supreme over half a thousand miles of hills, mountains, valleys and twisting rivers of the high Himalaya, a small, warlike people who, in defence of their own independence, have for two centuries shielded India from the swelling power of Tartaric Asia.

The End-papers map of 1816 shows from left to right Kangra, the Twelve Lordships, Sirmoor, Garhwal, Kumaon and Yumilla (Jumla), the Baisia (twenty-two) Rajahs, Malebum and the Chaubisia (twenty-four) Rajahs, Gorkha (Gurkha), Nepal and Makwanpore, Khatang (Kiranti), Sikkim, Bhotan. Running along the whole southern extent are the lands of the independent Sikh King, the Lion of the Punjab, Ranjit Singh; the possessions of the Sovereign Nawab Vizier of Oudh, and the territories of the Company.

The Gurkha authority was never exerted over the Dogra state of Kangra and only for a short while over Sikkim, so it is with the peoples between the two that we are mostly concerned and, of these, our attention naturally turns at once to the region with the most ancient known history, Nepal. Up to the time of the Gurkha eruption in 1768 the history of this whole wide area is only the history of this one valley, the Valley of Nepal: this volume is simply an account, as mingled as their criss-cross ravines and mountains, of the origins, the petty strife and the fusion of the clans who were the fighting men of the Gurkha nation whose infantry is a byword for gallantry and battle-skill in the world today. These clans, or sects, are the Limbus, Rais, Sunwars, and Lepchas, the Khas or Chettri, the Magars and Gurungs, salted with the most typical specimens of the Gurkha, the Thakurs or squirearchy, the hereditary aristocrats of Nepal, blood descendants of her highland lairds, ranking above all others except the Brahmans.

The spelling 'Gorkha' and 'Gorkhali' was usual up to recent times and is, in fact, the correct spelling, now again adopted by the present Indian Army for its 'Gorkha' regiments. However, as the British adaptation 'Gurkha' and 'Gurkhali', is more usual, I will employ that spelling throughout this present history, except for the town itself which, to distinguish it from the clansmen, will be spelt 'Gorkha'.

The chronicler slights a people's legends and traditions at his peril for, as often as not, they are founded on fact. In compiling this account of the Gurkhas, I have, as far as I know, given full weight to their own tradi-

viii

tional beliefs and, where there is doubt, have chosen that account which I have found to be the most likely. There is one factor which confuses all who try to fit together the history of Nepal and the Gurkhas, and it is that their method of computing dates was altered several times, in the carefree manner that one would associate with these mountaineers. Thus, Captain Kirkpatrick, who visited Nepal in 1793, the first Englishman to do so, recorded from what he was there told the dates of the kings' reigns. A typical statement was that a King Yellung Kherraut (a Kiranti prince) of Nepal reigned for ninety years and three months, while twenty-five of his successors claimed together 1,581 years and one month, an average of sixty-three years apiece! By checking and cross-checking, European investigators have brought some sort of order into this wilderness so that a reasonably credible tale can be told.

In telling the story of the Gurkha nation of modern Nepal, one cannot avoid starting with some sort of record of the ancient Newar nation who dwelt, and still dwell, in the centre of Nepal — in the Valley of Nepal — who were conquered a short two hundred years ago by the Gurkhas of Western Nepal, and who are now rising once more to political prominence in the country at the expense of those same Westerners, the Gurkhas . . . the pen is asserting itself against the sword. To cover all those thousands of years of Newar history in a few chapters, I have had to select the personalities and the events that were most concerned in the making of the modern Newars and those that have a bearing on the later period of Gurkha supremacy. It has, too, been necessary to weave in the story of the Eastern Nepalese — the Kiranti, the Limbu and the Rai tribes — who were also subjugated by the Gurkhas at about the same time as the Newars, for they are today, by virtue of that conquest, loosely spoken of as Gurkhas.

*   *   *   *   *

Taken all in all, the Gurkha must, for his unusually fine qualities, be nearly unique in the modern world. For this alone the story of his race must be worth telling. Let any enquirer be assured that if he seeks to understand the meaning of courage and selfless devotion, then he should soldier with a Gurkha regiment. He will return an enlightened and a better man from the experience.

CONTENTS

Contents

APPENDICES

ILLUSTRATIONS

Illustrations

The Author is indebted to Major J. O. M. Roberts for Plates 1, 5A, 6, 9, 10, 11, 14A, 14B, 15, 16B; *to Major R. Richardson for Plates* 5B, 7A, 7B, 12, 13A, 13B; *to Captain A. D. Carter for Plate* 8; *to Major P. T. Prentice for Plate* 16A; *to Panora Ltd. for Plate* 18; *and to 2nd Goorkhas Regimental Association for Plate* 17.

MAPS

ACKNOWLEDGEMENTS

FOR the ready help they have afforded me, my thanks are due to Captain R. N. W. Bishop, Major P. T. Prentice, the Presidents and Secretaries of all the Gurkha Regimental Associations, to Colonel G. R. Leonard, to Majors J. O. M. Roberts and P. Richardson and to Captain A. D. Carter for surpassingly fine photographs, to the Editor of *The Kukri* for permission to reproduce those already published; and to the Librarian and Staff of the India Office Library who have taken infinite trouble to find me answers to my many queries and to discover and send me so many books and documents.

For some important passages in later chapters I am indebted to the pages of *The Economist*.

The manuscript has been read by Mr. John Morris and Colonel Andrew Mercer whom I have to thank for their useful suggestions.

I

Nepal: Land of the Gurkhas

———————— ❈ ————————

At the end of this book there is a map. The shaded parts are those outer provinces which were under the authority of the Nepalese sovereign in his heyday until 1816, when British power exerted itself to set a limit to his ambitions. By the Treaty of Segouli he ceded Sikkim, Kumaon, Garhwal, and the Terai to the west of the Gandak River, the shaded territories. If a name is wanted, then the kingdom in the first few years of the nineteenth century up to 1816 may be called Greater Nepal. Nepal of today includes all the unshaded portion and the Terai from the Gandak River westwards to the Sarda River. Up to 1768 the country spoken of as Nepal was, as often as not, just the Nepal Valley, and it had been known at times that the King of Nepal only reigned over one of the City States of the Valley — Kathmandu, Bhatgaon or Patan — and no more. When men spoke of Nepal in olden times, they meant the Nepal Valley. It is only since 1768 that the Kingdom has been expanded, by warlike kings leading warrior clans of highlanders, to include the wide regions of today, five hundred and twenty miles long and about one hundred miles deep, from the Sarda, a tributary of the Ganges, to Sikkim, with a population of over eight millions.

Kathmandu has been the recognised capital of Nepal since 1768. It is a considerable town mostly built of wood, of many temples, and has been for centuries a market and trading centre.

The northern and southern borders of Nepal settle themselves: they should be nowhere else. The northern lies along the eternal snows of the Grand Himalaya, at 16,000 to 29,000 feet, with such towering peaks as Kanchanjunga, Makalu, Everest, Nanda Devi and a dozen more mounting up into the clouds. The southern is at the foot of the hills looking across the Indian plains, with a narrow belt of the Terai about twenty miles wide, partly of sal forest and partly of cultivation, lying along the south side of a low range of sandstone hills, the Churiaghati, and seething with the malignant *awal* fever.* Eastward the boundary is with the State of Sikkim, westward it is at the borders of the Indian district of Kumaon.

Ever since the East India Company came into contact with the mountain kingdom two hundred years ago, up till 1947, when India was given her independence, the Nepalése saw to it that all Europeans, except a favoured few who were from time to time invited by the Court, were excluded from the country. The movements of even those few were strictly confined to the Valley of Nepal. Only very occasionally and with special permission were any of these privileged Europeans permitted to travel in the country. The result is that in describing Nepal, reliance has had to be placed on information given by the natives themselves or on Asian travellers. This exclusiveness is by no means entirely a policy of modern times. Nepalese rulers have never gone out of their way to make things easy for those who would come up from India: they were far too jealous of their position and far too well aware of the rapacity of their cousins on the plains below. The Nepalese made no attempt whatever to improve the rocky, steep, narrow footpaths on which sweating porters carried anything from rice to the bits and pieces of motor-cars and steam rollers, from Bimphedi, over the Chandragiri highland down to Kathmandu.

Piece by piece, despite lack of personal exploration, a fairly sufficient picture has been built up, but there is still much more to be known. In these days the 'much more' is of course the character, quality, location and extent of Nepal's mineral deposits Various reasons have been given for the banning of Europeans and the obvious one is the best, namely, that the rulers feared that, if too much were known of their country, it would fall into the clutches of the British power, expanding fast and inexorably across the face of India. The people of Nepal are intensely patriotic and have a deep love of their mountain home, just as it is, however primitive, however 'undeveloped' and however 'backward'.

Another reason, advanced some thirty years ago, is given by Landon from a conversation he had with the Prime Minister of Nepal, Maharajah Chandra Shamsher. Said the Maharajah, 'My friend, the English have at times difficulty with the government of India. Those difficulties arise in no small measure from the fact that in these easy days of travel all English Sahibs are not Sahibs. Now I am convinced that the prosperity of Nepal is bound up with the maintenance of British predominance in India, and I am determined that the sahib who is no sahib shall never enter Nepal and

* Referred to as 'the deadly miasmata' by a British chronicler of 1850.

weaken my people's belief that every Englishman is a gentleman.' Landon, later on, speaking of the Sherpas of Nepal who helped British climbers on Mount Everest, writes, '. . . Odell's very gallant rescue of a small body of these men from a height of nearly 27,000 feet, when they had fallen exhausted and were waiting for death, will never be forgotten by their kinsmen.' It is no insignificant thing that the relations between British and Gurkha, civilian or soldier, have from the beginning exhibited the natural devotion of the men of both races for each other.

This exclusion of Europeans, which grew stricter as the contacts between the two powers grew closer, was not only insisted upon by the Gurkha State but also, as strictly or more strictly, by the British Government of India, in deference to Nepalese feelings and in order that that country should not suffer prematurely from contact with 'modern civilisation'. It is a mistaken idea and a rather conceited one, prevalent among those who claim to be progressive, that other people cannot be contented, happy or 'fulfil themselves' under an autocratic régime — the more inefficient, often the better for its subjects. These democrats cannot believe that, up to 1947, most of the inhabitants of Nepal were happy in their simple circumstances and, what is more, respected their rulers, the Maharajah and his Rana relatives, and wished to continue to live under them. Happiness is not necessarily the companion of modern sanitation and the vote, nor is honesty necessarily to be got from listening to radio or reading the daily newspaper. In fact, if we were to judge by the Gurkha soldier, then we would conclude that mankind is happiest and most honest where these civilising influences are least.

Permission to shoot and explore among the lesser folk of the Terai was readily granted and sportsmen and archaeologists paid frequent visits to that fever-ridden strip in the cold season when the mosquito was inactive. But the highlands have remained very much of an unknown land to the British, simply because they respected the scruples of the kings and their people. They would have given much to hunt the great sheep, the Ovis Ammon, the thar, the burral, the red bear and the snow leopard, as they hunted tiger and, sometimes, rhinoceros among the swamps of the Terai.

Strategically and politically Nepal was, of course, with Tibet, in the position of a buffer between China and British India. It must be remembered that in 1792 the Chinese Tartar General, the Duke Fu Kang'an, brought one army through Tibet and the Himalaya to within ten miles of Kathmandu and another through Sikkim to within hail of Darjeeling. Though victorious, he retired — was, in fact, compelled to retire by the hammering the Gurkhas had given him and by the onset of the snow

3

which was closing behind him those terrible passes through the Himalaya. Though the Chinese might raid, they could not stay: the high country was too much for them.

Nepal steps down sharply in its whole length from the 25,000 and 29,000 feet above the sea of its Himalayan border to the two thousand feet or so of the foothills, looking down in turn to the almost zero of the flat Terai. Tracks there are, running across the grain of the country from east to west, but very tortuous ones, the most important being that from Darjeeling in Bengal to Pithoragarh in Kumaon, over five hundred miles away. This track wanders through passes up to nearly 7,000 feet as it winds down into Kathmandu, over the hills to Gorkha and on through Dailekh. It is a fairly well-trodden route. To us in this story its interest lies in the direct link it affords between Gorkha and Kathmandu: for centuries past the two States have thus been brought closer together.

Some account of the stupendous passes between Tibet and Nepal will interest those who have a romantic failing for mountains. The descriptions given by Christian priests* who have in the past endured the terrors of this passage will freeze the marrow of the less adventurous. Landon writes, using Sylvain Lévi's translation of Father Georgi's narrative of his journey in the mid-eighteenth century through the Kuti Pass from Tibet into Nepal, '. . . the very narrow track lies along the edge of precipices and is continually turning the corners of extremely lofty mountains. Often the yawning gulfs between the rocks are bridged by narrow and trembling constructions of stick and undergrowth. The traveller shudders to see underneath him immense sheer precipices and to hear the noise of the water tumbling at the bottom among the stones. There is one specially difficult point which reduces timid or inexperienced men to terror, and the more they fear, the greater is the risk of a fall. Here a prominent rock about sixteen feet long slopes downwards over an abyss, and is the more slippery for the dripping waters which continually wash and polish it. It is true that holes have been hacked out upon its surface where the traveller is able to place, if not his entire foot, at least the ball of it; but Father Georgi does not seem to think that this much reduces the terrors of the passage. The river Nohotha is spanned by iron chains. Here people cross in safety upon the footway of the bridge grasping, on the right hand and on the left, two cables which are riveted into the rock at each end, but the oscillations of this rough bridge are fearful — especially when there is added to them the vibration caused when several persons are passing at the same time out of step. Then . . . one can scarcely endure the terror . . .

* Capuchins expelled from Lhassa by the Chinese Emperor.

farther on is Khangsa. . . . Once more the fathers encountered a wretched and dangerous path, worse even than that of the day before. There were no less than twenty-nine gangways to cross, and the mountainside to which they clung in desperation was as dizzy as ever, and the hazards more numerous.'

Father Marc reported that, so terrible is the crossing by some of the chain bridges, that many travellers are blindfolded and bound to a plank, which is slung to the cables and manoeuvred across by a local expert.*

An Indian traveller's description of this pass is no more comforting. He maintains that it is one of the most perilous in the whole Himalaya. The track cuts through a terrible gorge, crossing the river fifteen times. The rocky cliffs of the gigantic chasm are so close together that at one place a bridge of only twenty-four paces spans it. In another, the track runs along a perpendicular wall of rock. It is of stone slabs covered with earth, only eighteen inches wide, and climbs thus for a third of a mile fifteen hundred feet starkly above a raging torrent.

Kuti village is about 14,000 feet above the sea, not so very high as Himalayan villages go.

When one ponders these descriptions, one sympathises with the noted Chinese travellers of the seventh century A.D. who, rather than face the then utterly barbarous people of Tibet and these horrid passes, preferred the toils of the Gobi Desert, Central Asia and the Khyber Pass for their journeys to India.

Georgi tells us that the Jalap-La Pass in Sikkim was the easiest route from India to Tibet. It is still the easiest route and is commonly known as the Chumbi Valley route.

It is almost a tradition to believe that the passes from Tibet into Nepal are so difficult as to be virtually impenetrable. Admittedly in winter, from January to March, when the heavy snow lies on the higher passes, it is not feasible to travel that way but there are others which are very seldom snowbound and there are passes by which Tibetans bring their salt on laden yaks, and Nepalese, perhaps more hard-working or less addicted to labour-saving devices, carry rice by human porterage out of their country into Tibet. It is worth while to see what a few of the better-known passes have to offer. There is the Nangpa La just west of Mt. Everest. This takes the traveller from Namcha Bazar to Rongbuk: it is 19,000 feet high and is barely practicable for any sort of commerce. Then there is the Popti-La, which is only about 14,000 feet high; it is in normal seasons a commercial route of sorts, though authentic accounts of the retreat of the Gurkha

* *Nepal*, by Perceval Landon.

5

Army by this way in 1792, before the Chinese advance, show that snow blizzards can render it dangerous. The Kuti Pass Father Georgi has already described for us: a mountaineer would not find it as daunting as the Father, but it is difficult, for its highest point is 17,000 feet and pack animals find the narrow passage impracticable. The Kirong Pass is easy: laden animals carrying salt from the Lakes of Changtong in Tibet pass freely back and forth and large herds of sheep are driven down this track to the slaughter houses of Nepal. It is only 6,000 feet at the frontier and thence rises fairly gently to its greatest height of 9,000 feet in Tibet. The Chinese army invaded Nepal by this route in 1792, for it is the best route to the capital at Kathmandu. Further west there is the pass at the head of the Buria Gandaki River: this is in most seasons a fairly easy passage. Then there is the pass running up from the Kali Gandaki River by holy Muktinath and Mastang: this is quite a reasonable route for by it come the salt-laden yaks, the sumpter mules, donkeys and horses for Western Nepal. West again one leaves the Marsiangdi or the Buddhi Gandak River by the Larkaya Pass, over which again the laden yaks pass at 17,000 feet.

As a guide to distances, the village of Kirong is one hundred miles from Kathmandu, and Kuti is ninety miles.

These are some of the ways by which the present inhabitants of Nepal entered from their grazing grounds in Tibet and by which the flow of immigrants was maintained until the settlers decided it was time that they called a halt to this reinforcement.

There is every reason to support Brian Hodgson's opinion of 1831, 'It is only necessary to observe the due season for passing the Himalaya, and there is no physical obstacle to apprehend; so that the journey from Kathmandu to Peking may be surely accomplished in five months, allowing for fifteen days of halts . . . the Nepalese have used the Chinese commerce *via* Tibet for ages, and our Indian subjects might deal in concert with Nepalese by joint firms in Kathmandu.'

But Sikkim, the Jalap-La and the Chumbi Valley route have been preferred, one good and sufficing reason being that the British in India provided easy and efficient access by rail and then by road far into Sikkim, while the Nepalese government has as yet provided nothing more than existed in Hodgson's day except a meagre, rather primitive little railway from Raxaul to Amlekhganj, and a short stretch of motor road thence to join the bridle track that runs from the foot of the hills to Thankote near Kathmandu. From neglect and from ignorance of the tracks out from Kathmandu into Tibet, the legend has grown up of their impassable nature and of the strategic and political security that Nepal is supposed to enjoy from this illusion. This buffer state is now tight up against a Chinese Communist Tibet and is one of the most tender of the frontier problems of the world, particularly when related to that of Kashmir. If for no other reason, an understanding of its history and people has become profitable to anyone interested in international affairs.

There are four great rivers in Nepal; in the west, the Karnali, better known in India as the Gogra: in the middle, the Gandak, then the Baghmati in the Valley of Nepal itself: and, easternmost of all, the Kosi. These rivers are squeezed out by lofty mountain ranges branching as huge spurs southwards from the main east and west Himalayan system. The basins of these rivers and their tributaries provide the four divisions of the country. The Gogra basin represents the Baisia or Twenty-two Lordships: twenty-two little states in the hills. The Gandak basin contains the Twenty-four Lordships, among which was that of Gorkha, the most famous of all, from which the title of this book is taken. Both the Twenty-Two and the Twenty-Four Lordships were nominally subordinate to the Rajah of Jumla but, in fact, riotously independent of him except when it suited them. The Baghmati waters the densely populated Valley of Nepal, the heart of the country and of its history. In the Valley are the very ancient towns of Kathmandu (Kantipura), Patan and Bhatgaon, noted places of pilgrimage for Buddhists and Hindus. About the Kosi is the Kiranti civilisation, Khambus, Limbus, Yakkas, Rais.

The Valley of Nepal is 4,500 feet above the sea and but three hundred square miles in area. About it on all sides is a circle of hills from 500 to near 5,000 feet above the Valley. The southerly edge is formed by Mount Chandragiri, over which goes the road leading to the plains of India. Between Mahabharat and Chandragiri the sacred river Baghmati breaks out on its way to the Ganges, taking off the whole drainage of the Valley. The population is about 400,000. Every inch is intensively cultivated; villages, hamlets, farmsteads dot the plain.

The rainfall is high, about sixty inches, most of which falls in the monsoon period from early June to late September. December nights are frosty, so that the Court and its establishments used to move for the winter to Nawakote, about fifteen miles north-westwards, where at 2,000 feet above the sea, there is a milder climate. Before summer heat set in, bringing with it into the Nawakote Valley the deadly *awal* fever, the Court moved back to Kathmandu.

Kath-mandu, the building or temple of wood, was a lodging house set up by the king in 1596 for the accommodation of Sadhus, holy men.

7

From that endowment the city takes it name. It is generally composed of a number of open squares or *tol*, paved with brick and tiles, used in most cases as a market, with a maze of narrow streets and alleys all about. It is a dirty town, as one might expect our English towns to have been five hundred years ago. Beside the streets run kennels, stinking, up to a man's knees in slime and refuse. The houses, mostly of wood and brick, are two to four storeys high, tiled, with a marked pagoda influence in the slope of the roofs and the projecting eaves. The greater houses are built about a courtyard, usually a noisome enclosure with domestic animals and fowls on the ground floor. The small, low rooms are chronically overcrowded. The wooden pillars and house fronts are elaborately carved with animals, birds and flowers, figures from Hindu mythology, and grotesques of various characters. The carvings are finely executed and are of considerable artistic merit. These are all of Newar origin, that is to say of the aboriginal and still thriving tribe of the Valley. All are more or less ancient, for the Gurkha masters care little for any of these things.

There are numbers of pagoda-style temples, all heavily ornamented, many with utterly obscene Tantric carvings. No outcaste, that is, none of the Untouchables, is allowed to live within the city boundary.

Outside the city are the parade grounds, such few barracks as there are, and the great, modern, rectangular, white-washed piles, of no particular character, in which lived the erstwhile ruling family of Nepal, the Ranas. They compare ill with the admirable Newar architecture of nearby Kathmandu.

The other two cities, or rather, towns, worthy of notice are Patan and Bhatgaon. Patan is but two miles from Kathmandu, and Bhatgaon but nine miles, so it can be imagined what squabbling and armed bickering went on when each of the three had a 'king' of its own. Patan was formerly essentially a Buddhist city: it preserves many of the relics of that faith, so suffered more cruelly than any other city at the time of the Gurkha invasion of the Valley, when the whole fanatical ferocity of the Hindu Gurkha king was turned upon it. The temples were torn down, its noblemen executed; rubble still disfigures the little town.

Bhatgaon fared better, for it was in the main a Hindu place and its venerable king was more or less of an ally of Gorkha. Kirtipore, three miles west of Patan, was razed to the ground and has never revived. Patan and Kirtipur are still desolate: Bhatgaon is prosperous.

Until 1947, the only roads in the Valley fit for wheeled transport were those about Kathmandu, those connecting the towns I have mentioned, and the road to Thankote at the foot of Chandragiri, from where porters carry their loads out of the Valley and over the hills down to roadhead on the south side where the little metre-gauge Nepalese railway rattles the traffic on to Indian railhead at Raxaul.

To supplement the porters, a wire ropeway, fourteen miles long, was built in 1925 from Dhursing, near Bimphedi, to Khisipidi in the Nepal Valley, rising 4,500 feet and from there dropping 3,500 feet on the Nepalese side.

Since 1947, but never before then, aircraft serve the Valley, landing at an airfield near Kathmandu; a start has been made to cut a motor road through from Bimphedi to Thankote. These, and other 'civilising' innovations are spoken of in Chapter 29.

2

Nepal and the Newars

---------------------------- ❈ ----------------------------

F A R down the ages, in the half-light of history and fable, the Great Manjusri,* the One from Manchuria, made out from Mount Sirshain Maha-
china (China) in the distant north, passed over the flat roof of the Tibetan
plateaux, through the mighty gates of the Himalaya, and descended upon
the Lake Naga Vasa, a fine, blue, oval sheet of water within a closed valley.
He strode along its banks to the southern end, raised high his sword and
ripped the rocks apart,† letting the sacred waters of the Baghmati River
foam out through Mount Mahabharat down upon the plains of India to
join the Ganges below Patna. In the drying Valley, he and his companions
settled: from their loins sprang the Newars, the original inhabitants of
Nepal, a tribe of highly-skilled craftsmen.

Later, as the centuries passed away, so say the Vamshavalis, the
notoriously inaccurate family trees, Ne Muni, an ascetic from India, entered the valley bringing with him a prince of a Gupta line to reign over
the Newars. Such respect did Ne Muni command that the valley was called
after him while the dynasty he founded, his own or the prince's, added
the title of Gupt to their Sanskrit names to mark their descent. Ne-pal,
raised by Ne, cherished of Ne.

Apart from the Gupt titles of these Nepalese rajahs, there is little
foundation for all this outside the traditions and legends of the Newars.
Certainly, the Newars still bear marks of Mongolian origin, both physically, and in their many customs which are similar to those of other races
akin to the Mongols. There is no reason why a Chinese, even a Manchu-
rian, immigration may not have reached the Valley in remote times. That
the Valley was anciently a lake geologists will confirm, and the lake has

* According to Hindus, the God Vishnu.
† Still known as the *Kot-Bar* or 'Sword cut'.

certainly burst its bonds. Nepal is spoken of in the old Hindu writings, in the Mahabharat and in the Tantras as a land of infidels, of impure barbarians.

It has had a long and frequent acquaintance with Indian princes of the Gupta sect. In the fourth century B.C. the Maurya King, Chandragupta, conquered Bihar and Oudh and it is very likely that he stretched his hand out to Nepal, but we have no full record of his conquests. Perhaps Ne Muni did indeed traverse the deep forests of the Terai, cross torrents and climb the tangled hills to Nepal, in company with a chieftain of a Gupta family. Chieftain or priest, he is the patron saint of Nepal and in his time, possibly by himself, a Gupt, Gopala, or cowherd, line of kings was established and Buddhism may at the same time have been introduced into Nepal.

But perhaps the scholars who derive the word 'Nepal' from Chinese or Tibetan sources are right, and it means, 'The land leading to Paradise.' Passing up from the hot, khaki plains of India or down from the snow and rock of Tibet, the cool, green Valley may indeed seem to be on the road to Paradise. To a Hindu from India with his eyes on the height of Mount Kailasa, the Himalayan resort of the gods, their Olympus, it might well claim to be on the way to Heaven.

Doubtless the Newar blood is thickly mingled with that of many a migration and invasion from India. Another account of this people's origin, quite unacceptable to so old a people as the Newars, is that among the soldiery who invaded Nepal with Nanda Deva in the ninth century A.D. were Nair soldiery from southern India and these, settling in the Valley, gave their name to the Newars. Certainly, as Captain Kirkpatrick was quick to observe in 1793, the Newar women had one strange custom in common with their Nair sisters, and it was that they could have as many husbands as they pleased, 'being at liberty to divorce them on the slightest pretence.' It would, however, be rash to suggest that the Newars derive from any one movement from India into the hills: there were many of these incursions and many comings and goings of pilgrims and traders even in historical times. The Newar tongue is related to the Tibetan, a fact that belies any suggestion of an Indian origin.

Yet another story is that during the Muslim supremacy in India, in the thirteenth or fourteenth century A.D., the Rajah of Tirhut* quarrelled with his brother, who went off to Delhi, enlisted the aid of the Emperor,

---

* In Bihar, between Nepal and the Ganges River, it covers roughly the area of the ancient Kingdom of Mithila. The capital was Simraon, Sumraon, or Garh Samaran.

and returned with a powerful Muslim army. The Hindu Rajah, apprised of the approach of an impious host of beef-eaters, resigned his throne to his tutelary deity, Kangkali, and departed for a pilgrimage to all the holy places. Not unnaturally, his subjects deserted Tirhut on their own and set off on an exodus through the hills towards the refuge of Nepal, taking with them the image of Kangkali. On the road they were in danger of perishing from hunger, when Kangkali appeared to one of their chiefs in a dream and told him that in the morning she would provide for them, and gave them permission to use thereafter the kind of food she would send. The next morning there appeared a large herd of buffaloes: the people fell upon them and killed and ate their fill of the flesh that hitherto they had held to be forbidden. They afterwards settled in Nepal and are the people now called Newars, somewhat lax observers of the Hindu faith with a reprehensible addiction to buffalo meat. There is a glimmer of truth in this legend, namely, in the enforced flight of the Indian inhabitants from Tirhut about that time, but no self-respecting person of the ancient Newar race could accept the latter part of such a story.

Taken all in all, the probability is that the Newars of historical times are a tribe that came in from Tibet, or even China, and in the course of time acquired a strong dilution of Indian blood, Indian habits and religions, through invasion and immigration. The Himalayan barrier and the barbarous state of Tibet kept the northern approaches, but from the Indian side, though difficult, the means of access were not too formidable. Thus, the Buddhism which they had themselves received from India and introduced among their Tibetan progenitors has in fact given place to Hinduism with its caste rules, and is year by year yielding ground to the influence of the latter. The Shivamargi are submerging the Buddhamargi. With the coming of the new religion, the Buddhism of the Valley degenerated. It was not long before Hindu influence invited the hitherto celibate monks to take unto themselves wives.

A valley which controls the history of so extensive a country as Nepal might be expected to be of impressive size. It is nothing of the sort, for it is but fifteen miles long by thirteen miles across. An industrious and ingenious race of farmers and artisans, living in an equable climate at over 4,000 feet above the sea has made it what it is, a fertile valley with many temples of pagoda style built mainly of timber, elaborately, albeit often obscenely, carved and ornamented.

Far and wide into Tibet, China and Tartary travelled the craftsmen of Nepal leaving for all time the memorials of their skill in the countries they visited, taking with them the trades, arts and manners of the people

of India from whom they had learnt. Many authorities claim, and probably rightly, that even the pagoda style was introduced from India
among the Newars and not from China or Tibet. This is reasonable if the
Newar contribution is also recognised, for they must at least have developed the style from the less interesting original that was offered to
them. Thus was this small mountain tribe the ambassador of the arts between southern and central Asia. It is a fine tribute that we must pay to
the Newars of Nepal. The achievement is impressive.

Down below the foothills, among the swamps, the forests and the
farms of the Terai, live the Tharus, the very poor relations of the Newars,
an undersized and weedy people who have acquired a strange immunity
from the fearful malarial scourge, known to our forbears as the *ayul*, or
awal, which infests their country. These humble folk have exerted little or
no influence on the history of Nepal.

Historians, among them Captain Kirkpatrick, would have it that the
Newars were a most unwarlike race, but their valiant resistance for
twenty long years in the mid-eighteenth century to the persistent and
ferocious attacks of the Gurkha armies surely belies their detractors. For
their age, civilised, cultured, skilled as architects, builders and craftsmen,
they may have been more wedded to the works of peace than to the arts of
war and so in the end have wearied of warfare and fallen victim to the
more single-minded, lusty and crude tribes, the Parbatiyas or highlanders
of the west, who thrust in again and again across the high hills till the
Valley was theirs and its people enslaved.

Before the time of Ne Muni the Valley had had a long enough history.
A prince of Nepal is supposed to have fought alongside Arjuna in the
great battle of Kurukshetra over three thousand years ago. A trace or two
of real history invades the fables. The Manjusri is said to have brought
with him from China a pious and virtuous man of the name of Dharmakara, known at that time by reason of his high character as 'The
Treasure of the Law'. Dharmakara became the first King of Nepal. With
him came the customs, crafts, commerce and manners of his native land
and these he introduced among the Nepalese.

After Dharmakara there follows a confusion of rajahs and princelings,
many from the outer world, from Bengal and distant Madras. Among the
latter was one Dharmadatta from Conjeveram, twelve hundred miles
away, who stormed into the Valley with an invading army, subdued it and
colonised it with the four castes of Hindus for whom he raised the most
venerated of all its shrines, the temple at Pasupatti.

At last came Ne Muni. With him and his Gopala kings there starts

13

something like coherent Nepalese history. The eighth prince of this dynasty was overthrown by a pastoral tribe from India led by the Ahir, shepherd, chieftain Bhul Singh. Meanwhile a power was rising in the hills five or six days march to the eastward, where the rough highlander, Yalambar, had centuries before subdued the sheep farmers, probably the Lepchas, and installed his tribe, the Kiranti — the Khambu, with their fellow clans, the Yakka and Limbu — always spoken of even in those primitive times as a shockingly barbarian people. Led by Yellung, down they came upon Bhowani Singh, his ploughmen and scholars of the Valley and rolled them under. The Ahirs sank in the flood and the Kiranti ruled in their place. About 250 B.C., during the reign of Stunko, the fourteenth Kiranti King of Nepal, the famous Buddhist Emperor of India, the devout Asoka, grandson of the Maurya King Chandragupta, came to the Valley to visit the haunts of the Gautama Buddha. Asoka's four stupas still stand at Patan. His daughter, Charumati, later made her home in Nepal, then undoubtedly vassal to Asoka, and founded the shrine of Devapatan close by Pasupatti. That Charumati and her Kshattriya husband chose to settle in so remote a place is a tribute to the confidence placed in the protective power of the great Asoka.

At Lumbini, now Rummindei, fifty miles south west of Palpa, the Emperor set up a pillar and inscribed it, 'King Piyadasi (*he thus names himself*), beloved of the Gods, having been anointed twenty years, came in person and worshipped here, saying "Here Buddha, the Sakya ascetic, was born"; and he caused a stone capital in the shape of a horse to be constructed and a stone pillar to be erected, which declares "Here the Blessed One was born". King Piyadasi exempted the village community of Lumbini from taxes, and bestowed wealth upon it.'

The Blessed One was the Gautama Buddha, or Sakya, who journeyed to the Valley in the sixth century B.C.

The Buddhist Chronicle records Asoka's visit thus:

'Asoka, accompanied by the ancient and venerable Upagupta, the recipient of all the knowledge and traditions of the faith, visited Lumbini in great state. With him went four battalions of troops, and the perfumes, flowers and garlands of due worship were not forgotten. Arrived at the garden, Upagupta extended his right hand and said to Asoka, "Here, O great king, the Venerable One was born," adding, "At this site, excellent to behold, should be the first monument consecrated in honour of the Buddha." The king after giving 100,000 golden coins to the people of the country, raised a stupa pillar and retired.'

In accordance with Indian custom, Maya, the mother of Buddha, had been on her way from her husband's capital city of Kapilavastu that her first child might be born in her father's house at Devadaha. Here, she and her maidens rested in a grove of sal trees. She bathed in a pool near by, and, as she started to walk back, the pains came upon her. With her face to the east, grasping the branch of a tree, she gave birth to her child.

The savage Kirantis were in their turn cast out of the Valley back into their hills by yet another Hindu invasion from India. The fifth prince of this new line, Bhaskra Varman, itching for fame, led his mountaineers out through the passes on to the plains of India and, the chroniclers have it, spread confusion and terror as he passed his victorious horde right across India to Sagar and far to the southward. In after years the throne for once passed peacefully to another family, Chettris of the Race of the Sun, Surajbansi Rajputs. Long wrapped in peace, the Newar people pursued their orderly, productive way, reaching the zenith of this dynasty with Mahadeo, the twenty-first prince, a man of personal charm, well-educated and cultured. Under him the arts, literature and commerce flourished as never before, in a Nepalese kingdom which now extended outside the Valley to the eastward and as far to the westward as the Gandak River. The last of these rulers, Shivadeva Varman, had no son so gave his daughter in marriage to one of his Councillors, the *maire du palais*, a Vaisya Thakur of pure Rajput descent named Amsu Varman, probably from Oudh in India.

As Shivadeva's reign drew to a close and the sixth century A.D. passed into the seventh, confusion, distress and civil turmoil possessed the Valley. This luckless prince seems to have divided his realm into fiefs which he granted to his relatives, withdrawing into a monastery and a life of contemplation, from which he in turn hurried back to the fleshpots and bickerings he had left behind him. His return failed to restore order before death removed him. Another cause to confound the confusion was probably the spread of lawlessness in eastern India and the resolute measures of suppression taken by the young king Harsha from Kanauj on the Ganges, followed by his lightning incursion into Nepal and swift withdrawal back to India.

3

The Thakurs of Nepal

———————————❀———————————

IN the year A.D. 627 Hiuen Tsang, a learned Chinese gentleman of high birth visited Nepal in the course of one of the most astounding journeys ever made, right through Central Asia, to Kabul and into India, thence home by the Pamirs and Yarkand. From this invaluable chronicle we learn that the pious, scholarly Amsu Varman reigned in the Valley: either he had thrashed Harsha's men out or they had withdrawn on their master's orders. Hiuen Tsang's narrative has this to say of the Newars, 'The inhabitants of Ni-po-lo are all of a hard and savage nature; to them neither good faith nor justice nor literature appeals, but they are gifted with considerable skill in the arts. . . . Among them are true believers and heretics. Buddhist convents and temples of the Hindu gods touch each other.'

The title 'Thakur' now occurs in Nepalese annals with the founding of Amsu's Thakur dynasty. 'Very strong limbed and restless and people feared his power', records the Chronicle. He must have been one of the most brilliant rulers that Nepal ever had, for both in China and in Tibet history and legend mention his name and his achievements. Science, literature, education (the publication of the earliest Sanskrit Grammar), the expansion of commerce and the development of administration are a part of these achievements. King Amsu's Valley radiated over the Himalayas and across the Indian plains. His virtues, 'spread his glories over the entire earth,' announces the admiring Chronicle. It goes on to record that, 'Down to the reign of this monarch the gods showed themselves plainly in bodily shape: but after his time they became invisible,' pointing out with pride that this, at any rate, in this blessed Valley, was at least three hundred years longer than the period fixed for all other lands. Certainly Hun and Turk were on the rampage in Southern Asia.

16

And now we look northwards to the snow line. Tibet was a land known to the mountaineers, then and now, as Bod or Bhot. Slowly Bod had been crystallising into a single national unit from a tough, untutored, people of strongly Mongolian features with large, round, pink, wind-weathered faces, taller and bulkier than the men of Nepal. Chief Namr Srong Btsan and his able son, Srong Btsan Sgam Po, confirmed Tibetan sovereignty and power at this time, raising an army of 100,000 men, conquering through Sikkim and Bhutan to the confines of India and installing ambassadors at the courts of China, India and Nepal. Srong Btsan, the younger, thirsty for knowledge and to emulate his contemporaries in other lands, sent a mission into India to visit all the places of learning and to return to Bod with an alphabet. It is easy to imagine the excitement at the rude court in the new capital at Lhassa when the long-awaited mission returned with this invention, and the eagerness with which the simple, stiff-fingered elders in their homespun, prodded on by an impatient young king, applied themselves to adapting the letters to suit their own language and so to embark upon their first attempts at scholarship.

Tibet now advances on to the Nepalese stage, first as master, then as rival, then as prey to the marauders of Nepal, and lastly as tributary. Amsu's people had to bow their heads to the overlordship of the mighty Bod, an easy enough yoke when lightened by the payment of tribute and by Amsu's compliance with the Tibetan monarch's demand for the hand of his daughter in marriage. Srong Btsan had been smitten by the beauty of this girl, the Princess Bri-Btsan, when on a visit to Nepal, and had carried her off with him.

The Nepali princess took with her relics of the Buddha and other holy symbols in order to convert her warrior husband, a task in which she succeeded so well that he saw to it that his subjects accompanied him into the Buddhist faith. Srong Btsan Sgam Po, now equipped with the three necessities of polite society, an alphabet, a respectable religion and a well-bred wife, seems to have been so impressed with the result that he issued to the Son of Heaven, the Emperor Tai Tsung of China, a peremptory order to yield up to him one of the Imperial princesses. On the Emperor flatly and impertinently refusing the demand, the Tibetan Chief at once invaded China and advanced his standards through Kansu to Ch'ang-an, Tai Tsung's capital, where the princess, Wen-Chang, was tardily delivered up to him in the year 641. With her came all the books and appurtenances of her faith, including an image of the Buddha, on the long and rough road to Lhassa. Both she and Queen Bri-Btsan so earnestly en-

C

gaged in spreading the faith that Lamaism canonised them as the White and the Green Tara.

Nepalese, and so Indian, culture and craftsmanship took a lasting hold on Tibet to the exclusion of Chinese influence. There are still today in Tibet the Nepalese families of craftsmen imported by Srong Btsan, producing the fine metal work for which Tibet is so renowned.

Increasing commerce struggling through the passes from Lhassa, Nepal and Sikkim into India led in the natural course of events to the visit of a Chinese Mission to Nepal in the years about A.D. 650, soon after Amsu's death, during the reign of Narendra Deva, a ruler whose wisdom and benevolence have been handed down in the folklore of his people. With courtesy and hospitality he received the mission of Wang Hiuen Tse, in severe contrast to the manner in which it was received by Harsha's usurping successor. There, Wang and his companions were roughly handled and almost lost their lives. While at the Indian Court, they and their escort of thirty men were suddenly set upon by the king's minions who plundered the mission's goods and killed and captured the soldiers of the escort. Wang made his escape to Nepal, then a vassal of Tibet, and laid his quarrel before Narendra. The Tibetan overlord, sometimes called the Alexander the Great of Tibet, now wedded to a Chinese as well as a Nepalese princess, at once assembled his army, marched into Nepal, there picked up a Nepalese reinforcement, crossed the passes into India and poured out over the plains to avenge the insult. Advancing straight upon Tirhut, he stormed the capital, defeated the Indian Army with great slaughter and seized the monarch and his family. These he despatched to China and, if Father Georgi is any judge of Himalayan tours, the journey must have been a harsh new experience for them. Perhaps expectedly, the usurper died in China.

King Narendra, in the next year, returned the compliment with a Nepalese mission, thereby starting the flow of Chinese pilgrims to the renowned shrines of pious Nepal, along the routes already well trodden by merchants of both countries, and of India and Tibet. Prosperous Nepal restored its sacred buildings, Buddhist and Hindu, dug canals and fountains and reformed its system of taxation. Life was untrammelled and king and people happy and united. But sorrow was in store. Narendra's son, Vara Deva, succeeded.

Sankara Acharya, a brutal, fanatical Brahman, entered Nepal, must have wriggled himself into the young king's confidence and thereupon launched a bitter persecution of all, regardless of age or sex, who professed the old religion so dear to the Newars — Buddhism. As part of this wicked persecution, he destroyed all Buddhist literature, gave their temples to the flames and slew their priests — but he failed to wipe out the religion for it was too deeply and dearly planted in the hearts of the humble folk of the Valley. The loss through the destruction of these old Newar archives is tragic and utterly irreparable. Much that today is unknown or is conjecture would be common historical fact. It is good that the names should be recorded of those who disperse or destroy great libraries and the archives of nations. The name here is Sankara Acharya and that of the feeble or conniving king is Vara Deva.

During the long Thakur dynasty the Valley gradually turned from subsisting mainly on agriculture to living in great part by trade, and the market towns of Kantipura, later to be the capital of modern Nepal and to change its name to Kathmandu, and of Patan rose among the ricefields and the melon patches.

For many years now it is impossible to see through the dense tangle of dynastic changes. It is more profitable, therefore, to concentrate on those events which impinge closely on our story, whose object still remains to account for the Gurkha nation. At present we are with the Newars in the Green Valley, whose kings are still of the noble race of chieftains, the Thakurs.

Unwisely, some of these rulers saw fit to will this paltry realm to their sons in equal shares, so that there came on the scene the Kings of Kantipura or Kathmandu, Patan and Bhatgaon. In 1097 one Nanda Deva, a Rajput from the Indian Deccan, who had installed himself at Simraon, or Tirhut, twenty miles east of Raxaul, put an end to this parcel of princelings, at least temporarily, by invading the Valley, taking Bhatgaon and, from there, seizing the other two principalities. Of more interest and importance than this, however, is the appearance about now of migrants from the mountains of the west, people of the Khas tribe. This is the first we hear of them and, apart from a former incursion from nearby Nawakote by a small Thakur chieftain, it is the first time we have become acquainted with the Parbatiyas,* the hill folk from the west by whose hands modern Nepal has been moulded. These few Khas settled in the Valley, passing back and forth on their business, and in the course of time some of them became men of importance.

At the Court of King Hari Deva in A.D. 1100, one of these highlanders from the west, of the Magar tribe, held an important position. He was un-

* The term 'Parbatiya' really covers all the highlanders right out as far as Garhwal and Kumaon. In this book it is used to mean the Gurkha highlanders only.

welcome to some of the native-born ministers. They intrigued and he was dismissed. Raging, he trudged off westwards over the divide towards his home and to his chief at Tansing.* There he poured out his wrongs and spiced them with tales of the Valley, of the gold in the streets of Kathmandu, of the treasures in the bazaars and of the riches of the great merchant houses. Makunda Sen, the Parbatiya, Lord of Tansing, listened and envied. He looked about him at his spruce farms and then down on the farms of his Khas and Magar warriors sprinkled sparsely, white and red, among the little terraced fields of the steep hillsides in the glittering mountain light. He weighed the chances — and decided to march. Dismissing the suppliant with promises, he summoned his men. One fine morning he led them out on to the plains heading for the capital. Alarmed, Hari Deva beat to arms and the two forces met among the rice-fields.

But nothing before had been seen in Nepal like the disciplined ferocity and courage of the Chettri and Magar soldiers under their terrible chief. The Nepalese Army was dashed to pieces and terror and confusion rolled through the three cities.

The impious conquerors exacted dreadful retribution, committing bloody atrocities, smashing and disfiguring images of the gods and removing sacred relics to their own country.

The story goes that Makunda Sen arrived before Patan as the priests were about to celebrate the holy festival of Machendra Nath. The outraged Brahmans fled. At this, the serpent-mouthed fountains above the God spouted fine jets upon their idol and Makunda Sen, marvelling, cast over the image the golden chain from about his horse's neck. God Machendra Nath caught it and wound it about his own neck and, it is said, it remains till this day.

But the shrine of Pasupatti, indignant at the horrors committed by these infidels, sent upon them the Goddess of Pestilence, Mahamari, and within fourteen days the remnants of Makunda Sen's invincible army dribbled, stricken, away from the accursed Valley. Their Lord, disguised as an anchorite, barely made his way to the hills, to Devighat, where the swift Tadi and Trisul rivers meet. There he lay down and died.

Thus Nepal first tasted the fighting qualities of the highlanders of the west. For a decade the Valley was left shattered, devastated and torn by jealousies, from this stunning visitation.

The Thakurs from Nawakote then re-entered the Valley, easily as-

* Palpa.

sumed the reins of government and restored the demoralised administration. For over two hundred years they ruled in Nepal, from the twelfth to the fourteenth century A.D., when there appeared yet another race of chieftains who were destined to carry the kingdom along for the next hundred years. Just how they arrived in Nepal is not known for certain but there is a reasonable explanation, one given as having been derived from the Muslim chronicler, Ferishta.

India had for long been subjected to the pressure of Turki and Mongol invasion. A line of Turki Muslim emperors had held sway in Delhi since the end of the twelfth century when Muhammad Ghori of Afghanistan, having a year before been utterly routed at Tarain, north of Delhi, by the Hindu confederacy, returned and inflicted upon Prithiraj a terrible defeat at the very same place, not far from the famous battlefield of Panipat. Here, on this field, the fate of India was three times decided in later years. Cruel, ruthless and bigoted, the Muslims laid about them to exterminate and send to hell the infidels of Hindu India. Their most resolute and devoted opponents were the Rajput princes whose blood had been filtering for centuries through the hills into Nepal to enrich that of the warlike mountaineers. The struggle between the noble Hindus and the wild invader rocked all central and eastern India for a hundred bitter years, the Rajputs slowly, inch by inch, foot by foot, yielding desperately before the storm. It was a proud man who, in later years, could claim descent from these men or even to hold himself a fair measure of Rajput blood. Mahratta chief and Gurkha prince pride themselves in this legacy.

The harshest of this bloody stock of conquering emperors was one Muhammed bin Tughlak who extended his conquests into the Deccan and to the Coromandel coast. His father, Ghyass-ud-din Tughlak, had been a slave in the royal household and had had the distinction of being elected to the throne on the death of the usurper, Khusru. In the course of settling his dominions Muhammed bin Tughlak* marched into Eastern Bengal, to Sunargaon, near Dacca, to intervene in a disputed succession. In 1322 he turned for home, again passing close to the foothills of the Himalaya.

In Tirhut (or Garh Samaran, as our eighteenth-century writers have it), there ruled a Rajput prince, whose lands had been shorn from him by Tughlak's forbears, nursing his wrongs. As the Emperor's great host passed that way, Harsinha (Hari Singh), with the reckless, dauntless courage for which Rajputs are famed, shot out from his forests at the head of his little band and sprang like a panther on the Muslim force. The

* Ferishta, indeed, attributes this episode to Ghyass-ud-din.

outcome was inevitable. Tughlak threw him off and turned savagely upon him, driving his warriors back through the woods into their high-walled fortress, with its seven rings of moats. Calling up his siege train the Muslim prepared for the assault. After three weeks of hard fighting he carried the place to find that Harsinha had broken through his enemies and made off with his followers into the forests, abandoning his principality to Tughlak,

He must then have made his way into Nepal and cast the last of the Thakurs from the kingdom, to reign in his place 227 years after his famous ancestor, Nanda Deva, had seized the same throne. Once more the Valley provided a refuge and a prize.

The year is A.D. 1326.

During the closing stages of this, the Ajodhya dynasty, chaos once more prevailed, so that it is difficult to sift truth from legend. Certainly one of the Thakur Malla princes, Jyasthiti, of a very ancient line from India which had long before settled and at times ruled in the cities of the Valley, held the supreme power as chief minister to the King Jaya Singh Rama. It is quite likely that his position in relation to his master was the same as that of the Rana Maharajahs in the nineteenth and twentieth centuries to the King of Nepal. They were the power: the King was the figurehead. Jyasthiti thus set a significant and ominous precedent for the Prime Ministers of Nepal

Jyasthiti Malla and his son introduced into Nepal a definite Brahman predominance, thus changing the whole outlook of the people.

In time the sceptre passed to yet another Thakur prince who had married the daughter of the last Ajodhya king. This, the third Thakur dynasty, produced one great man, Yaksha Malla, 1429–1460, who annexed to his small patrimony of Bhatgaon, during the breaking up of the Muslim empire in India, Morang, Tirhut and even, it was chronicled, distant Gaya on the plains of Bihar, the Buddhist holy of holies. Northwards his armies invaded Tibet and seized Shekkar Dzong: westwards, significantly enough, he made war on the formidable Himalayan city-state of Gorkha, and conquered it. The refractory Rajahs of Patan and Kathmandu were brought to heel. The conquest of the haughty and independent, albeit primitive, Gorkha is interesting in view of the tornado it provoked which was three hundred years a-brewing before it finally broke.

Yaksha Malla, who should have been wiser, on his deathbed divided his empire into four kingdoms, Kathmandu, Patan, Bhatgaon and, to the east, only ten miles from Kathmandu, Banepa. These were the capital towns, all within a few miles, and here, with their domains behind them stretching far to the north, west and east, the four brothers and their descendants sat snarling nose to nose. The natural outcome was that the distant territories fell away altogether and the strongest of the brothers' successors, after strife and bickering, bit by bit swallowed the territory about them until but two kings remained, in Bhatgaon and Kathmandu. Matters stayed somewhat thus until 1769, although at one time even the diminutive kingdom of Kathmandu (or Kantipura) was divided between two sons.

On Yaksha's death, to his third son, Ratna Malla, was bequeathed the duchy of Kathmandu. He had some little difficulty in assuming his new state for there were a dozen Thakurs in control. With no qualms whatsoever Ratna therefore poisoned the lot. The Nawakote Thakurs took revenge by repainting the statue of the Goddess Rajyastvari, in defiance of their chief. Ratna accepted the challenge, marched on them and thrashed them soundly in a battle fought in 1471. Later, he quarrelled with Tibet and Bhutan and would have been beaten had not the Rajah of Palpa, the Parbatiya, descendant of the ill-starred Makunda Sen, come to his aid. In thanksgiving for his salvation he endowed the Brahmans of Kathmandu, thus taking the important step of 'establishing' the Hindu Church, an act which had a deep and lasting effect on the history of Nepal.

One of Ratna's successors, Mahendra, visited the Moghul Emperor, Humayun, at Delhi, taking with him presents of a white swan and falcons. Another, Sada Shira, was flung out of Kathmandu by a popular revolution incited by his letting his horses, of which he was altogether too proud, graze upon the growing crops, and by his abducting any good-looking woman who caught his fancy.

There are two events of note to be recorded at this stage, between now and 1769.

The first, when the imbecile king of Kantipura, Lakhshmi-Narsingh, built at this capital the great wooden lodging-house, the Kath-Mandu, from which his city now took on its modern name of Kathmandu. The *Nepalese Chronicle* thus records the building of this pile.

'In this reign, on the day of Machendra Nath's *jatra*, the Tree of Paradise was looking on at the ceremony in the form of a man and, being recognised by a certain Biseta, was caught by him, and was not released until he promised the Biseta that, through his influence, he would be enabled to build a *satal* with the wood of a single tree. On the fourth day after this, the Tree of Paradise sent a *sal* tree, and the Biseta, after getting

23

the Rajah's permission, had the tree cut up, and with the timber built the *satal* in Kantipura, and named it Madu-satal. From this being built of timber of one tree it was also named Kathmado. This *satal* was not consecrated, because the Tree of Paradise had told the Biseta that, if it were, the wood would walk away.'

Lakhshmi-Narsingh, in a fit of jealousy, slew one of his ministers, Bhima Malla. Bhima's wife burnt herself, committed *suttee* on her husband's funeral pyre and, as the flames licked about her, high above the noise created to drown her last words, she uttered the curse, 'Never more shall there be sound judgement in this Durbar.'

Lakhshmi, torn with remorse and superstitious dread, went mad.

In 1702, this, the Solar Dynasty, became extinct on the death from plague of Bhaskara Malla, due, it was said, to his celebrating the Dussehra festival in the unlucky month which was from time to time inserted in the Nepalese Calendar to coincide with the astronomical year. Bhaskara did all he could to avoid his fate, even going so far as to give every one of his subjects one good square meal out of his own pocket.

The second event of note occurred in 1736 when Narbhupal, the rebel King of Gorkha, pursuing the claim of his family to the throne of Kathmandu, extended his territory by force of arms eastwards as far as Nawakote, a bare fifteen miles from the capital, to be driven back on his homeland by the resolute Nepalese leader, Jaya Prakash Malla. Jaya Prakash had succeeded his father Jagat Jaya, in 1732. That father had died of anxiety and religious dread. Jaya Prakash was of tougher fibre. For thirty-seven turbulent years he held his own.

Narbhupal, the disgraced King of Gorkha, died in 1742 and his son, Prithwi Narain, was raised to the throne at the early age of twelve.

One day a wandering fakir strolled into Kathmandu and warned King Jaya Prakash that he had seen the soldiers of the young prince of Gorkha in Nawakote, just over the hills.

Mention of the name of Gorkha had for long had a menacing significance for the Nepalese kingdom.

*   *   *   *   *

We have brought the story now to the year 1742, to the point at which ancient Nepal and young Gorkha at last face each other for a struggle to the death. Gorkha is hammering heavily at the gates of Nepal, insistent, gathering strength, and the ram bears the image of the young chieftain, Prithwi Narain, Gorkha.

Let us leave the story of Nepal and its Mongol-Rajput Newars, its Thakur princes of Rajput descent and their two kingdoms in the Valley, Kathmandu and Bhatgaon.

Who were these Gorkhas or Gurkhas?

4

Gurkha

———————————❂———————————

ALL who write on the true, the original, Gurkhas complain that too little is known of the origin of the tribes that compose the Gurkha race, of their clans, and of their early history. That is so. Anyone, however, who knows the Khas or Chettri, Magar or Gurung men who comprised the armed host which laid Greater Nepal at its master's feet from Sikkim to the Dogra country, can affirm that the Khas are heavily impregnated with Rajput blood, sometimes almost submerging the Tartar strain. They note, too, that Gurungs and Magars, in that order, exhibit far more of their Tartar ancestry than of the Rajput admixture. Also, the Magar and the Gurung are typical Gurkhas, short, sturdy, hairless of face, often mistaken for Chinese or Japanese peasants, and eternally cheerful: the Khas, though below the average height of, say, the English, are comparatively tall, slight of build, of sharp features and as hairy as most other races. Furthermore, Hindu orthodoxy is obviously powerful among the high caste Khas rather than among the common people, the Gurungs and Magars, who retain, particularly the Gurungs, much of the freedom of their old Buddhist faith.

An account of the Gurkhas must explain how and when these people became what they are, Indo-Mongol in blood, Hindu with a varying taint of Buddhism in religion but, above all, how and why a Hindu caste system came to be applied to them, in which the predominantly military Magars and Gurungs are placed in caste half way down the system, whereas in the Hindu organisation of India they should be next only below the Brahman. In caste terms, they should be Kshattriyas or soldiers, no lower; they are, in any case, certainly not Sudras or menials as has been stated in a widely read book on Nepal. The aspect, the whole mien, of the Sudra of India is of a humble, rather cringing man, but the Gurkhas

26

of the Magar and Gurung are proud, self-respecting, genial little men, the equal of any other men on earth, including the Khas, and the superior of most. They are men of legendary courage and of a cheerful endurance that has to be experienced to be believed. Like most other gentlefolk and men of the countryside, they are lazily aggressive. These are not the qualities of the Sudra by any manner of means: they are the qualities of sturdy yeomen, the qualities of warriors and Kshattriyas — no less.

It is impossible here, and it would be tedious for a reader, to enter into any long discussion of the Hindu caste system. Those who wish to know more of it may read Hutton's masterly little book, *Caste in India,* or the multitude of longer and more confusing works that have been written on the subject. All we will do here is to fix one thing and it is that, generally speaking, the Brahmanical thread round the neck is only worn by the two highest Hindu castes, the priestly, or Brahman caste, and the warrior, or Kshattriya or Chettri, caste. Between those who are entitled to wear the thread and those who are not so entitled there is a great gulf fixed, both religious and social. Of those below the thread, the Sudra is the lowest caste within the Hindu system. After them come the outcastes, the Harijans, those who are hardly regarded as human beings and barely allowed the privilege of owning a soul.

Where do the Khas, Magar, Gurung, Limbu and Rai, the principal clans from which the British recruited their Gurkha soldiers, fit into this system?

In this chapter we will confine ourselves to an explanation of the rise of the Parbatiyas, the highlanders of the west, who have already appeared in the story of the Valley and whom we left in the 1740's threatening its independence. Among the Parbatiyas were the original Gurkhas, the men of the little state of Gorkha. In a later chapter we will turn to the easterners, the Kiranti, and see how they came to be included under the name of 'Gurkha'.* So far it has been recorded how, centuries ago, under Yellung, they invaded the Valley and placed their own man on the Nepalese throne, establishing a dynasty that lasted for some hundreds of years. From then onwards the Easterners, Limbu and Rai, had had closer relations with the Newar kingdom than had the more remote men of the West. In the perspective of history the Kiranti conquest of Nepal those long ages ago is probably more important than the Gurkha conquest of the eighteenth century A.D.

We must now answer the question asked: Who were the Gurkhas who lived in the mountains of the West, the people of the young chief Prithwi Narain?

* In Appendix I there is a note on some of the aboriginal tribes of Nepal.

27

The word 'Gorkha' or 'Gurkha' is probably the same as 'Gaekwar'. A Gaekwar is one who tends the cow, the holy cow. This title of Gaekwar was assumed by the Mahratta Chief of Baroda, the Gaekwar of Baroda. The name of Gurkha is one that has expanded from British usage. It was the British who applied it to all the military tribes of Nepal from whom they recruited their soldiers, whereas it should properly be applied only to the tribe of the district of Gorkha, the Gorkhalis. However, it has now come to be accepted as the name of the whole nation which inhabits the country known as Nepal.

The town of Gorkha, and later the district, is said to have derived its name from a saint called Gorkhanath who dwelt in a cave, which still exists, in the hill upon which the village of Gorkha was built. The ancestors of the Gorkhas or Gurkhas took their clan name from this village. They are the Gorkhali.

The Magars and Gurungs were animists with a veneer of Lamaic Buddhism, with Lamas for priests, and their religion and culture were similar to those of Bhot, Bod, or Tibet. In times of trouble they prefer even now to appeal to their animistic exorcisers, their *Damis*. Their languages are distinctly Tibetan in origin. In fact, in many cases the words are the same as the Tibetan. Their tradition is that they came over the hills from Tibet and that tradition is true, without any doubt.

Some time or other, with this rather barbarous material was welded the more refined metal of the Brahman and the Rajput. From the map it is clear that the routes of access from India to, say, the important little town of Palpa were few and uninviting to a plainsman. There cannot, therefore, have been Hindu movements of any magnitude except under severe compulsion, for the hill country had little or nothing to offer in the way of riches either in the soil or in the accumulated treasures of a cultured people. It is more than probable that the one great incursion from India was the first that was measurable, and the last. That incursion took place about A.D. 1300 when the Turki Muslim terror had India in its searing clutches. There are rumours of earlier movements, notably in the first century A.D. but, for want of anything like firm, or even corroboratory, evidence, these rumours must be set aside.

Whatever the final verdict, there are grounds for accepting the tradition that, after the sack of the Rajput fortresses of Ranthambor and Chitor, numbers of the inhabitants of the Rajput states, the famous fighting clan-castes, Rathors of Rajputana, Chandels and Bundelas of Bundelkand, Rashtrakutas of the Deccan, emigrated and found refuge from the fierce persecution in the mountains of the Himalaya. The tale of the particular family that wended its way to Riri and then to Palpa in the Magar country, is this.

Rishi Raja Rana was the Rajah of Chotogarh in India. For thirteen generations his successors ruled, until the Muslims came. They assailed Chotogarh, and Deva Sarma Bhattarak went down before the storm. The Muslim forces retired, leaving an administration to run the country. Deva Sarma's son, Ayutaban, now a puppet prince, discarded the title of Bhattarak and retained only his caste surname of Rana, synonymous with Rao or Rava, denoting a nobleman, chieftain. The title, Rana, is important for it occupies a prominent place in the history of Nepal from 1768 to this present time.

A chief of this Rajput Rana stock, Bhupati Rana, had three sons, among whom was Fateh Sing Ranaji Rava. Fateh Sing had a daughter, Sadal, of surpassing beauty, who unluckily attracted the attention of Alau-d din, the Muslim Emperor. He demanded that Fateh Sing render her up to him. Fateh Sing, with Rajput courage, proudly and firmly refused, whereupon the infuriated Muslim launched an attack on the Rajput stronghold of Chitor. The defenders stubbornly resisted. When all seemed lost, her father and uncle slain, food and water exhausted, Sadal threw herself into a cauldron of boiling oil to avoid capture and to remove the cause of quarrel. The unyielding resistance of these Rajputs, man, woman and child is quoted by Vincent Smith in his history of India, '... there can be no doubt that the defenders sacrificed their lives in a desperate final fight after the traditional Rajput manner, and that their death was preceded by that horrible rite, the *jauhar*, where the females are immolated to preserve them from pollution or captivity. The funeral pyre was lighted within the great subterranean retreat, in chambers impervious to the light of day, and the defenders of Chitor beheld in procession the queens, their own wives and daughters to the number of several thousands. ... They were conveyed to the cavern, and the opening closed upon them, leaving them to find security from dishonour in the devouring element.' Chitor fell in A.D. 1303.

Fateh Sing's brother, Manmath Ranaji Rava, is supposed to have cut his way out through the enemy and made for Ujjain. He had two sons but they unfortunately quarrelled, the elder staying at Ujjain, the younger, like so many younger sons, setting out to seek his fortune in the very wide world of southern Asia. His steps led him to the north-east into the Himalayas. After months of wandering along narrow mountain tracks, round and about the heavily forested hills and gorges, he emerged upon the terraced fields about the village of Riri in the province of Palpa, the

country of the Magars, the warrior tribe which had followed Makunda
Sen two hundred years before on his violent foray into Nepal. He and his
followers were cordially welcomed. It may seem strange that a foreigner
from a distant land could safely penetrate into these hills but the reason
is not far to seek. Between the Magar country and the plains and sprinkled
over the hills there lived a people called the Khas: they were by then
Hindus and claimed Rajput descent. Not only was the young Rajput
prince well received by these, his compatriots, but, on leaving their country and entering that of the Magars, he found a people already accustomed
to intercourse with men of his race. Thus, in Palpa, the Thums, or clans,
under their twelve headmen gave him a ready welcome.

He sought and found a home at Birkote, close to the border of the
Gurung provinces, where he bought land and settled down as a farmer.
But his high lineage and his Kshattriya caste marked him out as a leader
among the rude cultivators about him. Here, two sons were born,
Khancha and Mincha, both to rank as chiefs in the country of their adop-
tion and to pass the Rana title to its noble familes.

The Rajputs found here a primitive people with no idea whatsoever of
caste, a free community, and exerted no pressure upon them to adopt
Hindu ways, leaving them to enjoy their customs and religion, in contrast to the proselytising by intermarriage undertaken by their fellow-
countrymen who had penetrated into the mountain states of Kumaon and
Garhwal, west of the River Kali. In those parts all men claimed Rajput
descent and disclaimed with abhorrence any connection whatsoever with
the impure, infidel aboriginals, whom they virtually extirpated. Socially,
this purity may have helped them: tribally or nationally it has tended to
deprive them of the pride of race so apparent in the mountaineers of the
Magar and Gurung clans.

Among the immigrants from India there were numbers of Brahmans,
either entering the hills on pilgrimage to Himalayan shrines or fleeing
the Muslim terror and, as Brian Hodgson says, 'The Brahmans found the
natives illiterate, and without faith, but fierce and proud. They saw that
the barbarians had vacant minds, ready to receive their doctrines, but
spirits not to stoop to degradation, and they acted accordingly. To the
earliest and most distinguished of their converts they communicated, in
defiance of the creed they taught, the lofty rank and honours of the
Kshattriya (warrior) order. But the Brahmans had sensual passions to
gratify, as well as ambition. They found the native females nothing loth,
but still of a temper, like that of the males, prompt to resent indignities.

'These females would indeed welcome the polished Brahmans to their embraces, but their offspring must not be stigmatised as the infamous progeny of a Brahman and a Mlechha [an impure infidel]. To this progeny also, then, the Brahmans, in still greater defiance of their creed, communicated the rank of the second order of Hinduism [Kshattriya]; and from these two roots [converts and illegitimate progeny] mainly spring the now numerous, predominant, and extensively ramified tribe of Khas, originally the name of a small clan of creedless barbarians, now the proud title of Kshattriya, or military order of the Kingdom of Nepal. The offspring of the original Khas females and of Brahmans, with the honour and rank of the second order of Hinduism, got the patronymic titles of the first order [Brahman]; . . . It may be added, remarkably illustrative of the lofty spirit of the Parbatiyas [highlanders], that, in spite of the yearly increasing sway of Hinduism in Nepal, and the various attempts of the Brahmans in high office to procure the abolition of a custom so radically opposed to the creed both parties now profess, the Khas still insist that the fruit of commerce (marriage is out of the question) between their females and males of the sacred order, shall be ranked as Kshattriyas, wear the thread and assume the patronymic title.'

In other words, if the Brahman had to gratify himself he must deny his principles by exalting the family concerned, otherwise he could go elsewhere. Thus, from the advent of these thousands of foreigners and their numerous progeny of mixed blood, there sprang up a new race of Khas, and with this new race came a new language, a kind of Hindi patois, which was called the language of the Khas, or Khas-kura, and which became in after years the *lingua franca* of the whole of Nepal.

The Khas tribe is popularly supposed to have originated at the town of Gorkha which, tradition says, was founded by the Chitoria Ranas, Thakurs, who established their rule therein. Exactly what is meant by this is by no means clear. A Khas tribe already existed. Perhaps it was at Gorkha that the mixed offspring were first inducted into that tribe and given the Kshattriya privilege.

Thus the Khas or Kshattriya or Chettri tribe or clan arose in Nepal. It may be said to be founded on the original Khas tribe who are mentioned in the records of the Valley of Nepal as visiting that place about A.D. 1000. To them the Brahmans conceded the honour of wearing the thread.

As has already been said, the Gurung clans were very tardy in accepting Hinduism and therefore virtually no Gurung entered the new élite, the Khas clan. All the promotion went to the Magars, but by no means all the Magars clamoured for promotion: many of them declined for years to embrace the Brahman faith. These tardy ones, when eventually accepting the new creed, were not admitted to the now closing ranks of the Khas. Some place, however, had to be made for them and for the Gurungs, later converted, in the caste system, but it has never been clearly defined and no one knows precisely where they are to be fitted in. The difficulty is that these careless Magars and Gurungs came to provide the bulk of the fighting men of Nepal and, as warriors, they should in all justice have been classified as Kshattriya. However, that was not to be, and these tardy souls have been relegated to an undefined position below that of the Kshattriya or Khas and above that of the Vaishyas, the merchant caste or caste of the common man, and above that of the lowliest of the low, the humble, menial Sudra. As far as the army goes this relegation is all to its advantage, for it means that virtually no caste prejudices, such as plague regiments of high caste, interfere with the efficient performance of their military duties. Furthermore, these genial warriors care little for any of these things and have a fairly hearty contempt for priests.

We can now see how it is that today there are Khas who bear Magar clan names such as Thapa, Gharti, Rana, etc. as well as Magars of the same clan names. That leaves only one confusing point: it is that there are Thakur, very high caste, Ranas as well as Magar Ranas. This needs investigation. The Ranas who came from Chitor were Thakurs, a caste above the Khas. Sahis and Sens, as often mentioned in this book, were Thakurs: the present King of Nepal is a Thakur. The Ranas of the Magar tribe were an order of chivalry and socially respected in the tribe but bore no higher caste than the rest. They derived from the Magar Thapas among whom any Thapa whose three direct forbears had been killed in battle changed his clan name from Thapa to Rana. His family might later on have become Khas in the manner already described, or they may have been among the careless ones and remained Magars.

It is obvious that the Khas must be sprinkled widely over the Magar country and not necessarily concentrated in any one or two areas. They are indeed to be found all over Nepal. Up to 1947 Magars and Gurungs were not usually given political employment or high military command: these were reserved for Khas and Thakurs. In the Nepalese Army, Magars and Gurungs could rise to the rank of Captain only in the specifically Magar or Gurung corps, such as the Purana Gorakh, Kali Bahadur and the Kali Parsad.

Magars and Gurungs retain their ancient tongues of Tibetan origin, Magar-kura and Gurung-kura, while employing Khas-kura, of Hindi origin, for general use and so have spread it wherever they have conquered.

2. *Kathmandu, in the Valley of Nepal*

3A. *The Road to Kathmandu*

3B. *A Street in Kathmandu*

4A. *A Scene in the Square at Patan*

4B. *Pasupatti Temple*

5A. *Dhaulagiri*

5B. *Crossing the River Kali at Thiblang*

6. *A Thakur*

7A. *Gorkha. The Villiage Home of the Gurkha Race*

7B. *Gorkha. The Temple of Gorkha Nath*

8. *Gorkha District. Bridge across the Daroundi Khola*

9. *A Gurung Village in Western Nepal*

10. *Gurung Boy from Lamjung in Western Nepal*

11. *A Rai from Okhaldunga in Eastern Nepal*

12. *A Magar Rana*

13A. *Magar Girls at Gulmi*

13B. *Gurung Girls at Kaski*

In olden days these two tribes were accustomed to eat all sorts of animal food, including beef, and for long continued to do so until the Hindu customs of their Rajput squires and their Brahman clergy made them doubt for their immortal souls and question the piety of continuing in their ancient habits. Nothing, however, has ever come in the way of their addiction to spirituous liquors. Each tribe had its Lama priesthood and its own deities and worshipped spirits and, as Hamilton in 1800 calls them, 'ghosts'. Of later years, while eating copiously of the flesh of wild hogs, goats, sheep, ducks and fowls, they abstain from eating beef. They are small men of great bodily vigour, carrying heavy loads over the high mountains, used to frugality and hardship, while their cheerful and happy natures are a household word among all who know them.

While the Magars were a settled people who farmed their land, the Gurungs were to some extent pastoral and nomadic. Like the Ghilzais and other Pathan tribes from across Pakistan's western, or Pathan, frontier they drove their flocks and brought their families down from the upper highlands as the autumn chill set in and the snow of winter threatened. In spring, to escape the heat and for new pasture in their rocky highlands, they followed the retreat of the snow line up the Himalaya before the warmth of summer. They were a tribe of warriors, preferring the spoils of war to the tedium of weaving blankets, tilling the fields and minding their flocks. Moving about amid the remotest Himalayan steeps and valleys, at the tender mercies of the wild spirits who infested these harsh places, the Gurung shepherd clans more slowly absorbed the new teachings of their Rana guests. Even today there are numbers of these men whose understanding of Hinduism is of the vaguest. Perched on the heights, with their flocks roaming the sheer, grassy slopes below them, climbing nightly to the *goth* or stone corral to sleep, the more solitary herdsman seldom comes into conversation with other folk. Sometimes a man will present himself, grinning with good nature, to a Gurkha recruiting party who find that they cannot understand what he has to say — he is talking the language he speaks to his goats high up in the clouds.

To all and sundry, all over the world, it is the Magar and Gurung who are typical . . . they are the Gurkhas.

Historians have discussed and argued as to whether this or that line of lairds or chieftains among the Khas, Magar and Gurung came from the Rajput country in India. The matter is of little consequence. The truth is that Rajput blood is by now spread all through the mountains where these people dwell, thicker in the more accessible Magar homelands, thinner among the more remote Gurungs. Where it is thickest, the Brahmans

D

have seen to it that the Hindu caste is highest: where it is thinnest, it is the lowest. That is to say that families sired by Brahmans, Thakurs and Kshattriya from the hill women, and so brought up in the Hindu faith rather than in the Buddhist, are the Kshattriya or Chettris, the high warrior caste.

We must return once more to history to discover how the Gurkhas finally emerged.

The two young Rana chiefs, Khancha and Mincha, were not backward in extending their overlordships among their new friends, and as these same friends loved nothing more dearly than soldiering, they found their retainers only too zealous to forward their designs. Their father had left to Mincha lands at yet another Nawakote, on the boundary between the Magar and Gurung territories, not far from Palpa, and to Khancha lands about his own home at Birkote among the Magars. Of the two brothers Mincha took Hinduism as his religion while Khancha and his descendants became true Magars and inclined towards Buddhism. Mincha and his successors thus married into the best of the Rajput-Mongol families. With these two lairds begins what may be termed the Gurkha supremacy. Khancha, in his lifetime of clan squabbles, gradually pushed westwards, crossed the Gandak River, and seized control of the Mangranth (Magar land) country which added such districts as Gulmi, Dhor and Ghandrung, all Magar strongholds, to his patrimony. Mincha, from Nawakote, seized Kaski, Lamjung and Tannahung, the heart of the Gurung country.

As time went on, the descendants of Mincha set themselves up as separate and independent rulers at Lamjung, Kaski and Tannahung, Lamjung being the strongest whose authority came to be grudgingly acknowledged by the others. The Thakur King Hasobad of Lamjung had two sons. The elder succeeded his father, whereupon the younger, Drabva Sah,* who was his brother's chief minister,† determined to seek for himself a crown of his own. As in the Valley, all that is happening is on a miniature scale. Only ten miles from Lamjung, straggling about on a hill at the foot of a semi-circle of mountains which enclose a wide and well-cultivated plain, lay a sleepy little town of the name of Gorkha

---

* Sah. The origin of this title is not certain. It may have been assumed by certain Rajput noblemen or it may be the title 'Shah' conferred by the Muslim Emperors of India on influential Rajputs. Sah and Sahi are Thakur.

† Chauntriya. The Chauntriyas were the ruler's relatives and automatically held positions in the state government. The extent of the authority allowed to them varied with their master's wishes.

governed by a rajah of the Khas race, a vassal of Yasobam. Gathering some of his brother's hirelings, Drabva fell upon the hapless Gorkha. In the scrambling fight that ensued, he came face to face with the rajah and slew him with his own hand. Gorkha fell to the rebel's assault. The line of Drabva Sah, the House of Gorkha, was established.

The history of Nepal was being written about the Valley, oblivious of the little tragic happenings in the little town of Gorkha, hidden by the spurs of the Himalayas, not fifty miles away.

The year is A.D. 1559.

*   *   *   *   *

We have told the tale of the Valley and of the Parbatiyas, the western highlanders, but have yet to see what has been happening in the south and the east.

5

The Kiranti of Eastern Nepal

———————————— ✦ ————————————

THE Vamshavali, or genealogical chronicle, records:

'Dwapar Yuga lasted 834,000 years. . . . The Kiranti came into Nepal at the 15,000th year of the Dwapar Yuga, and they ruled over the country for 10,000 years. The Gods came into the country after the Kiranti. . . .'

Doubtless, there is in this wide tale much of truth: that, in ages before man recorded clearly, savage Kiranti tribes overran the Valley of Nepal: that they were cast out by more civilised tribes of a pure faith, Buddhist or Hindu.

Who were the Kiranti? Today we know them as the Limbus and Rais, both of which warlike clans were enlisted as 'Gurkhas' in the British Army.

In ancient Hindu writings, in the Vedas, for instance, mention is made of the Kiranti. Whether it was merely a generic name to cover all sorts and kinds of yellow-skinned races who dwelt in the hill and mountain regions from the Valley of Nepal eastwards and southwards to the Naga hills of Assam and to the Arakan on the borders of Burma, is not certain. On the other hand, there may actually have been a vast race of true Kiranti hillmen covering this area. Whoever the people were, they were more familiar to Indian scribes than were Magars and Gurungs. During the upsurge of Hindu power and its consequent expansion, these Kirantis were forced back on to their hills by the Indian princes . . . 'drives back the Kiranti to his caverns.' Dr. Sylvain Lévi says: 'The mountain is, in fact, his domain. It is there that he continues to live and to dominate during the epic (Hindu) period: Bhima meets the Kirantis on leaving Videha during his victorious march towards the eastern regions: Nakula meets them also on his journey when he conquers the west: Arjuna, whilst penetrating the Himalaya towards the north, is arrested and defied by a Kiranti, or rather by Shiva in the guise of one. The word Kiranti occurs times out of number in the Mahabharat in company with the names of strange people whose territories border upon the frontiers of India — the Yavanas, Shakas, Pahlevas — but it is, above all, with Chinese that they are associated. Kiranti and Chinese fraternise under the banners of the glorious Bhagadatta, Emperor of Pragyotisa (Kamrup). They form a contingent of the yellow men! The Chinese and Kiranti soldiers seem to be made of gold. Their troops gave the impression of a forest of yellow flowers! The Ramayana also makes note of the golden colour of the Kirantis.'

If reliance is to be placed on any of this, then the Kiranti came in from Tibet rather than from India. Judging by the Tartar features of the modern Limbus and Rais, we may accept this origin, and so may find more than an element of truth in the Kiranti tradition or legend quoted by the Indian traveller, Sarat Chandra Dass:

'The village of Yangma, from whence spread the Kiranti race, in ancient times was not inhabited. Once upon a time a cowherd from Tashi-rabka (in Tibet) lost one of his yaks, which, grazing in towards the Kangala Chen pass, entered the Yangma Valley. Here the cowherd, having followed the tracks, found his hairy property lying on a rock with a full stomach. In the morning he again missed his yak and, proceeding further down into the interior, met it at a place called Shophug, grazing in a rich pasture land. Here, being charmed with the luxuriance of the pasture as compared with his own bleak and barren country, he sowed a few grains of barley which he had obtained from a certain priest as a blessing.

'On his return to his village in Tibet he gave a good account of this place to his fellow-countrymen, but nobody would believe him, nor would anyone undertake to visit the place of his discovery on account of its position beyond the snows.

'The cowherd, however, with his wife went to the Yangma Valley to tend his flock, and to their surprise they found the barley well grown. On his return he showed the barley ears to his friends, who were now induced to emigrate to the new land to grow corn.

'Thus was the village of Yangma first inhabited. It is indeed a purely Tibetan settlement as the houses testify.'

Let that be the origin of the Kirantis. It is then the origin of the Yakhtumba, the Limbu, and of the Yakkas and other Rais. The language of the Yakhtumba is of the Tibetan group though quite distinct from the many tongues of the Rais. '*Jatti Rai, Utti Kura*.' For every Rai a different language, the Gurkhas say. In the course of time, these Yakhtumbas came to be known generally as the Limbu and are still so known.

Out of the Khambu and Yakka sections of the Kiranti grew the Rais. This is a recent designation originating in the 1780's when the Gurkha King of Nepal, wishing to conciliate the Kirantis after their bloody defeat at his hands, raised influential chieftains up to govern, under his seal, certain districts of their country. To these men he gave the title of Rai. The title was hereditary but, like the nobility of certain Latin countries, it spread widely among the descendants until the true entitlement was lost in confusion and many who have no legitimate right to the dignity are now Rais and accepted as such. For the same reason the title of Subha was granted to the Limbus and has spread in the same way

The Sunwars or Sunpars live wedged in between the Rais and the Gurungs. Their name is derived from their inhabiting the two banks of the Sun Kosi River. They are, like their neighbours, of Tibetan origin and they show in every way the admixture of the blood of the Gurungs and Rais, though they may have been originally quite a separate people who settled independently to the north of the Valley of Nepal.

These tribes are more or less indifferent to religion, Buddhist when it suits them to mumble the 'Om Mane Padme Hung' and to propitiate their Lama priests: devotees of Shiva in a Hindu country.

Until the great Gurkha explosion of 1768 the Kiranti were independent in their country to the east of the kingdom of Bhatgaon. Today, compressed as they may have been, they still occupy all that area from the Arun River eastwards to the Nepalese frontier with Sikkim and spill over into Sikkim itself and to Darjeeling in Indian territory. The Limbus inhabit the hills from the River Arun on the west to the Singalila ridge on the east: the Rais predominate in the country to the west of this, extending almost to the Nepal Valley.

Limbus and Rais have somewhat the same physique and qualities as the Magars and Gurungs: they are more quarrelsome and hot-tempered, and more Tartar in appearance, but otherwise there is little to distinguish them.

Something of their history is told in the chapters on the Valley of Nepal.

6

Palpa, the Kiranti and the 46 Lordships

———————— ✦ ————————

THE principality of Makwanpore, or Palpa, plays some part in the story of the Valley, not so as materially to influence the course of events, but at least to render that story incomplete without an account of the doings of its ruling family.

The year is about A.D. 1300.

South of Nepal and lying along the hills athwart the tracks that led into India were the domains of an impure or pagan chieftain of the name of Karma Singha, who ruled over a section of impure people called the Bhawars. These Bhawars had at one time possessed a great territory embracing the whole of Gorakhpore, with their capital at the by now, to us, well-worn site of Sumraon, or Garh Samaran, or Tirhut; but assault from without and, probably, quarrels from within had splintered the tribe. Thus, Karma Singha, the impure Rajah, ruled over one remnant on the west of the Gandak River, with his capital at Rajpore where that great river enters the plain. He had two brothers, the one on the Kosi River and the other nearer at hand, in Tirhut. Any rajah in India or Nepal who was unlucky enough to have brothers within hail, was under compulsion to keep a hand on his sword-hilt and to maintain a sufficient army to accommodate the advances of his kinsmen. Karma Singha accordingly kept as his military power a force of mercenary Kiranti and other barbarians, in occupation of the hills adjacent to his capital.

Chitor fell to the Muslims. In the Rajput exodus from that fortress into the Himalaya were those bands that found their way up into the Magar country as already related, and also one band of seven hundred soldiers who turned aside to sell their swords for a living, honest or otherwise, to Karma Singha. This potentate was only too pleased to accept the reinforcement, especially as it came to him under two Rajput chiefs, Jil and

Ajil Rais, men of high birth. For twenty-two years these noblemen and their troops served 'this low man', until at length the opportunity offered for them to raise a mutiny and slay the venerable heretic.

Ajil Sen was declared king. It is sad but true, as these pages show, that the Rajput was so often guilty of base ingratitude and treachery to gratify his ambition. Rajputs were a fierce, ruthless people who would stop at nothing.

Ajil's son, Tula Sen, built on the hills the fortress of Makwanpore, a post whose name is prominent five hundred years later in the days of the Honourable East India Company. From that firm base he set out to conquer. By the mid-century he had fairly reunited the old Bhawar country and had a foothold in the higher hills at Rishing in the Magar territories. His successor extended his conquests over this region, seizing the town of Palpa, where, in the fifteenth century, Rudra Sen was the first of the Makwanpore line to style himself the Rajah of Palpa. Rudra's son, Makunda Sen the First of Palpa, inherited a considerable kingdom stretching from Makwanpore along the plains and foothills over most of the Magar territory and well into the Gurung areas, but he, with peculiar imbecility, willed his possessions to his four sons: to the eldest, the provinces west of the Gandak River: Palpa, to the second son, Manik: to Bihangga, Tannahung: to Lohangga, Makwanpore.

We will follow Lohangga, in whose soul was greatness. Somehow the name lends a savage splendour to this prince.

To the east of him reigned the proud Rajah Vijayanarain, whose ancestors had come from Kamrup, under whose sceptre lay the Morang country between the Kosi and Kankayi rivers, and part of the Terai as far as the Mahanaddi. He was both proud and perhaps foolish or eccentric. The title of the Kamrup chieftain was that of Harbhang Rajah. This chief's minister was Bharbhang Mantri. In the provincial dialect it seems that Harbhang-Bharbhang disrespectfully and popularly came to imply feather-headed. However that may be, the tale goes that Vijayanarain took into his service one Singha Rai, a hereditary chief, or Hang, of the Kiranti along with his rough mountaineers. By them he was enabled to expand his power and to found Vijayapore, a new mountain capital, whereupon he dubbed himself Vijaya Bharati, the Victorious over the Earth. Having achieved his aim, he wished to be rid of the encumbrance of those who had helped him to it. Perhaps their demands became more exacting. Kiranti Singha Rai, the Hang, was no good Hindu: he and his men swilled their beer and *raksi*, a rowdy, barbaric lot of ruffianly heathens. Worst of all, this Hang was an impure beef-eating monster and there were stories of his having presumed to defile a Hindu lady. The Rajah seized on the latter pretext, caught Singha Rai and executed him out of hand.

No mountaineer of the Kiranti would bow the knee to a *desi* (low-lander) with his silken raiment and his scents. Baju Rai, Singha's son, drew off his highland contingent and went hot-foot to Lohangga, the young Rajput King of Makwanpore. Into his attentive ear he swore revenge if Lohangga would help him. He and his men, with Lohangga's aid, would lay Vijayapore and the whole Harbhang-Bharbhang edifice in bits at the feet of Makwanpore. Lohangga found this a heaven-sent opportunity to humble 'The Victorious over the Earth' and, more than that, to extend his dominions over a most desirable reinforcement to his fighting power, the barbaric, truculent and aggressive Kiranti tribes. But between Makwanpore and Vijayapore, which lay in the hills west of the Kosi River, there were numerous petty chiefs. Their existence, innocent or otherwise, did not deter Lohangga. He now proceeded to engulf them one by one, starting with a couple of minor rajahs of Magar extraction, and progressing therefrom to a Bhawar chieftain. Swallowing half-a-dozen more, each in turn, he found himself opposed by a devil during his attack on Gidha. Thrown back with serious loss he was near to utter disaster when a holy man, Ramanath, intervened in the nick of time and ordered the God Ramkrishna to hew the devil's head from his shoulders. The god obliged and the battle was won. All this would mean that the rapacious Lohangga had more than he bargained for at Gidha and would have lost the day if a lucky bolt had not killed the opposing commander.

From there he swung down upon Vijayapore, only to learn that 'The Victorious over the Earth' had died. For once, he entered peacefully into another's possessions.

Baju Rai, the Kiranti, was killed leading his men in these campaigns and his son succeeded to the chieftainship. Lohangga, whose meagre resources at Makwanpore would never have permitted such vast conquests, had been placed by Kiranti arms in authority over an extensive empire from the Adiya River on the west to the Mahanaddi on the east and from the alps of Bod to the plains of India. He was now Lord of the Kiranti, of the Yakhtumba, Yakka, Limbu and Rai, and these heretic folk began to receive the Brahman's creed and customs to digest into their half-Buddhist, half-animistic systems.

In the normal pattern for these regions, it was not long after Lohangga's death that his descendants were at each other's throats.

The last word lay with the Kiranti Hangs, who more than once cast down the Rajput king of Vijayapore and set up another in his place. One of these kings, Kamdatt, was on such bad terms with Bichitra Rai, the Kirant Hang of those parts, that he was chased off the *gaddi* (royal cushion) all the way to Lhassa and only dared return when Jagat, the king raised up by Bichitra Rai, managed to soothe the wounded Hang's incensed feelings. Bichitra's son took up the torch on the old man's death and he and Kamdatt shot each other out of Vijayapore whenever the one or the other could collect sufficient partisans with whom to enforce his authority. Finally, the Kiranti sought aid from Sikkim, tricked Kamdatt into a meeting with twelve ruffianly Bhotiyas, as they were styled, lent by the Chief of Sikkim for the purpose, and had him done to death. The Kiranti then sought out the legitimate heir to the throne of Vijayapore, Karna Sen, and installed him. In 1772 Karna Sen died, leaving an only son, under the care of the faithful Agam Singha, a Kiranti chieftain at the Vijayapore Court.

In 1772, the scourge of Gorkha fell upon Vijayapore.

* * * * *

Now we must return to Palpa, the inheritance of Lohangga's brother, Manik. The line of Manik faded out and the descendants of Binayak, Lohangga's eldest brother, succeeded to the title of Palpa. With the customary quarrels and attempts to rape each other's estates, the Magar-Rajput rajahs of Gajarkote, Rishing, Ghiring, Argha, Kachi, and Gulmi clung together in uneasy league under the leadership of Palpa, despite the violent attempts of Palpa to annex the last-named.

Narbhupal of Gorkha, claimant to the throne of Kathmandu, the rebel hero of the disastrous attempt to conquer the Valley in 1736, obtained in marriage the hand of a princess of Palpa, the sister of Gandharba Sen, the Rajah. Narbhupal's son, Prithwi Narain of Gorkha, was, therefore, cousin to Makunda Sen, Rajah of Palpa, who succeeded Gandharba on the *gaddi*.

To the east and south of the Valley of Nepal there were in the year 1742, the fragments of Lohangga's empire, with a capital city at Vijayapore: in the mountains to the north-east and east were the independent and very impure Kirantis: to the west lay Gorkha, still nominally a vassal to Kathmandu, solitary, scowling, licking its wounds; to south-west, Palpa and the Magar League.

Further west were the Twenty-four Lordships and the Twenty-two Lordships. The Twenty-four, the Chaubisia, spread in an arc embracing most of the Gurung and Magar country: the Baisia, or Twenty-two, Rajahs were due west again of these, their largest duchy, that of Jumla, sitting uncomfortably on their north side on the high slopes of the Grand Himalaya.

These forty-six duchies had slowly developed through the centuries from the inflow of Brahmans and Kshattriya Rajputs from India. Each one of them had as its ruler one who professed to be, and was accepted as, a Rajput. Split up into these little clans in the remote glens, the life of bickering and family feud so typical of highlanders must have suited well the turbulent Rajput squires from Oudh and Rajputana. To one who knows the independent spirit of the martial Magar and Gurung, it is not easy to understand how these tribes came so meekly to accept the supremacy of a handful of lowlanders. There can be only one explanation and that lies in the cunning with which the Brahman missionaries followed their self-imposed vocation of conversion. By holding out to a select proportion of the population the chance to gain Kshattriya caste in the new system, and by then conferring on them every privilege of that class, they bound to themselves and to their Rajput fellows by self-interest a powerful body of newly-created aristocrats who were not slow to exert their power over baser men and quick to preserve jealously their own privileges and position and those of their sponsors. As time went on the tree spread its branches so that nothing that grew below could rival its size.

Many of the duchies were insignificant. Hamilton in 1816 describes Ghandrung, whose capital was a village of some sixty or seventy huts lying about the chief's brick-built stronghold. Satahung had one 'town' of two hundred and fifty thatched huts. The 'city' of Gorkha, on the other hand, one of the more recently formed, contained some two thousand houses.

Some of the states were in alliance or formed themselves into uncomfortable leagues for their own protection. The Palpa League has been mentioned: Lamjung and Birkote each headed a league, and so on. Only Gorkha stood proudly and defiantly aloof, nominal vassal in bad times to the King of Nepal, but nominal only and manifestly at liberty not only to rebel but also to invade its master's territory. It was no mean state, its western boundary being the Marsiangdi River and its eastern, the Trisul.

All forty-six Rajahs were supposed to be subject to the largest state, that of Jumla, but, in fact, all had rebelled at different times. Jumla they used as a convenience only, acknowledging its leadership whenever they had anything to gain by doing so, but usually ignoring it.

7

Prithwi Narain of Gorkha

———————————❖———————————

IT was A.D. 1559 when Drabva Sah rebelled and stormed Gorkha. Within two hundred years, as has been recorded in the story of *The Thakurs of Nepal*, Narbhupal Sah, the ninth of the House of Gorkha, seeking to profit by the quarrels and factions of the kings of Kathmandu and Bhatgaon, seized Nawakote and raided the Valley but was beaten back into the hills. In 1742 he died and his twelve-year old son, Prithwi Narain Sah, came to power. Thus, in 1742, the centre of the stage is occupied by five groups — the two kings in the Valley of Nepal: Prithwi Narain, the boy-chieftain of Gorkha holding sway over many clans of the Magar, Khas and Gurung highlanders; the rajahs of the Chaubisia; and, lastly, the Kiranti chiefs to the east of the Nepal Valley, with their quarrelsome clansmen.

Advancing to take the centre of the stage is the valiant, cunning, ambitious, energetic and ferocious stripling in the lime-washed villa-palace below the great square wood-tiled hall above the Pokri Tol on the sunny hillside at Gorkha. As Gurkha hillmen go he was an inch or so above the usual height, slighter of body but lithe and strong, sharp-featured, brown-eyed, with rather semitic nose.

His first business was the obsequies of his father and attendance at the *aghun*, the wake. For the mourning period, as was the custom, he dressed all in white and shaved his hair and eyebrows.

The young ruler was confronted with a situation of some danger to his kingdom. Gorkha had always been resolutely independent of all other leagues in the hills. For this reason, Nepal had from time to time prevailed against Gorkha and had periodically been in a position to treat her as a vassal. This thraldom, Prithwi Narain was determined to throw off once and for all. He knew that release could only in the end be got by utterly crushing Nepal and that this was an undertaking little short of madness. His father's terrible disaster had proved that. He knew too that he must rely absolutely on his own resources to effect his aim and that during the struggle he must be prepared at any time to withstand the hostility of any of his rivals in the highland leagues. His kinsman at Lamjung, for instance, was leagued with Tannahung, Kaski, Dhor and Satahung, and Gorkha had in years gone by been reft from Lamjung by Prithwi's ancestor. Birkote led Ghandrung, Paiyung and Nayakote: Palpa had Gajarkote, Rishing, Ghiring, Argha, Kachi and Gulmi: Malebum of the Mallas was allied with Gulkote, and Piuthan with Musikote, Isma, Khingri and Bhingri. The Chief of Gorkha stood alone, nominal vassal to Kathmandu but holding in his family some sort of claim to the throne of Nepal.

The moment he assumed the *gaddi* of Gorkha, Prithwi Narain Sah began preparations to expand his dominions. While these were in progress, he made a journey to pay his devotions at the sacred shrines of Benares, in order that his designs might prosper. Thither he went, stopping on the way to visit the military establishments of the English Company and, in his journey, acquainting himself with the training and system of its regiments. The firelocks which served him so well, he must have procured from the gunsmiths of Lucknow and Cawnpore. Travelling in his splendid *palki* (palanquin) and on his broad Tibetan pony, escorted by his Khas bodyguard dressed in blue, red and green, flying before him the yellow battle standard of Gorkha with its embroidered figure of the monkey god, Hanuman, he came to broad, brown, Ganga-ji, the Ganges River, opposite Benares. Here he will have crossed in the magnificent, two-masted, green and gold pinnace of the Rajah of Benares, flying its master's red pennant and rowed by a score of good oarsmen standing in the fore well. His devotions ended, he set out to return to his own country.

At the frontier of Benares State, he fell foul of the Customs and in the quarrel the masterful youth slew a customs official with his *khora*, the vicious, broad-bladed, curved scimitar of the hills. He was saved from retribution by a Bairagi, a Hindu ascetic of a wandering sect, many of whose members were little better than highway robbers and common thieves. It is romantic to read that this man hid Prithwi, disguised him as a fellow mendicant and travelled with him through Oudh and into Nepal. The two pilgrims passed through Palpa where they were hospitably entertained by Makunda Sen, Prithwi's cousin. The story goes that in later years the Bairagi, with a numerous band of his uncouth brethren, came to Prithwi, now a powerful king, and demanded with menaces the reward that was their due, whereupon the ingrate monarch threw some of the party into prison and sent others to execution as a pack of worthless rogues.

Prithwi Narain's chief minister, or Chauntriya, was one Ahiram Konwar, a Khas Gurkha, the man who sired the long line of Rana statesmen who ruled Nepal for over a hundred years. While Prithwi reigned, Prithwi was King and no other dared to dispute his authority: in later years the right of the King to rule in Nepal was called in question and successfully denied.

Gorkha had no resources of wealth: it was cut off by other states from both Tibet and India so never acquired importance on a trade route, nor did it, as many others of these mountain kingdoms, possess silver or copper mines. Its chiefs were, therefore, considered as insignificant. Thus Prithwi Narain found that his only wealth lay in the martial spirit and warlike ardour of his highland subjects, and his significance in the terror he could inspire around him. He decided to lay out that wealth for profit. His father had attempted to reap a harvest in Nepal from the dissensions among its princelings. The dissensions, despite the lesson of 1736, continued and grew worse. Prithwi Narain watched like a cat. His one great asset was the hatred that Jaya Prakash, the King of Kathmandu, deliberately inspired in all his subjects and in the breasts of his two rivals of Patan and Bhatgaon. The Gurkha prince inserted a 'fifth column' into the people of Kathmandu to work the downfall of their king.

These are some of the sins of Jaya Prakash: the worst, the Kirtipore outrage, is told later. They are the sins of madness.

Offended by Jaya Prakash on some matter of Court etiquette, the Durbar officials set up his brother in a rival principality carved by them out of Kathmandu's estates. Jaya Prakash acted at once and his brother fled. Intrigue against him continued, the Durbar winning over his wife, the Princess Dayavati, so that the king was forced out of his palace and compelled to submit to the disgrace of having his own infant son proclaimed in his place. By assiduous counter-intrigue he got the better of the Durbar so that he returned once more as king. The Princess, at once grasping the situation, had the minister hanged who had proclaimed her infant son. Nevertheless, this did not serve her. Jaya Prakash forthwith cast his faithless spouse into a cell in her own palace, where her life came to an expectedly abrupt end.

At Nawakote, there lived a nobleman, Kasiram Thapa,* of a much respected family, the ancestors of those Ranas who ruled Nepal through-

---

* The deadly feud of this man's family with the family of Pande decisively influenced the history of Nepal.

out the nineteenth and the first half of the twentieth centuries. Nawakote was an uneasy subject of Kathmandu, always balancing its loyalty between that state and Gorkha and inclining to the latter. In 1743 Jaya Prakash summoned Kasiram to his presence at Court, and, despite his protestations of innocence, put him to death there and then for treason. This was treachery. The *Nepalese Chronicle* writes that from that day the King's fortunes began to worsen. 'He ought not to have put Kasiram Thapa to death.' Nawakote, the forward sap for the assault on Kathmandu, was now there for someone's grasping.

Jaya Prakash's second brother was King of Patan. Six Pradhans (Newar magnates) of that place conspired and put out the eyes of that prince, so the Kathmandu ruler enticed these six men and their wives to his city and secured them. For some insane reason or other, he spared their lives, but made of them a public mockery. The Pradhans were driven round his city and forced to defile themselves by buying a handful of rice cake at each stop; their wives, dressed up as witches, had to accompany them on the humiliating tour. After further ignominies, he let them go. The *Chronicle* has it, 'These Pradhans, after their release, tried to dethrone Jaya Prakash,' and then, significantly, 'The Gorkhali Rajah was very pleased to hear of all these happenings.

Next came the turn of Bhatgaon. Ranjit Malla, the ruler, threw some visitors from Kathmandu into prison on the silly pretext that they were too proud of their dress. Jaya Prakash protested: on that, they were released. He then imprisoned some of Ranjit Malla's subjects who had come to pray at Pasupatti and only let them go on payment of heavy ransoms.

Later, in financial straits, he robbed the Hindu temples of their lands and treasure in order to pay the Indian mercenaries he had hired to defend himself against Gorkha.

Thus, Jaya Prakash, already at odds with his own Durbar, had earned the undying hatred of the important strategic town of Nawakote, had set the ruling clique of Patan against himself and had alienated the King of Bhatgaon. In a crisis he was not entitled to expect assistance.

Meanwhile, in Patan, the rebellious and autocratic Pradhans, after expelling one ruler after another and cutting down the last in order to make room for Prithwi Narain, invited that firebrand to take the throne. He refused, but sent his brother Dalmardan Sah in his place. The Pradhans, then realising the danger of having called in Prithwi Narain, set Dalmardan up as King of Patan in opposition to Gorkha and declared war on Gorkha. Four years later, in 1765, they tired of Dalmardan and threw him out, putting in his place a figurehead of a monarch.

47

Thus Patan drew down vengeance upon itself.

Bhatgaon, as has been said, was in constant and futile quarrel with Kathmandu. From spite, he called upon Prithwi Narain in 1749 to invade the Valley and attack Kathmandu. So Bhatgaon also prepared his own funeral.

Watching these antics was the most dogged opportunist of his time, obsessed with an overweening ambition and a cold determination to wipe out all memory of his father's defeat at the hands of Kathmandu.

The Gurkha Army was now being organised by its young leader for the great task ahead of it. As in our own Scottish highlands in days long gone by, the fighting unit was a small one. In the case of the Gurkhas, it was the Company of some one hundred and fifty men, each Company having a band of about ten men and an establishment of 'artificers'. The Company carried two flags. The armament came to be mainly firelocks, but in place of bayonet these highlanders carried the *khora* and the *kukri*. The bow and arrow were still in use on both sides in the days of Prithwi Narain.

It was an army such as this, organised in companies, for there were no battalions even in 1814, which marched into Tibet and faced the Chinese hordes in the 1790's, and with such intrepid courage fought the British from 1814 to 1816.

In the year of Prithwi's accession, 1742, the casual ascetic had strolled into Kathmandu and told its king that the young prince of Gorkha's soldiers were in the streets of Nawakote. Jaya Prakash took alarm and sent a force to drive them back to their own country. This was easily done. They were not in strength.

Gorkha tried again a year later, relying on his friendship with Kasiram Thapa, to have the keys of Nawakote handed to him, but Jaya Prakash had stepped in, and Kasiram lay dead. Nevertheless, the Kathmandu chief did not march. Enraged at the death of his friend, Prithwi launched his first major operation, determined at any cost to seize once more the forward sap of Nawakote. In force he assailed the place, drove Kathmandu from it and finally secured it. It was his and the death of Kasiram Thapa sealed its people to him for ever.

Nawakote in his hands, the next step in his plans was the capture of Kirtipore, a town on an eminence three hundred feet above the plain, in the south-west corner of the Valley, about three miles from Patan and under the sovereignty of that duchy. The Gurkha Army now descended from the hills to fight its first campaign upon the plains of the Nepal Valley. Expecting the place to fall to them, they launched a precipitate attack upon it. But the men of Kirtipore were Newars of mettle. Their resistance was fierce and stubborn. The Gurkhas fell back, only to be set upon by Jaya Prakash who now led an army far more numerous than theirs, reinforced by some thousands of soldiers from India under Saktibalabh Sardar. Weight of numbers bore the hard-fighting Gurkhas and the intrepid youth who led them back upon the hills they had come from. The slaughter on both sides was heavy, and so was the Gurkha defeat. Prithwi barely escaped with his life.

There, in his hills, the Gurkha prince nursed his wounds, restored his power and gradually pushed his Trojan horses into the three principalities of the Valley. He had set his hand to the plough. While he breathed he would never turn back.

The nobles of Kirtipore, deserted by their overlord of Patan in time of need, came in deputation to their saviour, Jaya Prakash, to swear the fealty of their city to him. It is incredible that his sole response to this was to arrest the deputation and to slaughter others of the nobles of Kirtipore. Again he ventured to make a mockery of his victims. The chief of the deputation, Danuvanta, was compelled to parade through the streets of Kathmandu dressed as a woman at the head of his fellows similarly apparelled. Those who survived were thrown into prison. Yet Kirtipore's famous resistance had saved the Valley and saved its states, including Kathmandu.

Prithwi now found time to marry. Hamilton tells us that Digbandan, a Rajah who ruled in the western part of the old kingdom of Makwanpore, had a very beautiful sister, Maya, for whom Prithwi offered himself as a suitor. He was rejected with scorn as a match far below her rank. Although later accepted, the rejection rankled and the Gurkha chief set to work to suborn the feeble Digbandan's minister and army chiefs. In 1761 the time was ripe and Prithwi openly attacked his brother-in-law, Digbandan, seized him and his family, appropriated his estates and put to death all those who had resisted his onslaught in their endeavours to save their master. Some, it is said, he flayed alive. Digbandan, his wife and children, he imprisoned while, to retaliate on those dignitaries who had scorned his suit, he handed their children over to low-caste families to be brought up in low-caste trades. Digbandan's family would have starved, had not their kinsman, the Rajah of Palpa, provided a pittance to keep them alive.

Gorkha now realised that she could not meet Kathmandu in the open plain until she had further sapped the resources of her enemy. But at least that enemy did not again dare to climb the hills to clear Gurkhas from Nawakote. She had instilled that much respect into Nepal and, in doing

E

so, had her foot inside the door to heave it open when she willed. Had the Gurkhas possessed artillery and a siege train, Kirtipore, Bhatgaon, Patan and Kathmandu itself, would have fallen to assault, but there was none in all the hills and, had there been any, no roads by which to move it. Without the means of breaching the walls, there was no way of entering these cities except through treachery, a *ruse de guerre* or by starving them out.

So the Gurkha commander now applied a blockade to the Valley, to weaken it, make its people discontented and even perhaps to starve them. He also sent his spies and Brahman agents into the three cities to contact all discontented, disappointed and disloyal men and to bring them into communication with him. Danuvanta, the humiliated aristocrat of Kirtipore, eagerly swallowed the bait.

The Gurkhas established military posts on each of the seven passes that entered the Valley to prevent supplies of any sort whatsoever reaching the inhabitants. Jaya Prakash either dared not or was too apathetic to resist his determined tormentor, however weakened by the recent defeat. Year after year, at all seasons, the blockade continued. Father Giuseppe relates that the King of Gorkha's 'orders were most rigorously obeyed for every person who was found in the road, with only a little salt or cotton about him, was hanged upon a tree, ... even the women and children did not escape, for having supplied a little cotton to the inhabitants of Nepal; and when I arrived in that country ... it was a most horrid spectacle to behold so many people hanging on the trees in the road. However, the King of Gorkha being also disappointed of gaining his ends by this project, fermented dissensions among the noblemen of the three Kingdoms of Nepal, and attached to his party many of the principal ones, by holding forth to them liberal and enticing promises; for which purpose he had about 2,000 Brahmans in his service. When he thought he had acquired a party sufficiently strong, he advanced a second time with his army to Kirtipore and laid siege to it by the north-west quarter, that he might avoid exposing his armies between the two cities of Kathmandu and Patan. . . .'

As Father Giuseppe relates, Prithwi Narain swarmed down upon Kirtipore for a second time, after years of ceaseless preparation, activity and scheming. Kathmandu was but four miles away: Patan was closer still. But neither state lifted a finger to aid the stricken and valiant town. 'After a siege of several months,' wrote Father Giuseppe, 'the King of Gorkha demanded the regency of Kirtipore; when the Commandant of the town, seconded by the approbation of the inhabitants, dispatched to

him by an arrow a very pertinent and exasperating answer.' Prithwi was
so enraged by this that he ordered a general assault from all sides, only to
be again beaten back by the resolute garrison. In the assault his brother
Sarup Ratna was seriously wounded in the eye by an arrow and would
have been killed, had not his companions appealed to the Nepalese soldier whose sword was raised to despatch him. . . . 'Kings we may not kill:
this is a king.' He was borne from the field by some low-caste men to the
house of Father Michael Angelo, where he was cared for and cured of his
wound. Foiled once more, the Gurkha Army wound its way back up to
Nawakote.

Jaya Prakash did not interfere. Prithwi, vowing revenge for both insult and injury, consolidated at Nawakote and turned his restless attention westwards, marching with a considerable force on Lamjung where
his jealous kinsman was once more threatening to break the peace. Lamjung now felt the lash of the frustrated king. Prithwi attacked at once and
after several hard-fought actions brought Lamjung to terms such as to
ensure the quiescence of that chieftain while the Gurkha power was engaged to the east. He then swept south-eastwards, thrust the Rajah of
Makwanpore from his capital, seized his dominions right down to the
plains of the Terai and drove Abdullah, the Rajah's Muslim liegeman, in
a tearful rage to Calcutta, unavailingly to demand restitution of the twenty-
two villages seized from him in the Saran district.

The Gorkha now returned to his first love, the Valley of Nepal. In
1767 he launched his third attack on Kirtipore and met with the usual
stern opposition. The army was commanded by his brother Sarup Ratna:
the King himself conducted operations from the tall, square, brick-built
Darbar Hall at Nawakote. The siege proceeded for several months during which the two kings of Patan and Bhatgaon had leisure to compose
their quarrels and to combine at last to assail the invader. But it was too
late. The Gurkha Army, supported by defecting noblemen of Kathmandu,
beat them off with severe loss. Danuvanta, the disgraced aristocrat of
Kirtipore, burning with hatred for Jaya Prakash, escaped and deserted to
the Gurkhas. He then treacherously introduced them into the town.

The Gurkhas crept in and seized all the gates and strong points, but the
citadel still held out. Prithwi Narain, Father Giuseppe tells us, offered a
general amnesty and the gallant but exhausted inhabitants surrendered
when they could still have resisted. There follows a fearful tale of treachery and horror. '. . . Prithwi Narain, who was at Nawakote, issued an
order to Sarup Ratna, his brother, to put to death some of the principal
inhabitants of the town, and to cut off the noses and lips of everyone,

even the infants, who were not found in the arms of their mothers: ordering at the same time all the noses and lips to be preserved, that he might ascertain how many souls there were, and to change the name of the town into Naskatipore, which signifies the town of cut-noses. The order was carried into execution with every mark of horror and cruelty, none escaping except those who could play on wind instruments: although Father Michael Angelo, who, without knowing that such an inhuman scene was then exhibited, had gone to the house of Sarup Ratna, and interceded much in favour of the poor inhabitants ... (They) came in great bodies to us in search of medicines: and it was most shocking to see so many living people with their teeth and noses resembling the skulls of the deceased.' It is related that the noses and lips were weighed at 80 lb.

Captain Kirkpatrick, in 1793, on his way to Kathmandu from Patna, wondered why so many of his Nepalese porters lacked lips and noses.

The Gurkhas, now under Rama Krishna Rana* — for Prithwi Narain had marched eastwards — turned on Patan. Laying siege to it they beat the Patan forces in repeated engagements until, finally, under threat of the same fate as befell the inhabitants of Kirtipore but with the additional loss of their right hands, and with a promise that their lives would be respected, the people of Patan gave in.

In the meantime Ranjit Malla of Bhatgaon had implored help from the English Company. The response was a typical compromise, for it amounted to sending a meagre detachment of troops under Captain Kinloch into the foothills about Segouli where it was lost in the immensity of the mountains and forests, took the deadly *awal* fever and had to get out as best it could before the threat of the whole Gurkha Army which had marched from Patan.

At Patan Prithwi treated the Pradhans with much consideration until he had them all in his power when he executed them, on the principle that 'once a traitor: always a traitor'. It was they who had invited him to assume their city.

Kathmandu, rotted out by treason, fell an easy prey while the Indra-Jatra festival was on and all the garrison seduced from their duties. Jaya Prakash fled to Bhatgaon, taking with him on the way the King of Patan.

The Gurkhas now 'mopped up' in the Valley against the brave and despairing resistance of village after village. In July 1769, they appeared in force before Bhatgaon, whose king had befriended the Prince of Gorkha

* Nepalese genealogy shows him as the son of Ahiram Konwar, the King of Gorkha's minister. From him descends the celebrated Rana family of Nepal.

in his younger days. Bhatgaon had seven illegitimate sons, all traduced for gold by the agents of Prithwi Narain.

At the western gate there was no opposition at all to the Gurkhas' entry. The Tibetan mercenaries enlisted by Jaya Prakash were in no state to oppose his enemy for, distrusting their loyalty, he had burnt them alive in their barracks. The town was carried and the palace surrounded. Jaya Prakash here boldy confronted the soldiers of his old rival, determined to resist to the end. He was cut down but not killed. Mortally wounded, he rebuked with dignity the Gurkha soldiers who mocked at the three hapless and defeated Malla princes of Kathmandu, Patan and Bhatgaon.

Jaya Prakash died upon the royal slab at the temple of Pasupatti and Ranjit Malla withdrew from all the violence, bloodshed and confusion of the Valley to a holy sanctuary at Benares, while the unlucky King of Patan lay till his death in irons in a prison cell. As he stood on the summit of the Chandragiri Pass, Ranjit Malla looked back and cursed the seven traitors who, by every bond of blood and gratitude, should have stood by him to the very bitter end.

Prithwi Narain summoned to his presence the seven traitorous bastards, sternly denounced them, severed their noses and robbed them of their possessions.

While operations were delayed at Patan by the despatch of Gurkha forces to search for Captain Kinloch's column, Prithwi Narain, disdaining any further military action on the part of his adversaries in the Valley, sent north his Thakur general, Kahar Sing, to subjugate the country right up to the Kuti and Kirong passes and to secure those entries against Tibetan interference. He himself marched east with Rama Krishna to measure swords with the Kiranti tribes. These warrior highlanders were fighters after the pattern of the Parbatiyas of the western hills. The struggle was a grim one and the skill displayed on both sides of a high order. At last the Gurkhas drove the Kiranti forces back on Dulikhel, where the able and courageous Mohindra Rai barred the way. Most of the inhabitants had fled. Mohindra was urged to retreat but contemptuously refused. Here he stood at bay with ever diminishing numbers for six long months while the Gurkhas hung doggedly on to him thrusting and probing to break in. Worn out at last by the ceaseless battering, his forces depleted, he was broken in a furious battle in the hills on 21st June 1768. Mohindra fell where he had fought. The Gorkha King, as he rode over the battlefield, paid tribute to the body of his gallant enemy.

Recognising that he could never again undertake such savage fighting without severe damage to his power, he acted with a generosity that is all too unusual in his ruthless nature. He showed every kindness to the dead chief's family and took them under his own protection. The Kiranti on this fringe of the Valley he treated with equal consideration, setting their leaders up as Governors of their own provinces under his over-lordship. He thus secured their loyalty. It was left to his grandson to complete the subjugation of these stubborn tribes.

In the Valley he sought to terrify: in the Eastern mountains to pacify. The Kiranti now became Gurkhas — subjects of Gorkha.

Returning to the Valley, the victorious King established his capital at Kathmandu and had himself proclaimed King of Nepal. At last the Valley, with the fall of Patan, was united under one king and that an able, energetic, resolute and courageous, but cruel, monarch. Nepal soon came to imply the Valley, the great expanse of hills up to Sikkim comprising the Kiranti country, the stretch northwards to the Tibetan border from the Kirong to the Kuti, the old Gorkha Kingdom and the lands between it and the Valley. All within these borders were Gurkhas and Nepalis, the subjects of Gorkha and of Nepal.

But Gorkha, the proud, the independent, was set about with clans jealous of her newly-won power, smarting from wounds she had inflicted, ready to move in if the Gorkha King too long absented himself and his armies. He marched westwards on the Chaubisia, the twenty-four lordships. Taking them piecemeal, he crushed them with a succession of swift, powerful strokes, until he turned south on Tannahung where he met his match. The Chief of Tannahung dealt him blow for blow, steadily and unflinchingly. Prithwi knew when to stop: it was his great asset as a commander. He drew off to consolidate his gains and, as it happened, never again returned to settle with Tannahung.

The next year his forces moved on Vijayapore to extinguish that kingdom which lay inconveniently close to the Nepalese routes into India. It will be remembered that at this time its prince was a boy in the care of his mother and of the Kiranti Chauntriya, Agam Singha. The Gurkha flail fell on Vijayapore. The Queen Mother fled with her five-year-old boy and Agam Singha into the Company's territory. Prithwi Narain considered the boy to be a danger while he lived, so attempted to inveigle him into his power, promising to restore him to his throne. Failing in this, he then offered to hold the territories himself, paying an annual tribute to the Company for he was fearful lest the British should take up the boy's quarrel. Again failing, he is said to have paid one of his Brahman minions to insinuate himself into the favour of the Queen Mother.

Under pretence of inoculating the boy against smallpox, this priest inserted a poison which brought out the most dreadful ulcerations on the child's body, from which he perished. At any rate, to lend colour to the report, the Brahman is supposed to have retired to Nepal.

The Rajah had paid one elephant a year to the British as rent for the Makwanpore Terai: this the new Gurkha ruler continued to pay.

Prithwi Narain's life was drawing to a close. In 1772* this violent man, the hero of Nepal, the tireless and astute warrior, passed away at Mohan Tirtha on the Gandak River.

This record is in itself an assessment of his achievement in the making of modern Nepal. During those few years between the conquest and his early death, he organised the administration of his extensive dominions and reformed its currency. As a soldier he may well have owed success to his introduction of firelocks which, until his time, were unknown in the hills. In so far as he could, he adopted the Company's methods of discipline, fully realising their value in war, but he was no lover of the British in India and distrusted all Europeans. On his assumption of power in Nepal, the Christian Fathers asked permission to leave the country and departed into British territory.

He was the founder both of modern Nepal and of the Gurkha nation, as well as of the fighting prowess of that highland people. He is the national hero.

* The date of Prithwi Narain's death is given by different authorities as anything from 1771 to 1775.

8

Expanding Nepal

———————————❊———————————

IMMEDIATELY on King Prithwi Narain's death, his elder son, Pratap Sing Sah, clapped his only brother, Bahadur Sah, in gaol to ensure his own peaceful succession. From there he exiled him.

Nepal now entered upon a period of expansion, combined with confusion at the summit, where the usual struggle for power ensued until another outstanding personality emerged to control the jealous and unscrupulous disputants. As the two aspects of Nepalese life were not interrelated, they will be treated separately. Had there been a resolute monarch in charge of affairs, there would have been better calculated direction of strategic policy, and chaos in government would not have been there to prevent proper consolidation of Nepal's position. As it was, the military, and so the administrative situation, on her borders were loose-knit and unstable. She over-reached herself as has happened to other expanding nations before and after her.

It was not to be expected that the lesser rulers who followed the great King would refrain from employing the war machine that he had left to them in the full flush of its triumph. With varying success Pratap Sing attempted to expand his territory at the expense of Sikkim, while at the same time seeking to settle affairs with the truculent Chaubisia rajahs. The hill states of Someswar, Upadrong, and Jogimara fell to him. He died in 1777 and was succeeded by his infant son, the notorious Ranbahadur. The exiled Bahadur Sah at once returned from Bettiah to assume the office of Regent and a deadly feud arose between himself and the boy's mother. The Queen's party won. Bahadur Sah had to flee the country.

During the regency of Rajendra Lakhshmi, the Queen Mother, her famous general, Rama Krishna Rana, had pressed Nepal's borders further west to Kaski and Gurrumkote. Lamjung and the gallant Tannahung had fallen.

Rajendra Lakhshmi died and Bahadur Sah hastened back to Nepal to seize the reins of government. His regency and the later reign of Ranbahadur are notable for the series of daring, almost reckless, expeditions undertaken in the Kiranti country and into Sikkim and Tibet, and for the brilliant operations of Generals Damodar Pande, Sarup Sinha, Rama Krishna Rana and Amar Sing Thapa, resulting in the subjection of the Chaubisia and Baisi states—all except the influential Palpa—the Kiranti, and the conquests of Garhwal and Kumaon in the far west.

In 1788 Bahadur Sah set in motion the Gurkha Subha of Morang to invade Sikkim with a force of 6,000 men of whom 2,000 were regular fusiliers. Launching the operation from Kiranti country he encountered little opposition until he approached Gangtok, the capital, where the Rajah of Sikkim came out in force to meet the Gurkhas. The Subha won a complete victory, but not without severe loss. He then invested the city, from which the Rajah had made good his escape to the Tibetan frontier, whence he sent out urgent appeals for help. The Lhassa Government begged aid from China for it, too, was by now beset by Gurkha forces, which had penetrated through the perilous Kuti pass in order to compel the Tibetans to cease circulating debased coins in Nepal at an unfair rate of exchange.

The Chinese Emperor, somewhat alarmed at these Gurkha advances, the one into the territory of his rather shadowy vassal at Lhassa and the other threatening to command the Chumbi Valley route, prepared to respond to the call for help.

The Gurkha account of this Tibetan campaign is full of sweet reasonableness towards the 'Bhotiyas' of Tibet, relating that right from the days of Prithwi Narain they had complained without result to the evasive Tibetans about this business of the coinage. The fact of the matter was probably that they found the quarrel over coinage a good enough pretext, if any were needed, on which to invade Tibet with a chance of raiding some of the vast wealth hidden away in her monasteries. However, the serious view of this incursion taken by the Chinese Court induced them to come to terms with Lhassa. Their army had penetrated to Shekkar Dzong and laid siege to that place, beating off several attacks made by Tibetan forces, but failing to crack the nut of the defence. Loot, the Gurkhas did secure: enough to whet the appetite. The Chinese General, Chan-chu, arrived in Lhassa 'with three or four Umbas, or general officers, and a large force'. His duty was to drive the invaders out of the country. At this juncture, it would be well to quote the Chinese historian, Wei Yuan. '... the Gorkhas, using as the pretext the increases of taxes on merchandise and the admixture of dust in the table-salt, sent troops and invaded the frontier area. ... As for the officers whom the (Chinese) Government appointed, in order to help in the extermination of invaders — e.g. Officer of the Guards Pa-Chung, Tartar Generals Ao-Hui, Ch'eng-te, and others—they tried to settle the matter amicably and to get peace through bribery. So they secretly advised the Tibetan Abbots and other ecclesiastics privately to pay the Gorkhas a yearly subsidy of 15,000 in gold in order to stop the military operations.

'At that time the Dalai Lama could not agree to the suggestion. Nevertheless, Pa-Chung ventured to deceive the Emperor by presenting a memorial to the effect that the rebels had surrendered.'

The upshot was that Tibet guaranteed to abandon her nefarious juggling with the currency and ceded to Nepal a strip of much-coveted territory on the frontier at the heads of the Kuti and Kirong passes. She also undertook to pay annual tribute to Kathmandu, but paid only once and no more, an omission which led in 1791 to a much more serious assault from Nepal and to more far-reaching consequences.

Meanwhile, in Sikkim the Subha and his forces were rather more successful. The Rajah did indeed obtain 'Bhotiya' reinforcements and the Gurkha Army did not have everything their own way. In the end, however, they overran most of the country. Hamilton, in 1808, said that there were Gurkha troops 'at Sikkim and Darjiling, the two chief places in the district'.

In 1791, defrauded of their promised tribute and this time determined to exact it in plunder, the Gurkha Army once more advanced on Tibet.

The circumstances were these. The Tashi Lama of Tibet had gone on a visit to Peking and there died, leaving great wealth in Lhassa. The elder of the two surviving brothers seized upon this treasure, denying the younger, Sumhur Lama, any share in it. Sumhur Lama hastened into Nepal to lay his complaints before its king and to crave help to secure the fortune that was his. The Lama told the needy Bahadur Sah of Tibetan gold and silver mines and of all the stored wealth of that vast mountain plateau, which would be his for the taking. The avarice of the Nepalese Court was stirred to its sensitive depths. A force of 18,000 men was organised and moved at great speed up through the Kuti pass to Nilam and on to Digarchi (Shigatze), burning to see that justice was done to the wronged Lama!

Pao-Tai, the Chinese Resident at Lhassa, panic-stricken, tried to remove both the Dalai Lama and the Panchin-Lama to sanctuary outside Tibet, intending to abandon the country to the invaders. There was no defence of the tactically strong city of Digarchi as the Lamas ordained that divinations showed that the Heavenly Mother was opposed to fighting. So, it must be accepted, were the Tibetan commanders.

Digarchi was captured and it and the monastery of Tashi Lhumpo well and truly plundered. The loot was immense and well worth the trouble. The Gurkhas, heavily laden and therefore fully satisfied that the complainant's wrongs were righted to their own personal satisfaction, now started to retire. With the treasure, they had also secured as a hostage a high dignitary, a Vizier of Lhassa. Behind them, as they retreated, they left strong rearguards.

News of the outrage was sent hotfoot to the Son of Heaven who despatched a special envoy to Nepal. It happened that the before-mentioned Officer of the Guards Pa-Chung was walking with the Emperor when the news came that 'the rebels had invaded Tibet. He committed suicide by throwing himself into a river.'

The Chinese General Ao-Hui now made a demonstration against the invaders and seized a small outpost, 'held by 100 men, and memorialised the Throne to the effect that the enemy had retreated. They intended that the matter should be regarded as closed, and did not mention the presence of rebel forces at such places as Chi-Lung and Yung-Hsia,' wrote Wei Yuan. The Throne did not credit this report, so despatched the Tartar General, Fu Kang'an, with 70,000 men and batteries of leathern guns to Lhassa to deal with the situation. Meanwhile, the envoy was on his way to Kathmandu, sending ahead of him his credentials with a demand that the Nepalese ruler should come out to meet him, to which Bahadur Sah replied that he would do him no such honour: if he wished to come on, he could; if he did not so wish, he could return to his master. The envoy swallowed the rebuff and came on into Kathmandu, where he was treated with little civility. A Nepalese Silver Stick (*Chobdar*) was sent to bring his letters to the palace: the envoy was kept waiting. To the astonishment of the Nepalese the letters were found to contain the outrageous demand for the restitution to Lhassa of the fifty-two crores (some forty million pounds) of plunder, as well as for the release of the important hostage and the surrender of the renegade Lama. The Regent refused and told the Emperor he could do what he pleased about it.

On the return of his humiliated envoy, being informed of the insolence of the Nepalese ruler, the Emperor urged the opening of operations.

Marshal Fu Kang'an now repeated to Kathmandu the demands of the

Celestial Empire, but the only satisfaction he obtained was an offer to hand over the Vizier on condition of peace. The Chinese thereupon opened the war. Bahadur Sah, thoroughly alarmed, sent one of Nepal's most distinguished Generals, Damodar Pande, to take command. The account of these operations varies considerably according to which side, the Chinese or the Nepalese, has the telling of it.* The Chinese Emperor, making his record in the Male Water Rat Year, refers to the event as 'the submission of the Gurkhas in the Female Earth-Bird Year', to the Gurkhas as 'the thieves', to Nepal as 'the country of the thieves' and to their Ruler as 'the Robber Chief'. In his view they did not apparently qualify either as enemy or as a hostile army.

The Chinese Army advanced, headed by Resident Pao-Tai, now wearing a large wooden collar as a mark of Imperial displeasure. Marshal Fu Kang'an directed his advance in three more or less co-ordinated columns. The Gurkha forces, undismayed by the size of their opponent, put matters to the test in a series of hard-fought rearguard actions on the Tibetan plains, but were each time thrown back by the vastly superior numbers of the armies of the Heavenly Dynasty. At Tingri Maidan they suffered a serious reverse. The thought of that bitter struggle high up on the roof of the world inspires awe, and admiration for those Gurkha Commanders and the men they led against the Chinese horde. Forced on to the great passes, they fought stubbornly, destroying tracks and bridges as they deliberately withdrew and inflicting more than one local defeat on the advancing Chinese. Even Wei Yuan admits this. In August 1792, for instance, at the crossing of the Betravati close to the forward sap of Nawakote, Damodar Pande lay in wait on the Gurkha bank of the ravine, let the Chinese troops advance upon the narrow bridge and then assailed them. With the Gurkhas before and their own men pressing down the hill upon them from behind, panic seized the invaders and, at this crisis, Damodar severed the chains of the bridge and sent it spinning into the torrent below.

The eastern Gurkha column was heavily laden with the booty of Digarchi. It should have withdrawn by the Kuti pass but its commanders knew full well that, if they took that route, the Nepalese customs guards would examine their baggage and most of their treasures would go to fill other pockets and the royal treasury. So they decided to pass down by the Hatia or Popti-La, even more perilous than the gaunt track that so scared Father Georgi. Here in the deep snow and the blizzards, they lost two

---

* The account written by Captain Samuel Turner is in Appendix III. Turner having been well received in Tibet, may be somewhat partial to that country.

thousand men from exposure and sheer exhaustion. But they came through. The horrors of that passage are burnt deep into the nation's memory and are spoken of to this day. As a feat of endurance it would be hard to match. It is also memorable for another reason. The army was reduced to such straits from starvation that the men killed and ate the flesh of the Chouri bullocks — the yaks. This apparent transgression was later justified by the Nepalese on the score that the sacred bull of the Shastras was distinguished by its long dewlap, whereas the Chouri animal had no such feature.

Bahadur Sah, in September 1792, with a Chinese army only twenty miles away near Nawakote, sued for peace. He surrendered the Vizier and ordered Sumhur Lama to return whence he came. But the renegade inconveniently poisoned himself and thereby not only ceased to be an asset in the negotiations but also forfeited his right to a share in the treasure of Digarchi, if indeed any had ever been intended for him. However, Bahadur Sah had fallen into the familiar error of believing the enemy to be in better shape than his own forces. The fact was that the Chinese had had enough of this war. They were at their last gasp and were on the wrong side of the high passes, so they readily came to terms by which Nepal was to send a delegation with presents or tribute to Peking every fifth year. Reports vary as to whether the Nepalese handed back their loot, or any part of it. Chinese writers say that Fu Kang'an forced them to do so, Nepalese say that they did nothing of the sort. The former wished to show that everyone everywhere was humbled before their Emperor: the latter, that they cared not a fig for the Celestial Empire or any of its doings. If Bahadur Sah was mistaken in seeking for terms with the Chinese, many of his warrior subjects had no illusions at all about the sorry conditions to which the toil and fighting of the campaign had reduced the Tartar General's armies. They were ill pleased with their Regent.

Tibet, the only aggrieved party, came out of the affair worst of the three, for she received no compensation, apart from being handed back the region at the heads of the Kuti and Kirong passes, but was given the questionable satisfaction of having Chinese garrisons stationed for many years all over her country to afford her protection from 'the thieves'.

However, the war was over and the Chinese soldiers thankfully withdrew.

During this affair, Tibetans and Gurkhas both appealed to Lord Cornwallis, the Governor General in Calcutta, to countenance their cause and to lend his aid. He refused military aid to Nepal on the grounds that for years Britain and China had traded on the coasts and that he would not impair the friendship that existed between the two countries. To Tibet and the Chinese Vizier at Lhassa he pointed out that his Government was friendly to Nepal, having only recently signed a commercial treaty with her. He had some difficulty in replying to the Tibetan despatch, written in Tibetan characters, because none could translate it and so it was sent to Benares to be interpreted. In the early autumn of 1792, therefore, he replied to both complainants that he would send a representative to Kathmandu. There were, moreover, certain clauses in the commercial treaty about which the Nepalese Government was not being too scrupulous and it was as well to send someone to clear up misunderstandings.

In February 1793, Captain Kirkpatrick set out from Bankipore at the head of a British mission. With him went Lieutenants Samuel Scott, W. D. Knox and J. Gerrard, with Mr. Adam Freer as surgeon, and Maulvi Abdul Kadir Khan who had previously been in Kathmandu to negotiate the commercial treaty. It was hoped that the Regent would accept Captain Kirkpatrick as Resident at the Court of Kathmandu — perhaps a rather sanguine hope as the Nepalese Government were not unacquainted with the accidental but nevertheless familiar fate of those states to which the Company appointed its residents.

In March the mission reached Nawakote, where the Nepalese Court was hibernating, only to find that the war was over and that Bahadur Sah had made terms, a circumstance which he had not thought of reporting to the British Government. Kirkpatrick's reception by the Regent was polite, non-committal and rather frigid. It might have been warmer a few months earlier. 'I had now ascertained with sufficient certainty that my residence at this Court was not to be hoped for.' So he made his journey homeward by way of Segouli, crossing into India in mid-April.

He was the first Englishman to enter Nepal. Though politically fruitless, his visit was the subject of a long report on the country which is a tribute to the keen observation, and tireless and politic investigations made by himself and his companions of the mission during those few weeks in the Valley and at Nawakote.

While this distant and severe campaign was in full swing, the Gurkhas out to the west under Rama Krishna Rana and, later, Amar Sing Thapa,* were assailing Kumaon and Garhwal, more than five hundred miles from Kathmandu across the lower Himalaya. Kumaon had fallen to Gurkha

---

* Not to be confused with Amar Sing Thapa, father of the Prime Minister, Bhim Sen Thapa, who was later Governor of Palpa and died in October 1814, just before hostilities broke out with the British.

arms. In 1792 Amar Sing was recalled just as Garhwal was about to collapse. The Chinese were at the very gates of the Valley. The resources,
military and in sheer character and enterprise, of this infant State of Nepal
are astonishing, especially when one remembers that the fighting men
were almost entirely the few Khas, Magar and Gurung of the Parbatiya.
Damodar Pande, and Amar Sing Thapa after him, assuming supreme
command in the west, the Gurkhas by 1803 had crushed both their victims, the Garhwalis being destroyed in a decisive battle near Gurundhana
in the Valley of the Doon, where their rajah, Pradyumna, was slain. He
was unfortunate because he had already sold the family throne for
150,000 rupees, wealth which he did not live to enjoy.

Thus, by this year of 1803, the Gurkhas held sway from the heart of
Sikkim to the borders of Kashmir and the Dogra State. Palpa was a
little island of quasi-independence in the turbulence. Mahadatta, its rajah,
in conspiracy with his brother-in-law, the Regent Bahadur Sah, had sold
out his old allies of Gajarkote, Rising and Kachi. These were engulfed at
leisure by Nepal, and Palpa itself would have gone the same way had it
not been for Mahadatta's friendship with his big neighbour to the south,
the Nawab Vizier of Oudh.

Hamilton, writing at this time, has some searching remarks on the
making of war by the Nepalese. 'Garhwal enjoyed a respite until Ranbahadur returned from Benares, when he sent Amar Sing Thapa with
3,000 fusiliers, and an equal number of regulars, to extend his territories
to the west. No pretext, I believe, was held out for the attack; indeed, so
far as I can learn, the natives do not consider the holding out of any pretence as at all necessary or proper in war, although, in treating with
Europeans, they have now learned to make very appropriate observations
on the subject. Ranbahadur, on the contrary, when collecting this force,
I am credibly informed, gave out very publicly that it was destined to
go either to Calcutta or Pekin, he had not exactly determined which;
and had he considered the force adequate, there is no doubt that he would
have made the attempt, although he was on very good terms with both
Governments.'

The restless Amar Sing Thapa now moved west again. He and Bhagte
Thapa crossed the border into the Dogra country, Amar Sing directed
on the hill fort of Kangra with its sheer cliffs on all sides, Bhagte on
Sujanpore. The Rajah of Kangra, Sangsar, refusing to be locked up in his
fortress, hovered with his forces on the flanks of the two Gurkha columns.
Kangra and Sujanpore were besieged and it seemed that the invaders
would in time prevail, so Sangsar appealed to the powerful Sikh King at

Lahore, Ranjit Singh, the Lion of the Punjab. Amar Sing called on the British at Ludhiana to help him but Colonel Ochterlony refused to move. Ranjit, always ready for a quarrel, especially one that might enrich him, passed a considerable force into the area and Amar Sing's little army was beaten and hustled back towards Sirmoor, where a Rajput rajah, Karna Prakash, ruled with his capital at Nahan. He was lucky to be independent; he seemed to have been passed over by the Nepalese Generals. A year or so before, assailed by Sangsar and by the Rajah of Hindur, he had implored Amar Sing to help him. This General sent Bhagte Thapa with a thousand fusiliers. Sirmoor advanced but, defeated by the combined forces opposed to him, he was forced to flee to Amar Sing's camp. Amar Sing then took over the operations and, separating Hindur from his ally, thrashed him. Thereafter, as related, he had moved on Kangra. Amar Sing now sent to the Rajah of Sirmoor to come forth and confer with him, so as to combine in the best course to be taken. This man, thinking Amar Sing's bolt was shot, insolently refused, whereupon the Gurkha, shattered as his army was and in extreme danger, turned savagely on him, putting a detachment under his own son to bring the Sirmoori to his senses. This the young leader did; the Rajah fled and Amar Sing annexed his state to Nepal. He would have gone further, to Hindur, but Ochterlony, then in the neighbourhood, threatened to interfere.

Colonel Ochterlony and Amar Sing Thapa were destined to become better acquainted.

During these years of expansion, and of menace to the peace of China, Tibet, the Punjab and British India, the Court of Nepal had been behaving in its customary manner. The feud between the Queen Mother and Bahadur Sah has been mentioned. After her death, Bahadur Sah, as Regent, deliberately set out to debauch her young son, Ranbahadur, so that he would never be thought fit to rule. It is disputable whether it would not have been kinder to have had him assassinated: politically, it was merely inexpedient to make him a martyr. He never was fit to rule but the treatment, the encouragement to indulgence and vice of all kinds, deranged his weak mind and he grew up little better than a criminal lunatic. He had married Tripura Sundari, daughter of the Gulmi Raja, whom he neglected out of disgust that she had no children, and cohabited with other women. He first had a son by a common slave girl, a *keti*, his mistress.

In the year 1795, suddenly declaring himself sovereign, he arrested, confined and murdered his uncle, the Regent Bahadur Sah. His first act was to open a campaign against the Jumla rajah, whom all the mountain chiefs looked to, if not as their liege lord, at least as the doyen of their order. This chief he drove out of the hills to refuge with the Vizier of Oudh. He then kidnapped and forcibly seduced a Brahman girl, a deadly sacrilege in the eyes of the faith. His object, it has been said, was to raise the caste of all future sovereigns of Nepal. The priests damned him and her as incestuous. She fell ill of small-pox: he poured treasure upon the priests in costly rites and she recovered but, at the first sight in the mirror of her ravaged beauty, she killed herself. The King went berserk. He rained curses on Brahmans and on the very Gods themselves. He scourged the Brahmans to disgorge his money: he tore images of Devi from the temples: in excrement he ground them to dust with his artillery, cutting down the gunners who refused the sacrilegious work.

The Valley rose against him. In superstitious dread for his own fate under the Brahmans' curse, he abdicated, handing his throne to the infant, Girvan Judha Bikram, his son by the Brahmani girl, and retired as a Swami to religious devotion at Benares to procure for himself a place in heaven. This was in A.D. 1800.

The *keti*, his mistress, remained in Nepal as Regent to the boy king. Tripura Sundari, the legitimate queen, went with her husband into exile. Despite her loyalty, he treated her no better. The religious life ill suited him: in fact, before his departure he had already repented him of his decision and tried to reverse it by shutting himself up in Patan. Damodar Pande acted quickly, set upon Ranbahadur's adherents at Patan, scattered them and saw to it that Ranbahadur crossed the Churiaghati range into India. The exile bore no friendship to Damodar and his house.

At Benares Ranbahadur ran up considerable debts to the British Government which supplied him with his needs. For repayment of these debts, the British in 1801 entered into a treaty with him, one of its clauses being that the Court of Kathmandu should accept a British Resident. In February 1802 Captain Knox, taking with him Dr. Francis Hamilton, entered Kathmandu as the first British Resident. It seems that the slave-girl Regent was willing enough to accept him but the nobles, for that very reason and because the hated Ranbahadur had agreed to the arrangement, would have none of it. Captain Knox found his position so futile and difficult that in 1803 he went back to India. The second treaty of commerce which had been negotiated in 1801 became a dead letter: a new treaty brought by Captain Knox had, at the urging of Damodar Pande, been signed by the Regent but very soon afterwards abrogated.

The ex-king soon found consolation with one of the frail beauties of Benares on whom he bestowed Tripura Sundari's jewels, having stripped them off that long-suffering queen. With no means, and deprived by the Slave-Regent of the allowance which was her due, the poor lady was reduced to the utmost distress. She wandered off with her maidens towards her beloved mountains.

In Nepal, the *keti* had elevated to the post of Prime Minister a nephew of Damodar Pande. This young man, far from supporting his uncle, deliberately contrived to weaken his position by removing from every command they held in the army, especially of fortresses, the whole of his Pande relatives.

Feeling ran high against him. His aristocratic enemies sought their chance and assassinated him. Damodar, probably quite innocent, was suspect and a faction formed, a dangerous one led by the Regent who detested the Pande. To replace the dead Prime Minister the Regent now raised up a man of low degree, to the infinite discontent of the Court. Not far away, with the season of the dreaded *awal* of the Terai closing in upon her, was the distressed Queen of Nepal, a woman of high character, birth and probity, and an object of popular sympathy. In authority in Kathmandu was a slave woman, the target of derision and contempt.

The distinguished houses of Pande and Thapa had been in bitter feud for generations. Kaji* Damodar Pande now invited the Princess Tripura Sundari to return to Nepal. Thus he blindly hastened the quarrel to a dreadful crisis.

* General.

9

Nepal and the Hon'ble Company

———————❋———————

HEARING of the approach of the Princess, the Regent sent soldiers to bring all her male adherents in irons to Kathmandu. This was done and it was hoped that, thus deprived, the Queen would perish in the forests. But Tripura Sundari was daughter of a Gurkha chieftain. She would not turn back, but came on with a handful of female attendants to Chisapani, where the little fortress stands on the hill by the cold, clear spring. 'An additional company of Seapoys was sent to Chisapani, as if soldiers were the proper persons to stop the progress of a few helpless women. The officer commanding had received positive orders to refuse the princess admittance; but he contented himself with executing merely the letter of his orders. He took in all his garrison, shut the gates, and allowed the lady and her attendants to walk quietly round the walls. Much anxiety was now evident at the capital, and another company of Seapoys was dispatched to Chitlang, with positive orders to prevent the princess from advancing farther. . . . The officer commanding the Company met the poor princess and her attendants on the road, and, being a man of true honour, with a good deal of difficulty mustered courage to disclose his orders. When he had done so, the highborn lady, unmoved by fear, pulled out a dagger and saying, "Will you presume to oppose the lawful wife of a Gorkhali Rajah, while going to her own estate?", she struck him on the arm; on which . . . he immediately retired, quite ashamed of the service on which he had been employed; . . . The princess that morning entered the Valley of Nepal, and halted about five miles from the capital. No sooner was this known than she was joined by Damodar Pande, and all ranks flocked to pay their respects, and among them all the officers of Government, except the low favourite, who immediately fled towards Tibet. The Regent, thus deserted, retired with the [young] Rajah and her son to the sanctuary of a temple, taking with her all the money in the treasury and the jewels of the crown.' Thus runs Hamilton's account and, as he was in Nepal at the time, there can be no better.

The Princess assumed the Regency. She conducted herself with dignity and clemency, allowing an income to her rival and abstaining from the only too common massacre of those opposed to her régime. As her chief minister she appointed Damodar Pande. Both she and he were apprehensive of the possible return of her husband, Ranbahadur, and suspected that the British Embassy might intrigue to bring him back. It was this suspicion, among other causes, which led Captain Knox to conclude that his mission was *persona non grata* and that it had better leave, the new Regent having refused to ratify the treaty, to the clear disappointment of her Minister. Damodar wrote to an influential personage in Benares begging him to see that the exile did not quit that city, for Lord Wellesley had informed the Durbar that, since there was no treaty with Nepal, the ex-King was now free to go where he pleased. It is said that Damodar's letter fell into Ranbahadur's hands who, stung into activity, departed immediately and was in Nepal before anyone suspected that he had left Benares.

Damodar, having summoned his troops, hurried out to oppose the King's progress to Kathmandu. As the Nepalese force approached, Ranbahadur turned to a junior secretary, Bhim Sen Thapa, the son of Kaji Amar Sing Thapa of Palpa, for advice. Bhim Sen gave it. Boldly, the King called out loudly to Damodar's officers and men: 'Now show whether you will have me or Damodar Pande for your lord!' At once the whole army ran to him and the gallant veteran, champion of many a hard-fought field in his country's cause, patriot and statesman, was, with his son, bound as a common felon.

Ranbahadur seized the supreme authority, ruling as 'Swami', master or regent, in name, but in fact as King.

The new Swami was cordially received by his wife but did not neglect the frail beauty of Benares, for whom he sent and on whom he lavished his treasure.

This ferocious sovereign's vengeance and the claims of the deadly feud with the House of Pande now met together in common cause. Bhim Sen Thapa's father, the Provincial Governor, Amar Sing Thapa, lay in prison, cast there by his old enemy, Damodar Pande. Ranbahadur forthwith released the Thapa and despatched him westwards to his home in Palpa.

Jumla, the nominal head of the Chaubisia, was attacked, but proved a match for the army of Gorkha. For two years, with a force, it is said, of

22,000 men, he held his own. Ranbahadur then drew off until Jumla had released most of his men to their homes. He then suddenly assailed the Rajah, using such savagery 'that no force durst afterwards to assemble', wrote Kirkpatrick.

The Swami, incited by Bhim Sen, confronted Damodar with the letter he had written to Benares, denounced him and handed him and his son to the executioner. As the two were being led to their death, the son proposed resistance, for by a sudden attempt they might have gained possession of arms and, with their undaunted and well-known courage, they might well have found a following from among the Guard. But the veteran counselled resignation as he feared that violence might lead to the extirpation of the rest of his family. He may have been right, for this is not the last that is heard of the feud with the Thapas. And so he died.

But this was not enough. There was another rival at Palpa. Ranbahadur despatched an embassy to request the Rajah's sister in marriage, offering, in the event, to increase the domains of his prospective brother-in-law. Palpa sent the lady, and his younger brother to escort her. Prithwi Pal, fearing treachery, did not come himself. The brother and sister were kindly received but Ranbahadur was not satisfied; 'I have been a King and should therefore think myself degraded by worshipping you, (according to the Hindu custom) when I receive your sister from your hands; it will be therefore very pleasing to me, if your brother, Prithwi Pal, who is a prince superior to me in birth, would attend to give away his sister.' The priest in the girl's suite was sent to persuade Prithwi Pal, giving the most solemn assurances from Ranbahadur as to his safety. Prithwi Pal came. On arrival at Kathmandu his four hundred followers were set upon and disarmed and he himself was cast into prison. Ranbahadur thus laid claim to the extensive lands of Palpa including Butwal, a district ceded by Palpa to the British Company, an enroachment which sprung a dire conflict ten years later. To Butwal he sent his officials to exact the land rent and followed them by soldiers to occupy the territory. No more was heard of the impending marriage. Too much sympathy need not, perhaps, be wasted on this dastard because, in order to ingratiate himself with the monster who was to be his brother-in-law, he brought with him and delivered up to this butcher the widow and only surviving son of his old friend, Damodar Pande.

Sherbahadur, illegitimate brother of the now detested and feared Ranbahadur, was hailed to the presence to answer charges of conspiring to raise Palpa to the throne. He was ordered to leave Kathmandu and to join the army. 'We are sons of the same father,' said he defiantly, 'Go you

69

and I will follow.' In a towering rage, the King ordered him for execution. Sherbahadur whipped out his sword and cut his brother down. Balnar Sing Konwar, father of the great Jang Bahadur, slashed at the assailant and killed him. As he died, Ranbahadur confided his boy, Girvan Judha Bikram Sah, the illegitimate by the Brahman girl, to the care of Bhim Sen Thapa.

Bhim Sen promptly rid himself of the slave-queen by compelling her to commit *suttee* on the King's funeral pyre. With customary thoroughness, he used the occasion to extirpate his enemies. Fifty army officers and many nobles came under the executioner's sword. His father, Amar Sing, he sent to seize the estates of Palpa and to govern the whole region in the name of the King. Close by Palpa was the great Prithwi Narain's daughter, married to the Rajah of Saliyana. Bhim Sen confiscated her estates and carried her and her boy off as captives to the Valley. The throat of Prithwi Pal he slit, there in Kathmandu. To his own staunch supporter, Queen Tripura Sundari, he confided the regency.

With the death of Ranbahadur there ends the legitimate line of Prithwi Narain Sah, King of Gorkha.

As soon as the King breathed his last, Bhim Sen hastened to the Royal Guard to seek their support. He addressed them. Being acclaimed, he immediately surrounded the great hall where the Court was assembled, and massacred every one of those who might stand in his way, under pretence that they were partners in Sherbahadur's conspiracy. To some extent his claim may have been justified.

Bhim Sen Thapa, Prime Minister of Nepal, was now all-powerful. He had acted swiftly and thoroughly, through the medium of the villain who was his master. From now onwards the authority of the Prime Minister in Nepal transcends that of the King until the royal personality ceases to be felt altogether in the country's affairs and the bearer of the empty title is a state prisoner, generation after generation, in his white palace at Kathmandu: so it is until King Tribhuvana in 1950, on the pretext of ill-health and with Indian connivance, reaches Delhi by air.

*   *   *   *   *

The reign is now that of King Girvan Judha Bikram Sah. His Prime Minister is Bhim Sen Thapa, no friend of the British, suspicious and jealous of them. The Regent is the King's stepmother, the Princess Tripura Sundari. Kaji Amar Sing Thapa is fighting in Kangra, six hundred miles from Kathmandu. The year is A.D. 1804.

Gurkha power is at its zenith: it has spread east and west and north, but it has not pushed its way southwards so has not come into rivalry with that other growing power, the phenomenon of the nineteenth century, British India. It is not surprising that Bhim Sen should have failed to assess the immense thrust, military, administrative and spiritual, of this new force in Asia. Some day a historian will explain this unique period in India, why it was unique and how it was that the men matched the period. To Bhim Sen it must have been confusing, for in the end only the cool head and good sense of the incredible Merchant Company preserved to his land its national identity, and saved it from itself.

The story of Nepal is till now a sad tale of brutality and greed: there is still more to come of the same sort. The Parbatiya are a biddable people and must have been so throughout their history. In Chapter 11 are tributes to the men of these tribes. How does one reconcile the high character attributed by so many others with the cruelty and bloodshed of the history of their highlands? In the first place, the history until 1736 is that of the Valley of Nepal in which the Parbatiyas had no part. In the second place, the leaders between whom the atrocious conflicts were waged were Rajputs and the Rajput, brave as he was, and even chivalrous in so many respects, was a cruel and subtle man. He lived in fearful times of conflicting barbarity and civilisation in which the savage brutality of Central Asia had to be met by an equal cruelty. The habit and the example became normal and widespread. In so many parts of the world two hundred years ago horrors were still the ordinary commerce of life, even of so-called civilised peoples. The Parbatiya was led by these men: he followed. Knowing the Gurkha well, one is left to question how far the rank and file of any army are ever to blame for the atrocities of war, the deliberate war policy of the leaders.

* * * * *

Bhim Sen could now look around him. In India he saw a British power in a position of some peril; all about it, India was in ferment. The Mahratta Confederacy was on the warpath while Sindia and Holkar were persecuting the Rajput principalities left over from the Turki expansion. The former was at grips with the brilliant commander, Lord Lake, had been heavily defeated near Delhi and was about to receive the *coup de grâce* at Laswari. Holkar was about to administer a beating at the Mikund Dara Pass to the small force under Monson, an operation which made a far greater noise in the India of its day than its insignificant scale warranted. But there it was: a widely reported defeat of British forces. Soon afterwards, the Mahratta chief combined with Bhurtpore in an attack on

Delhi, stoutly and successfully defended by Lieut.-Colonels Ochterlony and Burn. Then came the British victory over Holkar at Deeg, counter-balanced by Lake's repeated failures to capture the great moated fortress of Bhurtpore. Along the frontiers beyond Bihar and with Gwalior and other native states, the robber Pindari horsemen were making chaos worse confounded. Sikkim, Garhwal, Kumaon, Sirmoor, the Doon, the long strip of the Terai were under the heel of Gorkha. If anything, Bhim Sen must have seen Nepal as a strong and progressing state and British India as one suffering from grievous wounds, any one of which might, if inflamed, be fatal. Addressing the young Rajah in full court, he said, '. . . The Chinese once made war on us but were reduced to seek peace. How then will the English be able to penetrate into our hills? The small fort of Bhurtpore was the work of man, yet the English, being worsted before it, desisted from the attempt to conquer it. Our hills and fastnesses are formed by the hand of God and are impregnable.'

Every Prime Minister of Nepal, from this time until 1858, was faced with the problem as to how to keep the army employed. Every year the whole army was virtually disbanded and raised again. This threw a large number of men out of employment. These men were termed the *Dhake-riah*. There was thus a great reserve of trained soldiers, many of whom would be recalled before long to the colours in the usual course, but who, belonging to tribes whose sole delight and profession was that of war, ardently desired a campaign and so a swift release from their no-pay condition. Added to this, the whole of the upper classes were in the army holding army rank. In 1816, after the Gurkha war was over, Hodgson pressed the Indian Government to recruit these men extensively into its ranks but it was many years before anything of the sort of any material account was done. He saw that a Nepal, bent on expansion, bereft of Sikkim, Kumaon, Garhwal and the Terai, must find some outlet for her ambitions and that outlet must unfortunately be into British India unless another were provided.

In 1801, the cession of the Gorakhpore territory to the Company by the Nawab-Vizier of Oudh, had brought British India into direct contact with the Nepalese frontier. Nepal now started a deliberate policy of infiltration through the Terai, slowly absorbing village after village which was situated either in territory under dispute or in British territory itself. For seven years this seeping away went on, until Bhim Sen began to see it as something usual and not to be resisted by the British victim. However, at length the Governor-General came to realise the dangers of allowing the process to continue, so sent word to Kathmandu that he wished a commission on which there would be a Nepalese representative, to visit the frontier, investigate what encroachments had already been made and make recommendations for the future. The Commission duly assembled and found in favour of the British claims, whereupon the Nepalese delegate returned to Nepal and rendered to his government so misleading a report on the decisions that Bhim Sen not only took no steps to follow the recommendations, but, on the contrary, directed that the gradual policy of assumption was to continue. Kaji Amar Sing Thapa, who had realised the significance of Colonel Ochterlony's intervention at Hindur and who, as a soldier, was more of a realist than the Prime Minister, warned him not to stir up the English to the point of their resorting to arms to settle differences with Nepal. Bhim Sen knew better: he would not listen. He continued his provocative policy and prepared for war. Lord Moira, receiving nothing but evasive answers to his protest, broke off negotiations and abruptly demanded the evacuation within twenty-five days of the Nepalese troops who were occupying the disputed villages in the Gorakhpore Terai. Receiving no satisfaction, he instructed the District Magistrate to send a force to drive the usurpers out. The Gurkhas offered no resistance and withdrew.

In Kathmandu a council was held and the question of war or peace fairly debated. From nine in the morning till eight at night the twenty-two councillors consulted, and the decision was for war. Amar Sing wrote from the distant west, 'We have hitherto but hunted deer: if we engage in this war, we must prepare to fight tigers. . . . The advocate of war (Bhim Sen) who proposes to fight and conquer the English, has been bred up at Court, and is a stranger to the toil and hardships of a military life.' He voted for peace and the cession to the British of the disputed villages. But the revenue from the villages was passing into the coffers of Bhim Sen Thapa's family.

The area was taken over by the British in April 1814, but in May affairs took a more serious turn when Gurkha troops suddenly raided three frontier police-posts in the Butwal District, killed eighteen policemen and put the Darogha to death with singular brutality. These posts had been set up in the normal administrative pattern on the withdrawal of the soldiers from the fever-stricken Terai at the onset of the *awal* season. Bhim Sen now received an ultimatum from the Governor-General at a time when the war party was rampant at Kathmandu, so he disdained, or did not venture, to answer the demand. 'If the English wanted war against the Gurkha conquerors, they could have it.' He then made use of the special position of Nepal as a tributary of the Celestial

Empire to spread the alarm that the Hon'ble Company was contemplating the seizure of the high Himalayan passes leading to Tibet and thus to China, and, posing as the shield of that Empire, to demand Chinese reinforcements. News of this leaked into Calcutta, producing a spate of diplomatic activity and inflaming feeling against Nepal. Lord Moira set his army in motion to assemble at Dinapore, Benares, Meerut and Saharanpore, and Ludhiana. He planned to split it into four columns: from the Dinapore area General Marley with the main force of 8,000 men, directed on Kathmandu by way of the passes of Bichia Koh and Hataura; from Benares, General Wood, with 4,000, on the frontier districts of Butwal and Sheoraj, thence into Palpa; from the Saharanpore area General Gillespie, with 4,000 men, to invade the Valley of the Doon, pass a detachment to the east of Mussoorie by Sansadara directed on Srinagar, the capital of Garhwal, and, with his main force, turn west on Nahan to cooperate with Ochterlony; General Ochterlony, with 6,000 men and twelve guns to move up the left bank of the Sutlej and engage Amar Sing's main forces in Malaun.

The Company's army so disposed, including some Sikh allies and other detachments, amounted to 30,000 men with sixty guns, and a levy of irregulars.

Bhim Sen, being informed of the assembly of enemy forces, prepared to meet them. He had available 12,000 men. The eastern flank opposite Marley and Wood, he held lightly: the western he entrusted to the Governor of the region, Kaji Amar Sing Thapa. Amar Sing had his staunch lieutenant and nephew, Balbahadur, in the Doon Valley at the stockade of Kalunga, or Nalapani, with six hundred men, mainly of the Purana Gorakh Regiment, entirely Magars. Kalunga barred the track to Sansadara and Garhwal. The fort was on a wooded hill, some five hundred feet above the surrounding country.

To hold the western approach by Nahan, the Kaji appointed his son, Ranjur Sing, with 2,000 picked regulars.

He himself, with 3,000 regulars, faced Ochterlony.

If Lord Hastings, formerly Lord Moira, had stretched the English forces wide over a six-hundred-mile front, then so had he stretched those of Nepal. The Company's Commanders had this great advantage in addition to their marked superiority in numbers, namely that, in the opening phases at least, their forward and lateral communications were more efficient so long as their four main columns could be easily supplied and reinforced from the plains.

The general strategy was to sever Amar Sing's lines of communication and so of reinforcement, from Kathmandu, already nearly two months distant over the mountain tracks. To this end Gillespie was to occupy the Doon Valley and so compel the Gurkha Kaji to shift his lateral communications with the east up into the hills: then to push them still further back into the snows by seizing Srinagar in Garhwal. Later, a small force under Gardner was directed on to Almora in Kumaon with the same intention. Thus weakened, Amar Sing was to be assailed and destroyed by Ochterlony, reinforced by the main body of Gillespie's column. In the east the two columns under Marley and Wood were directed on Kathmandu and Palpa, taking advantage of Gurkha preoccupation in the far west.

This was the first mountain campaign in which the British-Indian Army was to engage. Any experienced soldier will readily agree that those who do not understand the mountains face one of the most difficult military problems in the world, when first confronted with them. In these days we read of so many recent reputations made by those who have conducted 'small-war' operations, that it comes as somewhat of a surprise to find men from the past whose names are virtually unknown today, whose exploits were accepted by themselves and their contemporaries as being all in the day's work, but who were, in fact, more imaginative, competent and skilful than some of those minor moderns whose military reputations, deserved or undeserved, have been exalted to the front rank. David Ochterlony's is one of many of those names from the past. He was a born master of operational technique, adaptable, highly efficient and bold. Lacking any sort of experience of mountain fighting, he yet devised the stockaded post and was interested, but no whit deterred, to discover on first contact with his enemy that that was precisely the accepted Gurkha method of conducting their defence, in fact, the basis of their whole tactical system. To other columns these stockades came as an unwelcome surprise for, on the plains, outposts and camps were seldom fortified as the fate of Marley's detachments only too sadly demonstrated.

Lord Moira, the Governor-General, busied himself in the preparations for this unaccustomed campaign, taking a personal interest in all proceedings and seeking advice where he could get it. A Mr. Rutherford, a temporarily unemployed merchant whose calling had kept him for some years close to the Nepal border, and Captain Hearsey, a well-known character on this northern frontier, were two of his most trusted counsellors. Rutherford's opinion was that, 'Even in the equipment of a military force destined for operations in Nepal, a previous knowledge of the local peculiarities of the country will be indispensably necessary. The mode of warfare will have scarcely any points of resemblance to that to which our troops have hitherto been accustomed. The formidable arms of artillery and cavalry can be no longer employed. Instead of a baggage train conveyed by elephants and camels and horses and bullocks, they must be content with such articles as can be conveyed by men and goats. Instead of tents, they must be content with the covering of warm clothes and a thick *rauẓee* [quilt]. In the conduct of the commissariat, instead of foraging in the invaded country, supplies must be brought with labour, difficulty and expense from the plains.' Hearsey recommends 'bullocks, mules, *tattoos* [ponies], jack-asses and elephants, the mules being also employed as officers' chargers. The number of servants common in an Indian Army will not be able to subsist in the mountains. Subalterns can have three, captains five. . . . Every five men to be allowed one *paharee* [hillman] to carry cooking utensils and ten seer [20 lbs] of provision.'

Rutherford counselled the adoption of our modern battle-dress. 'The best kind of clothing for the limbs would, in my opinion, be a pair of trowsers, very loose, and made to tie at the ankles with a running band, and in the same manner perhaps at top, like parjamahs. . . . This kind of dress would be found very convenient, and afford great facility to those contractions of the limbs which occur in the steep ascent and in setting down to rest in the course of a fatiguing march. To meet these, little ankle boots, especially of *sabur* [deer skin], would be capital things . . . the trowsers tied over them. Each soldier should carry with him a second pair of trowsers, composed of some thick stuff quilted with cotton, and sufficiently large to admit of being drawn over the former. At the close of the day these should be put on.' The soldier would thus not only be warm at night but ready for immediate action, 'for I consider it very probable, from the nature of the country and the character of the enemy, that ambuscades and night attacks will be often tried.'

Our business man took strong exception to the Commander-in-Chief's recommendation and the Governor-General's order for four thousand pairs of shoes of 'deer skin dressed soft, double upper leather, wax cloth interposed if for the rains: not necessary if for the cold season . . . high at the heel with a strap to pull on by. . . . The sole thick; a little tip of iron at toe and heel. Every man should have a piece of fine cloth pressed out of hot wax: the moment a little tenderness of foot is perceived, the part is to be covered with a piece of cloth. By this shoe and precaution the feet will be kept sound.' However, he obediently undertook to try and procure them. This led him into a heated quarrel with Mr. Salter, the Collector of Customs at Bareilly, whose letter to our indignant merchant is worth notice. The Collector suspected him of trying to get his own private goods through the Customs under cover of the 'public authority'.

(Para) '9. The second paragraph of it [Rutherford's letter] jumbles together deer skin provided by public authority on an emergency proceeding to Cawnpore and your hempen cloths proceeding to Moradabad, couched in an ambiguous style, leaving a person the choice of imagining that the hempen cloth also was provided under authority and on public authority, or not. I chuse the latter: therefore shall not further notice it.

'10. The following sentence, "And since, from my inability to discover any grounds for your refusal, without imagining any motives which I should be sorry to impute etc.," which I quote from the same paragraph, appears to me a very impertinent and arrogant style of language for you to use... merely to have an opportunity of using disgusting and affronting language... ,' [and so on].

'11. I desire you will not address me in future, except as you may be authorised by the Government in your official duty.'

On Rutherford appealing to Lord Moira, the latter figuratively knocked their heads together, the Collector for standing on red tape, the merchant for insulting the Collector.

'The hat of the sepoy,' wrote Rutherford, 'is ill-adapted for the service, and had better be altered. Something that will set close to the head, (a helmet for instance), and be a defence against stones and not liable to be brushed off in the thickets, should be contrived... on the present service a martial air should give way entirely to convenience, comfort and efficiency.' He was demanding a jungle hat something superior to and more battleworthy than our soldiers wore in Burma against the Japanese.

Of the Gurkha Army, Hearsey says, 'Their muskets are infamous, and their gunpowder the same. The made-up ball cartridge I have seen exceeded seven inches in length, flints are bad, little or no clothing, and very ill paid. They are armed with a musket, with or without a bayonet, a sword, and stuck in their girdles is a crooked instrument called a kookuree. ... They are hardy, endure privations, and are very obedient, have not much of the distinction of caste, and are a neutral kind of Hindoo, eating in messes almost everything they meet with, except beef. Under our Government they would make excellent soldiers.' The irregulars, of whom there were many attached to their small army, were armed almost entirely with bows and arrows.

The men had no tents; the officers, only bivouacs; the chiefs used small tents carried on the backs of six porters, and those tents no bigger than an Indian subordinate official of the Company would take with him on tour.

So they were an ill-equipped force but a mobile one.

The Commander-in-Chief in India sent words of advice to his army. His troops were warned to be on the alert against night attack and ambuscade for which the Gurkha soldiers were celebrated. 'The Commander-in-Chief has frequently had occasion to observe in the course of service, the security to be derived from causing large fires to be kept up during the night, about two hundred yards in front of the piquets. Anybody passing between them is bewildered by the glare and at the same time sufficiently exposed to be a fair mark for the fire of artillery from the outposts. Another precaution, . . . considering the nature of the country you will have to enter, and the peculiar modes of warfare by which it will be defended, is not to bring your columns under the fire of matchlocks from adjacent heights, where musketry could produce little effect in return.' This last injunction, suitably amended, might as well have been applied to operations on the North West Frontier of India ever since the tribesman armed himself with a small-bore weapon.

Ochterlony, in one of his earlier despatches, from his post as a Political Officer in Ludhiana, not far from the westernmost outposts of Greater Nepal, had explained thus the Gurkha successes in those regions. 'The conquests of the Gorkas in the north are recent, and their government by no means popular. The Rajahs who have been expelled did not maintain any, or only a very small number of troops, but depended for the defence of their country on the inhabitants themselves; and to this and the want of concord among the chiefs, may be in a great measure attributed the success the Gorkas have met with. At Nahan, the principle government of the hills in this quarter, they were first called in by the Rajah himself, to subdue an insurrection of his own people, and from there made their way to the Sutleje, more by the discord existing between the chiefs than by force of arms; and every place of strength has fallen, not by attack (for they have not guns of any calibre), but by famine, the consequences of blockade.'

Ochterlony on the west and Bradshaw on the east, as political officers, made contact with all the expelled chieftains, issuing proclamations urging the dissidents to rally to the British, not only approaching the Gurkha 'allies', but setting the print for later dissemination of leaflets among the Chaubisia and the Baisia Rajahs and in Makwanpore and Palpa. Among the allies, the appeal gradually succeeded as Gurkha fortunes fell: in the Chaubisia and the Baisia it had no effect: in Makwanpore, with its exiled chief and Kiranti people, there was a moderate secession. The Sikkim chieftains soon rose against the Gurkha power and from them a Kiranti corps was formed in the Morang by Captain Latter. Efforts to seduce the Kiranti soldiers from the Gurkha Army failed, partly because of the brutal punishments meted out to those Kiranti leaders caught in correspondence with the British enemy.

From Lucknow on the 1st November 1814, the Governor-General in India issued the declaration of war with Nepal.

10

War with the British

———————❋———————

THE four English Columns advanced from their points of forward concentration in the late autumn of 1814, only to meet with severe checks all along the line.

The aged and nerveless Marley and Wood stepped delicately forward. Wood bumped into a stockade just short of Butwal, there suffering some casualties in a fire fight. His main force coming up, the stockade was enfiladed. Colonel Ujjar Sing, Bhim Sen's nephew, started to withdraw, but so did General Wood, to the disgust of his soldiers, leaving the now returning Gurkhas in possession of the battlefield. It was therefore a Gurkha success and a British reverse. The latter withdrew before an army half their size who now gaily followed them up and harassed them. Marley established three strong posts of about five hundred men each, at Baragarhi, Samanpore and Persa respectively, covering his assembly in three columns. The two last posts were out of supporting distance, so Colonel Rundher Sing surprised them and wiped them out. So dumfounded was Marley at this aggression that, fearing for his artillery train and his line of communications, he stepped his force back to cover them. Lord Hastings sent him reinforcements and promptings for action. Marley's interpretation of the Governor-General's incitements was to march to and fro out of range of Rundher Sing's weapons. Before long, however, he found the responsibility of this operation altogether too much for him so, without telling a soul or arranging for anyone to act for him, he quietly rode away by night into self-imposed retirement. On being acquainted of this, the Governor-General placed this officer on the invalid or non-effective establishment — a merciful end.

Meanwhile, on the Nepalese side there was some dissatisfaction. Bhagat Sing, who had approached Marley's front with a few hundred

80

men, was given forthright orders to attack. He demurred, in the face of an enemy nearly ten times his size, so Bhim Sen ordered him back to Kathmandu to face a court martial which directed that he should be made to attend open Durbar dressed in petticoats.

There were no further activities hereabouts until Ochterlony came east in early 1816.

West of these two shuttlecocks a small irregular force under Colonel Gardner* was making good progress up into the hills towards Almora. Lord Hastings, who was on an extended reconnaissance of his huge front, with a tactician's eye for success, here spotted a vacuum in the Gurkha defences so at once reinforced Gardner with Colonel Jasper Nicolls, Quartermaster General of the King's Troops in India, and some artillery. These two stormed Almora and moved rapidly into Kumaon where they consolidated their position astride Amar Sing's communications with the Valley of Nepal — a brilliant operation which not only cut Amar Sing from his reinforcements, but, furthermore, drew additional Gurkha reinforcements in towards Almora.

The gallant Gillespie, now ageing but still as brave as a lion, seized the Timli Pass and led his column through the Kheri defile into Dehra Doon with the object of introducing a detachment into Garhwal.

Thus Amar Sing, the Gurkha Commander-in-Chief in the west, found himself four hundred miles from Kathmandu defending a wide front in recently subjugated and therefore bitterly hostile country. His opponents' strategy may have had its faults, but it had the merit of aiming to penetrate into regions where the population would afford most aid to the invaders and do most damage to their highland masters.

Balbahadur, from the tower of the low and ill-found stockade of Kalunga, watched General Gillespie's formidable column of 4,000 men with a train of twenty guns moving out on the Rajpore road from the little town of Dehra Doon, the white dust rising high and blowing away to the east. His six hundred defenders manned the walls.

That night a message offering terms came from the British commander. Balbahadur, remarking that he did not accept letters at that late hour, tore it up. The English force arrived before Kalunga on 29th October 1814: before daylight on the 30th the bombardment was opened with ten guns and the leading troops assembled for the assault. The intrepid and im-

---

* Gardner's force was mainly of Pathans, Rohillas from Rohilkand in India. He, and Major Hearsey who commanded a parallel and unsuccessful column, were both irregular officers recently in the pay of the Mahratta Army. Hearsey was defeated and captured by the Gurkhas.

G

patient Gillespie had given the signal for the attack some hours before he had notified that it should be given. The British and Indian regiments therefore attacked piecemeal and were thrown back. The General then led in person the second assault. That, too, was defeated with severe loss.

At the height of the bombardment a Gurkha suddenly appeared advancing through the shells and smoke, waving his hand. The firing ceased and he was welcomed into the camp. A shot had shattered his lower jaw, so he had come for treatment to the British surgeon. When discharged from hospital, he asked for permission to return to his own army in order to fight the British again.

Gillespie then put himself at the head of his old regiment, the Royal Irish Dragoons, and a party of the 53rd Regiment and made his third attempt. With him were his A.D.C. and one Lieutenant Frederick Young of the 13th Native Infantry, of the Guide and Intelligence Department of the Field Army, now commanding a Company of the 53rd. Dashing at the gate, Rollo Gillespie was shot down thirty yards from the palisade. He fell dead into the arms of Lieutenant Young.

Again the attack failed. The British column waited until 24th November for its siege train to arrive from Delhi. With that, it renewed bombardment and assaults, to meet with no more success than before. At last a breach was made but the Gurkhas each time drove the assailants back from it with bullets, arrows, stones, any missile, the women hurling them as they stood by their men. Food and water were running out in the beleaguered and battered post and the ranks of the defenders were thinning fast under bombardment. Balbahadur was in desperate plight, beyond hope that Amar Sing could come to his aid.

'To capture the Fort was a thing forbidden but now I leave of my own accord.' With his last seventy hale men he slipped away on the night of 1st December through the besiegers' lines and they saw him no more. The British entered to find the place empty, save the dead and the grievously wounded, among them women and children. They rescued the living, then razed Kalunga to the ground.

Balbahadur had lost 520 men: his enemy, 31 officers and 750 men. On the hills at Kalunga, or Nalapani, are two small white obelisks, the one to Gillespie and those who fell with him, the other to 'their gallant adversary'. 'They fought in fair conflict like men, and in the intervals of actual combat, shewed us a liberal courtesy . . .', wrote the British historian.

General Martindell, who had failed dismally at Rewa in 1813, was appointed to succeed Gillespie. The Governor-General's reason for honouring him with this appointment was unusual — that his previous failure 'would have stimulated him to exert himself in regaining the ground he had lost in the public estimation on that occasion'. It had no such effect. Martindell fell back on Dehra Doon, abandoning the projected advance up into Garhwal, then, leaving a detachment to garrison the Doon, he marched westwards along the Valley towards Nahan, under orders to co-operate with Ochterlony.

In the meanwhile Ochterlony's advance on Malaun was progressing against his old acquaintance, Amar Sing Thapa, who opposed him with 3,000 picked troops. Amar Sing could appreciate good generalship and in his despatches to Nepal he paid tribute to Ochterlony's, saying that for once he could never fight at the time and place of his own choosing. Seeing the danger that Ranjur might be caught and trapped between the more powerful Martindell and Ochterlony, Amar Sing drew him out of Nahan northwards on to the fort of Jaithak. Martindell followed Ranjur up through Nahan and into the hills. On 27th December he attacked up the ridge seeking to secure positions on the flanks of the main fortress. The approach up the long, narrow spur had to be frontal for it would have invited disaster to drop down into the valley and, therefrom, up the steep hillside, attempt to drive in an attack from the flank. Before the fort, dotted along the spur, were stockades and fortified villages, each of which must be taken by assault. Elephants carrying heavy guns were levered up the hill from Nahan. The bombardment opened and village after village went up in flames as the red-coated, blue-trousered men of the Company, with their black chimney-pots hats, wound for miles along the single narrow track. The smoke puffed about the mountain meadows. Though their enemy secured a footing the Gurkha garrison of Jaithak did not suffer them to keep it. Finally, Martindell, having lost a third of his force, drew his men off, sat back and appealed for help. Though he outnumbered Ranjur by two to one, he decided to starve him out. Martindell's operations, while not coloured with the timidity of Wood and Marley, can only be described as lethargic.

By the end of October 1814, on the day that Gillespie died, Ochterlony was at Plasi at the foot of the hills where Amar Sing's small force was posted. The Kaji had seen to it that his enemy would have to advance 'against the grain of the country', over ridge after ridge, each one well defended with stockades and fortified posts. By 5th November the first ridge with the forts of Nalagarh and Talagarh had fallen to the British. The enemy was conducting a carefully deliberated series of operations by which to force Amar Sing into his final defences about Malaun. Amar Sing stood firmly on the second ridge. Ochterlony, in no mood to waste life, cut roads and step by step brought forward his artillery, to bear on the Fort of Ramgarh. Then Amar Sing found this second position neatly and methodically turned so that he had to evacuate it and fall back to the last, Malaun, ridge. Still clinging to Ramgarh Fort itself he consolidated for his final defence. Hitherto it had been possible at most times for his opponent to reap his harvest by manoeuvre rather than by head-on battle, but there had been severe fighting for all that. The Gurkhas were now cheered by Amar Sing's surprise attack on a forward detachment in which he wiped out a clear hundred of the enemy at one blow. With remarkable tenacity, however, their opponent was pursuing a policy of attrition, stabbing first here and then there to seize the points of vantage he needed. Casualties on both sides were heavy but the enemy's continued local successes were bringing to his side the hesitant chiefs of the district and gradually detaching others from Amar Sing.

On 2nd March Amar Sing had sent to his King, Girvan Judha Bikram Sah, stoutly condemning his monarch's proposals to appease their enemy. His letter was intercepted by British agents and is reproduced in Appendix IV at the end of this book. It is the letter of a stout-hearted soldier, written as he faced a better equipped and more numerous enemy.

That wily enemy now applied himself to his final operation. His first step was to pass a force round the south of the Malaun ridge to cut the Gurkha line of supply from Bilaspur on the Sutlej, their only life-line at this time, whereupon the Rajah of that place defected to the British. The Malaun position ran from Malaun Fort along a series of fortified peaks south by east to the Fort of Surajgarh. But two of the peaks, in the very centre, were not fortified, Ryla and Deothal. It was a chance that Amar Sing might take with most of his opponents, but not with this one. On the night of 14th–15th April he learnt that both points were being stormed in great force, that Ryla had fallen at a blow and that Deothal was yielding. By dawn he had lost both and his position was carved in two. On the 16th he launched at Deothal all he had, under his courageous Sirdar, Bhagte Thapa — 2,000 men. 'The Gurkhas came on with furious intrepidity, so much so that several were bayonetted or cut to pieces within our works. Umur Singh stood all the while just within musquet range, with the Goorkha colours planted beside him; while Bhugtee was everywhere exciting the men to further efforts.'* Gallant, fruitless, disastrous, at the end of the day five hundred Gurkhas lay dead on the field, Bhagte Thapa among them. The defenders, in their fortifications, had lost three hundred and fifty men.

* Prinsep's *Political and Military Transactions in India,* 1825.

Amar Sing was in sore straits. The remnants of the great counter-attack fell back on Malaun. His Sirdars, learning of the loss of Almora, came to plead that he should sue for peace. He refused. So they left him to his fate. With two hundred men he drew himself in on the Fort of Malaun for a last stand. Ochterlony, reinforced, mopped up the outer posts and faced Amar Sing's citadel set high upon a steep, conical peak overtopping the ridge. In itself, the fortress was of great strength, but it needed a garrison to hold it.

Bhagte was dead: he had but two hundred men. Deserted, Amar Sing asked Ochterlony for terms.

Malaun and Jaithak fell to the enemy.

'. . . in consideration of the bravery, skill and fidelity with which he had defended the country entrusted to his charge,' Ochterlony agreed that Amar Sing should march out with his arms, accoutrements, colours, two guns, and all his personal property. Similiar terms were granted to Ranjur Sing, beleaguered at Jaithak, but he was only allowed to take one gun and two hundred men. Father and son were to meet wherever they wished on the road and to march by Saharanpore, Hardwar and Najibabad to cross the new boundary, the Kali River. Apart from the bodyguard the British were to be free to recruit from all troops 'in the service of Nepal'.

Ochterlony's other terms were definite and severe. Amar Sing could but accept them. Turn where he would, he could not find the means to fight on. Nepal was to cede the Terai, to cede those districts which are today Kumaon, Garhwal and Simla, to quit those parts of Sikkim that she had reft from the Rajah and, bitterest draught of all, to accept a British Resident at the Court of Kathmandu.

Bhim Sen delayed ratification until he heard that Ranjit Singh at Lahore was mobilising against the British, that Amir Khan's Pathans were threatening from near Agra, and that Mahratta activities were on the increase. Gurkha successes were turning the heads of all the Company's enemies in India. He then refused the terms, and not without reason for his eastern army had defeated its enemies on the main approach and beaten them back across the border. Only in far-distant Malaun had there been failure — while the incursion into Kumaon was little more than a foray by a handful of irregulars. Why, then, of all regions, surrender the Terai, the buffer zone of Nepal's security? Bhim Sen would have none of this clause, nor would he entertain a British Resident like any subject state on the Indian plains.

Amar Sing, arrived in Kathmandu, set himself at the head of the party opposing ratification of the very treaty that he had been prepared himself to accept far away in Malaun, besieged, defeated and awaiting the *coup de grâce*. Brave as he was, he yet lacked the courtly chivalry of David Ochterlony.

During the height of the operations of 1814, Ochterlony had addressed the Commander-in-Chief recommending the enlistment of Gurkhas in the Company's army, a strange idea at such a time. On 1st December 1814, Mr. Adam, Secretary to Government, wrote to authorise Ochterlony to raise local levies of irregulars to harass the Gurkha armies, by cutting off small bodies, for guarding convoys, protecting friendly districts and other similar services. It must be remembered that Gorkha had conquered vast territories, that many of its soldiers were recruited from these peoples and that they were by no means all happy to be fighting on the side of Gorkha. Even the Nepalese tribes of the Chaubisia and Baisia were of varying loyalty. Mr. J. B. Fraser, who was with the Dehra Doon column, wrote, 'This gave rise to the measure of forming a light irregular corps, to be raised chiefly among the highlanders of these friendly districts, the old soldiers and dependants of the ex-Rajas, to whom arms were distributed and native officers attached, chiefly their countrymen . . . which, though not to be much relied on in cases of importance and danger, were in many cases very desirable.' As Gurkha positions and fortresses were taken, their garrisons were allowed to join.

On the far western flank the raising of irregulars was entrusted to Lieutenant Robert Ross of the 6th Native Infantry, the nucleus of whose forces was the contingent of 2,000 men of the Hindur Raja. There came to join him a number of 'Nasiris', or friendlies, bits and pieces of the garrisons of captured forts and deserters from the 'allies' of Nepal. Lieutenant Ross employed the Nasiris in the operations before Malaun. That same autumn of 1814, Lieutenant Frederick Young, 'peculiarly qualified for the charge', was selected to raise and command an irregular force of 2,000 men for operations on Ochterlony's inner flank. These were of all sorts, from plains and hills, from near and far, from the by-ways and the hedges, and they were very bad soldiers. Early in 1815 a small reinforcing column of two hundred Gurkhas was found moving westwards towards Jaithak, and Young was ordered to move out into the hills, intercept and drive them back. The Gurkhas met this force of irregulars and at once attacked. The irregulars fled, leaving Young and his handful of officers standing forlorn on what should have been a battlefield. The Gurkhas gathered round. They laughingly asked him why he did not run off with his men. 'I have not come so far in order to run away', replied Young, 'I came to stop', and he sat down. 'We could serve under men like you', observed their leader.

They held Young as an honoured prisoner, treated him well, made friends with him and taught him their language. When he was released, he was sent to look after prisoners of war in Dehra Doon. He there applied for permission to go to the prisoners' camp and ask for volunteers to form a Corps of Gurkha soldiers. Permission was granted. As he said afterwards, 'I went there one man and I came out 3,000.' From these men the Sirmoor Battalion was formed. At about the same time another regiment of two battalions was being raised at Subathu, near Simla, called the Nasiri regiment, and a third at Almora, the Kumaon Levy. The Kumaon Levy was actually being formed on local enlistment by another Gardner, a political officer, a relative of Colonel Gardner, while the operations against Almora were in full swing. Many of the men of all these three, the first battalions of the famous Gurkha Brigade, were therefore at that time Garhwalis and Kumaonis and not strictly Gurkhas. This was the seed from which grew a splendid tree of twenty regular Gurkha battalions in the British-Indian service.

On 27th July 1815, General Orders were issued by the Commander-in-Chief for Ochterlony to form the Nasiri and Sirmoor Battalions, 'The uniform of the Nasseree and Sirmoor Battalions to be a close green jacket without facings, red cuffs and collar and trimmings, blue loose trousers, and a bonnet, the whole according to a description which has been published to Major General Ochterlony. . . .'

On 7th October 1815, the Court of Directors of the Hon'ble East India Company directed the establishment of the 'Nasseree Goorkah' of two battalions, of the 'Sirmoor Battalion' under Lieutenant F. Young and of the 'Kumaon Battalion' . . . 'to be composed of the Goorkah corps late under the command of Soubah Jye Kisheen, of natives of Kumaon, and other corps of hillmen.'

Bhim Sen paltered and evaded. Negotiations broke down before Lord Hastings' absolute insistence that a large part of the Terai, Nepal's granary, should pass into British hands. For this cession of territory he offered compensation of from £20,000 to £30,000 a year. No matter what else was agreed upon, without acceptance of this one vital clause the war must go on. But Bhim Sen's nobles drew their incomes from the lands they owned in the Terai. They and he refused the terms. The British Army assembled at Dinapore and the experienced and proven commander Ochterlony, was given command. The Nepalese reply was to reinforce its eastern flank to bar the passes over the Churiaghati range and to garrison the great fort of Makwanpore which stood on the road to Kathmandu.

This had been the hardest fought campaign of all those that the Hon'ble

Company had engaged upon since the first arrival of English merchants in India in the seventeenth century. From the days of Clive to those of Lord Lake no one amongst its enemies had dared to make such a stand. It had come as a shock to the Government whose very existence was now challenged, and it gathered its resources for the next phase. Thus, in January 1816, Ochterlony advanced from Saran in command of 14,000 regulars, about 4,000 irregulars, and eighty-three guns, with one objective only — Kathmandu, and the route the same as the ill-starred, unenterprising Marley was to have taken. As Ochterlony came forward he met the Nepalese envoy bearing letters renewing the war. Between Saran and Kathmandu there was one very strong position, the fortress of Makwanpore, originally built in the fourteenth century as has been related in Chapter 6.

The Dinapore column, under its tall, spare Commander, plunged into the dismal forests of the Terai, heading for the Bichia Koh Pass, through the Churiaghati range. This he knew would most certainly be held in strength. Being a soldier, he was determined not to risk a head-on battle for the possession of this mountain defile. He therefore reconnoitred for a track to turn its flank. Captain Pickersgill, one of the few to find the opportunity to distinguish himself in the earlier campaign in these parts, discovered a little-used path through a deep ravine, leading to the heights of the ridge and turning the main position on the pass. Ochterlony, the deliberate and systematic commander, now changed his technique to suit his new situation, taking what the conventional would regard as a grave risk. At night he led his whole infantry force with a couple of guns on elephants in single file up through this gorge, and by dawn he was shaking it out on to the high ground. It was an operation after the Gurkha Commander's own heart and he knew it directly his patrols reported that morning. He had been out-manoeuvred and outwitted.

Ranjur Sing, the hero of Jaithak, withdrew on Harihapore and Makwanpore leaving rearguards to delay the enemy advance. In due course the British closed up on the Makwanpore positions and here the fighting was intense and bitter. Lieutenant John Shipp of the 87th (The Royal Irish Fusiliers) has a long description in his Memoirs, one feature of which is his personal combat with the Gurkha Commander, or Subah, Kisnabahadur Rana, whom he at length killed with a sabre blow on the neck, nearly severing the head from the body. After the guns came up, 'The havoc was dreadful for they still scorned to fly. . . . On going round the hill afterwards, the dead bodies there astonished me. It was scarcely possible to walk without stepping on them.' Despite the severe task they

88

were setting their enemy, the Gurkhas had little heart to continue this interminable campaign. On a rainy night, Ranjur Sing and the remnants evacuated the fortress of Harihapore. Despite his former services, Ranjur never lived down what was regarded as his desertion of this post.

With the fall of Makwanpore there remained two higher passes before Ochterlony could march into the Valley. On 28th February Bhim Sen's envoy sued for peace. Bhim Sen would not have an enemy setting foot in the Valley in 1816 any more than would Bahadur Sah in 1792. On 4th March 1816, he signed a treaty of peace with General Sir David Ochterlony. The peace was that which he could have had a year earlier but there was one clause more heavily underlined than before. In Ochterlony's words, 'You must take either a Resident or war;' words which for years were bitterly resented in Nepal and which made the Resident's task of gaining the Court's confidence none too easy. Fortunately for all, the third of the British Residents in Kathmandu, successor to Edward Gardner, was a man in every way outstanding, Brian Hodgson, statesman, scientist, student and man of affairs. To Hodgson the world owes its first real knowledge of this ancient mountain state and of the Lamaic Buddhism which is spread over such vast regions of Asia.

It is A.D. 1816. There is an uneasy peace between Nepal and British India, the one smarting from military defeat and shorn of territory on which her warrior people prided itself, the other suspicious of the future along these five hundred miles of rough borderland and still beset by enemies on all other fronts. Bhim Sen remains unconvinced that the good of his country and the safety of his own position can best be served by befriending the infant colossus so rapidly growing out of the delta of Bengal, despite the wise restraint it has shown in leaving Nepal with her sovereign independence.

The Treaty of Segouli has been signed on 4th March 1816. Nepal attends to India and turns her back on the Himalayas.

I I

Gurkha Soldier

———————— ❈ ————————

Now that the tale has come to the year 1816 and Gurkhas are being for the first time enlisted under the British flag, it will not come amiss to give some description of the men who were presenting themselves to the recruiting officer, and it is right that a start should be made at the time of the Gurkha war, when the British first tested the mettle of Nepal's fighting men.

In 1816 Ensign John Shipp, himself termed 'the bravest of the brave', of His Majesty's 87th Regiment, wrote in his Memoirs:

'. . . I never saw more steadiness or bravery exhibited in my life. Run they would not, and of death they seemed to have no fear, though their comrades were falling thick around them, for we were so near that every shot told. . . .'

After this same war, General Sir David Ochterlony expressed an opinion confidentially to Lord Hastings that, '. . . the Company's sepoys, then Hindustanis, could never be brought to resist the shock of these energetic mountaineers on their own grounds.'

In 1832, Brain Hodgson, who had been for some years in Nepal:

'These highland soldiers, who despatch their meal in half an hour, and satisfy the ceremonial law by merely washing their hands and face and taking off their turbans before cooking, laugh at the pharisaical rigour of the Sipahis [Sepoys], who must bathe from head to foot, and make puja [worship] 'ere they can begin to dress their dinners, must eat nearly naked in the coldest weather, and cannot be in marching trim again in less than three hours.

'In war, the former readily carry several days' provisions on their backs: the latter would deem such an act intolerably degrading. The former see in foreign service nothing but the prospect of glory and spoil: the latter can

90

discover in it nothing but pollution and peril from unclean men and terrible wizards, goblins and evil spirits. In masses the former have all that indomitable confidence, each in all, which grows out of national integrity and success. . . .

'In my humble opinion they are, by far, the best soldiers in India; and if they were made participators of our renown in arms, I conceive that their gallant spirit, emphatic contempt of madhesias [people residing in the plains] and unadulterated military habit, might be relied on for fidelity; . . .'

Captain E. Vansittart, 1894:

'The Magars and Gurungs have already been referred to as being of the Tartar race; they, in Nepal, follow agricultural pursuits; they are square-built, sturdy men, with fine, muscular, and large chest and limb development, low in stature, and with little or no hair on face or body, and with fair complexions. They are a merry-hearted race, eat animal food, and in Nepal drink a kind of beer made from rice, called *jaur*, and a kind of spirit, called *raksi*. In our battalions they will drink any English wine, spirits or beer. They are intensely fond of soldiering. They are very hardy and extremely simple-minded. They are kind-hearted and generous and, as recruits, absolutely truthful. They are very proud and sensitive, and they deeply feel abuse and undeserved censure. They are very obstinate, very independent, very vain, and in their plain clothes inclined to be dirty. They are intensely loyal to each other and their officers in time of trouble or danger.

'On service the Gurkhas put aside the very small caste prejudices they have . . . Gurkhas will eat all and every kind of vegetable and fruit. . . . They will smoke any English or Indian tobacco and are very fond of cheroots. . . .

'The kukri, a short, curved, broad-bladed, and heavy knife, is the real national weapon of the Gurkhas, and it is worn by all from the highest to the lowest. In our regiments they are carried in a frog attached to the waist-belt. From the beginning of the handle to the end or point of the blade it averages about 20 inches in length.

'Where wood is plentiful they are very fond of practising cutting with the kukri. . . . A really skilful cutter will cut off slice after slice from the end of a piece of green wood, each slice being not thicker than an ordinary piece of shoe leather. . . .' [*There is a legend from the First World War that a Gurkha, encountering a German soldier, took a slash at his neck. The German laughed and shouted, "Missed again!" "Try waggling your head," was the Gurkha's reply.*]

91

'They are also skilful with the *gulel* [pellet bow] knocking down and killing the smallest birds with ease. All who can manage to raise the funds try to possess themselves of some sort of fire-arm.

'Gurkhas delight in all manly sports — shooting, fishing, etc., — and are mostly keen sportsmen and possess great skill with gun and rod. They amuse themselves in their leisure hours either in this way in the field, or in putting the shot, playing quoits or football, and they are always eager to join in any game with Europeans.'

General Sir Charles Reid, K.C.B. (who commanded a Gurkha battalion in the Mutiny at the Siege of Delhi), says:

'All Gurkhas are keen sportsmen and are never so happy as when they are on a tiger's track. A man I lost at Delhi had killed twenty-two on foot; they never waste a shot; they call ammunition "Khazana" or treasure.'

The following story (of about 1820) is given as illustrative of their coolness and amenability to discipline:

'A tiger had been seen within a few miles of Dehra and Colonel Young (then Captain and the gallant Commanding Officer of the Sirmoor Battalion), accompanied by Colonel Childers, of His Majesty's 11th Dragoons, mounted an elephant and hastened to the spot. They, however, were unsuccessful in rousing him, and after a long and tedious search were returning home.

'A Gurkha sepoy was following the elephant with his gun on his shoulder, when he suddenly dropped on one knee and presented his rifle as if in the act to fire. Having, however, roused the attention of the sportsmen, he did not pull the trigger but kept his gun fixed in the same position. He had suddenly caught sight of the fiery eyes of the tiger who was crouching among the underwood, within three paces of his gun. In this situation they steadily regarded each other. The elephant was immediately pulled up close to the kneeling Gurkha, but neither of the sportsmen could succeed in catching a glimpse of the animal. In order, if possible, to observe the direction more accurately, Captain Young called out "Recover Arms!" The sepoy came to the recover as calmly and collectedly as if on his own parade. "Present!" Down went the gun again; this was repeated, but still the tiger was invisible.

'Captain Young exclaimed, "That gallant fellow shall not be left unassisted!" and in a moment dropped from the elephant and placed himself close to the sepoy. He looked along the levelled barrel, but to no purpose; the brute was not to be distinguished.

'Cocking his gun, therefore, he told the Gurkha to fire: there was a terrific roar, a rush forward for one instant, and all was still. When the smoke had just cleared away, there lay the tiger perfectly dead. The ball had struck the centre of his forehead and entered his brain.'

'. . . Gurkhas are bold, enduring, faithful, frank, very independent and self-reliant: in their own country they are jealous of foreigners and self-asserting. They despise the natives of India, and look up to and fraternise with Europeans, whom they admire for their superior knowledge, strength and for their courage, and whom they imitate in dress and habits.

'They have the following saying: *"Topiwar Kamwar, Lungiwar khan-newar"* — The cap-wearer works, the lungi [turban]-wearer eats! [*Needless to say, the Gurkha wears a hat.*]

'They are very jealous of their women, but are domestic in their habits, and kind and affectionate husbands and parents. As a consequence, their wives are less shy and reserved, and have more freedom, and reciprocate their affection, carefully looking after their uniform and all culinary and domestic matters.

'As a rule, recruits on joining are very unsophisticated, very truthful, but dirty, and the first lesson that has to be taught them is that "cleanliness is next to godliness".' [*This is hardly to be wondered at among boys whose lives are spent on the cold mountain side with their flocks and in their fields.*]

'The great vice of Gurkhas is gambling, to which they are greatly addicted. Though hot-tempered and easily roused, they are in general quiet, well-behaved men, and extremely amenable to discipline. . . . No officer can be too strict with them in parades, but they hate being "nagged at".

'From the warlike qualities of his forefathers, and the traditions handed down to him of their military prowess as conquerors of Nepal, he is imbued with, and cherishes the true military spirit.

'His physique, compact and sturdy build, powerful muscular development, keen sight, acute hearing, and hereditary education as a sportsman, eminently capacitate him for the duties of a light infantry soldier on the mountain side, while his national weapon, the kukri, has in Burma and other places proved itself invaluable.

'The bravery displayed by the Gurkhas in their contacts with the British has already been alluded to, and their own traditions afford ample proof of the dogged tenacity with which they can encounter danger and hardship.

'The return of the Nepal army from Diggarcheh in the year 1790, amongst other instances, affords a distinguished proof of their daring and hardihood.'

Gorkha

The following extracts from Captain T. Smith's book of 1852 are very characteristic:

'At Bhartpur [1826] it was an interesting and amusing sight to witness the extreme good fellowship and kindly feeling with which the Europeans and the Gurkhas mutually regarded each other.... At the assault of Bhartpur, the Goorkhas were ordered to follow in after the 59th.

'These directions were obeyed, with the exception of going in with them instead of after them; for when the British Grenadiers with a deafening "hurrah" made their maddening rush at the breach, at that glorious and heart-stirring moment, it was impossible to restrain them, and they dashed into the thick of it.

'In the morning after the storming of Bhartpur, when being praised for their gallantry by their British comrades, they returned the flattering partiality of the latter by the following characteristic remark: "The English are as brave as lions; they are splendid sepoys, and very nearly equal to us!"'

'Dr. Oldfield [1860] in his book points out that there is not a single instance of a Nepal chief taking bribes from, or selling himself for money to the British or any other State. This loyalty to themselves is only equalled by their loyalty to us during the fiery ordeal of the Mutiny, the records of which, as well as of Ambeyla, of the Kabul Campaign, and many other wars and battles, amply testify the value of the services rendered us by our Gurkha regiments since incorporation in our army in 1815.

'Their fighting qualities, whether for sturdy, unflinching courage or enduring *élan*, are *nulli secundus* amongst the troops we enrol in our ranks from the varied classes of our Indian Empire, and no greater compliment can be paid to their bravery than by quoting one of their sayings:

*Kafar human bhanda manny ramro!**
It is better to die than to be a coward!'

* Written today: '*Kafar hone bhanda morne ramro!*'

'Kafar' is an unbeliever not a coward —
(urdu)
busdil — coward 'urdu'
dar } — " hindi.
kauf }

12

The House of Thapa

———————— ❈ ————————

WITH the Regency of Lalita Tripura Sundari and the ministry of Bhim
Sen Thapa Nepal enters upon an era of consolidation and progress. The
whole thirty years are governed by five factors, the unquestioned ascen-
dancy of Bhim Sen; the Thapa-Pande feud, fed by Ran Jang Pande
(whose life Bhim Sen had spared in 1807), a son of Damodar Pande; the
rivalry of the two queens, the wives of King Rajendra Bikram Sah; all
bedevilled by the treachery of Bhim Sen's younger brother, Ranbir Sing,
and the discontent, or worse, of the powerful Brahmans of Kathmandu.
Throughout, Mathbar Sing Thapa, Bhim Sen's nephew, behaves loyally
and with courage, a clear stream through a dirty pool, while Ran Jang
Pande and Ranbir Sing crawl about the obscure depths. Bhim Sen Thapa
had bathed in blood on the road to power. The price of power in Kathmandu had always been, and still was, eternal vigilance: this price he paid,
but even that was not high enough.

King Girvan Judha Bikram Sah died of the small-pox in 1816, while
still a minor, and his infant son Rajendra Bikram Sah reigned in his stead.
The baby's step grandmother, the childless Queen Tripura, continued as
Regent and Bhim Sen was Prime Minister. Bhim Sen's absolute supremacy
enabled him to rebuild Nepal so that his great successors of the Rana
family could complete the fabric to their hearts' desire. His measures
considerably increased the revenues, bringing much-needed innovations
in the standing army and an increase in its strength from 10,000 to 15,000,
with a sufficiency of arsenals and army workshops to support 45,000 men
in its mountain campaigns. To the east of the city he constructed the
Tundi Khel, the great parade ground, with its barracks, arsenal and artillery cantonments. All who ever wished to address the army — and they
were many — assembled it here.

In 1816 the second British Resident, the Hon. Edward Gardner, an able officer, assumed his duties in Kathmandu. Soon after came Brian Hodgson as Assistant-Resident, later to be one of the most distinguished of all Residents produced by that distinguished body, the Indian Political Service. From the first, Gardner laboured under the handicap of having been appointed, not by an act of friendship, but under duress. It must be years before a British Resident could gain the trust and confidence of vanquished Nepal under so astute and able a Prime Minister as Bhim Sen, whose character had been moulded in the traditional violence and intrigue of Valley politics. Bhim Sen had good reason to trust in no one about him: there was even more compelling reason that he should mistrust a foreigner, representative of an all-absorbing power from over the seas. With an Assistant, two army officers and an escort of two companies of Indian soldiers, Gardner took up his residence in the Valley of Nepal to conduct relations between a Government in India whose main object was trade accompanied by the law and order which make trade possible and profitable, and a Government at Kathmandu whose traditions and most recent successes had been those of militarism. A warrior people equipped in no manner to profit by a life of peace, was seeking its very existence by expansion through war and from the plunder which would follow. Any Prime Minister who was deaf to their clamour or who never sought to gratify their hopes, would pursue other policies at peril of his life. This, Bhim Sen knew.

In 1832, Queen Tripura Sundari died, the able, constant and far-seeing Regent and friend of Bhim Sen. Till that day his position was unchallenged and secure: from that day his enemies gathered strength and multiplied. Seven years earlier the one man who was to understand this vital character had returned to Nepal to his old position at the Residency. In 1829 Gardner retired and Hodgson took over as Acting Resident, to be officially appointed by Lord William Bentinck in 1833.

Within the above framework it is possible to unravel the story of Bhim Sen, Prime Minister for thirty-three years, from 1804 to 1837. His role, well understood by himself, was to carry with him the military tribes of Nepal whose great fear was that the British would establish their supremacy over the mountain kingdom, and whose prime ambition was to expand its borders at the expense of British India. Throughout his career Bhim Sen toyed with this latter sentiment by a constant pin-pricking of the British, quietly assimilating a village here and a village there. This policy was not too harmful of relations with the British unless it were pursued severely and became such as to scandalise them. The

Nepalese Minister, unfortunately for his country, at first took too seriously his jealousy of the Hon'ble Company and the ambitions of his people and, moreover, underestimated the resources in wealth, military power and skill of his foreign neighbour. He plunged too deeply when, in 1814, he virtually invaded the Gorakhpore district. Stiff as was the medicine administered to him and his people, it may well have prolonged his career by rebuffing the war party and cooling their demands for aggressive action. Thereafter, pinpricks against British India sufficed to keep the highlanders from becoming too restive. It was a nice balance that Bhim Sen had to keep: the British, tutored in Wellesley's system of protectorates, had to be discouraged from attempting to extend it to any part of Nepal: the Pande faction had to be kept in a state of suppression, but, as Brahmans, they were always in a position to call on powerful support: the Pande and Brahman anti-British alliance had to be kept in check short of stirring up another war: the Chinese overlord must not be goaded into action by too stiff a Nepalese policy towards the always provoking Tibet or a too cordial one towards the very alien British. No sooner was the Treaty of Segouli signed than Bhim Sen conspired with China to cast out the British Resident. The intrigue was fruitless: he probably meant it to be so. It was a handy gesture to his Celestial overlord to make up for the signing of the Treaty.

Bhim Sen scored his first point in a somewhat odd diplomatic exchange. Pleading the infancy of the Maharajah, an utterly irrelevant argument, he induced the Marquis of Hastings to restore to Nepal that part of the Terai between the River Gandak on the east and the Barhni tributary on the west, in exchange for the annual subsidy of £20,000 at that time due from the Company to Nepal. The yearly revenue of this ceded area yielded four times that sum to the treasury at Kathmandu. On the surface, the bargain was one-sided: in fact, it brought a rich return to the Company in the goodwill of Bhim Sen's people. Despite the improved relations, Gardner found himself boycotted in his Residency at Kathmandu and almost completely shut off from sources of information. And so matters were to continue so long as British resources were stretched by the exigencies of the Mahratta Campaign, the Pindari war and the Expedition to Burma in which, according to Burmese chronicles, '. . . the Kula pyn, or white strangers of the west, fastened a quarrel upon the Lord of the Golden Palace.' Bhim Sen was yet, in his balancing act, to make up his mind on which side the scales were to be weighted, on the Company's side or on the side of its formidable enemies. From 1816 until the disasters of 1840–41, in Afghanistan, British power was in the ascendant.

H

Mahrattas and Pindaris had been brought to heel; Burma had ceded important areas, notably the Arakan, and paid an indemnity; Bhurtpore, that hardest of fortified nuts, had been taken. *The British reserve of power so far impressed Nepal that she made an effort to improve relations with her neighbour. But, until those slightly cordial times arrived, Gardner had to be content with being 'sent to Coventry', helplessly watching the most flagrant violations of the Treaty of Segouli and smiling wanly at the obvious military preparations being made for another onslaught against his country's position in the Terai and on its Indian borders.

Bhim Sen now made his first and deadly serious false step. He needed money for military establishments and for his administration. Like the daft Ranbahadur before him, he raided the Brahmans, the natural friends and the kinsfolk of the Pandes, extorting from them the endowments they had so long enjoyed. Soon after this the wise Queen Tripura Sundari died, leaving Bhim Sen unbridled in his power and uncovered in his vital spot, where the Pande-Brahman dagger was now pointed. King Rajendra Bikram's senior wife ranged herself with the Pandes and the Brahmans: the junior, with Bhim Sen and the Thapas. The King, after a youth of indulgence, irresponsibility and vice, came of age a year later. Wearied of his suppression by Bhim Sen and determined in his wild and headstrong way to assert himself, he was only too willing to hearken to the Senior Queen and to side with her and the now re-forming Pande faction, led by Ran Jang Pande, Damodar's son. In Ran Jang's ranks were the descendants of those who had so cruelly suffered in the Prime Minister's purges of 1804 and 1807. All that Maharajah Rajendra Bikram asked for was to see Bhim Sen, whom he envied in his weak, moronic way, brought to his knees, no matter how or by whom. All that Ran Jang wanted was revenge against the man who had butchered his great father and in brutal fashion almost extirpated his line. All that the Brahmans looked for was the return of their wealth and the degradation of the man who had bereft them of it. All that the Elder Queen hoped for was to shatter the influence of her younger rival and, with it, the omnipotent Bhim Sen. Yet none dare do in the open what they planned in secret — seize, torture, degrade and slay Bhim Sen.

The strangest ally to attach himself to the conspirators was the younger brother of Bhim Sen, Ranbir Sing Thapa, jealous of his brother and of the talented nephew, Mathbar Sing, now Governor of Gorkha.

It is fair to admit that the position of the King, if he were to be king at

*No inconsiderable part of the force consisted of regular Gurkha soldiers in the Indian Army.

all, however imbecile, was utterly intolerable. At the time, Hodgson had reported to his Government, 'The Raja is hemmed into his palace, beyond which he cannot stir unaccompanied by the Minister, and then only to the extent of a short ride or drive. Even within the walls of his palace the Minister and his brother both reside, the latter in the especial capacity of "dry nurse" to His Highness. Last year the Raja desired to make an excursion into the low hills to shoot. He was prevented by all sorts of idle tales and obstructions. This year he proposed visiting his palace at Nawakote, the winter residence of his fathers: again he was prevented as before. Of power he has not a particle, nor seems to wish it. Of patronage he has not a fraction; and is naturally galled at this, as well as at being sentinelled all round by Bhim Sen's creatures, even within his own abode, and at being debarred from almost all liberty of locomotion, and of intercourse with the Sirdars and Gentry of the country.' The Senior Rani was by no means willing to accept this royal servitude and, irritated by the King's supineness, 'has, it is said, avowed to his friends her resolution, should he not soon be moved to assert either his personal or political liberty, to claim the rule of the kingdom in his name as the mother of two male children.'

Thus goaded, the King made his bid for power.

The Prime Minister being in no way disposed to allow his young king to override him, the Senior Rani snatched at this opportunity to strike. Her husband was now fairly in the camp of the opposition, the Pandes. Supported by the Brahmans, she blared forth an unexpected and violent denunciation of Bhim Sen. But Rajendra Bikram, still afraid of open contest with his powerful servant, awaited the yearly Panjni ceremony, at which all public offices had to be surrendered into the hands of the Sovereign for election of new holders or re-election of old. He refused to reappoint Bhim Sen. For the first time he had asserted himself against his formidable custodian; it was an insidious draught for a weak constitution, despite the necessity which made him recall Bhim Sen only a few days later.

Disregarding his Minister, in 1838 he entered into a secret understanding with Ranjit Singh, the powerful Sikh Rajah at Lahore, and then committed the folly of sending a messenger to Teheran to make contacts against the time of the rumoured Russian invasion of India, intrigues duly reported by the observant Hodgson.* These negotiations

---

* Despite these sly dealings, there was at this time a battalion of Gurkhas under British officers serving in Shah Sujah's army in Afghanistan and fighting alongside the British forces. This provided the redoubtable garrison that in 1841 held Charekar fort, 40 miles from Kabul, led at first by Codrington and then by Haughton.

coloured the British attitude to Nepal all through the critical days of
the Sikh wars in the later '40's and right up to the time of Nepal's signal
gesture of support and friendship in the days of the Mutiny of 1857.
Dalhousie, Sleeman and many others voice their suspicion of the
hostile intentions of the mountain State, sitting menacingly on the
right flank of British armies operating away up into the Punjab and
beyond. Egged on by the anti-British Pande party, a policy of nibbling
aggressiveness on the Company's borders was once more begun, for
the time being ignored by the British victim, who probably recognised
it as a sop to Nepalese militarism and to the Pande-Brahman combin-
ation.

Adversity, or at any rate a sense of danger, began to have its influence
on Bhim Sen. Hodgson appeared in a new light, . . . almost as a friend or
at any rate, a refuge. The Prime Minister even went so far as to warn the
Resident that the Durbar were preparing 'for hostilities in October
should it be found that the accounts from Ava, Pekin and Lahore were
favourable.' The war party were pressing the King to expel the Resident
at once. Although his life was in danger, Hodgson remained imperturb-
able, a quality in him which seems more than once to have confused and
disarmed his opponents in Kathmandu. His friends among the ministers
had told him that Nepal had sent an emissary to Burma by way of Sikkim and Assam and that what the Durbar supposed to be highly secret
negotiations were proceeding with the Indian States of Udaipore, Jodh-
pore, Gwalior, and Hyderabad, and with the Mahrattas and Sikhs, Peking,
Kabul and Teheran. Although he knew that there was no armed force
available to back him from India, he always seemed to the Durbar in
Kathmandu to be leading from a strong hand. Hodgson had played this
hand with nice calculation. He had at first tried to draw the teeth of the
Pandes and to divert Nepalese ambitions for territorial expansion by recommending to his Government that it should extensively recruit Gurkhas
into its regular regiments, men of the 'Khas, Muggur and Gurung tribes.
I am not sure that there exists any indispensable obstacle to our obtaining,
in one form or other, the services of a large body of these men; and such
are their energy of character, love of enterprise, and freedom from the
shackles of caste, that I am well assured their services, if obtained, would
soon come to be most highly prized.' Having failed by this means to
syphon off into India a large part of the excess of trained and untrained
military manhood restively kicking its heels in Nepal, he next conceived
the plan of turning Nepal into a trade route and market for India and
Tibet, instead of an interposing obstacle to the commerce of the two

countries. From his proposals there grew a marked increase in the exchange of commodities.

He then turned his attention to the delimitation of the frontier between Nepal and Oudh, rendered necessary by the cession in 1816 of a part of the Nepalese Terai to the King, or Grand Vizier, of Oudh, and by the more recent partial restoration, at Bhim Sen's request, of the western Terai. The Prime Minister accepted the setting up of a Commission consisting of representatives of Nepal and Oudh under a British chairman. By 1833 the work was done and the demarcation accepted by all parties. A common cause of friction and standing excuse for Gurkha aggression was at long last removed.

The Resident had for some time been in negotiation with the Governments of India and Nepal to agree upon a commercial treaty. Having worked it out to the satisfaction of Bhim Sen, he failed to obtain the agreement of the Indian Government. This setback tended for a time to draw the Briton and the Gurkha a little closer together. Hodgson's high opinion of this minister, expressed after the latter's death, cannot have been built up in a few months. It must have been an appreciation formed over years and formed in spite of the bloody beginnings of 1804 and 1807, the early intrigues against the British, and the harsh character of Bhim Sen's autocratic administration in Nepal, which made him more feared than loved.

Pricked on by his senior wife and the Brahmans the King found increasing cause for disagreement and quarrel with Bhim Sen. As the crisis approached, more and more Pande malcontents gathered under the Queen's banner. Bhim Sen's unscrupulous younger brother, Ranbir Sing, soon saw fit to encourage the conspirators by successfully intriguing to gain the position of Commander-in-Chief, from which he at once importuned his weak-minded and now conceited sovereign to dismiss his elder brother and to instal himself in his place. At the height of this latest plot there entered a man with whom all had to reckon, to cast his weight on the side of the sorely beset Prime Minister — his nephew, Mathbar Sing, the idol of the army, overbearing and headstrong. The Pandes now changed their ground, relying on the thirty-year-old popularity of their celebrated forbear, Damodar Pande. They demanded from the King the restoration of the family estates and honours; this, at the expense of the very man who had expropriated and almost extinguished the family. The King was thus pressed to choose between Bhim Sen and those who conspired against him. He hesitated, for he still feared the man he wished to ruin.

They then sought to detach Mathbar Sing by bringing against him a charge of having cohabited with his late brother's widow, no sin in the eyes of the Buddhists of Nepal among whom a woman also married her husband's brothers when she married her husband,* but a deadly sin in the eyes of the Hindu Rajput ruling class. The charge was made and abandoned for want of foundation, but significantly the false accuser was never brought to book; Mathbar was still Governor of Gorkha.

In 1837 Nepal was due to send to Peking the quinquennial Embassy and presents, under the terms of the treaty of 1792. It had been for Bhim Sen to choose the delegation, but this time the King insisted on his prerogative. Not daring to go so far as to insult his Prime Minister by appointing a Pande to lead it, he selected one of his own cousins, a Chauntriya. On this, the whole edifice of the Thapas began to crumble. The importunate Brahmans obtained for one of their men, Raghunath Pandit, the appointment of Chief Justice: Ran Jang Pande received from the King the lands, goods and honours the family had lost to Bhim Sen: Mathbar Sing was dismissed from his post at the head of the Government of Gorkha and another son of Damodar Pande took his place. But Bhim Sen remained untouched. The King and all others feared him.

Then came the end. The Senior Queen of all people, his enemy, suddenly lost her youngest son. At once the Pandes spread about the rumour that Bhim Sen had attempted to poison the Queen, but missed his mark. The court and administration at Kathmandu were plunged into confusion. Ran Jang Pande, at the King's ear, persuaded him to strike at once. Forthwith, the jealous prince seized Bhim Sen, degraded him and cast him in irons into prison. Mathbar was secured and thrown in to join his uncle. Ran Jang Pande seized supreme power, consumed with the lust for vengeance. Evidence against the tyrant was needed. The Baids — the doctors — were put to the torture. Then one confessed, falsely, to having been ordered by the fallen chief to administer the poison. To seal his mouth, he was then either tortured till he died or, more mercifully, just crucified. Another was burned on the forehead with hot irons till the brain was exposed, and on the cheek till the bone was laid bare. Yet another, a Newar, was impaled and his heart cut out while he still lived, but no corroboration of the one poor confession could be obtained. The King was an enthralled spectator of these doings. Landor says that four years later the Pandes confessed that the whole charge was false.

* This may have been the basis of Kirkpatrick's observations about Newar and Nair women. See p. 11.

To join Bhim Sen and Mathbar and for good measure, the treacherous brother, Ranbir Sing Thapa, was shorn of his offices and gaoled.

Fear and consternation gripped all who held office. Ran Jang embarked on a systematic spoliation of all who had by any means showed even the smallest sympathy for Bhim Sen. He called in all lands that had been granted on rent-free tenure since his father's death over thirty years before. He also levied forced loans from the chiefs of anything up to £80,000 for a single family. These noblemen began to turn their eyes towards the British and the Chauntriyas protested to the frenzied king. Courage failing him, he dismissed Ran Jang Pande. A cipher, Raghunath Pandit, took his place. The junior Rani, Lakhshmi Devi, interceded and Bhim Sen and Mathbar were set free, amid the public rejoicing of the Army. To bring the Army to a better frame of mind and to console him, the King appointed Ran Jang Pande its Commander-in-Chief. The Pande applied himself to remove Thapa influence and popularity.

Mathbar Sing, taking advantage of the favourable moment, set out for Lahore to the Court of Ranjit Singh, the Sikh; for what purpose has never been known, but in all probability to invoke the aid of that wily chief. If so, he failed in his purpose. Ranbir Sing made off to Benares to live as a fakir. Bhim Sen retired into private life, an object of popular sympathy, as well for his outstanding services in the past as for his pitiable condition in the present.

The half-lunatic King strove to govern: a posse of puppet Prime Ministers passed one by one in and out of office. In 1839, the insatiable Ran Jang Pande again seized the office. This time, he made sure of his old enemy. The two-year old charge of poisoning was resurrected with only a show of trial, and Nepal's one outstanding personality since Prithwi Narain lay once more in a dungeon, a subterranean cell described as simply a ditch of filth. Without light and almost starved, there he lay. The cowards did not, even then, dare to execute him. Ran Jang gave orders that by savage treatment he was to be brought to suicide. Beside him they placed a kukri, hoping. Bhim Sen held out against all they could do. They then brought him news, true or false, that his wife had been compelled to walk naked in broad daylight through the streets of Kathmandu. With the kukri so handy, he pierced his throat. For nine days he lingered, then ended his tragic life. The date is 29th July 1839.

Hodgson's despatch read, 'His corpse was refused funeral rites but dismembered and exposed about the city, after which the mangled remains were thrown away on the riverside, where none but the dog and vulture dared further to heed them.' 'Thus has perished the great and able

Statesman, who for more than thirty years had ruled this kingdom with more than royal sway; ... the uniform success of nearly all his measures had been no less remarkable than the energy and sagacity which so much promoted that success. ... Nor am I aware of any native statesman of recent times, except Ranjit Singh, who is, all things considered, worthy to be compared with the late General Bhim Sen of Nepal.'

*   *   *   *   *

Whatever the commotion and fury in Kathmandu, the villages away in the hills were little affected by it. Whatever the supposed oppressions of the system of government and of justice in the Kingdom of Nepal, we have the word of Sir Henry Lawrence a few years later that the people outside the horrors of the Court circle lived happy and cheerful lives. Still a hundred years on from Lawrence's time, the boys who came into Gorakhpore and Ghoom to enlist were a merry, carefree crew. Life was simple in the hills but it was a happy life.

13

The House of Pande

—————————— ❈ ——————————

AGHAST at the possible consequences of Bhim Sen's death at his hands, the foolish King hurried to the Residency to offer excuses for the atrocious deed. Hodgson received him in stony silence, ignored the excuses and kept his own counsel. Lord Auckland, from Calcutta, told his Resident to express his own opinion and that of his Government to the Court of Kathmandu: 'The Governor-General views with feelings of extreme disgust and abhorrence the measures of indignity, insult and cruelty which the Government of Nepal has adopted towards the late and able minister of that State.' This message, driven home by Hodgson in a personal interview, shook Rajendra Bikram's confidence in himself and in those around him. He began to question the wisdom of his new Prime Minister Ran Jang Pande, and of the military party that this man controlled.

Ran Jang and his fellow-conspirator, the Senior Queen or Maharani, applied themselves to the consummation of their labours. By edict they confiscated the dead man's lands and those of his family and annulled all land grants that he or Queen Tripura had made to anyone whomsoever during the past thirty-five years. The half-witted sovereign returned from the Residency to find himself compelled to sign a decree debarring the whole clan of Thapa from holding public office or enjoying state employment for seven generations. Ran Jang, perceiving his royal master cooling towards himself and his party and judging that he had better commit him forthwith to a policy of war, concocted a census of Nepalese military power, showing that the country had available the preposterous number of 400,000 trained men. He ordered the construction of a great foundry to cast all calibres and natures of weapons and put in hand the manufacture of a quantity of gunpowder. He then gave publicity to recent Brahman prophecies of the coming collapse of British power in India.

All this was, however, in no way committing the King actually to war. The Maharani and the Prime Minister now tried to involve the Resident in a Court intrigue, so as to bring about his disgrace and removal. To them Hodgson not only represented Britain, but he also represented the friends of Bhim Sen and the anti-military party. Hodgson's good sense kept him clear of all interference with the inner life and intrigues of the palace. The pin-pricking policy had been resumed after Bhim Sen's fall from power, so the next move was to prod the lawless frontier bands into activity. Ramnagar was raided and held to ransom. Hodgson insisted on reparations, withdrawal and an apology to the Governor-General. Ran Jang and the Queen procrastinated while maturing a plot by which they hoped to have the Resident killed without their being implicated. On 21st June 1840 a parade of the Kathmandu garrison was ordered and an announcement read out to them that their pay was to be reduced by orders of the Government of India. The irritant worked: the army marched off to the Residency to slay Hodgson. Arrived there, ardour cooled in face of Hodgson's popularity. Whisperings began. They decided that they must have the Royal Seal on an order to dispatch so important and influential a foreigner. They went to the palace to obtain it. The Queen had already removed herself from the capital, in order to create her alibi. The King, as confused as his soldiers, tried to put the best face on the business and appeared before them to tell them that the real fact was that their pay was being cut in order to provide funds for an invasion of India. He could hardly have made a bigger mistake if he had searched his imagination for the most inflammable lie in the circumstances. The soldiers had seen little service for twenty odd years: they were itching for war and plunder, Their spokesman clamoured to be led on Lucknow and Patna, to sweep the Nepalese frontier forward to the Ganges. First they must destroy the Resident. But the Court's heart failed it when thus called upon to give official sanction to the massacre of Hodgson and his household. The intended victim at once sent to tell the King that he had been aware of the whole plot and that word of it was by now far outside the confines of Nepal and speeding to Calcutta across the plains of India. On this, the conspiracy collapsed. It had been too richly mixed to succeed.

Lord Auckland, the Governor-General, awakened from his habitual boredom, instructed the Resident to tell the Nepal Government to remove its armed followers from the Ramnagar district before he took steps to have them removed. He further directed Hodgson to ensure that the war party was put out of office. Hodgson presented the ultimatum and the Queen meekly withdrew her men from Ramnagar. On this, dissension broke out at the Court. While all were at sixes and sevens the Resident chose this time to insist on the removal of Ran Jang Pande, a procedure decidedly more forthright than would have been permissible for his successors at the Legation. Ran Jang was dismissed and one of the Chauntriyas appointed, who brought with him a considerable backing of Brahmans and landowners, by now grown tired of the squabbling, wilting Government. The King presented the list of his new Cabinet to Hodgson for approval, urging its acceptance as consisting entirely of ministers pledged to renew the friendship between Nepal and India. So Hodgson had advanced far in Nepalese confidence since 1833, so far indeed that his adversary, the Senior Rani, left for a pious course of devotion at Benares. The King, unsure of himself, set off in pursuit. Lord Auckland, amused, and apprehensive of causing confusion, refused her a passport, directing Hodgson on this pretext to persuade King and Consort to abandon the project. The royal pair returned to the capital where the recently detested Maharani was given an unexpectedly enthusiastic reception. Characteristically, this was accompanied by a demonstration against the now sinful Cabinet who must have so oppressed the lady that she was desirous to seek spiritual comfort at the holy place. The immediate response of the would-be postulant was to plot to oust her husband from the throne, seizing for herself supreme power as regent during her son's minority.

Failing in yet another scheme and suspecting the most unpleasant results from her failure, she set out once more for Benares. But this time she was overtaken. On 6th October 1841, she died in the Terai, victim of the deadly *awal*.

As the Queen faded out, so died the hopes of the war party that they could enlist the help of the enemies of the British with whom she had corresponded — the Mahratta chieftains, Sikh and Rajput lords and Afghan Amirs.

The turnover of Nepalese policy was almost violent, the King offering the services of his forces in Afghanistan or in Burma, as Lord Auckland would desire. The offer was not accepted but the refusal bore in it terms of friendship such as had not before been honestly expressed by either party. It is here at this point in 1841 that the seed of mutual trust and of comradeship, so fruitful of good for both peoples, was first sowed. Doubtings and suspicions there were to be from time to time between the two countries, but they were of short duration and finally allayed by the Indian Mutiny of 1857. It is impossible to assess too highly the part played by the remarkable man who was Resident in Nepal, Brian Hodgson.

Whatever the external situation, the internal hardly changed at all. With the Senior Queen out of the way for ever, her son, Surendra, the Heir Apparent, found himself fighting for his very life against the Junior Queen who had succeeded to his mother's authority and who was determined that her own son should succeed their father. With good grounds, she insisted that the Heir Apparent was feeble of mind and unfit to rule. A ludicrous incident now occurred which went far to prove her right, not only as regards the Prince but as regards the King, her husband. In a newspaper published in India there appeared a rumour that the Senior Rani had been poisoned. This so incensed Rajendra Bikram that he rushed off to the Residency to demand the life of the slanderer. It so happened that, the Court being in mourning for the Senior Queen, it was at that time forbidden to them to ride a horse in Kathmandu. So these two, King and Prince, appeared at the Residency in ridiculous fashion riding upon two very decrepit old chieftains as 'saddle-men'* instead of horses. The King, in a frenzy of rage, stormed at Hodgson, 'Tell the Governor-General that he must and shall give him up. I will have him and flay him alive, and rub him with salt and lemon till he dies. Tell the Governor-General that if this infamous slanderer is not delivered up, there shall be war between us.' The Heir Apparent, shocked at his father's behaviour, intervened, when the former turned upon him. The two rained blows on each other until they fell off their human mounts and into the puddles where they rolled together at the gate of the Residency. The son prevailing, the father was forced to apologise to the Resident. A little later the Prince Surendra saw fit to use force once more on his father, this time to compel him to violate the extra-territoriality of the Residency in order to arrest a British-Indian subject who had sought refuge there. On this occasion the King brought a large party of soldiers and followers and demanded the immediate surrender of the man, Kasinath. Hodgson, having been warned by friendly Chauntriyas of the coming of the King, paraded his own small escort as though to pay the usual compliments to royalty. He then went to the gate to meet the King. After he had repeatedly rejected the demand, the King himself rushed at Kasinath to seize him and bear him off. 'I threw my arm round the merchant and said sternly to the Rajah, "You take both of us or neither." ' The Rajah could not find the courage to arrest them both, despite the frantic urgings

---

* In the Valley of Nepal this was by no means an uncommon mode of transport. In fact, there were properly designed 'saddles' for fitting on to slaves, *ketas* for male riders, *ketis* for female. Forty years later the Residency Surgeon records the arrival to consult him of a noble lady so mounted.

and blows administered to him by the Prince Surendra. While this hour-long altercation was going on, friendly Chauntriyas were whispering to Hodgson as they passed, 'Be patient and firm. Everything depends on you.'

All were tiring of the antics of this strange sovereign. Hodgson had used patience and an understanding toleration in circumstances of irritation and no little personal danger, but matters could not continue in this way lest the wretchedness of the King's administration should lead it into collision with British Authority. Unhappily, at this very crisis Lord Auckland retired and Lord Ellenborough arrived as Governor-General. New masters are distrustful of old servants. Ellenborough thought Hodgson took too much upon himself, was too big for his boots. He first recalled him. Then he cancelled the recall, on wiser advice. Then he tied his hands by limiting his powers of intervention in the Government of Nepal, despite the thousand miles and the mountain track that divided Calcutta from lonely Kathmandu. Hodgson probably, to our later thinking, had come to take more positive action in Nepalese affairs than is the custom for a British Resident, but by his fruits he must be judged and those fruits were wholesome where all about was rot. With reason it may be argued that there were later times when another Hodgson, with Hodgson's powers, would have worked with great profit to the Nepalese kingdom, not least in its last days before Indian independence and in the months succeeding.

In place of his mother, the late Senior Rani, Prince Surendra assumed the role of opposition to the British connection. Hodgson's hand being tied by his new instructions, this young man launched out upon an unbridled career of license and of oppression of his father's subjects and of the King himself. The latter came to have no say whatever in the Government of the State, nor could he in any manner control the youth. Late in the year 1842, nobles and people rose. 'The people complained that they could not obey two masters, adducing numerous instances in which the Maharajah had allowed them to be punished by his son for obedience to his own commands, whilst for all the murders, maimings, beatings and insults perpetrated by the Heir Apparent the Maharajah had evaded authorising prevention or making atonement in a single instance.' At last, and for once, all parties combined against the King. They compelled him to resign his chief authority and he did so . . . to the surviving Maharani, Lakhshmi Devi, ambitious and without scruple. She found herself stiffly opposed to the Pandes and the Chauntriyas. Always a partisan of the house of Thapa, she saw the chance of supressing her enemies, the Pandes, and of ridding herself of their shield and buckler, her dissolute stepson, the Heir Apparent. She acted swiftly with a *coup d'état* and Mathbar Sing Thapa, exiled nephew of the illustrious Bhim Sen, suddenly appeared in Kathmandu, joyfully acclaimed by populace and army, 'a strikingly handsome man with keen eye and lofty brow.'* He had been living at Simla in British territory on a comfortable British pension.

The inducement that the King and his Maharani had placed before Mathbar Sing was the execution of every one of the Pandes who might possibly disturb his peace of mind on his return. Very thoroughly they saw that the task was completed, the Pandes obligingly bringing their own kukris in order to be certain of a clean, unbungled execution. Ran Jang Pande, when at the place of death, was rather contemptuously reprieved as a thing of no merit or importance, for he was even then a-dying in the natural way. Kurban Pande, Kubrai Pande, the two Thapa renegades, Indrabir and Ranbam, and Kanak Sing Mahat, the judge who had condemned Bhim Sen to death, his case unheard, were beheaded. Bodman Karki lost his nose and lips, Bansraj Basnet his nose. In return, Mathbar was to destroy those who had rendered themselves obnoxious to the King and Queen, the Chauntriya ministers.

In 1843, the year of the Pande slaughter, Brain Hodgson retired and Henry Lawrence took his place.

Sir William Hunter, in the biography, describes Hodgson's departure from Nepal. 'At Hodgson's final audience with the Durbar the Rajah burst into tears and, referring to the exertions by which Hodgson had so often averted war, called him "the Saviour of Nepal". Then, taking a jewel from his turban, he turned to Major Lawrence (who had just re-received over charge) and said. "I know that it is your custom for Residents not to accept presents, but I owe so much to Mr. Hodgson's prudence and patience under many and great provocations, that I beg you will make my earnest request to the Governor-General to the effect that he may be permitted to accept this hereditary jewel of mine to become an heirloom in his own family." This request could not, of course, be complied with. But no official repression could prevent the affectionate farewells of the chiefs and people which made Hodgson's march to the frontier one long triumphal progress.'

Brian Hodgson had certain unusual characteristics which smoothed his path in Nepal. His health was wretched, so he lived the life of an ascetic, eating no meat and drinking no wine. There was a certain other-

* Laurence Oliphant, *Journey to Kathmandu*, 1852.

worldliness which thus attracted high-caste Hindus. As a born scholar his researches into Lamaic Buddhism brought him into friendly communication not only with Buddhist intellectuals of Nepal but also with those of Tibet. He was thus able to command sympathy in influential circles of the Himalayan country to which he was deputed. There is no doubt whatsoever that Hodgson saved Nepal from committing the suicidal folly of launching an aggressive war against the British during those dark days of 1838 to 1841.

*   *   *   *   *

Ambition must be stern indeed that would lead a Thapa back to Nepal in 1842, to take control of his country's destinies. In 1843 Mathbar Sing assumed the office of Prime Minister.

He came, attended by his nephew, Jang Bahadur Konwar.

14

The Return of the House of Thapa

———————— ❖ ————————

WHEN in 1742 Prithwi Narain Sah strolled from his father's funeral pyre up the track towards the Pokri Tol in Gorkha, he was accompanied by the Khas, Ahiram Konwar, his chief minister. Ahiram was a mountain Rajput with mountain, or Magar, blood in his veins. He was of fighting stock on both sides for Gorkha was well laced with clansmen of the Magar and Khas. From the loins of Ahiram Konwar came Rama Krishna, one of Prithwi Narain's most trusted generals, commander in the wars against the Chaubisia and Baisia Lordships. Rama Krishna's son, Ranjit Konwar, made his name in the campaigns in Kangra and Batoli. Ranjit had three sons. The eldest was Balnar Sing Konwar, who slew Sherbahadur when, in open court, the latter cut down his own half-brother, the King Ranbahadur Sah, in the year 1807. Honours and land were showered upon Balnar and to him was granted the privilege of carrying his shield in the presence of the Sovereign with the title of Kaji, to become hereditary in the family.

Balnar Sing married the Prime Minister Bhim Sen's niece. They had seven sons, of whom Jang Bahadur was the second. He was born on 18th June 1817. His parents wished to call him Birna Sing but at the special request of his uncle, Mathbar Sing, he was named Jang Bahadur, the Brave in War. With this same uncle, Mathbar, in the year 1843, Jang Bahadur came to Kathmandu.

There are many stories told of the youth of Jang Bahadur. His father, Kaji Balnar Sing, was the military commander of the north-western district, so the family spent its days far removed from the seat of government at Kathmandu. Jang Bahadur's six brothers were Bombahadur, Badri Nar Sing, Krishna Bahadur, Rana Udip Sing, Jagat Shamsher, and Dhir Shamsher. Jang was courageous, resourceful, unscrupulous, petulant and, with these qualities, without affection and lonely. His thoughts were his own; his plans for no other man. His delight was to sow discord among others, even among his nearest relations. Physically he was slight but athletic and strong. His appearance was that of a Tartar rather than of a Rajput, with broad face and pugnacious, short nose. The face did not belie the man: it was not an agreeable face.

He was an autocrat with most of the impatience of the character, quick-tempered and, towards the end of his life, dangerously so on the slightest opposition. As might be expected in such a man he was for long illiterate, despite his taking so close an interest in world affairs that he insisted on having the newspapers of India and England read to him whenever possible. His illiteracy was not due to laziness for he made several essays to learn English but never mastered the language. Perversely for a gambler, he was not only economical but inclined to be mean: and, for a soldier, he kept no settled time for anything from when he rose in the morning, very early or very late, until the time when he went to bed, just as variable as his rising.

Jang was commissioned into the army where he led a chequered and turbulent career. As an Ensign his reputation was not unknown at Kathmandu where his independence and restiveness under discipline were common report, more especially because he was the son of a nobleman, a respected Kaji of the royal army. But the Kaji could exercise no control over his wayward son. He was a law to himself and utterly reckless of any consequences of his escapades. For all that, his place in the respect and affection of the rank and file was second to that of no other officer. Flouting his superiors and regardless of such rules and regulations as the Nepalese Army had for its aristocracy, he yet seems to have possessed a personality and been able to evince a charm that wove a spell about those below him. After all, he was a dare-devil. He was a soldiers' man. He was an inveterate gambler and remained so till late in life. His reputation as a hunter and sportsman was common knowledge in an army where the private soldier was a born sportsman to whom his games and the hunting of wild things were second nature.

In 1837, on the fall of Bhim Sen, Balnar Sing and his son, being of the Thapa faction, were both deprived of their appointments. Jang Bahadur thought he would finance himself and pay off his gaming debts by catching elephants, so made his way down into the Terai to herd and capture his quarry single-handed. Very fortunately for him he was soon recalled to the colours for his elephant operations had been a dismal financial failure. Elephants seem to have had an attraction for him: they were a test

I

of his cunning and strength. Later, in Kathmandu a male elephant went 'must'. Anyone who has watched a 'must' elephant will appreciate the herculean savagery of the great beast. A mahout usually sees warning signs of the approach of this temporary madness and in good time double-shackles his charge with heavy chains. It is an awesome sight to watch 'must' elephants weaving ceaselessly to and fro, hauling at the clanging irons as they go, first with this leg and then with that. This one had killed its mahout, went raging through the town and quickly out into the countryside where, in bursts of frenzy, it terrified and ravaged the neighbourhood. No one could summon up the courage to attempt its recapture. So Jang Bahadur went out alone to take it. Daily the animal would range the same area passing through a certain village on its way. The young officer posted the royal mahout near by, climbed a tree over the road and lay out on its branch waiting. As the mad brute passed below him, he dropped lightly on to its neck. Then came the struggle as it strove to rid itself of him. Once thrown and he was a dead man. Jang Bahadur, hanging on like a limpet, managed to slip a wide cloth over its eyes, blinding it. At length the Court mahout seized his opportunity, rushed out, threw a shackle round one leg and secured it to a tree. Jang Bahadur slipped off the way he had come, lucky to be alive.

The little army of Nepal offered no scope at all for the vaulting ambition of this youth. He left it.

Characteristically, he took French leave. Perhaps the Pandes still had their eye on him after Bhim Sen's fall. Of all places to which he might have felt himself impelled to go, he chose Lahore. What he did there and why he went are questions unanswered. If his object was to bestir the Lion of the Punjab, the cunning, besotted, ruthless ruler of the Sikhs, to take arms against the British, then he failed. If he wished to procure for himself some responsible position in that potentate's army, then he failed again. At Lahore were men who could cozen the devil himself and the mountain stripling had not yet achieved that measure of skill. He ran out of money. With an effrontery that only he could have employed, he walked over the border and reported himself once more to his own army, where, far from being punished for his sins, he was received with open arms and given immediate promotion. Perhaps the Kaji, his father, was relieved to welcome the prodigal son: perhaps the youth had something to offer as a result of his stay in the Punjab with the Sikh Army.

He found he had well timed a triumphant return to his own country, because at that very moment his favourite uncle Mathbar Sing had been summoned by the Maharani to the coveted post of Prime Minister and was on the lookout for a trusted assistant. He accepted Jang Bahadur, the man of decision, discretion and courage and his own nephew. The youth once more deserted from the army in order to travel to Kathmandu. Under his uncle he at first spent most of his time designing uniforms for the soldiers instead of taking any serious part in affairs of state or army. Henry Lawrence, Resident in Nepal at this time, seems to have found this a rather surprising way in which Jang Bahadur should occupy himself. When it is remembered in what dangerous company he found himself and how inexperienced he was at that time of the devious ways of the Court and of its factions and plottings, it is not surprising that he preferred for a time not to let an all too decisive and active character break into the life about him. He needed time to watch and to consider.

His first steps in diplomacy were unhappy ones. Mathbar Sing Thapa, who made a serious underestimate of the permanence of the Company's system, reversing the later policy of Bhim Sen, calculated that much was to be gained for Nepal if the British in India were crushed. He wished to be free once again to overrun Sikkim, Kumaon and Garhwal and to steal a goodly slice of the fertile plains to stock his larder. Only too readily were the stealthy overtures of the Court at Lahore received in Kathmandu. Very soon his nephew found himself on the old, old trail for Benares, bound for a meeting with a representative of the Sikh State, there to coordinate plans to bring under one standard all the discontented and apprehensive independent rulers for a fresh unheaval to throw the British into the sea. The local authorities at Benares were too wide awake for such clumsy conspirators. Jang Bahadur and his mission found themselves being bundled off back to Kathmandu under the Governor-General's orders, while the Sikh mission was being politely seen off on its way to Lahore. None of them had been taken seriously by the high authority at Calcutta, which was at the time in supposedly friendly relations with the Sikhs and Nepalese.

Jang Bahadur returned to Kathmandu to kick his heels once more. As his uncle's nephew he was too well known to mix in palace intrigues so he went back to his uniforms and buttons and to a quiet and innocent routine of employment. The King was mentally ineffectual, quite unfit to take any part in the administration: the Maharani, still a devoted adherent of the Thapas, was hand in glove with Mathbar Sing: her lover, Gagan Sing, was jealous of the Prime Minister's influence: Surendra Bikram, Heir Apparent, was as before an equally stubborn partisan of the Pandes. Jang Bahadur was perforce a Mathbar man: he was also openly treated by the Heir Apparent, insanely jealous of Jang's abilities and rising power, as his deadly enemy. If the young soldier had not had his wits very much about him his life would have been a short one. Surendra Bikram made no bones about it ... he wanted to kill him. He hated him as a madman hates. His first attempt was made when Jang Bahadur was out riding with him in the rainy season when all streams are raging torrents. They arrived at one of these, spanned by a narrow wooden bridge formed simply of two logs laid together. The Prince ordered his escort to cross. Jang Bahadur proceeded to do so. Surendra, seeing that he might easily succeed without crashing headlong into the rapids, and then implicitly dare his master to follow, shouted to him when half-way across to return at once. Jang Bahadur, sportsman and good horseman, who knew better than any man in Nepal what a mountain-trained horse could do, promptly lifted its forehand, swung it round on its hocks, and walked it back whence it had come.

Later, the Prince's star being at the time in the ascendant, he obtained on some pretext or other an injunction to execute Jang Bahadur by throwing him down a well. Mathbar Sing must have been nodding or else cared not to lift a hand to save his nephew. Jang seems to have had warning of this proposal and had made a study of wells from which he had learnt that few round Kathmandu were so nicely constructed that an agile man could not obtain some sort of help from the walls. He had gone so far in his studies that he actually practised jumping down wells, legs crossed in professional style. Perhaps he had studied this very well, or had even been given a choice of the manner of his death and had chosen this quite usual but insanitary means of departure. Arrived at the selected well, he found the Prince and a fair retinue assembled to witness the end of the detested little Thapa. Jang modestly pleaded that he might be spared the indignity of being picked up and thrown down the shaft. The Prince, willing at this triumphant moment to display to his courtiers his magnanimity, permitted the prisoner to leap down without assistance. Jang leapt.

The audience waited to hear the pleasing splash and then filed off, well content with the afternoon's amusement.

The would-be suicide, on bobbing up, found a good grip in the bricks lining the side of the well and, with the friendly buoyancy of the water, held on. Some hours later, when it was dark, his friends arrived with a long rope. The young man, once more at the surface, sped out of Kathmandu to a place of concealment, and there lay quiet until he might be forgotten and the see-saw of intrigue and political juggling raise the Thapas high in the air and bump the Heir Apparent and his cronies on the bare ground. In due time he came forth from his refuge.

In such circumstances Jang Bahadur, even if he had had it in him by nature, had no chance of becoming a tolerant, easy, simple man. He was for ever in the midst of enemies: it was his life against theirs. He could, of course, have shaken the blood-stained dust of the city off his feet and gone home, but if he did so and the Pandes returned to power, then he and his whole family were doomed. It seems that he must live on precariously where he was, rather than quit and certainly die.

For two years uncle and nephew directed the Government of Nepal under the rule of the Heir Apparent to whom his father, Rajendra Bikram, had by now delegated his authority, such as it was. In fact, father and son sat together in audience in the great Durbar Hall of Kathmandu: nominally their decisions were those of the father, in fact they were the son's. Jang Bahadur, we are told, attended the Durbars in the simple sable robes of a first class Chinese official. The father was virtually an imbecile: the son a licentious profligate with no morals whatsoever. The Maharani had foisted Mathbar into authority because she believed that he would prove to be malleable in her hands. She wished that Surendra Bikram's claims to the throne should be set aside and that of her own son recognised. But the new Prime Minister would have none of it: he went further and hitched his wagon to the star of the Heir Apparent, the Maharani's opponent and Jang Bahadur's persecutor. Had Mathbar done as she bade, he would have been at least an accomplice to the murder of this woman's personal enemies.

Weak Kings, an intriguing Queen with a lover, and a dissembling Prime Minister could lead to but one end, another bloodbath. Since the Queen could not persuade Mathbar to acquiesce, he must make way for one who would. Gagan Sing considered himself the man, so he had every reason as the Queen's paramour to favour any plan that would rid the place of Mathbar Sing and leave him alone to bid for power. He advised her to tell the Maharajah that Mathbar was plotting to force him to abdicate in favour of his son, the Heir Apparent, Surendra Bikram, as a first step to Mathbar himself usurping the throne and 'liquidating' the royal family. She must persuade her husband to order the death of the dangerous Prime Minister. The King consented and thereby unwittingly ensured that all power was to pass to the Queen and Gagan Sing, the object which both these villains had sought to obtain. But who was to do the deed?

Why this choice of assassin should have fallen where it did and why they should have had reason to know that this very man would undertake the crime, will never be known. These pages may perhaps indicate a reason.

The King sent for Jang Bahadur, the man without scruple, the adventurer, the daring, the small, swarthy nobleman. He ordered him to kill his uncle, Mathbar Sing Thapa, on pain of death if he refused to obey. He remarked to Jang Bahadur that, in any case, Mathbar's days were numbered.

Jang Bahadur consented to commit the murder — and at once.

It is open to anyone to think what they will of this deed and of the man who did it. These, as far as is known, are the facts.

On 17th May 1845 the King sent word to his Prime Minister to come to the palace, to the Queen's apartment. Into the nephew's hand the King himself put a loaded musket and bade him hide behind a screen. Gagan Sing and Kaji Kulman Sing Thapa hid with him.

The strikingly handsome man with the keen eye and lofty brow, Mathbar Sing, entered the room.

Jang Bahadur shot him dead. He fell at the Queen's feet.

They flung the shattered corpse out of the window. Later, as a casual act of grace, it was dragged, bespattering the road as it went, to royal Pasupatti.

15

British Gurkha

———————— ❖ ————————

IT is a pity to break into the story of Kathmandu's misfortunes: it is, however, necessary to do so at this stage. Perhaps it may come as a welcome refreshment to some to turn their attention to other happenings, bloody perhaps, but at least blood spilt in the open field. The progress of those three hill Corps raised in 1815–16, by selective recruitment later to be composed almost entirely of Gurkhas, is important, for by them in the long run relations between Nepal and British India were to be governed. Article 5 of the Capitulation Act of 1815 read: 'All the troops in the service of Nepal, with the exception of those granted to the personal honour of the Kajees Ummer Sing and Ranjor Sing, will be at liberty to enter into the service of the British Government, if agreeable to themselves and the British Government choose to accept their services. . . .' For many years, even as late as 1835, the Nepalese Government were not at all cordial in the matter of recruitment so that recruiting parties had to get their new entries by hook or by crook and, when they were short, had still to accept other hillmen. The three Corps were at Subathu, Dehra Doon and Almora, all on the edge of Garhwal, and Kumaon territory. Their duties were for local security rather than for regular war. Thus it came about that in 1824 the Sirmoor Battalion had its first serious blooding when the civil authority sent for it to clear armed banditti from the neighbourhood of Roorkee. Captain Young led out a strong detachment of his battalion over the Kheri pass in the Siwalik hills where he found news of the position of the dacoits' main refuge, at Koonja seven miles north-west of Roorkee. With Young was the intrepid Superintendent of the Doon, Frederick Shore. By forced marches the column effected a surprise on the enemy but, having no artillery, they could not breach the walls to gain an entry. They therefore cut down a great tree and swinging this as a battering ram, under heavy and damaging fire, they burst in the gate. Young and Shore at the head, they stormed through into the fort and, against odds of three to one, routed the garrison and captured the place.

Two years later, in 1826, men of the Nasiri and Sirmoor Battalions were with the force under Lord Combermere in the siege operations and storming of the great fort of Bhurtpore, and there earned his warm commendation.

It is strange to realise that during all these years from 1815 onwards the Nepalese at Kathmandu had been playing such a fickle diplomatic game with the British, more often cold than warm in their attitude, more often than not intriguing with other chieftains against them, yet here in India were Gurkhas freely enlisting and loyally serving the hated rival. The fact is that then, as now, what went on in the Valley and at the royal Court at Kathmandu was of no concern or interest at all to the Parbatiyas. Kathmandu could be a veritable hotbed of intrigue and hatred but the highland villagers lived their own simple, cheerful, sunny lives. Stranger than all that had happened hitherto was to be the leading and gallant part played by the Nasiri and Sirmoor Battalions at the great battles against the Sikhs at Aliwal and Sobraon in 1846, at a time when Kathmandu was still in conspiratorial negotiation with the heads of the Sikh state at Lahore.

As these were the days in which the Gurkha was building up a military reputation in the outside world, it is apt to quote the remarks of some of those in high authority in the Company's service at this time.

Both the Nasiri and Sirmoor Battalions were strongly commended for their conduct at the taking of Bhurtpore.

Of Aliwal the Governor-General wrote: 'Great praise is also due to Brigadiers Godby and Hicks who, with the 36th Native Infantry and Naseree Battalion, H.M. 31st, and the 24th and 47th Native Infantry, stormed the village of Aliwal, drove the enemy from it, and seized the guns by which it was defended. The Governor-General has much satisfaction in observing the warm terms in which the Major General speaks of the Naseree and Sirmoor Battalions . . . under Brigadier Penney and Captain Fisher. . . .'

Sir H. Smith, 'The intrepid little Goorkas of the Naseree and Sirmoor Battalions in bravery and obedience can be excelled by none.'

After Sobraon, Sir Hugh Gough's despatch included these remarks, 'I must pause in this narrative especially to notice the determined hardihood and bravery with which our two battalions of Goorkas, the Sirmoor and Naseree, met the Sikh whenever they were opposed to them.

Soldiers of small stature and indomitable spirit, they vied in ardent courage in the charge with the Grenadiers of our own nation and, armed with the short weapon of their mountains, were a terror to the Sikhs throughout the great combat.'

And the Governor-General in a General Order of 3rd March 1846, 'The Company's Service has lost an excellent officer in Captain Fisher, who fell at the head of his brave Sirmoor Battalion, which greatly distinguished itself. The 29th Foot and the Sirmoor Battalion have entitled themselves by their gallant conduct to the thanks of Government.'

Thus British Gurkhas were building the reputation of their kingdom in the hills. At Delhi in 1857 they confirmed and established that reputation for all time. Of that epic we will later hear more; thereafter, the war services of these men became so frequent and varied that it will only be possible to speak in general terms. So long as there are only three battalions, it is practicable to keep trace of them: thenceforth, it is no longer possible to do so.

In 1850 Lord Dalhousie organised the three local battalions into regiments: in 1856, just before he left India, with his usual foresight, he strongly recommended a big expansion of the Gurkha forces in the Indian Army. His recommendation was ignored.

It must, one supposes, be credited to the Kumaon and the Sirmoor Battalions that two of their officers, Ramsay and Young respectively, first introduced the potato into the hills of Kumaon and Garhwal neighbouring on their Corps Cantonments.

Polygamy is not illegal in Nepal, but a Gurkha seldom has more than two wives. The British Gurkha would as a rule leave the senior wife at his home to look after the fields and the flocks and bring the junior with him to the Regimental depot. This younger wife, the 'leahita' as she is called as opposed to the elder or permanent wife, the 'beahita', had a somewhat insecure existence, the husband being apt to rid himself of her at short notice. Northey relates that while a young Gurkha was at the front during the war, another man went off with his wife. On his return to the depot after the war the husband took the case to his company commander. The officer noticed that, while the young soldier was somewhat indifferent about the abduction of his wife, he yet had something on his mind. At the end of the proceedings, the company commander asked him what else was troubling him, since he had been assured that the erring wife would be returned to him. 'Oh, I'm not bothering about that woman at all; what's worrying me is that the man's gone off with my umbrella.'

There is in eastern Nepal a custom of singing for one's bride at open competitions at which the girl or the boy starts the competition by singing a couplet, to which the other must answer. And so the contest proceeds, each couplet being, it is expected, more witty and apt than the last, until the scintillating wit of the one or the other wins the day.

From the early days of these corps it is apparent that the countrybred Englishmen who came to soldier with them found common ground with their men in their love of field sports of all kinds. They and their Gurkhas were mighty hunters.* Dehra Doon afforded big and small game of a wide variety and its rivers were full of fish: Almora and Subathu gave special opportunities for shooting in the hills, than which there is no more fascinating sport in a wonderful country. Young in Dehra Doon maintained and hunted a pack of foxhounds. The Gurkha never sees a forest or a mountain but he asks what 'shikar' [game] there is to be got in it: never sees a strip of water but wants to know what fish are to be caught. He is very much a man of the rod and the gun. The Briton being equally addicted to games of all kinds, found his men just as zealous on that score as he was.

Briton and Gurkha had one quality noticeably in common: both were honest and incorruptible.

* In Appendix V is Captain Thomas Smith's account of his two-hour battle with a 'must' elephant, about 1844.

16

The House of Rana

———— ✦ ————

JANG BAHADUR hastily summoned his brothers, Udip and Bombahadur, and bade them take Mathbar Sing's two sons at once to the most distant village in the Nepal Valley and set them on the road to India.

The Maharani had not yet done. More heads were to fall. This woman with the heavy, sensual face and cruel eyes would suffer no opposition to her one obsessive longing — to see her own eldest son on the throne of Nepal. There was no one to take Mathbar's place, for the palace could not agree on a successor and no one dare bid for the post. The King's accomplice and the Queen's man, Jang Bahadur, by tacit consent carried on the administration, with no official position which might bring retribution from one side or the other. The Maharani was determined to instal Gagan Sing, her paramour and tutor of her children: the dim-witted King was persuaded of the consequences of this course and prompted to forbid it. In desperation, with a disintegrating authority all about him, he sent for the Chauntriya, Fateh Jang Sah, but he had not the courage to appoint him in the face of the Maharani's tempestuous rage. Gagan Sing he would not stomach. With Fateh Jang as his tool, he hoped to have the Queen's lover murdered. Lacking determination, he in the end compromised so that no one need feel injured. There were four candidates, backed by different factions, and all four were to be appointed Commanders-in-Chief. Gagan Sing was to command seven regiments: Fateh Jang, Jang Bahadur and Abhiman Sing, three regiments each. Of these, Fateh Jang, *primus inter pares*, with wings clipped, became Prime Minister: the other three came after him in order of precedence. Fateh Jang and Abhiman were King's men: Gagan Sing was the Queen's: Jang Bahadur, strangest of all, was now the Prince Surendra Bikram's man. Politics have always made strange bedfellows but none more surprising than in Nepal.

123

Fateh Jang Sah was Prime Minister, but to Jang Bahadur was given the duty of modernising the systems and discipline of the army, and Jang Bahadur was a soldier's man. The other three and the Queen seem to have overlooked something.

Late in 1845 Sikhs crossed the Sutlej under arms. There was war between the Company and the Sikhs. The great Ranjit Singh was dead and a squabbling cabal was in power. Lahore appealed to Nepal for help. The Council met at Kathmandu. Fateh Jang Sah and Abhiman advised the King to send help to the Khalsa; Gagan Sing and Jang Bahadur opposed them. Jang Bahadur had seen Sikhs in the Punjab, he was not so impressed by what he saw there as by what he had heard of the Company's fighting men and what Amar Sing's veterans of Malaun had had to tell him. Furthermore, he remembered the remark of his kinsman, Bhim Sen, the great Minister, 'The English are a nation that crushes thrones like potsherds.' The King and Queen steered negotiations down the centre of the road. Nepal would send aid just as soon as Sikh standards flew from Delhi Fort. In a few weeks' time Gurkhas in the Company's service were to ply their kukris at Aliwal and Sobraon, and Kathmandu was to be spared the responsibility of making a decision.

The Adjutant-General of the army now trod the tight rope. Like his uncle, Mathbar Sing, he had come over to the side of the Heir Apparent, probably with complete cynicism. But still he kept a foot in the camp of the evil Queen and of her no less evil lover, Gagan Sing — indeed, an expert balancing feat, but one that was worth the trouble he gave to perfecting it.

It is hardly possible for those who have been brought up in the belief that murder is a deadly sin and that, if not here on earth, then in the next world, they shall be arraigned for it, to have any but the dimmest understanding of a society, a circle, a community in which to murder makes no impress whatsoever on the conscience of the being who commits it, who abets it or who orders it. Here in Kathmandu all of any authority used murder as they would eat their daily bread and walked in perpetual knowledge — not fear, one supposes — that this day might be their last.

No one would openly attack the formidable Jang Bahadur but many would kill him in secret. Never in all his days now did he go forth in the Valley of Nepal without a strong escort and even when he went on his favourite hunting expeditions he had his bodyguard with him, for not everyone was so intent as he on their skill at shooting only wild game. There is a greatness about this man of blood which somehow does not attune with the killing for sheer personal ends of Mathbar Sing Thapa. There is more in that story than we have been told. Jang would never have killed him because of the King's threat to his own life: he was too resourceful to be trapped by anything so simple. What is least easy to explain is his now attaching himself to the Heir Apparent, who more than any other man had desired his death at the time when Mathbar Sing himself was of that Prince's following.

The King, self-appointed Lord High Executioner of the Realm, on 12th September 1846 ordered his sons, Surendra Bikram and Upendra Bikram, to clear the stain from the family's name by murdering the Queen's low-born lover, Gagan Sing. This man had held a humble position at the Court as a Silver-Stick or official messenger. By his mistress he had been raised to be a General and Commander-in-Chief. Upendra, somewhat overburdened by the magnitude of this assignment to murder the Commander-in-Chief, went to the Prime Minister, Fateh Jang, to seek advice. Fateh Jang discussed the business with his colleague, Abhiman, and with the Pande member of the Council, Birkishore, in the course of their daily round and common task, and gave Upendra their expert advice which was to hire an assassin, since he himself was only a boy and Surendra almost a mental patient. They hired the assassin for him, the Brahman, Lal Jha. Two days later, while at his prayers, Gagan Sing was duly murdered: shot from a near-by roof by Lal Jha.

The Maharani's fury burst all bounds. She hastened to her dead lover's house and, that they might not appear as his lawful wives, forbade the three widows to commit *suttee* on the funeral pyre. She then summoned all chief officers of state, civil and military, to attend at the Kot or parliament square. Jang Bahadur went, attended by his three regiments, taking with him under this protection all his brothers and relatives, armed *cap-à-pie*. His was now a self-contained household force . . . for his own household. Being at Kathmandu at the time, Jang's was the first party to arrive, a more formidable array than the Queen had anticipated. She accosted him and demanded an explanation. The quick-witted Jang Bahadur not only allayed her fears, but also induced her to sign an order forbidding any other General to bring troops to the Kot. In the meanwhile his men outside surrounded the buildings. Thus Jang was left in a position of absolute power, the first occasion on which he is seen to outwit all his rivals — including his friend, the Queen. In flocked the other high officers of the State, into the courtyard of the Kot. The Queen was in no mood for discussion or parley: she was afire for vengeance.

Her accusing finger pointed to the Pande, Birkishore. She denounced him as the murderer and ordered Abhiman Sing to arrest him. Abhiman did so. Birkishore hotly denied his guilt and no threats from the Queen would extort confession from him. Raging at the prisoner she ordered Abhiman, of all men, to behead him there on the spot. The King, the arch-conspirator, intervened to say that there could be no execution without trial. Thankfully, Abhiman Sing propounded this neglected principle to the Queen. The King, equally thankfully, excused himself, hurried out and galloped to Fateh Jang's house. There, he despatched the Prime Minister to the Kot, then bolted off to seek refuge at the British Residency. The Resident, in no mind to mix himself up in King Rajendra's latest acts of policy, sent word to him that Europeans did not receive visitors at so late an hour and his request for an interview must be refused. The King then made his faltering way back to the Kot but, at the sight of blood trickling under the gate and along the gutters, he thought better of it and fled back to Fateh Jang's house.

Jang Bahadur, from the dominating position among his Guard and well-armed retinue of relations, had complete charge of the situation. He felt certain that Abhiman had conspired to murder Gagan Sing. Fateh Jang Sah hurried in. Jang Bahadur stopped him and told him that either Birkishore and Abhiman must be put to death or the Queen arrested. The latter, seeing that everything was not going her own way and that she was so hemmed in as to be inaudible, had discreetly removed herself from immediate bodily harm by entering the apartments. She now appeared at a window looking on to the excited courtyard, screeching to Fateh Jang below to tell her the name of the murderer. He shouted back that it must take time to find this out. To Jang Bahadur he whispered that he agreed that the Queen must be arrested but that this was not the time. The exasperated woman then rushed down from her vantage point, hysterical with rage and completely out of control. She elbowed her way into the crowd, flourishing her sword, to throw herself on Birkishore and kill him with her own hands. Jang Bahadur tactfully stopped her and sent her back. His was now the authority, but he would not offend the Queen. He might need her as a part of his design.

Report now came to him that Abhiman and Fateh Jang Sah had put their heads together without consulting him. He understood at once. He leapt up the stairs to the Queen and told her that Abhiman's men were on the march to overpower her party and to take her into custody. Would she order Abhiman's immediate arrest. She would. As Abhiman left to meet the troops he had sent for, the sentry stopped him. 'Whose orders?'

'The Queen's,' sent to him by Kaji Jang Bahadur. Abhiman, also understanding, tried to force the sentry. The Officer of the Guard prevented him. He then lost his temper — as the Queen again lost hers when she heard of his mutinous conduct, and lost it with dire results. She sent to the Guard to use their arms if Abhiman persisted.

The sentry, by now as excited as General Abhiman Sing Rana, snatched a musket and bayonetted him in the chest. Abhiman fell, rolling in agony. As he died he cried out loudly that Jang Bahadur himself had murdered Gagan Sing. Kharak Bikram, Fateh Jang's eldest son, hearing this, shouted to all to rally round him to sell their lives dearly, 'Jang Bahadur has betrayed us!'

Jang Bahadur's younger brother, Krishna, told him to hold his tongue. Kharak slashed at him. Krishna parried with an arm and lost his thumb. Kharak raised his sword for a second blow but Bombahadur, another brother, intervened and received a severe cut on the head. Dhir Shamsher, yet a third brother, a famous swordsman, had by now drawn his *khora*. With one slash he cut Kharak Bikram in half.

A hush fell on all.

Jang Bahadur stepped up to the stricken Fateh Jang and, pointing out that Kharak had started it, asked the father to forget and forgive. Instead, he and other ministers rushed to the Queen. Jang Bahadur following, again interceded, saying that he was innocent of Gagan Sing's death. But Fateh Jang elbowed him off and pressed on with his two companions. Jang Bahadur's staff officer, posted to guard the staircase, gave the order. The three ministers rolled back dead.

At the far side of the square Udip Sing, the fourth of Jang's brothers, was being assailed by one of the Chauntriyas. Hitherto, and now again, the assailants had caught the brothers unawares, their *khoras* sheathed. Bombahadur and Krishna sprang to his help and laid the Chauntriya on the stones.

A rush was made at Jang Bahadur.

Fateh Jang's brother shouted that no Rajput ever surrendered! Every man, seizing whatever weapon he could find to his hand, laid on and the blood flowed under the gate and out into the gutter for King Rajendra to behold.

Suddenly one of Jang Bahadur's companies broke into the courtyard from outside and swept all before it, the Chauntriyas escaping into the apartments which lined the courtyard, or over the courtyard walls. The slaughter became general, hundreds, noble and humble, perishing in this terrible massacre. Fateh Jang, Kharak Bikram, Abhiman, the minister

Dalbandhan Sing Pande, Ranjur Thapa, the hero of Jaithak, died in this square white-washed place.

Jang Bahadur, the enigma, saved the life of Fateh Jang's younger brother and smuggled him out to safety. During the fighting he personally stood by the Queen. She there and then, in all that turmoil, rewarded him with the coveted, and only now safe appointment of Prime Minister and Commander-in-Chief.

When the horror was done, she ordered Prince Surendra Bikram to her presence that he might be so terrified at what he saw that he would join his father in his now contemplated flight to Benares. But Jang Bahadur was in no mood to lose a pawn in his game. He met the Heir Apparent and told him to look round upon the dead, that he might be sure that all his enemies lay there among them. The Heir Apparent stayed on in Kathmandu, the puppet of the new Prime Minister and the opponent of the violent Maharani.

To secure the safety of Surendra and Upendra from the designs of the Queen two companies of Jang Bahadur's own regiments were posted on guard over their houses. The Queen was threatening a massacre beside which the Kot killing would be a pale thing, if the King did not place her son, Ranendra, on the throne.

The King, his host dead, returned to the Hanuman-Dhoka Palace, whither the Queen had also repaired. There, Jang Bahadur presented himself as the new Prime Minister. On the King's demanding to know who had ordered this fearful holocaust, he boldly threw the whole blame on the King himself, for 'All was done by the orders of the Queen to whom Your Grace gave sovereign power.'

Rajendra, startled out of his feeble wits, moved to Patan to prepare for his journey to Benares.

Jang Bahadur, in absolute authority, acted fast and thoroughly. He exiled from the country the families of all those nobles who had died in the massacre or who had fled, and forbade their return on pain of death: their lands and property he confiscated. When the annual Panjni came round and offices were to be surrendered to the King, he saw to it that every official who might oppose him was replaced by one who would afford him his support. His brothers and his relatives he placed in all the politically strategic posts.

At a great parade on the *Maidan** at Kathmandu Jang Bahadur had himself publicly proclaimed as Prime Minister and Commander-in-Chief.

For himself and his family he now, in 1846, assumed the proud title of

* Plain: open space.

Rana, conferred upon him by the King: Jang Bahadur Rana, Prime Minister and Commander-in-Chief of Nepal.

With all these bloody happenings in mind Henry Lawrence, the Resident, remarked, 'Who could have supposed it possible to combine a court delighting in blood and revolution, with a people dwelling in peace and happiness?'

17

Jang Bahadur Rana

———— ❋ ————

THE history of Nepal is for a time absorbed into the study of a man, the enigmatic Jang Bahadur Rana, the man who kept his own counsel in life and in death.

So far, this history has displayed him in no rosy colours. No attempt has been made to set up excuses for his conduct, but a few doubts have been expressed as to his motives and a few questions asked about them and about him. He is now in power: perhaps his use or abuse of the authority he wields may serve as a guide to his conduct in the days before that power came into his hands.

Whatever the outcome, Jang Bahadur maintained to the end of his life that the Kot massacre was caused by one person alone, the Queen, by her unbridled and tempestuous conduct in those early minutes in the white square.

She was still Regent of Nepal and from the Hanuman-Dhoka Palace wielded the authority of Regent. Under Jang Bahadur's tight grip there was peace in Kathmandu so that men went confidently about their lawful occasions, for a few days. Then the Maharani struck again as her wretched lord was leaving on his pilgrimage. His faithful servant, Bhowani Sing, seated on an elephant by his master's side, was by her orders murdered in cold blood. Kathmandu seethed: Jang Bahadur 'stood to' the army of the Valley against another dreadful outburst. From him, still her seeming confidant, she now demanded unceasingly the deaths of Surendra and his brother and the enthronement of her own boy. As often, the Prime Minister politely deferred, for one reason and another, ordering the assassination she so frantically craved. If King Rajendra Sah was mad, this woman was a monster. Jang Bahadur silently collected proof and perfected his plans against the deluded, bloodthirsty ghoul. One morning, as she sat brooding in the palace, a letter was placed in her hands.

130

'I have received Your Majesty's letter enjoining upon me the duty of perpetrating what I deem to be a horrible crime. I feel obliged to protest humbly that such an act would be, firstly, exceedingly unjust, inasmuch as the setting up of a younger son in supersession of the eldest is against all custom, and is directly opposed to all laws, human and divine: and secondly, the murder of the Princes would be a terrible crime against all conscience and all religion. For these reasons I regret that I cannot obey you. Above my duty to you as Regent, I owe another duty to the State which, in case of conflict, must override any personal considerations.

'My duty to the State bids me to submit that, *should Your Majesty again repeat this order, you shall be prosecuted for attempt at murder by the law of the land.*'

Surely the words in italics must have seared into the besotted brain of this queen. The letter ran as ran the man who sent it, at first in careful, modest terms, gradually rising to a crescendo of strength and firm purpose. She was defeated by her supposed ally before battle was joined, by the ally whom she had so confidingly raised up against herself. This, too, from the man who was by her side at the bloody Kot, '. . . *prosecuted for attempt at murder by the law of the land.*' So, after all, there *was* a law. With her there was only one solution to any difficult problem — to kill the individual who posed it — the law of the jungle. She prepared to kill Jang Bahadur and thus once more displayed her simplicity in dealing with this calculating master of political craft. She laid her plans with what she believed to be the greatest care, her creature, solemnly sworn by every oath dear to their religion, being Birdhoj Basnet. His reward was to be one of the most original ever devised for an assassin — or for anyone else. He was to be Premier, the appointment being made hereditary in his family. In order to maintain themselves in the office he and his descendants were to be each allowed without punishment a quota of up to seven murders, provided that no member of the royal family were included in the allowance. It is intriguing to imagine the scene while this bargain was being struck between the bloody Queen and her aspiring candidate.

The plan she propounded to her agent was that they should induce Jang Bahadur and all six of his brothers to take up residence with the two princes and thus to sleep in their apartments. One night the Basnet gang was to break in and murder the two boys and, if they could find him, her husband, the King, also. The Rana brothers would then be arraigned for the crime and certainly executed. This scheme, however, they abandoned: it certainly sounds crazy because, for one thing, the Rana brothers were not the country clowns who would so obligingly fall in with such a plan. The new plot was for the Basnets to decoy Jang into a private part of the Hanuman-Dhoka Palace where the Queen herself would be present, with the assassins suitably placed and hidden to kill him. The Queen used her agents, and so did her intended victim. The victim used his more efficiently.

In the Palace was a tutor for the royal children, Bijai Raj.

Birdhoj suborned him, promising him the post of High Priest if he could succeed in bringing Jang Bahadur to the assigned room in the Palace. Bijai Raj, a rather timid, scholarly man set out on his mission. Birdhoj and his band of Basnets concealed themselves and waited. Time passed. No Bijai Raj and no Jang Bahadur appeared.

Bijai, in some trepidation, had entered the formidable Kaji's residence the Lagantol. He was admitted at once. He delivered his message. Jang Bahadur looked him up and down and coldly asked him what precisely was his motive in making the request. Bijai Raj, a bad conspirator if ever there was one, jumped immediately to the conclusion that the Prime Minister was aware of the plot. In a fright he blurted out the whole affair. Jang Bahadur summoned six companies of his own regiments and set out for the Hanuman-Dhoka.

Birdhoj, taking leave of his senses, unable to understand why his messenger had not returned, rode off on the road to the Lagantol. He rode head-on into Jang Bahadur's escort. He knew that the game was up, yet he went on instead of turning back to warn his confederates to take to their heels. Krishna Bahadur met him. He asked to be brought to the leader. Krishna, depriving him of his weapons, brought him to his brother Jang. Birdhoj saluted His Excellency and announced that the Queen wished him to meet her at once at the Palace. His Excellency replied 'How is that so? You are Prime Minister. Not *I*. She has appointed you. What can she want with me?' He made a sign, Birdhoj's death warrant. The escort moved on.

At the Palace the soldiers rounded up the Basnet* gang. Those who resisted they killed: those who gave up their arms, they put in chains.

Jang Bahadur walked swiftly to the King's apartments, looking neither to right nor left. To her affrighted consternation the Queen saw the man whom she regarded as good as dead riding up to the Palace and demanding an immediate interview with the King, and the King alone. She sent messengers to him. He looked straight through them and they feared for their lives. He strode into the Palace and demanded to be

* Basnets are Khas Gurkhas.

brought to the King. The Maharani, still undefeated though now certain that all was known, joined her husband. Jang Bahadur should not see the King alone. She took her seat by him. The Prince Surendra stood with them.

She attempted to interpose but Jang, ignoring her with silent scorn, cast his headdress at the foot of the throne and spoke to the King. Coolly, clearly, without any trace of emotion, he demanded from the King his Queen's immediate deportation and exile. He turned to his staff. Decorously she was removed from the presence and jailed in her own apartments. The Prime Minister left the Palace, summoned the Council of State and sat in judgment on the red-handed despot. The King and the Heir Apparent set their seal to the sentence then passed and to the list of the woman's crimes. She was formally deprived of the Regency. 'You have caused the death of hundreds and brought ruin and misery upon your subjects, whose misfortunes cannot cease as long as you remain in the country. . . . For the offences we have mentioned you are ordered to leave the country and to prepare yourself forthwith to remove to Benares.'

The Maharani, out-manoeuvred and under sentence of exile, insisted on taking with her her two sons, Ranendra and Binendra, rather than leave them as hostages in Kathmandu in peril of their lives, should opportunity offer for her to return from Benares. Jang Bahadur unwillingly agreed. She then also persuaded the feeble King Rajendra to announce his intention to expiate his sins in the holy Ganges and so to join the party. With the King in her keeping, she held a court card of some considerable value. Jang Bahadur put the cortège in charge of six of his own battalions to see it well and truly over the frontier and that it did not return. The Royal Family left Kathmandu for exile on 23rd November 1846 and the Council of State appointed Surendra to be Regent in his father's absence. The Maharani took to herself a new lover, Dalbahadur, an exile from Nepal.

On this day begins the long reign of the Rana family with Jang Bahadur Rana as Prime Minister, and every substantial post in government and army in the hands of one of his Rana relatives. Surendra Bikram Sah, soon to be King, was less than a figurehead: he took his orders from the strong, taciturn master of Nepal, who resided at the newly built Thapatali. Jang Bahadur was not the only one who knew the depth of Surendra's former hatred for him and of the cunning attempts the new Regent had made on his life in days so recently gone by. The presence of Surendra, the lawful heir, on the *Gaddi*, lent countenance to the new régime and discouraged others from challenging for the throne, while it in no way hindered the plans and reforms of the great Prime Minister whose puppet he was determined the Prince should remain. Gradually, the farsightedness of Jang Bahadur is becoming apparent. What is left debatable is the extent to which the carnage at the Kot can be laid to his charge and the compulsion which made him kill his uncle, Mathbar Sing Thapa, the ally of the homicidal Heir Apparent, Surendra Bikram. On this last perplexity Landon sheds some light. He relates that in July 1851 Jang Bahadur, before an audience in the Court, read a lecture to King Surendra Bikram, in which he contrasted his own temperate conduct as Prime Minister with that of his uncle, Mathbar Sing. He showed that Mathbar 'had permitted Surendra, then Heir Apparent, to indulge in such barbarities as the mutilation of innocent persons, and the throwing of live slave girls down wells.' And not only slave girls, those present must have recalled. It is possible that the lives of Jang Bahadur Rana and of many other men and women of Nepal were not worth a moment's purchase so long as both Mathbar Sing Thapa and Surendra Bikram Sah remained alive. The only question may have been to decide which of the two should die. Mathbar Sing's death was desired by the King and the Maharani for one reason, by Jang Bahadur for another. This perhaps explains Laurence Oliphant's account of his visit to the Thapatali, Jang Bahadur's palace, in Kathmandu, in 1850. He says that Jang, showing him round the palace, drew attention to one of the pictures hanging there. 'It was a portrait of a strikingly handsome man whose keen eye and lofty brow seemed almost to entitle him to the position he held between the Duke of Wellington and the Queen. "See," said Jang enthusiastically, "here is the Queen of England, and she has not got a more loyal subject than I am." Then, turning to the picture of the man with the keen eyes and high forehead, he remarked, "That is my poor uncle, Mathbar Sing, whom I shot: it is very like him." ' This insouciance may have been due to Jang's callousness, or to his conviction that the only and natural course left open to him was to kill Mathbar. Of one thing we may be sure and it is that Jang Bahadur did not kill his uncle in order to crave his own life from the King, Rajendra. He was never a coward.

Benares was the centre of every intrigue in the Valley, centring round the 'Martyr' King. There were many who should conspire against Jang Bahadur — Pandes, Basnets, the Maharani's party, Fateh Jang's and Abhiman's families, the King's cronies, and others beside. Jang Bahadur who had never favoured the idea of letting virtually the whole of the Royal Family live together in exile, now set to work to split them up. His first move was to invite Rajendra back. At the Maharani's behest

Rajendra refused, unless he could bring her with him. This the young conqueror flatly refused to accept, saying that if the King did not return in reasonable time, he would set Surendra Bikram on the throne in his place. The Maharani, confronted by a difficult problem, sought her familiar solution — murder. She procured two professional assassins and sent them to Nepal to find out the state of feeling in Kathmandu against the Prime Minister and thereafter to murder him. Rajendra, in witless fashion, gave them a letter to say that they were deputed to kill Jang Bahadur and that anyone who hindered them would be flayed alive when he, the King, laid hands on them. They probably showed this letter round in order to invoke occasional aid and were arrested with loaded weapons and this astounding document in their possession. They confessed at once.

Jang immediately put to the best possible purpose this latest threat to his life. He paraded the garrison at the familiar spot by a well-known tree on the parade-ground. Holding up the King's document, he told his men that they were ordered by the King to kill him. 'Here I am,' said he. 'Come forward and execute the sentence!' With shouts of loyalty, the troops surged round him, demanding the deposition of their King. While popular feeling ran so high for him, he promulgated the order deposing King Rajendra and setting Surendra on his *gaddi*. That same day the usual ceremonies were completed for the coronation of the new King: salutes were fired and there was public rejoicing. On the following day the Council of State listed the ex-King's crimes, drew them up in due form and despatched them to Benares, together with an invitation to him to return to Kathmandu, for they still held that he would be less of a nuisance under their eye in the Valley, than in India with the scheming, murderous woman, his wife. Furthermore, if he came to Nepal he would bring with him a large part of his not inconsiderable private fortune and thereby deprive her of the sinews for her war against Jang Bahadur. Prominent in this list of the Maharajah's sins was his responsibility for the death of Bhim Sen. There was nothing strange about that for, without his royal authority, Bhim Sen could not have been deposed, cast into prison or treated with such savagery in his wretched dungeon.

On receipt of the Council's letter the Queen made yet another false step in her campaign. She persuaded the incompetent Rajendra to invade Nepal. Jang Bahadur was only too pleased to learn of the approach of this incoherent body of soldiers, bringing nearer to him the very man he wanted, the King. While it was still hovering about at Alau in the Terai he sent off four of his regiments under Sanak Sing to round it up. Sanak attacked, routed the royal army and picked up the King himself while he was seeking safety on an elephant. Sanak put his precious captive in a closed palanquin and took him up to Thankote in the Valley by way of the Sisagarhi and Chandragiri passes. Arrived at Thankote, Jang Bahadur treated his old master as a guest of honour, welcomed him cordially at Kathmandu and sent him off to Bhatgaon to live in custody as a privileged prisoner. Here he started again his silly plottings, so Jang had him brought back to Kathmandu where he was put under a trusted guard and kept in confinement in a manner becoming his royal blood. He was purposely encouraged to attend in state at all public functions and occasions, so as to keep alive his faction in opposition to that of his son and thus to split and weaken the royalist party.

So that the young Rana Chief of State should not enjoy too reposeful an existence, Fateh Jang's family took up the chase, with Guru Parsad as the chief huntsman. There were several attempts on his life until 1849 when Guru Parsad, seeing that the murder business was played out, sued for pardon — and for an annuity! Jang, nothing loath to hear the last of an assassin and his band, pardoned him, made him a Colonel in the army on full pay and restored to him his confiscated lands and goods. A quixotic act of generosity to a worthless man.

It was the Prime Minister's intention that the ex-King should live in obscurity and that his son, the King, should take no part whatsoever in affairs of State. All power and all patronage were to be in the hands of the Prime Minister: the King was to be no more than a name to the people of Nepal. And so it was. Jang Bahadur reigned supreme and the House of Rana was established for the next hundred years in the ancient seat of the Newars Kings at Kathmandu.

18

Nepal and the British

———————— ❋ ————————

THROUGHOUT his life the right-hand man of Jang Bahadur Rana was his brother Dhir Shamsher. This cheerful, smiling, loyal and courageous Gurkha was a man of affairs, a man of action, an accomplished swordsman and a soldier of skill and determination. Above all, he was modest and had no excessive personal ambition. His wise and tolerant counsel must have been invaluable to the solitary Chief, his brother.

The Prime Minister had always been a protagonist of the British. While realising the dangers of British infiltration into Nepal through their custom of letting the flag follow trade, he yet insisted that there must be some quality in them by virtue of which they maintained their position in India. He made up his mind to discover more about them and to do so personally. One day he would pay a visit to England. This decision was far bolder than most would understand. Its boldness calls for some explanation. It was a Hindu superstition that it was unlucky to cross the *Kala Pani*, the Black Water: it was more than a superstition, it was a religious precept, and those who crossed were liable to be told that they had broken their caste and to be outcaste. So strong was this feeling that at Barrackpore in India in 1824 the 47th Native Infantry mutinied when ordered to take ship for Burma. No Indian Chief had yet faced this peril by visiting England, so Jang Bahadur, with a fine display of moral courage, determined to do so.

In the summer of 1848 Nepal offered six regiments of Nepalese troops to the British as a reinforcement for the second Sikh war which was then brewing. Lord Dalhousie refused them, but said that if there should be need in the future, he would gratefully take them. Jang was not pleased at this rebuff so, that same December, when the British and Sikhs were at each others' throats in Multan and on the Sutlej, he set out for a shooting expedition into the Terai taking with him a great army of 30,000 men with fifty guns, cavalry and administrative train. His motive has never been discovered. It seems most likely that, apart from training his officers and men to operate in large bodies in flat country, he intended to demonstrate to the British and perhaps to the Sikhs that he had efficient forces of impressive size. For the time being Jang's presence in force on that flank gave Dalhousie and his Commander-in-Chief the unfortunate idea that Nepal might be about to intervene. The fears of British officials in the then North Western Province of this show of strength is recorded in many a contemporary letter and document. It is said that the Nepalese leader was distrustful of the loyalty of his troops so must have them with him rather than leave them at the chronic danger-point of Kathmandu, but this is belied by his absenting himself about a year later for his journey to England.

A few months afterwards the widow of the great Ranjit Singh of the Punjab escaped in disguise from British custody at Chunar and made her way up into Nepal, to the embarrassment of the Anglophile Jang. He interned her and set his agent to see that her house did not attract political malcontents.

The great event in the career of Jang Bahadur Rana and in the policies of modern Nepal was now about to take place. In 1850 the British Government extended an invitation to His Excellency the Nepalese Ambassador, Kaji Jang Bahadur Rana, to visit England. As self-styled Ambassador he came, but no one was in the least mistaken that this was the dictator of Nepal who came to visit the British Queen. He came to see England and everything in England, its system, its factories, its people, its agriculture, its armed forces, with his own eyes. For nearly a year he stayed. He saw all he wished and took back to his own country the benefits of what he had seen and heard. He then started the modernising of Nepal. Had others of his perceptiveness and determination followed him, Nepal would have progressed faster and further than she did and 1947 would not have found her unaware and slumbering. Disdaining the inevitable charges of defiling his caste, the Nepalese Ambassador to the Court of St. James set out from Kathmandu to go to London, a journey eagerly anticipated since he was a boy.

General Bombahadur, his brother, would act as Prime Minister, Badri Nar Sing as Commander-in-Chief, Krishna Bahadur to take charge of the Civil Department, and Udip Sing to act as Governor of the Eastern and Western Provinces. Two brothers, Dhir Shamsher and Jagat Shamsher, went with him. There were twelve members of the staff and twenty-six servants. As matters are handled in the Orient, this was a modest establishment. Captain Thomas Smith and Landon have been at great pains to tell of the journey and of Jang's visits and tours in England. There is room here only to summarise Landon's narrative. Jang Bahadur Rana's was by now a legendary and somewhat awe-inspiring reputation among enlightened Britons in England who had heard of Nepal and of the Gurkhas.

Passing through India he lived up to his reputation. At Bankipur was a vast granary erected sixty years before, a circular building with a spiral track thirty inches wide cut out of its twelve-foot thick walls. Jang and Dhir Shamsher, hearing that British officers sometimes rode up this ascent and wishing to admire the view, must ride their horses up this precarious and brittle way, to the consternation of the British officers of the staff standing about below.

Calcutta received them cordially and brilliantly. They concentrated their attention on the arsenals and foundries of Bengal, somewhat indicative of their habits of mind. On 7th April they embarked on the P. & O. S.S. *Haddington*. Jang Bahadurwas now nearly thirty-three years of age, a splendid, exotic figure in his magnificent ceremonial uniforms of bright silks encrusted with jewels.

On 24th May 1850 a salute of twenty-one guns was spontaneously fired by the Darbar's orders in honour of the birthday of the Queen of England, the first of a century of salutes.

From the Hoogly the *Haddington* sailed to Madras, thence to Galle in Ceylon, and eight days later called in at Aden. At Suez the party set out on the overland journey to Cairo, thence travelling by boat to Alexandria where they embarked on the P. & O. S.S. *Ripon*. The measure of Jang Bahadur's adventure can here be taken. His knowledge of contemporary western transport could only have been of the very rare river steamboat that he may have seen at Benares on his previous visit: he may not, in fact, have seen even that. He had plunged straight from the barbaric social and political climate of Kathmandu into the most modern and highly civilised community of the day, and had reached his destination across the wide Black Water over which brooded all the evil spirits that the Brahman mind could conjure from the depths. He had come among a people whose ways were strange to him and whose outlook, coloured by a thousand years of liberal development, was in no manner like his own. But he remained himself and unabashed. Tradition is a staunch pillar on which to lean. Added to this, his eagerly questing mind, intent to dis-

cover all things new to him, kept his attention fixed on everything outside himself. Quite apart from his eastern splendour, he exerted himself
to create an impression of a Nepalese nobleman, putting forth his undoubted grace and charm and the personal magnetism which, in another
land, unfailingly carried his soldiers with him.

His youthful ambition had been to meet the Duke of Wellington, the
greatest soldier of his age. The ambition was gratified with great cor-
diality, and to the end of his days he spoke of the Duke having treated him
in every way as an equal, urging this, whenever doubt arose, as the reason
for the fullest recognition of his, Jang Bahadur's, status. 'When that
great warrior called upon me, I felt it to be the proudest moment of my
life.' There is a certain modesty in this attitude when one recalls that it
was held by a man under whose solitary hand lay the fortunes of five
millions of people. There is modesty also in his reply to Lord Gough who
asked him what his name meant. 'Brave in war,' replied the Gurkha,
'but it is a mere trick of language. Your name is no trick, for it is associated with the conquest of the Punjab.'

On learning of the great Duke's death in 1852, Jang had eighty-three
minute guns fired in salute to his memory.

The genial Dhir Shamsher also seems to have distinguished himself,
by winning a notable victory over an English wrestling champion. No
one seems to know quite how he came to enter the ring for this occasion,
but Landon thinks he found himself there because the English, ignorant
of the habits and wishes of these Himalayan strangers, left them to roam
at their will. Dhir Shamsher roamed in the direction of the wrestling booths.
There is no doubt that Jang Bahadur was very pleased with his Commander-in-Chief's prowess.

The three of them went everywhere and saw everything.

Jang, the despotic little schemer from Nepal, was as much impressed
by Queen Victoria as she was by him. The Queen was quite delighted
with him. She invited him to be present at the christening of the young
Prince who was later the Duke of Connaught and a great friend of one of
Jang's successors as Prime Minister. Sitting by her side he talked and
played with the children and she told him how much her little ones ad-
mired his gorgeous jewels. His two brothers, Jagat and Dhir Shamsher,
attended a debate in the House of Commons and were surprised at the
peacefulness with which argument was conducted in that place. It so happened that, a day or two later, a lunatic name Pate assaulted the Queen.
Jang, at once feeling at home and that he knew all about this type of
business, went to the palace and demanded that the offender should be

executed forthwith. Pate had only a walking stick, so could have inflicted little harm.

The Gurkha prince had no use at all for opera: he regarded it as a rather silly entertainment and quite unintelligible. At a gala performance in London, the Queen noticed him enthusiastically applauding the *prima donna's* performance. 'But,' said her Majesty, 'you have not understood one word of what she was singing.' 'No, Madam,' came the prompt reply, 'nor do I understand one word of what the nightingales sing.' His was a quick wit and, for an unlettered man, all the more remarkable. He preferred the music of a military band, even the noise of his own rude company musicians, above any opera.

Jang and his brothers made a special point of inspecting arsenals, military establishments and everything agricultural. He even went down a mine to see how coal was gained from the soil. When he sailed, he took back with him to Nepal a number of pedigree sheep and cattle.

On 21st August he left England for Paris. There he visited the tomb of Napoleon Bonaparte and, Prince Louis Napoleon enquiring from him what he would like to see most, he requested a parade of 100,000 men. The French Prince did his best, a great parade, but not the 100,000 he had hoped for. They enjoyed themselves, visiting every place of sport and interest. At a shooting gallery a French girl laughingly said she could shoot as well as Jang Bahadur, so he handed her his pistol. Nervously fingering it, she let it off by mistake. The bullet lodged in Dhir Shamsher. Jang extracted it on the spot, for it was not serious and the stout soldier was soon about again. At Marseilles H.M.S. *Growler* met the party and returned them to Alexandria.

On 19th December Jang Bahadur left Calcutta for his home, wondering just what he would find there when he got back and, if no change, then just what had been the effect of the heady wine of power on the brothers he had left behind. On the way he stopped at Benares to see his old enemy, the Maharani. Her two sons called on him to complain that they were not receiving their share of the money that the ex-King, their father, had deposited in India for them, so Jang had it divided into three parts, a judgment to which the trio agreed, the Maharani thus losing financial control. On the way, too, news came to him that Fateh Jang's son, Guru Parsad, whom he had quixotically pardoned, was again plotting to kill him. On 29th January 1851 he entered the Nepalese Terai where his brother, General Krishna, met him with two regiments. Jang had a few days' shooting, then turned his face towards his capital driving up to the Thapatali on 6th February, having been away for more than twelve months. His route was lined with soldiers and the whole Valley went mad with rejoicing. He himself was in white silk, with silver coronet encrusted with jewels, and girt with the sword presented to him by the French Emperor. He advanced and took his seat in the midst of the pavilion, his bodyguard with double-barrel rifles close behind him, spoke a few well-chosen words to the great throng and drove amid a tumult of cheering to the Thapatali.

He knew the crowd of Nepal. He now awaited the inevitable conspiracy by the chosen few.

Little more than a week later, his brother, Bombahadur, who had been left in supreme charge during his absence, called at night at the Thapatali. Jang Bahadur and he sat talking until at last it all poured out. Bombahadur burst into tears and disclosed the plot long and carefully laid by his brother, Badri Nar Sing, backed by the King's family. Badri had hired an assassin who was to shoot Jang Bahadur while on his way to Basant-pore the very next day: Upendra Bikram Sah was to murder his own brother, the King Surendra, at the same time. Upendra would be King, Bombahadur Prime Minister, and Badri Nar Sing Commander-in-Chief. Jang warned his brother of the serious consequences if the story he told were false, 'stood to' the Thapatali guard and, under their escort, forthwith crossed the *maidan* and entered the Kot. Falling in the Kot garrison, he sent a hundred men to each of the conspirators' houses, under trusted officers — Jagat Shamsher, Ran Mehar Adhikari, Jang's oldest friend, and his brother, Udip Sing. Honest Dhir Shamsher stood ready to summon the guards and Jang's own regiment if trouble arose. But all went smoothly. Within two hours of Bombahadur's confession the conspirators were brought in chains to the bloody Kot to face a Council, ready seated, presided over by the King, with the ex-King in attendance and a number of high officers as members. Their houses were meanwhile searched and documents found incriminating them all. They denied all knowledge of the plot so the trial was postponed to the next day. Then Badri Nar Sing invoked before the Council the wrath of God upon all who might conceive such villainy — only to be shown the documents by his cold, hard-featured elder brother, who ordered the Captain of the Guard to smite him across the mouth with his shoe, a deadly insult. Badri's spirits collapsed. He confessed.

The Council thereupon sentenced the conspirators to death. Jang Bahadur would not accept this, so it then sentenced them to be blinded with red-hot irons but this, too, Jang refused. He would neither execute nor torture; nor would his mother, a humane and good woman, have allowed him this revenge. He seems to have sickened of bloodshed. His journey into the outside world had served him well. He wrote to the Governor-General requesting him to take charge of the prisoners. Lord Dalhousie, in full sympathy with Jang Bahadur's difficulties and willing to strengthen his position in Nepal, readily agreed. In June 1851 the conspirators were put on the march for Allahabad to an easy confinement as political prisoners.

History is indebted to Laurence Oliphant, whose father was Chief Justice of Ceylon, for a better acquaintance with Jang Bahadur, with the 'Minister Sahib' as he was termed by his entourage at the time of his return to Nepal from England in 1851. His ship called in at Galle in Ceylon at the end of 1850 and he there met Oliphant, whom he invited to accompany him back to Kathmandu for a short visit. Oliphant wrote an account of his journey and of all he saw and heard. He shot tiger and rhinoceros and trapped elephant with Jang in the Terai before going on up to Kathmandu. He tells us that time never hung heavy on the hands of the busy and active Minister. On board ship he spent two hours daily practising with rifle and pistol, then trained his hunting dogs and visited his horses. Of English he had but a few words. . . . How do you do? Very well, thank you. Will you sit down? You are very pretty. Fortunately, he did not use the phrases at random.

Oliphant's great friend was the fat brother, Colonel Dhir Shamsher. He used to play billiards with him and found him the most 'jovial, light-hearted and thoroughly unselfish being imaginable, brave as a lion, as recent events in Nepal have proved, and full of amusing conversation. . . .' 'My friend, Colonel Dhir Shum Shere, now came up whistling the Sturm Marsch and challenged me to a game of billiards: he was in his manner more thoroughly English than any native I ever knew and both in appearance and disposition looked as if he were an Anglo-Saxon who had been dyed by mistake. . . .' On one occasion Dhir demonstrated his skill by shearing off a buffalo's head with one blow of his *khora*. He then sent for another buffalo for the visitor from Ceylon to display his skill. 'This I declined as politely as I could. . . .' Again, '. . . I know of no one I would rather have by my side in a row than the young Colonel. Cheerful and lively, his merry laugh might be heard in the midst of a knot of his admirers, to whom he was relating some amusing anecdote, while his shrewd remarks were the result of keen observation, and proved his intellect to be by no means of a low order.'

Of Jang Bahadur he has this to say, 'But, while anxious to increase his popularity, with his attempts at conciliation is combined a patronising

143

air, which he cannot conceal and which is calculated to render him un-popular.' He recounts an instance of the Prime Minister taking the law into his own hands while on the journey to Kathmandu. A deputation of peasantry came to him to complain that two of the Sirdars of his retinue had defrauded them of 25,000 rupees, one of the Sirdars being a special favourite of Jang Bahadur. Jang inquired into the case, satisfied himself of the justice of the complaint, arrested the two defendants and confined them until they repaid the money. The whole camp was delayed awaiting the production of the full sum: it then moved on. Of the murder of Math-bar Sing, Oliphant writes, '. . . this detestable act, of which he [Jang] always speaks now in terms of the deepest regret, but asserts that it was an act of necessity, from which there was no escaping,' and then, of Jang's passage to power, '. . . though his path to greatness had been deluged with the blood of the bravest nobles of the land, it must be admitted that the peace and prosperity which Nepal now enjoys would never have been possessed by her while distracted and convulsed by the struggles of hos-tile factions; and much less would she ever have experienced the blessings of an enlightened administration, if these struggles had not resulted in the elevation of General Jang Bahadur to the office of Prime Minister, . . . [he] possessed sufficient daring and resolution to execute the bold, though unscrupulous schemes his undoubted genius had conceived . . . he is not I am convinced, naturally cruel; and in a companionship of two months I discovered so many estimable traits in him, that I could not help making allowances for the defects of character entirely self-formed by one ignorant of all moral responsibilities, the half-tamed son of an almost totally uncivilised country. . . . Upon becoming Prime Minister he could neither read nor write. Finding great inconvenience from his incapacity in these respects, he applied himself diligently to his alphabet, and was soon able to carry on all official correspondence of any importance to himself.' Oliphant further remarks on his amazing industry and his hard-working day.

The young King Surendra, he dismisses in a few damning words. 'The young King, capable only of aiding in nefarious schemes, such as those already recounted, can in no way comprehend the new-fangled philanthropic views of the Prime Minister. He cares little about the wel-fare of his country; his amusement seems to consist in concocting and executing bloody designs, and his mind must be so accustomed to this species of excitement that it can scarce be without it!' In other words, a homicidal maniac to whose hands it is not surprising that the Minister would not entrust any part of the cares of the State. From this stems the

14B. *Western Nepal*

14A. *Eastern Nepal*

15. *Gurungs in High Grazing* Got, *12,000 ft. Above Sea Level*

16A. *Dhankuta, Eastern Nepal. The Main Street*

16B. *Kiranti Boys (Limbu and Rai) at Their Dinner*

17. *British Gurkha Sepoy, 1817*

18. *The Queen's Gurkha Orderly Officers*

19. *The Maharajah Jang Bahadur Rana. 1846–1877. Wearing the Robe of G.C.S.I. Decorations G.C.B. and G.C.S.I.*

20. *The Maharajah Chandra Shamsher Jang Bahadur Rana. 1901–1929*

21A. *Leading Ranas with the British Minister, 1944*

21B. *Nepalese Generals (Rana) saluting King Tribhuvana, 1944*

22. *The Maharajah Judha Shamsher Jang Bahadur Rana. 1931–1945*

23. *The Maharajah Mohan Shamsher Jang Bahadur Rana. 1948–1951*

absolute subservience of Kings to Prime Ministers in Nepal. Without a Parliament, this means of controlling the royal power and abuse of power was inevitable.

'From Calcutta the journey was made in a roomy carriage built almost upon the model of an English stage-coach, in which, with my fellow-traveller, I had passed the night, . . . dragged along at the rate of about four miles an hour by ten coolies, harnessed to it. It was an excellent macadamised and perfectly level road, denominated the Great Trunk Road of Bengal', and quite fit for horses.

At Benares Jang Bahadur married the daughter of the ex-Rajah of Coorg and, despising as he did all restrictive customs, offered the next day to introduce his bride to Oliphant and his friends, but, as the meeting was about to take place, his outraged father-in-law hurried in in a great panic and, much to Jang's irritation, prevented it. Later, in the absence of the Coorgi, Jang did introduce her as his 'beautiful Missis'. This seeking of their brides of Rajput stock in a foreign country was later to estrange the Ranas from their own people. He was very European in his outlook. Oliphant relates that one day a local rajah came to see him, apologising for not having found any auspicious time to come before. Jang received him politely and replied that this was unfortunate as he could not, owing to his immediate departure and to his business with the English gentlemen, return the visit. So saying, in his most graceful manner he conducted the visitor to the door, and returned rubbing his hands and knowingly remarking, 'That is the way to get over an interview with one of these natives.'

A detachment of his own regiment had come to Benares to escort him to Kathmandu. The men were tall and well-made, dressed in light green with yellow facings. Their Company drill was good. Their platoon drill they performed to music with no word of command as the Maharani had complained that the shouting grated on her ears.

Oliphant remarks on the difference in the Terai passing from the Company's territory into that of Nepal, 'The villages looked more wretched, the people more dirty, the country was almost totally uncultivated, and nearly all traces of roads disappeared as we traversed the green sward of the Terai of Nepal.' Jang's brother, Krishna Bahadur, was Governor, 'an active and energetic officer. Any complaint of the peasantry is in the first instance brought to his notice and referred by him to his brother if his decision does not give satisfaction. . . .' He praises Jang Bahadur's management of the Terai by which in a few years he had increased its wealth tenfold. About the *ayul* or *awal* fever he says, 'It would appear that [it] might be obviated ... by going in search of and killing certain serpents, which are said to poison the atmosphere with their breath. I should be inclined to recommend cutting down the jungle in preference to the cutting up of the serpents.'

'The present policy of the Nepal Government is to keep the roads by which their country is approached in as impassable a state as possible ... in case of a war, the badness of the roads would offer an insuperable obstacle to our progress. Jang Bahadur is quite alive to the real state of the case, and sees at once the absurdity of the policy ... but he feels that any innovation of the sort would be too unpopular for him to attempt in his present position.' Jang's remark regarding war with the British, 'If a cat is pushed into a corner it will fly at an elephant, but it will always keep out of the corner as long as possible,' was sufficiently expressive.

Arrived in Kathmandu, Oliphant went about seeing the sights. 'My conductor was a brother of Jang Bahadur's, who distinguished himself about a week afterwards by a brave attempt to assassinate the Minister [Jang]. . . . Not that it signifies in the least in Nepal whether a man is a fratricide or proposes making away with more distant relatives. If you do not associate with assassins, you must give up the pleasures of Nepal society. Among the natives assassination is not looked upon as a crime, but as a matter of course; the Minister, however, with those of his suite who accompanied him on his recent mission have become more enlightened in this respect, and have found to their astonishment that indiscriminate murder is not the usual mode adopted in the civilised world for bringing about political changes or accomplishing private ends. . . . Already has one of them [his brothers] attempted his life: but the Minister has learned mercy in England, and, to the astonishment of everyone, Badri Nath Sing [Badri Nar Sing] and his fellow-conspirators are only banished for life. It is said that the Minister resisted all the representations of his friends as to the propriety of executing the conspirators by the argument of, "What would *The Times* say?" — which must have appeared to the majority of the members of the Nepal Durbar to be a very extraordinary reason for leniency.' In order that Bombahadur might not feel too keenly the loss of power and prestige after having held the post of Prime Minister in his long absence overseas, Jang created him Commander-in-Chief.

Laurence Oliphant's assessment of the aged King and of the great Prime Minister is probably as fair as any that has ever been made. 'The vacillating conduct of the imbecile old man throughout his whole reign, the apathy with which he was contented to remain a passive spectator of those bloody dramas of which his court was for so long a period the theatre, deprive him of all claim to commiseration in his present degraded position, which, in fact, is the natural result of his indifference to the game so eagerly played by the contending parties, and of which the stake was his own throne.

'If, on the other hand, in a country where common humanity and, still more, every kind of principle is unknown, daring and intrepid conduct merits reward, Jang has fairly earned for himself the position he now holds. . . . And now, for the first time in the history of Nepaul, the Durbar was to a certain extent united; internal machinations were no longer to be feared; and the country was ruled over by different members of that family, the elevation of which was due to one of their own number, who possessed sufficient daring and resolution to execute the bold, though unscrupulous schemes his undoubted genius had conceived.'

These personal notes on the Prime Minister, on his fellows and on his and their outlook are given here at some length because in them can be found the explanation of much that went on in Nepal during the next hundred years.

In September 1852 the Government of India notified Jang of the death of one of its prisoners, so he immediately sent permission for the return to Nepal of his brother, Badri, and of the Prince Upendra. Badri he kept at Palpa as a state prisoner for a short time, then pardoned him. Then to end the feud between the Guru Parsad and himself he recalled this priest from exile at Bettiah and, as an act of policy, and no more, married Guru's sister, the daughter of Fateh Jang who met his death at the Kot. Finally, to neutralise the royal family, he married his son, Jagat Jang, to the King's eldest daughter. He was now free to apply himself to the affairs of his country.

Every fifth year Nepal sent a mission to Peking. This mission was grossly insulted and ill-treated on its return journey through Tibet. This was not all. Always there was friction on the frontier: always the Tibetan authorities treated Nepalese residents and merchants abominably in Lhassa. The treatment of the mission finally brought Nepalese anger to boiling point at a time when the Chinese Army was away in the Eastern provinces suppressing the Taiping rising. Jang Bahadur, determined to settle the dispute once and for all, seized this opportunity to put his army in motion.

He sent orders to the Chaubisia and Baisia to raise contingents to join a force that he had directed westwards on Jumla to protect his left flank from attack through the passes of Yari and Muktinath, and posted a considerable force at Dhankuta on the Sikkim border to look after his eastern flank. To support his main armies he had already speeded up production from his arsenals, bought large stores of tentage and administrative equipment from India, installed great supply depots at the foot of the passes, and enlisted a whole corps of Kiranti tribesmen from the East. The Tibetans must have been very dense of mind if they had not grasped what was intended for them. While these preparations were in progress to cook the Tibetan goose, Nepal was negotiating a treaty with the British for the mutual surrender of prisoners, an agreement of some importance for the peace of the border, for the Company had had no little trouble in the past in extracting from the Governor of Palpa the fugitive criminals who led the atrocious bands of Budhuk dacoits driven into Nepal by the operations of Indian soldiers and police.

Twenty-seven thousand men, including 1,200 horse and light mountain guns, moved up into the Kuti and Kirong passes in March 1855, Dhir Shamsher leading the Kuti column. He defeated a Tibetan force near Khassa and seized the fortress protecting the pass, but was halted by thick snow. The next day he carried Kuti and, a month later, Suna-Gompa, with heavy losses to the defenders. Bombahadur took Kirong village without opposition, Jagat Shamsher capturing Jhanga after nine days of bloody fighting. At this stage Jang Bahadur himself left Kathmandu to take command, consolidated the positions, opened parleys and thereafter returned to his capital. That November, during negotiations, as was the Tibetan habit, their army suddenly attacked, carrying Kuti with heavy loss to the Gurkhas and inflicting casualties on the defenders of Jhanga, but suffering far more heavily themselves. Dhir Shamsher at once counter-attacked against heavy odds, drove the Tibetans out of Kuti, killing 1,100 of them, and threw them back another ten miles, retaking Suna-Gompa. This operation was conducted with much skill, almost entirely with the cold steel, and with few casualties to his own force, achievements which earned the compliments of the Prime Minister.

Simultaneously, Colonel Sanak Sing, marching to the relief of the now besieged Jhanga, forced the passage and dealt severely with the Tibetan forces, again with the kukri as the cold was too intense for the men to load and to use their triggers. The Tibetans came to terms by which both combatants were duly to honour the Chinese Emperor as hitherto; the two countries entered into a mutual security pact; Nepal was to place an envoy in Lhassa to look after her interests; Nepalese subjects were to have complete freedom to trade in Tibet and disputes between themselves were to go before Nepalese arbitrators. The most important clause, however, was that Nepalese subjects were not to be taxed and Nepalese goods were to enter Tibet free of all duty. Many years afterwards this last clause led to friction when Nepalese merchants took their goods into Tibet through Sikkim by the Chumbi Valley route.

On 1st April 1856 the Gurkha forces started to draw out of Tibet.

As in the expedition of 1792, so in this, the Gurkha armies were reduced almost to famine. Jang Bahadur, never at a loss, at once directed his Brahmans to declare the yak to be officially a goat, not a cow, so that his army might be fed without harm to its caste Hindus.

Jang Bahadur's next move has never been explained. In July of this same year he declared himself to be a sick man and resigned his office of Prime Minister into the hands of his brother, Bombahadur. His action would have been plain if he had in fact withdrawn from public life, but he did nothing of the sort, for every decision of any moment was still made by himself and duly executed by the dummy he had installed as head of state. One result of his nominal retirement was that an eminent deputation headed by Raj Guru Bijai Raj, the erstwhile incompetent conspirator, approached him with an offer of the Crown. To this he gave the astute reply that if he ever thought the offer would make for the happiness of Nepal, he would consider it, thus warning the King against misconduct: that he could conduct the country's affairs without the burden of a crown that he had given to another, thus impressing upon the King and Bombahadur that his was still the real authority: that if the country ever really needed him, he would not hesitate to return, thus warning would-be trouble-makers of future punishment. On his refusal to accept the Crown, the deputation asked him to accept the duchies of Kaski and Lamjung with the hereditary title of Maharajah* to pass from Prime Minister to Prime Minister, with authority to overrule or coerce the King. This he accepted. From now onwards Nepal boasts a Rana as Maharajah and Prime Minister who wields the power, and a Sah or Sahi as King, or Maharajadiraj, who is a cipher, a mere relic of the great Prithwi Narain Sah, a symbol that once there was such a man. By this treatment Jang Bahadur laid in a store of trouble for his successors in other times.

Conferred upon him now in retirement were such powers over the whole kingdom as only an absolute monarch would wield. He could appoint and dismiss all public servants, he could declare war and peace and sign treaties, he could himself make new laws and repeal old ones, he was given powers of life and death and of all punishments. He was, in fact, as

* There is little doubt that it was at the King's behest that Jang Bahadur accepted this title, for no one else could confer it.

much the sovereign as was Peter the Great of Russia. Jang, determined
to keep the Premiership for ever in the Rana family, insisted that the post
of Prime Minister should for ever pass from brother to brother, rather
than in the direct line to the eldest son, according to date of birth alone,
descending then to the eldest of the next generation and so passing along
and down. Failing these, provision was made for it to pass to cousins.
Thus he provided against the perilous contingency of a minor succeeding
to the office and against the honours and dignity passing out of the family.
At the same time, he also ensured that year by year a stream of disgruntled
and disloyal Ranas outside the privileged few proceeded from this polygamous family.

Retirement was not all a bed of roses. It nettled him that the British
Government stubbornly refused to correspond with anyone other than
the official Prime Minister, now Bombahadur. Ramsay, the new Resident,
was not allowed to recognise Jang in any official capacity. Between the
two men relations became more and more strained until Jang could not
abide this British agent who was, rather unfortunately, a cousin of the
Governor-General.

On 25th May 1857, Bombahadur died a natural death, the first Prime
Minister to do so. Jang Bahadur at once resumed the office, dealing by the
way with another attempt on his life.

In India the scrap of unleavened bread and the lotus bloom had been
speeding by night from cantonment to cantonment. The Bengal Army
mutinied.

19

Nepal and the Indian Mutiny

———————— ❊ ————————

It is a matter of history that the necessity to bite the cap from the greased cartridge was one of the causes of the Mutiny. Early in 1857 Lieutenant D. Macintyre was in charge of a squad of Gurkhas from the Nasiri, Sirmoor and Kumaon Battalions undergoing a musketry course at Amballa.

'After being encamped for some time with the Native Infantry details, a request was made by the Gurkhas, through one of their own officers, to be allowed to pitch their tents with those of the British soldiers. The reason stated for this was that they did not like being mixed up with the *Kala Log**, as they called the native Sepoys, whom they reported as showing a very bad feeling in their conversations regarding the use of the greased cartridges. At the same time, they requested that these might be served out to them, in order to show the Poorbiahs that they had no fellow-feeling with them in the cartridge question.'

They were permitted to encamp with the British soldiers and the greased cartridges were served out to them at their own request, though ungreased ones were available, had they wanted them.

On the 11th May 1857, Bengal units of the Meerut garrison rose in armed mutiny.

Firm as a rock in his friendship with Britain, Jang Bahadur, directly he knew of the outbreak, offered 6,000 Gurkha soldiers to Lord Canning. Ramsay accepted and two regiments marched at once from Kathmandu. But Canning, the Governor-General, unexpectedly, though in the kindest of terms, refused the offer on the grounds that the entry of Nepalese troops might encourage the rebels in thinking either that the British could not handle the situation or alternatively that Nepal was advancing

---

* Black folk.

Gorkha

to their aid, the ex-King of Oudh having appealed to Jang Bahadur for assistance against the Company.

A month later Canning gratefully accepted Gurkha help and asked that the first contingent should be sent to Lucknow. Jang despatched Dhir Shamsher with three thousand men, despite the havering and doubts of the Council of State.

At noon on 14th May a tired camel *sowar* pushed his way through the throng of the Dehra Doon bazaar, across the *maidan* and up to the orderly room of the Sirmoor Battalion, bringing the gravest news from Meerut and orders to march at once. Within four hours, not waiting for its baggage, the battalion was on the road with sixty rounds in their pouches and two elephants carrying the reserve of ammunition — 490 strong led by Major Charles Reid. The corps made for the Kheri, or Mohan, pass along the stony beds of the now silent torrents.

At Rawalpindi in the Punjab on 23rd June the Kumaon Battalion was ordered to Delhi.

Briefly we will follow the fortunes of these two Battalions of British Gurkhas* before we return to their brothers fighting under the staunch soldier, Dhir Shamsher.

* * * * *

Reid of the Sirmoor Battalion kept a diary. A few extracts may suffice to show the part his battalion played in these fateful days. Passing through Saharanpore, Roorkee and Bulandshahr, with occasional skirmishes on the way, he led his men into General Barnard's camp at Alipore outside Delhi. He then marched for the Ridge close outside the Kashmir and Mori gates of the city. After a smart battle at Badli-ke-Sarai in which he drove a large rebel force back on the city he was ordered to occupy Hindu Rao's House, which then became the Main Piquet of the force besieging Delhi, facing and within 1,200 yards of the Mori bastion. Here, in the scorching heat of an Indian summer, from June 8th to September 14th, reinforced from time to time by companies of the 60th Rifles, the Guides and Coke's Rifles, the Sirmoor Battalion held on, constantly counter-attacking and inflicting defeat after defeat on immensely stronger forces of trained units of mutineers.

'Hindu Rao's House was the key of the position . . . which the enemy were not long in discovering; they tried their utmost to drive me out of it the first day, and it became ever after the object of almost every attack. . . . June 9th: We were again attacked. We met the scoundrels coming up

* At Appendix VI is a note on the Gurkha Brigade.

152

the road. I threw out skirmishers on the right and left, and allowed them to approach. We were fighting till 4 p.m. when the enemy retreated with heavy loss. . . . 10th . . . the mutineers came out in force with guns and cavalry . . . I turned out the Main Piquet. . . . Whilst my men were advancing, the mutineers called out, "Come on, Goorkhas, we won't fire upon *you* — we expect you to join us." "Oh, yes," was the reply, "we're coming." They closed upon their centre, and when within 20 paces they gave the mutineers a well directed volley . . . the scrimmage lasted until 7.30 p.m. when the enemy thought they'd had enough of it, and withdrew. . . .

'12th. I was attacked this morning. The mutineers were driven back in a very short space of time with a loss to them of about 200.

'13th. . . . They fought most desperately. The Sirdar Bahadoor was killed by my orderly, Lal Sing. . . . The mutineers were about 5,000 strong, infantry and cavalry.

'15th. I was attacked this morning in great force, some 6,000 infantry and cavalry. . . . On they came and placed a green standard on the hill within a hundred paces of me. . . . I gave the word "forward"; our little fellows were up like a shot, and advanced in beautiful order to the top of the hill . . . on came the mutineers and we met just as I got over the brow of the hill. . . . I gave them one well directed volley. . . . We are under fire morning, noon and night. . . . We can hold our own. . . .'

And so, day after day and night after night, the struggle went on, Reid and his handful of Gurkhas never yielding an inch and always on the attack.

'23rd. I was attacked early this morning. The enemy turned out in greater force than I have ever yet seen them. . . . The mutineers about 12 o'clock made a most desperate attack on the whole of my position. No men could have fought better. . . . Thousands were brought against my mere handful of men. . . . I drove the enemy out of the Subzee Mundee no less than six different times. . . . We were fighting hard until sunset. . . . They retired, leaving about 800 killed and wounded on the field. . . .'

More accounts of daily attacks up to July 12th.

'July 12th. We had another grand scrimmage yesterday; . . . the enemy were about 8,000 strong, and fought desperately. . . . I had fairly driven the enemy inside their walls, and as nothing more could be done with my handful of men, we withdrew. . . .

'July 14th. Fighting all day . . . attacked the twentieth time. The attack commenced at 8 o'clock in the morning. . . . My total loss since 8th June . . . nearly half the regiment. . . .

'July 19th. . . . we all came home dead beat. I never was so completely done up before. . . . We drove the enemy within their strong walls . . . they hope to wear me out.

'August 3rd. . . . The engagement commenced at sunset on 1st, lasted the whole night and until 4 p.m. yesterday . . . the whole force, in all about 20,000, came straight at my position . . . they were very desperate indeed. . . . Before 12 o'clock we drove them back half-a-dozen times. . . .' [There followed an account of still more attacks.] 'Shortly after the moon rose came fresh troops from the city. . . . I passed the word from right to left to allow the enemy to come close up and to keep a dead silence in the ranks . . . round after round, with volleys of musketry had the effect of driving them back again. . . .' [After further fighting]. 'Thus ended the great Eed attack, being number twenty four on my position. . . . It was a glorious victory. . . .'

The struggle went on with hardly a pause.

'27th . . . again attacking me. They got a good thrashing.

'31st. . . . The great Mohurrum attack came off last night. . . .

'September 1st. . . . I drove the enemy from their breastworks last night. . . .'

Returning one day to the Main Piquet, Reid relates, '. . . I saw a boy squatting behind a rock with a rifle in his hands . . . he got up and saluted me, and said, "I . . . came here with the recruits. I have disobeyed orders, Sahib, but I could not help it. My father was on duty in the Sammy House, and I went there to assist him in getting out his cartridges. He was killed, and I then went to one of the 60th Rifles to help him in loading quickly. He was shortly afterwards wounded. He gave me his rifle, and told me to get a 'Doolie' and send him to the hospital. I did so, and then went at it myself. After firing a few shots a bullet struck me which made four holes in my legs, but I am not much hurt." He looked *quite* pleased. . . .'

On another occasion, having news of an impending attack, Reid went to the hospital to see if any men were yet fit to return to the ranks. The result was that every patient, sick or wounded, who could in any manner handle a weapon of any sort disappeared from hospital and appeared to answer his name before zero hour for the operation.

On 14th September Delhi was stormed, Reid and his men going in with the right column, with which there was also a detachment of the Kumaon Battalion.

In the Sirmoor Battalion eight officers out of nine had been killed or wounded and 327 men out of 490.

The Defence of the Main Piquet at Delhi ranks with the Defence of Lucknow among the epics of the centuries.

*   *   *   *   *

On 31st July the Kumaon Battalion, after varying adventures on the way, reached Rhye, two marches from Delhi. On 1st August, at 3 a.m. it marched into its position on the Ridge at Delhi as the mutineers started their great 'Eed' attack. On 12th August it was in the smart affair when the guns at Ludlow Castle were surprised and captured. On 14th September the main body of the battalion took part in the gallant action of the storming of the Kashmir Gate. From the Kashmir Gate it advanced, driving the enemy from the *Kotwali* and from Delhi's famous street, the Chandni Chauk, until it came up against the quadrangle of the Great Mosque, the Jama Masjid, where it stopped to await the artillery. Thereafter it occupied itself in clearing the enemy out of the narrow alleyways of the great city, a task that took some days to complete.

Before the Mutiny broke out the Nasiri Battalion had been far afield, its campaigning having taken it into the Kurram among the North West Frontier mountains and along through the remote Swat Valley away to the north of Peshawar. Bickering and fighting, it had been almost constantly on active service from 1851 to 1856. In the days of the Mutiny it was engaged in local operations below Naini Tal and Almora, at times co-operating with Jang Bahadur's Nepalese troops, and fighting an outstanding action at Chapoorah against a far superior force.

As a result of these achievements the reputation of the Gurkha as a fighting man was hailed in British and Indian Armies; these battalions had established Nepal in India. Before long the Indian Army was to recruit more battalions from Nepal until, by 1908, there were on its cadre ten regiments, twenty battalions. In 1857–58 two new battalions, to be later known as the 4th and 5th Gurkha Rifles, were raised at Pithoragarh and Abbottabad. It is no longer feasible to follow the services of individual units of this rapidly-expanding 'Gurkha Brigade'.

*   *   *   *   *

The time has come to turn to the Nepalese force under General Dhir Shamsher Rana. It had marched from Kathmandu at the end of June. Dhir advanced straight on Gorakhpore, where the mutinous soldiery were disarmed: he then threw out detachments to occupy the rebel towns of Jaunpore and Azamgarh. On 18th September, the latter place being threatened by a large force of rebels, Dhir took the Sher Battalion from

Jaunpore. It marched the forty miles that day. Arriving at Azamgarh at 6 p.m., he learnt that his enemy had taken position at Manduri, ten miles away. Not wishing to forfeit the advantages of surprise, he moved out at 1 a.m. that same night. As the sun rose his patrols reported the enemy in position, strongly fortified, immediately before him. Dhir at once formed up in five columns and charged in with the cold steel. The onslaught was so swift and fierce that his men swept into the enemy works and were among the defenders in a matter of minutes, plying their curved knives. On 29th September Nepalese troops from Jaunpore occupied Mubarak-pore, captured the rebel chief and handed him over for trial, then spread out and pacified the entire district, capturing Utraula, another rebel stronghold, and razing it to the ground.

In the meanwhile hostile forces had gathered once more in the neigh-bourhood of Azamgarh and Jaunpore. Dhir Shamsher's battalions turned on them and, in October, coming up with the enemy at Kudya and Chanda, administered to them two sound beatings. At Chanda the fighting was savage for the Gurkhas were only some 1,100 strong with two guns while their opponents had between 4,000 and 5,000 men strongly posted with seven guns. The battle rocked back and forth, but in the end the Gurkhas succeeded in forcing their way into the defences, winning a complete victory, the rebels leaving three hundred dead on the battlefield. The Gurkha Commander, Colonel Madan Mohan Sing, was killed and Gurkha losses were more severe than their small numbers could well afford. In this fight Lieutenant Gambir Sing, 'single-handed, took a gun, cutting down five artillery men and wounding and driving away the others.' He was covered with wounds but returned to fight again.

Lord Canning now asked that Jang Bahadur himself should take over command, bringing with him 9,000 men whom he had held ready for the purpose these last four months. Jang responded with alacrity: a fight was always to his liking. In later years he spoke of this campaign as the most important work of his life. In the meanwhile the Gorakhnath Regiment had marched from Segouli, and had engaged in a successful little battle at Sobanpore on the lesser Gandak River. Jang had his force at Bettiah eighty miles east of Gorakhpore by 23rd December, where he was joined by Brigadier-General MacGregor. On the 5th January 1858 the combined force was near Gorakhpore which had been re-occupied by the rebels. Jang attacked and carried the place, the enemy taking to his heels, leaving about two hundred dead and wounded. Passing a part of the Nepalese forces to British Command on the Gogra River, Jang now marched for Lucknow by way of Sultanpore. Crossing the Gogra on 25th February he stormed a small rebel fort on the road to Ambarpore, stoutly defended, the garrison dying to a man. Costly to him as was this small operation it had its effect elsewhere, for a much larger fortress which barred his way was evacuated without firing a shot. Passing the Gumti, Jang Bahadur on 11th March brought his men into the British lines outside Lucknow near the Begam's Kothi.

At this same time General Franks with a force of some 5,000 men, of whom over 3,000 were Nepalese, was clearing Oudh. His first success was the capture of the enemy position at Saraun against great odds, where 'Nepalese rivalled Europeans,' says Malleson. At Chanda in February he accepted battle with 8,000 rebels, closely supported by another 10,000, and defeated them: then turned on the 10,000 and put them to flight. At Sultanpore on 23rd February, by a brilliant feint, he turned the enemy position, captured twenty guns, all their ammunition and stores and won a complete victory. On the 4th March Franks' force joined the Commander-in-Chief, Colin Campbell, outside Lucknow.

On the 14th March Campbell requested Jang Bahadur to throw the enemy out of the Alambagh positions. Jang moved out, took the defences in reverse, and steadily cleared position after position from the Char-Bagh bridge up to the Residency gates, capturing the rebel cannon as he went. After some street fighting he threw his regiments in to help break the enemy's last stand at the Musa Bagh. A few days later Lucknow fell to the British assault and Jang Bahadur's campaign was at an end.

On 22nd March he left Lucknow for Allahabad where he and Lord Canning had a most cordial meeting, at which the Governor-General told him that a part of the Terai was to be returned to Nepal as a gesture for all he had done in those critical days. It is always disputable that the inhabitants of Garhwal, Kumaon and Sikkim benefited from the substitution of British for Gurkha rule. Henry Lawrence had written, 'The Gurkhas are the best masters I have seen in India. Neither in the Terai nor in the Hills, have I witnessed or heard of a single act of oppression since I arrived a year and a half ago, and a happier peasantry I have nowhere seen.' In 1851 Laurence Oliphant, on his visit to Kathmandu, says 'In talking to a man who acted as guide on our return through the Terai, we discovered that the popularity of Jang, arising from this cause [protecting the interests of the peasantry], had extended across the frontier, and had induced my informant to migrate into the Nepaul dominions, so that he might benefit by the paternal rule of its prime minister. He said the taxes were lighter and that he led altogether a more happy and independent life than in the Company's dominions. . . .'

Jang's Gurkhas had never in all their lives set eyes upon such wealth as there was in Oudh and especially in Lucknow; they were not likely to let pass such a heaven-sent opportunity for enriching themselves. By the time that they were due to leave India for their own country, they possessed a baggage train of several thousand bullock carts, all loaded well above the Plimsoll Line with the plunder of their year's campaigning. It soon became apparent that the Nepalese Army was but a baggage guard to its own transport for, once on the move, it had no troops to spare to go out and fight. It was unlikely that an army which had braved the Popti-La pass in mid-winter in order to evade its own customs, would abandon its easily-gathered plunder on the plains of India. Rather than leave it, it would have remained with it. With great magnanimity, complaining withal, Colin Campbell detached some of his own regiments to escort his over-laden and now opulent allies across the border into the Terai. Thus, slowly, the Gurkha, well content, wended his cheerful way back to the mountains.

On the 4th May the Maharajah Jang Bahadur drove up to the Thapatali in Kathmandu.

The next problem which presented itself to the Nepalese Government was that of dealing with the big influx of mutineers escaping from British retribution. Some 50,000, many of them armed and organised in their original regiments, crossed the border into Nepal. The first thing was to disarm them. By October Jang had collected a force of eleven regiments of infantry and a regiment of artillery. With these he moved west to Palpa where his formerly disloyal brother, Badri Nar Sing, held the local military command. He inspected Badri's brigade, a procedure perhaps embarrassing to the Brigadier. He found a somewhat alarming concentration of rebels in the neighbourhood, over 20,000, and more than half of them fully armed. They surrendered their arms to his force, as well as eighteen English hostages, all non-combatants, whom they had brought with them as counters for a bargain in which their very lives would be at stake.

Jang Bahadur returned to the Thapatali, his life and position now at long last secure as the supreme authority in Nepal. Despite his security he changed neither his habits nor his solitary life. His trust, to the very end, was in no man, and no man ever read his heart. He ruled absolutely and relentlessly, but, as always, he was ready to listen to the other point of view. He was busied with the administration of his country, establishing a postal system, touring here and there and satisfying himself of the efficiency and honesty of his officials, both civil and military. What Prithwi Narain Sah and Bhim Sen Thapa had founded was safe in the keeping of Jang Bahadur Rana. It was not in the nature of this dictator that he should fail in anything he undertook. Nevertheless he failed in one measure that was dear to his heart, the progressive emancipation of slaves, firstly by debarring anyone from being sold into slavery who was not born a slave and secondly by freeing all slaves who went to work on the estates that he was developing in the Terai. The first he found impossible to enforce in practice and, as regards the second, the country was too deadly from the *awal* fever to attract the labour he expected. His attempt at emancipation was made about the same time as the United States succeeded in abolishing slavery in its own territory and thirty years after Great Britain had done so. Of his legal reforms the most memorable was the abolition of twenty-two punishments for various crimes, principally those involving different types of torture. The mutilation of noses was forbidden.[1] A great gambler himself in former days, he prohibited all gambling except for five days during the Dewali festival.

In November 1860 the Indian Government handed back to him a narrow two-hundred-mile strip of the Terai between the River Gogra on the west and the district boundary of Gorakhpore on the east, in recognition of his generous services during the perilous days of the Mutiny. This region, reft from Nepal in 1816, had been conferred upon the Nawab Vizier of Oudh by the Company that same year in repayment of a loan of a million pounds sterling. With a cordial letter from the Prince Consort, Ramsay, the Resident at Kathmandu, on the Queen's behalf presented the renowned Maharajah with the Order and jewels of a Knight Grand Cross of the Order of the Bath. Replying to the Prince Consort's letter, Jang expressed his gratitude at the conferment of this high honour for his humble services and promised that if ever the Viceroy were again to need his services, they were his to command. As the years were to prove, this pledge binding his people was no idle one.

To counter the honours conferred on him by the British Queen, the Emperor of China, in 1872, invested him with the highest honour of the Celestial Empire accompanied by the Double-eyed Peacock Feather and the Sable Coat.

During these final, placid years in Nepal he was loyally served by his brothers Krishna, Rana Udip and Dhir Shamsher. On Krishna's death, Jang withdrew even further into his isolation, refusing even to see the members of his own family. In 1874 he journeyed to Calcutta to settle boundary disputes and there conceived a desire once more to visit England. All was made ready for six of his sons and nephews to accompany him on the tour, among them his son, Padma Jang, his biographer. That winter he passed in state through India, calling in at Benares to pay his respects to his old enemies, the ex-Queen Lakhshmi and her two sons. At Allahabad he was to have bathed in the Ganges but committed the gaucherie of appearing armed at the religious fair, a thing forbidden by law. Sir John Strachey courteously reminded the Maharajah of the regulation, but Jang was offended and left the place without observing the ritual for which he had come. The Viceroy telegraphed special permission for an exception to be made, but Jang's *amour propre* allowed him to relent only so far as to say that he would return the following year to fulfil his pilgrimage. On 21st January 1875, he arrived at Bombay and sent his baggage on board.

Ten days later he took his usual evening ride through the streets; his horse took fright, bolted and threw him on the pavement, seriously damaging his chest. The Governor sent a European doctor to him, his entourage sent him an Indian, meanwhile telegraphing for Maharanis and Nepalese doctors to come from Kathmandu. Nepalese medical opinion prevailed, so that Jang announced his decision to postpone the trip till the following year. Soon after, he set out to have his bathe at Allahabad on the road back to his own country. On the 20th April he was again in his house, the Thapatali. As it happened, the visit to Europe never came off for the very next year the Prince of Wales himself travelled out to India, to enjoy Jang's lavish hospitality in a great shoot in the Terai. Jang, though not well, was in great heart supervising the sport for his former host, but he took the opportunity of consulting the Prince's personal physician, the famous Fayrer, who had been medical officer in charge of the Lucknow garrison during the Siege of 1857. Fayrer warned Jang of coming heart trouble, a warning that was taken sufficiently seriously for the Maharajah to set his worldly affairs in order on his return to Kathmandu. Having done this, he went off again on his favourite sport, big game shooting.

On 25th February 1877, he fell ill with fever, so ill that he took the unprecedented decision to cancel the day's march. To his brother, Rana Udip Sing, he despatched a message to tell him to assume his office if the worst befell. There was just time to bear the semi-conscious Lord of Nepal to the banks of the sacred Baghmati, where the stormy spirit passed peacefully from the hard-driven body of Jang Bahadur Rana.

By the holy stream the corpse was burnt. The three senior Maharanis committed *suttee* on the pyre, a deed that Jang would probably have forbidden. The epitaph of this great and never-understood man may fittingly be the dignified words of the Senior Maharani before she laid herself down to die by her lord —

'Gentlemen, you all know the love the Maharajah had for you, and the zeal with which he devoted his life to the welfare of your country.

'If in the discharge of his duty he has ever by word, look or deed wronged any one of you, I, on his behalf, ask you to forgive him, and to join me in praying for the everlasting peace of his soul.'

20

The House of Shamsher

———————— ❖ ————————

IF Jang Bahadur died a natural death, then he was the second Prime Minister of Nepal so to succeed. If affairs were to take their usual course, then the death of a strong ruler was to be followed by a dreadful convulsion. There were enough reasons for catastrophe and to spare. Though schooled by Jang Bahadur for the task before him, his nominated successor, Rana Udip Sing, was a man of little account, sufficiently industrious and sufficiently capable under the authority of a man of the late Minister's calibre, but no leader himself. The ten sons of the late Maharajah were youths without self-control and self-discipline, for Jang, beyond demanding implicit obedience to his own wishes, had made no attempt whatsoever to cultivate in them any other virtue. How they conducted themselves with others seems to have been no affair or concern of his. The eldest, Jagat Jang, was utterly self-centred and without moral stability. Thus, despite the rigid settlement which their father had devised for the succession to his high office, to its emoluments from the estates of Kaski and Lamjung, and to the title of Maharajah, these youths, led by Jagat Jang, expected that their father's decree should be set aside and that his dignities and perquisites should be continued from him to his son. The descendants of the Pandes who met their deaths at the hands of Bhim Sen Thapa, the descendants of Mathbar Sing Thapa who fell by Jang Bahadur's bullet, and those of the noblemen who died in the carnage at the Kot, and of the executed Basnets, were there to join hands in opposition to the new régime.

Against these factions there stood one man only, General Dhir Shamsher, now Commander-in-Chief, but ageing and losing his old geniality and toleration. For seven years he held his brother, Rana Udip Sing, in place at the seat of power.

162

Those who are not aware of the traditional Eastern mode of conducting public affairs by torture and assassination, should not think too hardly of the nobility of Kathmandu. Twenty years before this the independent kingdom of Oudh, neighbour to Nepal, not only managed its affairs in this disgraceful way but also permitted and often encouraged the vilest of cruelties, torturings, extortions and other horrors in all its outlying districts and, furthermore, winked an eye at the widespread devastation of the fields and wholesale butchery of its peasantry. Had Dalhousie not stepped in and bluntly annexed the kingdom, these fearful doings would have continued — more, they would have worsened. The British in India, not unaware, faced the consequences of this act in 1857–58; a twelve-month of strife was worth the cessation for ever of the atrocities of Oudh. In Nepal, the horror was confined to Kathmandu. All outside that warped city were unaffected, even happy and contented: not so in Oudh, and not so in Mahratta Gwalior, where the very army ravaged its own countryside.

Rana Udip Sing had been Governor of the Eastern and Western Provinces of Nepal during the visit to Europe and, on Badri Nar Sing's disqualification through his attempted fratricide, had become next in succession to Jang Bahadur. It was Udip who brought Prince Upendra Bikram Sah to the Council to hear his sentence for the part he had taken in Badri's plot. After acting as second-in-command to his brother during the fighting in 1857–58, he had returned to Nepal as Commander-in-Chief until called to the Premiership.

As soon as he heard of his elder brother's death, Rana Udip went straight to the King for formal appointment in his place. Thereafter, attended by a strong guard, he called up the ten sons and informed them of their father's decease and of his own succession. In 1880 he paid a visit to India attended by far too large a household and staff, enough to cause grave inconvenience in the smaller places he visited — a little man who would appear as a great one. Soon after his return to Kathmandu, King Surendra died and the father, the ex-King Rajendra, at once laid claim to the throne he had forfeited years before. Fortunately for the hesitant Udip this quarrelsome ancient suddenly died, so that Surendra's infant grandson, Prithwi Bir Bikram Sah, was peacefully crowned King, or Maharajadhiraj, of Nepal.*

Both Jagat Jang, Jang Bahadur's eldest son, and the Thapas now began to conspire against the new Maharajah. It would be tedious to follow in detail yet another murderous plot. Suffice it to say that Jagat Jang, learning that the Thapas were plotting to kill his uncles, Udip and Dhir

* The heir apparent, Prince Trailokya Bikram Sah, had died in 1878.

Shamsher, and the whole of the latter's family, and then to wipe out himself and his nine brothers, adjusted his own plan so as to permit them to fulfil the first part of their quite unexceptionable programme, upon which he would in his turn make a clean sweep of the Thapas themselves. If the Thapa project went awry, then he would in the name of outraged justice wipe them out, thereafter himself executing the part of their programme left uncompleted. On 6th January 1882, the Thapas planned to kill Dhir Shamsher and then his sons, thereafter hastening to the Terai to murder Rana Udip Sing. Unfortunately for all concerned, they had forgotten that ex-Queen Lakhshmi's dead lover, Gagan Sing, had been assassinated before the Kot massacre by the very forbears of some of these plotters. Gagan Sing's grandson went to Dhir Shamsher and gave him details of the sordid business. Dhir, as may be expected, acted forthrightly. His enquiries brought to light the whole involved scheme of both Jagat Jang and the Thapas. Jagat, deficient of his father's courage, had left for India before the due date in order to establish an alibi, and now refused to return to clear himself of complicity or to answer for his part in the plot. Dhir exiled certain of the chief conspirators and handed twenty-one of the leading Councillors of State over to the public executioner. Thereafter there was peace and he and his brother could proceed with the administration of their country.

They introduced the militia system by which it became possible to expand their fighting forces at short notice, a measure which proved of the utmost value to the Allied cause thirty years later. Udip and Dhir saw to it that Nepal, while retaining its absolute independence, remained in close friendship with the Government of India. To cement this Udip, perhaps reluctantly, gave in 1885 a general permission to India to recruit freely for the establishment of the four new Gurkha battalions being raised for the Indian Army. Until then, the Nepalese Durbar had tended to regard all those who 'went for a soldier' in the British Gurkhas as deserters. It was long before this outlook underwent sufficient change to make any difference to the practical difficulties of getting recruits into the Depot at Gorakhpore. At first, the Durbar would send them to the Residency Surgeon to be examined before despatch to the Depot and they were a very poor standard of recruit, most of whom were cast as medically unfit. After representations from Simla there was some improvement. Unluckily Girdlestone, the British Resident for many years, was out of tune with Dhir Shamsher and the rest of the Durbar. This bedevilled relations at the level of the Durbar and the Residency, however cordial they might have been between the two Governments.

In 1884 there fell a dire event. Dhir Shamsher, Commander-in-Chief, the pillar of the State, sickened and, after a short illness, died. He was a great loss to his army. They recalled his rousing speech to the men who had been routed and thrown out of Kuti in 1854 by a treacherous Tibetan attack. Coming up, he rallied the fugitives, re-formed them and led them back to fight. Before the engagement he spoke to them. He praised them for their rapid and arduous march under his command. Death must come once to all and death in battle brought glory here and hereafter: it was better than a mean death on a sick bed. The Maharajah had ordered him to take Kuti at all costs and he pledged himself to his men that if he did not take it he, Dhir Shamsher, would never return alive: rather, he would immolate himself in the ruins. In the van he placed the men who had re-treated from Kuti. Dhir and his army carried the position by storm. The ancient warrior blood of Rajput and Magar flowed richly in this leader's veins.

Ramsay, no friend of Jang Bahadur's, when he retired from the Resi-dency had written to Dhir Shamsher thanking him for smoothing his way with the despotic Prime Minister, 'I admire your wisdom and fore-thought. . . .' To Dhir's credit was the first essay to start a public school in Nepal, the building of the road from Churia to Bimphedi, and an at-tempt, unfortunately unsuccessful, to prevent the three senior Maharanis from committing *suttee* on Jang Bahadur's pyre. He brought his sons up in a stern and salutary discipline which stood them and their country in good stead in the years to come.

He was a great man and he was dead.

Evil men who had feared to act while his brother lived, now sought to bring the compliant Rana Udip Sing into their toils and schemings. Jagat Jang obtained permission to return to Nepal. Within a very short time he was plunged deep in his plans to grasp the supreme power, Udip having committed the folly of replacing his name on the list of succession. In order to smooth his way to power he formed an alliance with the party of Badri Nar Sing, the would-be killer of his father, Jang Bahadur. Indeed, another strange mating. The alliance was directed against the Shamsher brothers, whose leader was now the eldest son, Bir Shamsher, in place of Dhir who had gone to a more peaceful world. The parties grew publicly and palpably hostile as it became crystal clear that one or other must be obliterated. Hand in glove with Jagat Jang in his plotting against these brothers was Rana Udip's own wife. A renegade from the party was Jit Jang, Jagat's younger brother, who on Dhir's death became Commander-in-Chief but preferred to live in India, resigning this high office as soon as he learned that Jagat was in Nepal and more than likely to clip Jit's wings or revenge himself for the latter's lukewarmness in the last conspiracy.

Dhir Shamsher's sons were as significant in Nepalese history as were the famous sons of Balnar Sing Konwar. These are their names — Bir, Khadga, Rana, Deva, Chandra, Bhim, Fateh, Lalit, Jit and Judha. Bir had been supposedly educated at Doveton College in Calcutta, where indeed he learnt very little. He inherited his father's military capacity and was a man of action and of quick decision. His wife was daughter of the traitor ex-Prince Upendra, King Surendra's younger brother, who was exiled for his share in the attempt on the life of the King and the Prime Minister, Jang Bahadur. When Bir Shamsher was eighteen years old, Jang Bahadur selected him as Nepalese representative in Calcutta, in preference to any of his own sons and to Dhoje Nar Sing, the only son of Rana Udip Sing. The preferment of Dhir's eldest boy over any one of themselves rankled with the sons of Jang Bahadur. They saw in it a portent. At the time of Dhir's death, Bir was his Chief Secretary. He faced a daunting situation in which he was the focus of all the hatred of the returned exiles whom his father had driven out of the Kingdom, and who, had that father been alive, would still have been forbidden the country.

Of the others, Khadga was well-educated, intelligent, capable and beyond all sense conceited. Of Chandra Dr. Gimlette, the Residency Surgeon, says, 'Chandra was a very wily young man, clever and capable.' He spoke English well.

At 9 p.m. on the 22nd November 1885, the Residency Surgeon heard a tumult coming from the Narain Hatti palace, much musketry firing and soon the bugles sounding the assembly, and then seventeen guns, the salute for a Commander-in-Chief, blasted out into the night. A little over an hour later there came running breathlessly to him for sanctuary relatives and adherents of the Maharajah Udip Sing, exclaiming that there was a plot and the Maharajah was dead. His last words were to send them to the Residency for protection. Dr. Gimlette armed the Residency guard and posted double sentries.

Ram Bikram Sah had himself seen the murder. The Maharajah was lying down in a small room dictating letters, with the Dowager Maharani, the senior wife and two other ladies seated nearby and a maid-servant anointing his feet. A knock at the door and a messenger asked that Khadga Shamsher be granted an interview. Permission given, Dhambar,* Rana, Khadga and Bir Shamsher entered the room. Dhambar said he had brought a rifle of a new pattern to show to his uncle, dropped

* An illegitimate son of Dhir Shamsher.

on one knee and shot him through the head. Khadga took aim and fired also. Rana, the family drunkard, fired and missed. A *keti* fell dead. Balbahadur, the orderly officer, and the one-eyed secretary fled from the room to the Residency. Later, the activities of the orderly officer showed that he was of the party of Bir Shamsher. Gimlette's opinion of the outrage was this, 'The murder of the old man seems to have been the most brutal and heartless of even any previous ones in the annals of Nepal. It was perpetrated at the hands of his nephews, whom he had always treated as sons, and loaded with favours and gifts of large sums of money.'

Khadga Shamsher came a day or two later to the Residency where he told Gimlette that the late Maharajah, with the connivance of his wife and the Dowager Maharani, had certainly planned to reinstate Jagat Jang completely, in fortune, position and succession, and that this would have sounded the death knell of the Shamsher family. They acted in self-defence. There is ample evidence to show that what he said was true in all respects. To most civilised peoples murder is murder and damnable, but they must at least put themselves in the place of the hunted to decide if the quarry may suddenly and secretly turn and kill the hunter, and be justified in doing so.

As soon as the murder was done, soldiers went to Manaura and Thapatali, and there killed Jagat Jang and his son, Judha Pratap Jang, while the conspirators carried off the young King and his mother to safe-custody at Bagh.

Bir Shamsher was proclaimed Maharajah. At once he exiled into the care of the paternal Government of India all those who might interfere with the supremacy of his family. Dr. Gimlette sighed with relief as he witnessed the departure of his unbidden and very prickly guests, male and female.

The plot had been well laid. Bir, in his position under his father, had carefully cultivated four regiments and a battery of artillery — the Bajr Bahadur, Kali Bakhsh, Purana Gorakh and Kali Bahadur with the Mahindra Dal Battery. This force he assembled ready to march into India to take part in training exercises to which the Government had already sent a contingent. The true purpose of the concentration was now apparent. The toll of the plot was probably quite considerable. Gimlette believed that at least twenty bodies were burned at Pasupatti on 23rd November — Sirdars who had been killed by special squads of Bir's regiment.

Bir Shamsher was in the saddle.

Rana Udip Sing's administration had carried the country forward somewhat. His contribution to progress was not inconsiderable. The more imposing achievements of his famous nephew, Chandra Shamsher, have tended to obscure the genuine advances of Rana Udip's time. He reformed the land settlement. Before his accession the system of 'farming' the land revenue worked grievous injury to the cultivators: he introduced the *ryotwari* system by which the farming community had a real and permanent interest in their lands. He established an efficient system for the collection of the national revenues and for the audit of the public accounts, thereby thrusting responsibility on the fiscal officers of the state for rendering true and accurate returns of their stewardship. He set up a Public Works Department and banks for facilitating the operations of trade and commerce. Criminal law was reformed, barbarous penalties being substituted by more rational methods of correction. He reclaimed waste lands, developed the tea industry, abolished monopolies in mines, tobacco and dry fish, waived the poll tax on pilgrims, encouraged the founding of Sanskrit-teaching schools, built hospitals and dispensaries for the sick poor and lent his support to local industries. Finally, he restored to the Brahmans the lands confiscated by King Ranbahadur Sah. Towards the end of his reign he became more interested in his religious devotions than in governing his country, and the reins were beginning to slip from his never too muscular grasp.

His enemies routed and a fairly up-to-date system ready to his hand with which to direct his country, Bir Shamsher's course was set for peaceful and progressive days.

Within sixteen months, Khadga Shamsher, the Commander-in-Chief and heir to the Prime Minister, was discovered plotting against the life of his brother, the Maharajah, in collusion with the sister of the Queen Mother. Bir Shamsher seized him and interned him near Palpa, a better fate than he deserved. Two years later Bir, out of sheer kindness, made him Governor of Palpa. But Khadga was clever yet a fool, no leader but a born conspirator. Early in 1888 Ranbir Jang, one of Jang Bahadur's exiled sons, tried to invade Nepal from India with a rabble of unarmed adventurers. In the Terai they secured some arms but a Nepalese regiment came upon them and scattered them to the four winds. At the same time his nephew stirred up a mutiny among the troops at Palpa. Bir's agents stamped on this. Fifty-four conspirators with their ringleader were arrested, of whom five were executed. The Brahmans among them could not be put to death so were submitted to the dreadful rite of defilement and degraded from their caste.

With Khadga in banishment, Rana Shamsher became Commander-in-Chief, followed by Deva Shamsher on his death in 1887.

Light seemed at last to be penetrating into the jungle of Nepalese politics. Bir Shamsher reigned as Maharajah until 5th March 1901 with no further attempt on his life or subversion of his authority. He was not a great man but he was a steady and a wise one. Like his uncle, the famous Jang, he was reserved: he was fond of music and imported European bandmasters to train his bands. Under the peace he brought, the country prospered in its simple way. The position of the Maharajah *vis-à-vis* the Viceroy and the Indian Government he finally succeeded in establishing. Lord Curzon would regard any visit of the Maharajah as a complimentary mission to himself as the representative of the Queen Empress. Bir would not countenance such a lowering of the prestige of Nepal or of his office and insisted that if he came to India to visit the Viceroy, then he came as an Ambassador of his country with all the dignity due to that honourable position. Then, as later, the Maharajah kept a watchful and suspicious eye on the attitude of India and of China and Tibet towards Nepal as a sovereign power.

His internal administration was marked by improvements in education, sanitation, hospitals, the building of bridges, of which the suspension bridge at Khuli-Khani is one example, and the supervision of the administration of the Law. By 1891 he had completed the new water supply to Kathmandu and by 1895 to Bhatgaon. At Narain Hatti he built himself a fine mansion designed from Government House at Calcutta. But there was still a curfew enforced in Kathmandu to keep evilly-disposed men from being abroad after dark. He paid two state visits to India to visit Lord Dufferin and, later Lord Curzon. In 1889 the Chinese Emperor invested him with the same high decoration as he had given to his uncle, Jang Bahadur — T'ung ling ping ma kuo kan wang, of which Dr. Gimlette writes, 'The most prominent ornament in the jewelled head-dress of the Nepalese Prime Minister is a large ruby and plume of peacocks' feathers, the insignia of the order. . . .'

In 1901 Bir Shamsher died of an aneurism and was gathered peacefully to his fathers. Deva Shamsher, Commander-in Chief, succeeded, an insignificant and frivolous man, luxury-loving and lazy. The revenue he wasted on brilliant durbars, processions and festivals: his time he wasted on sport and amusement at Nagarkote. There was no head of state while he was in charge. His intentions were often good but amounted to little in practice. He decreed a great increase in schools but neglected to find the means to provide them: he decreed the emancipation of slaves in Kaski, Lamjung and Kathmandu, but had to withdraw his decree for the uproar that greeted it, owing to his never having prepared either owners or slaves to accept one tithe of it. He was indiscreet and garrulous to a fault, losing friends and supporters by his unbridled tongue.

On 26th June 1901, his brothers invited him to the Narain Hatti to arbitrate in a family quarrel concerning their rights in the building. There they 'ringed' him as you ring an elephant and presented him with an ultimatum. He promised to reform, failed, and was made to sign his abdication and to retire to Dhankuta where he was interned for a short time. He was conveniently allowed to escape to India where he lived in comfort on 4,000 rupees a month paid him by his successor, Chandra Shamsher. This latter prince was the most distinguished, as the most enlightened, of all those who held the post of honour in Nepal since the stormy days of Prithwi Narain Sah.

But Deva Shamsher could not let his able brother work for his country in peace. He had to follow the jungle tradition. While Chandra was away in Delhi for the great Durbar of 1903, he launched his plot to murder him, but the Indian Government, who kept a fatherly eye on all Nepalese princes in their banishment, knew all about it and sent him to Benares for closer confinement while the Maharajah was in India. From then onwards the indolent prince lived happily enough in his home in the beautiful hill station of Mussoorie, on one side looking over the green Doon Valley with its silver ribbons of the Ganges and Jumna, on the other facing the white giants of the eternal snows. Those British officers who from time to time met these so amiable Nepalese exiles in India were seldom acquainted with the nefarious reasons for their banishment.

Of Deva all that remained in Nepal was the custom of the midday gunfire, as in all military stations of India, on which everyone set his clock. With the coming of Radio Delhi and Radio Nepal that too will have disappeared and Deva be remembered no more. Not so his younger brother, Chandra Shamsher.

Firstly by assassination and now by deposition the rule of succession instituted by Jang Bahadur Rana had been violated. As this system and its infringement were in the end to tumble down the Rana supremacy, something more needs to be said of it at this place. The custom of devolution to the eldest agnate, widely favoured in Muslim countries, was new to Nepal. Brother was to succeed brother until the whole generation had been exhausted, when the succession passed to the eldest of the next generation irrespectively of whether or no he belonged to the senior branch. This applied only to the Prime Minister's succession and not to the monarchy where the law of primogeniture still prevailed. The object of the Rana system of succession was to avoid at all costs the advent to power of an immature Rana. This object was achieved. Not only did it ensure that the monarchy could never prevail over a minor holding the office of Prime Minister, but it afforded a very good chance that, as so often before, a mature Prime Minister might dominate a King during his minority and, as Regent, handle all authority. Obviously, the rivalry between King and Prime Minister would be perpetuated and might at any time break into open conflict as had happened in Bhim Sen's and Jang Bahadur's days. The monarchy was suppressed but not yet smothered. Other disadvantages were that the Maharajahs tended to succeed at an advanced age, and great age is no guarantee of fitness to govern: furthermore, the knowledge that the succession might pass to some distant relative afforded little incentive to a Prime Minister to pass on a kingdom better ordered and more prosperous than he himself had inherited, rather it led him to exploit, to 'farm', the state for the sole benefit of himself and his own children, particularly as the custom prevailed that any surplus in the Treasury was transferred periodically to the Maharajah's private pocket. The Prime Minister Chandra Shamsher, when he died in 1929, left a fortune of some £40 million to his sons besides certain properties in land. Infractions of Jang Bahadur's law of succession led in the course of time to quarrels, feuds, intrigues and disunity in the Rana family itself, increasing as the prolific and polygamous family multiplied. In Chapter 24 there is more about these quarrels and their causes.

*   *   *   *   *

During these years of gradually decreasing turmoil in Nepal, the Gurkhas of the Indian Army were loyally serving their adopted mistress, the Queen Empress. In 1863 they were at Ambeyla on the North West Frontier. In 1864 they were fighting in Bhutan to restore peace to that mountainous and intricate frontier: thence, in 1868, up into the Hazara and Black Mountain country to suppress Pathan incursions. In 1871 they were storming Lushai stockades in the most inaccessible parts of the Assam mountains and forests. In the mid-eighties King Thebaw of Burma was intriguing with the French Government and had heavily fined the British Bombay and Burma Trading Company and imprisoned its employees. Gurkha soldiers marched with the army into Upper Burma and took Mandalay. In 1876 they went campaigning in Perak on the Malay Peninsula. In 1878–80 came a stern test when Lord Roberts led an army into Afghanistan. There, in the van, at the storming of the Peiwar Kotal, at Ali Masjid in the Khyber Pass, in the defensive battle of Ahmed Khel near Ghazni when a Gurkha square, standing as a rock in the battle flowing past it, held firm the British front; in the defence and counter-blow at Charasia, in Roberts' famous march from Kabul to Kandahar, and in the final, stubborn fight at Kandahar when the Gurkha rifleman rammed his cap down the muzzle of an enemy cannon to prove his regiment's claims, the newly-forming Gurkha Brigade had covered itself with glory. Between 1878 and 1888 one of its men, Kishanbir Nagarkoti, was decorated four times for gallantry; in the stiff rearguard action at Monghyr, at Charasia, Kabul and at Oghi in the Black Mountain. In the last episode he and two survivors fought a most gallant withdrawal after being surrounded.

There followed the 1888 reconnaissance on the Tibetan border to Niti, 18,000 feet up, with the campaign in Sikkim against the Tibetans which took Gurkhas through the Jalap-La pass; the relief of Chitral; the long four years of operations on the Indian North West Frontier from 1891 to 1895 when the forces penetrated to Wana, Kaniguram and Makin; then in 1897 the arduous campaign into the Tirah where the stout-hearted Afridi tribesmen fought to stem the advance. Here the steep, craggy hill of Dargai was gallantly taken by Gurkhas who were unaccountably ordered to evacuate it and then ordered to retake it. Dargai was finally stormed by Gurkhas, Highlanders and Sikhs at heavy cost and with great gallantry.

In 1891 fifty Gurkhas of the Assam Light Infantry, marching from Burma to the relief of the Residency at Manipore, reached a mound in the Manipore plains at Lang Thobal, where they were set upon by two thousand rebels with two cannon. Here they stood and fought for eleven days and nights and defeated their assailants. During the battle the Jemadar marched the camp-followers here and there armed with wooden rifles, to impress the enemy. On return to cantonments, the British officer in charge of the party reported, 'I recommend every man of the party for the Order of Merit. I think they have well deserved it. . . .'

As a result of the Afghan war Lord Roberts decided to expand considerably the Gurkha units of the Indian Army by raising second battalions for each of the five regiments. In 1885 Colonel Becher was sent to Darjeeling to examine the prospects of opening up a recruiting depot thereabouts similar to the one at Gorakhpore, for taking in young men from Eastern Nepal. A depot was later established at Ghoom near Darjeeling. It is probable that the 1885 rumours of Russian advances into Afghanistan may have speeded up the decision to expand, in preference to accepting Maharajah Bir Shamsher's offer of his own army to assist the British in this Russian contingency. The Nepalese Government at once agreed to provide the extra recruits, sweetened by a fair-sized gift in money and in Service rifles. We have already noticed Dr. Gimlette's experience of the recruits initially provided. One regiment, the 3rd Gurkha Rifles, the old 'Kemaoon' as it is spelt in the India Register of 1849, did not get its second Gurkha battalion until 1891, because it was at first ordered to raise it from Garhwali soldiers to be contributed from the other four regiments, and by further recruitment. Having started successfully to constitute this battalion it was, in 1890, then told to peel it off so that the new Garhwal Rifles could be formed alongside the 3rd at Almora, the scene of the old triumph of 1814 and the first raising of the Kumaon Levy.

By 1904 the three battalions of 1816 had swelled into sixteen battalions and Nepal was habituated to seeing the annual winter immigration of recruiting parties to bring the pick of the Magar, Gurung and Khas youth down to Gorakhpore, and into Ghoom near Darjeeling to take the boys of the ancient Kiranti tribes, Limbus and Rais. The Maharajah had concluded that every Gurkha trained in India who retired to his mountains added to the military strength of Nepal.

As these regiments settled back into cantonments after the Tirah campaign, the Maharajah Chandra Shamsher took his seat as Prime Minister of Nepal. In 1851 his famous uncle, Jang Bahadur Rana, had remarked to Laurence Oliphant, together looking at a portrait of Queen Victoria hanging in the palace at Kathmandu, 'See, here is the Queen of England and she has not got a more loyal subject than I am.' All his life Chandra Shamsher bore this in mind. What he believed to be due from himself to the British Crown, he believed to be also due from his Gurkha soldiers. With it all he maintained the independent sovereignty of Nepal, loyally assisted therein by the Viceroy and Government of India.

21

Chandra Shamsher Jang Bahadur Rana

———————— ✸ ————————

THIS is a 'reign' — for that is its true status — which lasted for twenty-eight years. The man to whose lot the highest authority of the State had fallen was the best fitted of all the Prime Ministers of Nepal to exercise the powers of that office. Like his father he was a sportsman, brought up to regard physical fitness as an end in itself. He was born on 8th July 1863, the fifth son of General Dhir Shamsher, the Commander-in-Chief. As a boy he was taught English by the palace tutors, at that time a language which was not in use at the Nepalese Court, later to become the usual language of the royal circle. At the age of fifteen he was married to a Thakuri girl. Four years later, after his father had stamped out the sparks of Jagat Jang's conspiracy, Chandra Shamsher journeyed to Calcutta to complete his education at the University. There, unlike his elder brother, Bir Shamsher, he acquitted himself with credit, but his studies were cut short by news of his father's sudden illness. He hastened back to Kathmandu and remained by him until the end came.

Just as Dhir Shamsher had been the right-hand man of Jang Bahadur, so did Chandra become the right-hand man of the Maharajah Bir Shamsher. Thus, Chandra became fully acquainted with the affairs of the State and the working of its administrative machine. On Bir Shamsher assuming power, he became Senior Commanding General. During Bir's tenure of office he served him as loyally and with the same self-effacement as his father had served his distinguished uncle. At Kathmandu in 1892 Lord Roberts reviewed the Army as reorganised by Chandra and reported on it favourably. By 1891 Chandra Shamsher had arranged with the Government of India for the increase of Gurkha battalions in the Indian Army from nine to fifteen. In 1886, the year of the first big expansion of the British Gurkha establishment, Captain C. A. Mercer, the British Recruit-

174

ing Officer for Gurkhas, reporting from Gorakhpore on the Season 1885–86, gives his opinion that the system by which the Nepalese Durbar was recruiting men for the newly-forming second battalions was most unsatisfactory. After Dr. Gimlette had discarded a high proportion of the recruits, the British officers at Bahraich, Segouli and Darjeeling, whither the Durbar despatched those that Gimlette approved, cast a further twenty per cent. Mercer strongly advocated the retention and expansion of the regimental system of recruiting, under which the regiment sent its own recruiting parties into the hills, provided that the Durbar would permit them to do their work 'without let or hindrance'. It was to this last purpose that Chandra Shamsher applied himself with success, to the removal of all 'let or hindrance' to the recruiting of British Gurkhas. It may appear, from now onwards, that too much space is given in these pages to matters concerning Gurkhas in the British-Indian service. The reason for this emphasis is that year by year the whole of Nepal's economy came to depend vitally upon the hiring-out of her military manpower, that she always had been and still remained essentially a military nation, that her reputation in the world was made by these same mercenaries, and that relations with her powerful neighbour in India were based on the loan of her men and governed by the friendship and constant intercourse that the transaction promoted. Chandra Shamsher's part in these early years in fostering that friendship, and so his country's interests, was of first importance.

The Nepalese, as these pages show, have always been tender about allowing any sort of deputation or even individual official from India to move freely in their country outside the Valley. The same tenderness which postponed the work which British engineers could have contributed to utilise Nepal's vast resources of water-power, interfered with the activities of Gurkha recruiting parties although every member of the parties was a native of Nepal. If we are to judge by the serious outcome of the incursions from India since 1947, we may accept the good reasons behind this apparent touchiness. Mercer wished to extend recruitment to the provinces of Eastern Nepal, to the Kiranti, on whom Colonel Becher had just reported. Maharajah Jang Bahadur had enlisted them into the Nepalese Army ever since 1847, while many of these men were already being recruited into the 42nd, 43rd and 44th Assam Regiments, later to be transformed into Gurkha Rifle Regiments — and into the Assam Frontier Police. From this period onwards, Nepalese revenue came to rely more and more on the money brought into the country by its fighting men serving as mercenaries under a foreign flag.

As a result of the dependence placed upon him by his elder brother, Chandra was very soon given the Nepalese Foreign Office and the task of overhauling the system of public education. At the Foreign Office his policy was firmly and unswervingly for the cultivation of friendship with British India and for absolute and devoted loyalty to the British Crown. Thus, in 1889, when the Rajah Sidkeong Nangyal of Sikkim attempted to prevent the establishment of a British political officer at Gangtok and, on being sternly reprimanded by the Viceroy, fled to Nepal, Bir and Chandra at once turned him out of their territory, letting him know that he could find no succour from them, but providing him with a full royal escort to see him away and to salve his wounded feelings. Chandra Shamsher's foreign relations will be dealt with later. It is enough here to note that in 1893 the Dalai Lama, Tubdan Gyatso, came of age. He was the first to reach that standing for some time, for the Regent and Council of Tibet had been in the habit of killing off all Dalai Lamas who so aspired, so that they could themselves retain the government of the country. Tubdan was allowed to live because the Regency at this time was planning to throw off Chinese suzerainty and it did not relish having, as was the custom, to submit for Chinese approval the name of a new Dalai Lama, thus acknowledging the paramountcy of the Celestial Emperor.

In 1892 Bir Shamsher took Chandra with him on a visit to India. Bir was ailing, so it fell to his younger brother to appear for him at many functions. The brothers here negotiated the purchase of a battery or two of mountain guns and some thousands of Martini Henry rifles, on the plea that Nepal was no good ally of Britain so long as she was too ill-armed to take her place on a modern battlefield.

On 5th March 1901, Bir Shamsher suddenly died. The light and ineffective Deva was given a few weeks in which to prove his unfitness to rule, was deposed, and Chandra Shamsher, the obvious choice, was raised to the position of honour. He was experienced, a good administrator, determined, honest and, above all, a patriot. He, too, was well served by his brothers, Bhim Shamsher, the Commander-in-Chief, and Judha Shamsher, Senior Commanding General, both of whom in turn succeeded him. Chandra Shamsher was a great Maharajah, the length of whose reign and the opportunities so given to display his eminent abilities to some extent overshadowed the achievements of the two loyal men who followed in his footsteps. He was an autocrat, a benevolent one to whom the poorest among his people could bring their complaints. No detail was too small for his industrious nature and little escaped his notice and his attention, particularly in the lives of the humble peasants of his mountain home.

Yet his vision was wide, his judgment on foreign affairs liberal and sound, and his foresight in handling them often remarked upon during his lifetime. Lord Morley described him as 'certainly much more than an ordinary man'. He was strong, slim and wiry, and, in Western eyes, small of stature, his manners those of a Rajput aristocrat, gracious and easy, his dress simple. It is little wonder that this prince was popular and respected in his army, among his officials and with men of business.

In 1905 Chandra's Maharani died, to his lasting grief and to the sorrow of many little homes in the Valley, in Patan particularly which owed to her and to her determination to wipe out the cholera, the provision of its water supply. Unlike other noblemen of his country, Chandra had but one wife. When she knew she was dying she insisted that he should marry again. He refused. She won the day by having a bride brought to Nepal from Benares and, on the day before she died, extracted from him a promise that he would marry this girl, the successor of her choice.

Jang Bahadur Rana had instituted the unalterable custom whereby all Ranas must marry women of pure Rajput blood. He himself and more than one of his brothers showed strongly in their physical traits that they were well laced with Magar blood, than which there is no finer in the Nepal highlands unless it is that of the Thakurs.

Slowly, in a country never yet exposed to the impact of the surging life of progress of the nineteenth and twentieth centuries, with infinite tact and care the Maharajah succeeded in introducing reform into the kingdom. Prithwi Narain had created from Gorkha the Kingdom of Nepal: Jang Bahadur Rana had from this created a power in Southern Asia, to be reckoned with by the British in India: Chandra Shamsher placed Nepal on the world stage, particularly by his military contribution to the First World War. His achievements in his own country were no less memorable, but it was apparent before he died that no one man could possibly handle the multitude of affairs and problems that were growing out of his reforms and the steps he had taken to modernise the administration of Nepal. He was fortunate when he took office that no need presented itself, as heretofore, to liquidate the administration: its officials had served his brother and himself competently for many years — they were tested men. His eldest son, General Mohan Shamsher, was responsible for the smooth running of everything in the Durbar: the second, Baber, was a popular General in the Army: the third, Kaiser, also a General, was a most cultured man of liberal education, famous as a hunter of big game and a first-class shot. Singha and Krishna Shamsher came into public life after the death of their father. His nephew, General Padma, son of Bhim Shamsher, was closely concerned in most of the Reforms. Eventually he commanded the Nepalese forces in India during the First World War.

As soon as he took office the Maharajah appointed Commissions to enquire into the essential reforms that were needed. While these were busily engaged, the wholly unreliable elder brother, Khadga Shamsher, already once banished and then so excused as to be created Governor of Palpa, embarked upon intrigue within the provincial garrison which could have but one meaning. Chandra dealt with the affair in a characteristically subtle manner. He ordered out Khadga's favourite regiment, the Sabuj, to attend army manoeuvres, thereafter to reinforce the Kathmandu garrison in view of the Maharajah's intended visit to India. Khadga took fright and fled the country, whereupon his brother was content to clean up the conspiracy by dismissing a few junior officers. Khadga, he pensioned off in some comfort at the delightful little lakeside town of Saugor in the Central Provinces of India.

The Commissions reported and the Maharajah at once set to work to readjust his whole administration transferring subjects as indicated from one ministry to another, introducing new departments to handle the Kingdom's expanding affairs and new offices to fill the gaps in administrative and executive services. While innovating, he made sure that the administration would keep its native character, for he saw that only by satisfying his subjects of this would it be possible for him to get ready acceptance of the measures that he was determined to introduce. He would not hurry. There was no desire among his people for a democratic government with all its trappings such as a free press* and a wide franchise, so he made no attempt to bring these institutions among them. Rather he persevered in improving their material benefits and eradicating those things that he considered to be retarding their political and economic progress. He would make no foolhardy experiments in government ahead of his people's desires and capacities. To these ends he chose his servants from men of good family, whose ambitions were to serve their country rather than themselves, and who were with him in stamping out corruption in government, at the centre and in the provinces. At the annual Panjni it had been the habit of those newly appointed to reward their supporters by gifts of office within their power to bestow. This system ceased, all offices, high and low, being in the hands of the Maharajah who saw to it that no honest and efficient man was relieved of his

---

* The only newspaper printed in the country, the *Gurkha Patra*, was under official auspices.

post and no dishonest or incompetent one allowed to continue in his. A permanency and stability not hitherto experienced was thus introduced into the administration.

The *Corvée*, the right of an official to requisition goods and beasts and to demand personal service for himself and his staff wherever he went, was abolished. Much of the land given out in *jagir* to pay for services such as those performed by officers and men of the Army was resumed by the State on payment of compensation. With the help of the Imperial Forest Service of India, the indiscriminate felling of the rich forests of the Terai was stopped and steps taken for periodical reafforestation. Large tracts of the Terai were reclaimed to agriculture. With a trade treaty between Nepal and India in 1923 came better regulation of customs affairs, while the free movement of goods within Nepal was assured by the removal of the ancient inter-provincial *octroi* posts. With their going, went a chronic source of corruption and malpractice. After long and patient negotiation with Tibet certain customs posts were also abolished on the main route from Nepal into the chief towns of that country.

The contests between the temporal powers represented by the Kshattriyas, and the Brahmans, were settled if anything in favour of the latter. Prithwi Narain had had little truck with his clergy. When he took Nawakote he confiscated all Brahman lands in the neighbourhood and turned the owners adrift to seek their fortunes in the Valley. Despite this rather resolute conduct, the Brahmans were ready enough to serve him as agents in the Valley cities. It was Bahadur Sah who saw to it that the consumption of Chauri bullocks on the march back from Digarchi in 1792 was condoned by the refusal to recognise this variety of kine as 'cows' in the spirit of the Shastras. Similarly Jang Bahadur saw to it that the yak was a goat. It has not been in the interests of progress in Nepal that, since those spacious and bloody days, the Brahman and his worn-out taboos have laid hands on the government and on its people. Superstitious fear of the Brahman's curse is a stiff brake on liberal thought and an insuperable obstacle to liberal action. It may be placed to Chandra Shamsher's credit that, strict observer as he was of the Hindu way of life, he yet succeeded in effecting all that he did.

In 1829 Lord William Bentinck had abolished throughout the territories then under the Company's control the inhuman ritual of *suttee,* by which a man's widow or widows burned themselves alive at his funeral. Jang Bahadur had issued a decree that no woman who had duties yet to perform to her children or to her husband's family or to the State was ever to commit *suttee*. Bir Shamsher went further, making *suttee* unlawful without his consent or, in his absence, that of the highest legal authority. In 1920 Chandra took advantage of the Acts of Bentinck, Jang and Bir Shamsher, to forbid the practice altogether. With his better-knit administration, he stamped it out.

The greatest achievement of his career was the abolition of the slavery mentioned in Chapters 19 and 20 and again in Appendix II. Where Jang Bahadur, belatedly enlightened, had failed, where Deva had done his feeble but kindly best, Chandra Shamsher with infinite skill succeeded. Slavery was the common and accepted practice in the East and it would be so today if the Western nations and Christianity had not frowned upon it, eradicated it from their own systems, declaimed against it wherever met and used the sword to sweep it away from Africa and Asia. If anything, slavery in Nepal was a more kindly institution than in most nations and brought with it in very many cases an intimate family relationship within which the slave was content with his lot. But slavery is slavery and, whether it is the absolute power of one individual over the fortunes of another or of a great organisation over the individual fortunes of its members, it is a relationship utterly to be deplored and utterly to be extinguished. In the East the absolute power of the organisation, the state, has usually, but not always, been tempered by the knowledge that, if pushed too far, its subjects would either resist passively or take the law into their own hands. In the West, having at last ousted the state as a slave-owner, the nations are confronted by organisations within themselves having most of the arrogant and oppressive qualities of slave-ownership, and wielding much of the power. Promoted by the principles of democracy, they have yet to be controlled by those same principles, almost as difficult a task as faced the Maharajah Chandra Shamsher in dealing with slavery for, in both cases, not only the people as a whole must be brought to see the evils inherent in the system but those who control it must also be persuaded.

By the twentieth century slavery was confined to the hill tracts: there was none in the Valley. It has been likened to the slavery which existed in the Southern States of America up to the 1860's, seventy short years before it was broken in Nepal. Only in rare instances were the slaves illtreated. As early as 1839 a law had been passed to prevent the enslavement of free men, women and children of the four castes and the thirty-six sub-castes. Jang Bahadur, as related, made it illegal for any free person to sell himself or his child into slavery, but the law was not enforceable even in his despotic day. Deva, limiting his edict for the freeing of female slaves to the seat of Government in Kathmandu and in his own duchies of Kaski and Lamjung, failed completely to obtain any liberations in the duchies and had only about one hundred nominal liberations in the capital. But Chandra's administration was by now stronger and closer.

His first step was to see that Jang's order was strictly enforced. Here he was on firm ground for the law had been passed and accepted by all, even if it was not observed. He then made it illegal for any existing slave to be sold without due notification to his or her relatives of the right to buy the slave out for a fixed sum varying from 25 to 120 rupees, according to sex and usefulness. With this went an order for the immediate freeing of any slave who came into the Government's possession by virtue of the law; he then selected a more healthy place in the Terai for state development to which any slave was at liberty to go and where, on arrival, he would automatically become free. Lastly, he decreed that any slave who had absented himself from his master for ten years could return as a free man and that those runaways who had gone to India could return and at once buy themselves out for the sums already stated, the heavy financial penalties previously enforced for the returning fugitive and his re-enslavement being totally abolished.

The culmination of this humane project came in 1924, when he at last believed himself strong enough, and the time ripe enough, to act. He had addressed a large open air meeting on the Tundi Khel and wrote to his friend, Landon, '. . . I look forward to the day, which I earnestly hope now will not be many months off, when, by God's grace, I shall have the supreme satisfaction of witnessing the fulfilment of my long cherished desire to see, not only the inhuman practice inherent in the institution stopped, but also the legal status of slavery totally abolished throughout the kingdom.' He had told his people that the whole civilised world looked to Nepal to abolish a practice that tarnished a brave, just and humane nation. He described to them the life of a slave as a mere chattel, with the right to marry but thereafter nothing to prevent parents and children being parted at any moment and for ever. His argument was a long and clear thesis on the whole question of slavery including the economic fact that a free man was a better investment for the work he produced than ever was any slave. Landon tells the story which the Maharajah related to the assembly to exemplify the intolerable cruelty flowing from slavery.

'The mother, a slave, had given birth to seven children, and her master, despite her protests and tearful prayers, had already disposed of one daughter and four sons by sale. The woman in her petition through the

Niksari Office wrote that the bitter lament of the children at thus being forced to separate from their mother sent a pang through her heart more acute than any she had ever suffered; that she summoned resignation to bear the misfortune and drew consolation from what was left her; that she submitted to it as the work of that fatality, the result of the accumulated *karma* of her previous births, which had followed her like a shadow to her present existence; but that when to her dismay the hardhearted master arranged to take away the baby slave that was still suckling at her breast, her endurance broke down completely. She supplicated and prayed — as parents do pray, as you and I pray to the Gods on high when the dearest of our children lies in the clutches of grim death — to her master, the arbiter of her destiny, and to her as omnipotent in this crisis as fell Death himself. But all to no purpose. The adamant heart did not melt: the master completed the transaction. Then, maddened by a treatment which is resented even by irrational beasts, she came all the way to see if the Maharajah, "the common father of all people", could do aught to allay the consuming sorrow at her breast. As this was so different from the ordinary run of complaints, the people concerned were sent for, and the matter on investigation turned out to be true to the letter of the petition; the child had been sold by a regular deed, the *Parambhatta*. The master was asked if he did not feel pity for the poor woman, though a slave; what would have been the feelings of himself or the mother of his children if such an infant of theirs were either forcibly taken away or sold elsewhere? What reply could he make to his Creator when summoned to His presence to answer this charge of inhumanity? He replied, and the purchasers replied, that that was the custom in the hills, and the law did not prohibit it. Now what does it mean to us all? That so long as we permit this sort of thing every one of us must bear a part of the sin, must share the curse of the weeping mothers, inasmuch as we tolerate the custom and uphold such laws. The poor woman was given the wherewithal to free her sold children according to the law which provides that on the sale of slaves their kith and kin or those interested can liberate them on payment of the legal amounts to their masters.'

The proportion of slaves in the population of some 5,500,000 was not, in fact, high. Slave owners were under 16,000 and slaves about 50,000. The Maharajah remarked that if the vast majority of the people could get along comfortably without slaves, then did these few need them? Had he not abolished the evil of *suttee* in 1920, despite the sour prophecies that ill would come of the decree? What ill had come? None, only good.

The conclusion was that he carried his people with him and slavery ended as soon as compensation was paid to the owners. The measure drained the limited resources of the Nepal Exchequer of close on £300,000.

During these years the law was reviewed and revised again and again in order to make it common to the country as a whole, and at last a distinction was drawn between civil and criminal offences. To some extent crime against religion was separated from civil crime but, in a country where so much depends on religious sanction, it has never been possible entirely to divorce the two from each other. A Central Court of Appeal, or Bharadari, was set up, the Prime Minister retaining in himself the final judicial authority, only approachable in serious criminal cases liable to heavy sentences. With all this, the old village *Panchayats* disappeared, perhaps to the regret of all and to cause delay in the settlement of minor cases.

The law remained strongly coloured by Hindu religious precept. Offences against parents and spiritual leaders were more heavily punished than those against others and heavy penalties were still inflicted on women who married into a caste beneath them. Certain old customs remained theoretically in use but in practice obsolete. Such a one was the husband's right to kill, at any opportunity whatsoever, his wife's adulterer. This right had been reduced to a sporting contest in which the plaintiff was armed and his quarry unarmed but given a reasonable start of him. The husband had to catch him and any onlooker could, if he wished, trip up either party as he passed in the race. Where the offender was a Brahman there was no such right, but on conviction he could be outcaste.

Chandra dealt with the vice of drink by cutting down the number of licensed shops, forbidding the sale of liquor at fairs and public gatherings, prohibiting its import and seeing that whatever liquor was sold was of good quality. To combat the other national failing, gambling, he forbade the giving of credit to the loser.*

His efforts to afford opportunities of education to his people were fraught with great difficulties presented by those very religious precepts and customs that he himself was bound to obey. He did make a start in expanding primary education and he did succeed in founding an English College, the Tribhuvana-Chandra College, in Kathmandu and sent large numbers of students to universities in India. His schools he affiliated to the University of Patna. He had made a beginning; the trouble was that

---

* At the Dewali when gambling is for once in the year officially permitted, the sport starts on the beat of a drum. All else is thrown aside and the whole population of the town, Kathmandu or wherever it may be, gives itself up to the greatest absorbing passion of Nepal.

most of the education centred about the sophisticated Valley: in plain words he was educating the wrong people, though he was not to know it. This mistake is made in nearly all 'undeveloped' countries of the world. The first need is for primary and technical education and in that sphere it is first required for those most able to make good use of it without it turning their heads, the peasants, the most stable and enduring element in every country and the element most bound to the traditions of its own nation.

There is not space to make more than a bare mention of other improvements in Chandra Shamsher's time. Looking at them in 1947, they are taken for granted, but in the 1920's they were long strides forward of all that had gone before. Whatever there was, was the work of the Rana family and mainly of this one industrious, patient and far-seeing Minister. He cut roads from Birganj on the India border to the foot of his hills at Bimphedi and into the Bichakoh pass from India, but never piercing the mountain wall of his country: that he left intact as he found it. He bridged the torrents within Nepal and built the Valley roads: he bought up the ropeway that the British used in the third Aghan War and installed it to lift goods fourteen miles over the hills from Dhursing, near the road-head on the Indian side, to Kisipidi in the Valley. He reformed the police and postal service, installed electric current and telephones in the Valley, furnished Patan, Jajarkote, Pokhara and Dhankuta with piped water, instituted the Nepalese forestry service, regularised land tenure and reformed the Army. All this was not the work of backward men in a backward country. It was a beginning of the modernising of a forward-looking Nepal.

For the Army he translated the British manuals into Khas-kura and distributed them to his regiments. Promotion examinations were started and a higher standard of efficiency demanded, while the whole administrative machinery was reorganised. The one great handicap to efficiency remained and that lay in selection of the officer cadre. Not only were the great fighting clans of Magar, Gurung, Limbu and Rai excluded from appointment to field rank and above but place had to be found for the progeny and relatives of the King and of the whole Rana family. Many of them never exercised executive command — they were permanently on the unemployed cadre — but many did serve with the Army and they lived in a past century, no good example to a magnificent body of men either in stamina or in skill. Payment by assignments of land, *jagirs*, and in kind, was abolished once and for all, and all ranks received their pay and allowances in cash. Another handicap to efficiency remained to the end in the paucity of barrack accommodation for the twenty-six battalions in the important District of Kathmandu, The men would assemble for a few days, billeted and fed locally, then disperse again. The corporate spirit required to weld officers and men into fighting units was absent. These deficiencies brought ruin in the end. Strangely enough, in this 'irregular' system controlling the lives of 28,000 men, the discontinuation of the *jagir* payment tended to cut away the foundation on which the very structure rested because the men thenceforth lacked the visible and obvious symbol of their dependence on the State for the well-being of their wives and families.

Arms and ammunition continued to be imported through India. Conscription, or compulsory service for the Nepalese Army was fixed at a period of three years.

Before dealing with the important subject of foreign affairs and with Gurkha activities in the First World War, there is one subject to be mentioned of much significance in later years, the relations of the King, Prithwi Bir Bikram Sah, and the Maharajah Chandra Shamsher. Ever since his grandfather, Surendra Bir Bikram, had been sternly and deservedly thrust out of public affairs by Jang Bahadur Rana, kings had played little part in the affairs of Nepal, but they had not necessarily been treated without respect or affection by their Prime Minister. During his last and fatal illness King Prithwi Bir Bikram Sah had received from Chandra Shamsher every attention the Prime Minister could give and all possible medical and spiritual comfort he could procure, in order to prolong the ebbing life. On his deathbed he read to his principal officers and officials a speech of gratitude to the man who had served him for so long, his Prime Minister. '. . . You have done your best for me, for my beloved mother and family, and I am sure you will continue to do so in the future. Myself, my mother, and those of my race to come will never be able to repay you for what you have done. Should it please God I may welcome you back after the shoot [with King George V in the Terai]. . . . The mind urges but the body fails. So long as God grants me consciousness — and may it please Him to allow me to take with me memories of you into the Spirit Life — I shall not cease to pray for the prosperity of one who ministered to my comforts more than my own father could. Maharajah, you have won my eternal benediction. . . .'

At least in the days of Chandra Shamsher, forty years before King Tribhuvana conspired and fled to India, the King and his Prime Minister had no quarrel.

On 20th February 1913, the boy, Tribhuvana Bir Bikram Sah, was crowned King of Nepal.

22

Nepal and World Affairs

———————— ❈ ————————

THE corner-stone of Chandra Shamsher's policy was loyalty and friendship to Great Britain.

The first test of his diplomatic abilities came in the last years of the nineteenth century when he attempted to pour oil on the troubled waters of the dispute between Britain and Tibet by advising Britain on the Tibetan attitude and probable reactions, and exhorting Tibet to see the British point of view and to fall in with their reasonable demands.

In 1890 China had acknowledged British interests in Sikkim and had agreed upon the frontier separating Sikkim and her vassal, Tibet. Then in 1893 the two powers had signed a commercial agreement regulating trade between India and Tibet. In 1895 the Tibetans, aspiring to throw off every tittle of Chinese suzerainty, refused to accept either of these agreements and demolished the pillars that the British surveyors were erecting to mark the boundary. In 1902 Tibetan aggressiveness led to raids upon the Sikkimese grazing grounds and loss of Sikkimese life. The Viceroy's letter of protest was returned by the Dalai Lama, unopened, that secluded potentate having been informed by his advisers that the Viceroy and his British were only vassals of Bhutan. Lord Curzon then addressed Peking to bring the Dalai Lama to his senses but that government disclaimed any responsibility for the wayward follies of Lhassa. Tibet was now set upon defeating both China and Britain, encouraged thereto by surely one of the oddest characters in all diplomatic history, a Lama called Dorjieff. Landon tells us that this efficient charlatan made the Tsar in St. Petersburg believe that Lamaism regarded him as the eagerly-awaited reincarnation of Buddha and persuaded the Dalai Lama that the Tsar was now a convert to Buddhism. The Kajis at Lhassa felt certain, therefore, of Russia's support in any dispute with Britain. A Chinese mission of mediation had set out to meet a British one on the Sikkim border but the Tibetan government refused it free passage, so the British mission also returned home. Russia, of all people, then sent a protest to Britain against the despatch of any mission into Tibet, threatening action if the *status quo* in that country were thereby upset. This made it quite certain that Britain would press her claims.

Nepal's position was invidious. She was bound by many acts, pledges, and national sentiment to friendship with Britain: on the other hand, there was the 1856 treaty with Tibet guaranteeing mutual defence if attacked. Chandra Shamsher, while endeavouring to find means whereby the two parties could be accommodated, held the opinion that if Tibet unfairly and unjustly provoked Britain into armed action, then Nepal could not stand by her. She was freed from her obligations under the Treaty of 1856. At a meeting of his Council he convinced his advisers that Tibetan policy was one of intrigue and provocation against Britain and that Nepal could not risk alienating her great neighbour by taking up a dishonest case on Tibet's behalf. All Britain sought was to negotiate an agreement: she would seize not one acre of Tibetan ground. He then strove by every means to persuade Lhassa to come to terms with Calcutta, reproaching the government for its folly. He told the Viceroy that any mission sent to Lhassa would be opposed. All his efforts failing, he was notified by Lord Curzon that the British mission must go and go under strong escort. To Tibet he wrote, 'It is well known that the sun never sets upon the British dominions, and that the Sovereign of such a vast Empire should entertain designs of unjustly and improperly taking the mountainous country of the Tibetans should never cross your minds.' He made it clear that Lhassa could not expect any help from Kathmandu. Tibet moved her forces forward to the border of Sikkim and prepared to fight in the Red Idol Gorge near Tuna, in the Gyantse Valley, and on the Kara La Pass. From Gyantse Jong her artillery bombarded the British post despite the existence at that time of an agreed armistice. In 1904 the British, under Younghusband, with a yak supply column provided by Nepal, crossed the border and, after some fighting, advanced to Lhassa where a treaty was signed, thanks to a great extent to the good offices and perseverance of the Nepalese Envoy at that capital. Thus was the Chumbi Valley trade route opened, draining off commerce from Kirong and Kuti. Chandra Shamsher's policy and help to Britain was seen to be all the more generous for the hurt it did to his own country's economy. With direct communication established between Tibet and India, Nepal lost her commanding position as an intermediary. But, for all these debits, she had one overwhelming credit, since she had bound the three countries together in a friendship which was all the more precious when in 1912 the fall of the Manchu dynasty left Tibet an independent country in full control of its foreign affairs. With China, Nepal remained on friendly terms, the Celestial Emperor conferring upon the Maharajah the same high honour as he had conferred upon Jang Bahadur and Bhim Shamsher.

The response from the British side has consistently been to confirm the absolute independence and sovereignty of Nepal and when, in 1910, there was friction on the Nepalese-Tibetan border, she warned Tibet that if Nepal was compelled to use force to end it, Britain would in no way restrain her.

In 1906 the Maharajah's friend, Lord Kitchener, paid a visit to Kathmandu where he was invited to inspect a full parade of the Gurkha Army. He recorded his impressions of the marble palaces lit by electricity and of the Nepalese officers, day in and day out wearing uniform like any Continental nation. In his farewell message he spoke of the Gurkhas of the Indian Army as some of our bravest and most efficient soldiers and said that, if ever his country were involved in a serious war he would be proud to have under his command the Army of Nepal and to associate it with their comrades already serving the British Crown. Chandra Shamsher remembered these words and honoured them, as he honoured the speaker with the minute guns of the Valley garrisons when the *Hampshire* went down in far northern seas.

In April 1908 the Maharajah drove out of Kathmandu among cheering crowds on his journey to England. He was bound on a mission to confirm absolutely the sovereign status of Nepal, to obtain free and unconditional import of arms and ammunition without reference to the Viceroy of India and to obtain the same liberty to import industrial, agricultural and scientific machinery into Nepal. There was peace and there was stability in Nepal, so he set forth on his travels. Under a salute of nineteen guns he sailed from Bombay in the *City of Vienna*, especially chartered and fitted out for His Highness and his suite. At Malta he was entertained by the Duke of Connaught. On 8th May the royal train drew into Victoria Station where the official carriage awaited him, a large, welcoming crowd clustering round to catch a glimpse of the fabulous Gurkha prince.

Chandra Shamsher, from the press accounts of his visit, seems to have made a marked impression on the British public, being greeted enthusiastically wherever he went. In the two short months he spent in England he and his staff visited every arms and munition factory, every type of industry which might be of use to his country, from Edinburgh to the South of England: as a Major-General in the British Army he inspected army formations and visited the fleet assembled at Dover. In Scotland, replying to the Lord Provost of Edinburgh, in his fluent and easy English he spoke of the close association in arms of his own highlanders and those of Scotland, ending with the observation that his personal experience now showed him that there was something deeper than the simple comradeship of camp and field which made brothers of Scotsmen and Gurkhas. Before he left he distributed considerable sums to the most deserving of London's charities.

On 21st July King Edward, who had found the Maharajah a most congenial and picturesque companion, invested him with the Grand Cross of the Order of the Bath, having had the Cross of the Order specially studded with diamonds as a mark of honour and respect to the Gurkha nobleman on whom he bestowed it.

On the same day Chandra Shamsher published a letter of thanks to the British people, 'Wherever we have gone we have found everyone anxious to make us feel that we were friends. . . . I want to and do thank the British people for all their kindness. . . . Yours is a great country. . . . But to me the greatness of your country is best seen in the good it has done for our great neighbour, India, in the peace, security of life and property, justice and numerous other benefits it has given to that country. So I take my leave, with the wish that God may prosper the people of this country and their work, and by again saying how much I and my people have enjoyed the kind hospitality which has been so fully extended to us and for which we are all so thankful.'

From England he went to Paris, to the tomb of Napoleon, thence to Milan to visit the Cathedral, to Rome to the Colosseum and to St Peter's and at last to Naples where he boarded the *City of Vienna* for Tuticorin and a visit to the holy shrine of Rameshwaram. On 27th August the Maharajah was back among his own folk at Kathmandu, greeted with public festivities and rejoicing. The King accorded him an official welcome in the great Durbar hall of the Hanuman-Dhoka. That day a letter was presented and read to the King, from King Edward VII, beginning, 'My dear friend,' expressing his great pleasure at the visit of 'Major-General His Excellency Sir Chandra Shamsher, Your Highness's Prime Minister,' and ending, 'I am, your Highness's sincere friend.' Chandra Shamsher rose and thanked the King and his people for their kind welcome: Colonel Macdonald, the Resident, spoke and the King himself, the Maharajadhiraj, gave a brief and warm address of congratulation to the returning Ambassador.

In 1908 China sought to stir up trouble in the Himalayan borderland. Her opening gambit was to demand that she should enlist from Tibet the Nepalese-Tibetan half-breeds. Chandra Shamsher flatly refused to permit such a thing. China then commenced overtures to Nepal for a regional alliance of China, Tibet, Nepal and Bhutan. Chandra would not listen and at once consulted the Government of India to solicit its support in giving a firm, if not provocative, answer. The Viceroy told him that he could count absolutely on India's support if he were ever threatened from Tibetan territory. The Maharajah thereupon curtly rejected the Chinese advances and furthermore repudiated all claims of China to any vestige of suzerainty over Tibet. The Chinese again claimed the right to enlist the half-breeds, so the Government of India stepped in and told them plainly that it would resist any attempt on the part of Peking to enforce this claim and would, in that event, not only undertake the defence of Sikkim and Bhutan but also render direct assistance to Nepal. The Chinese continuing truculent and aggressive on the Tibeto-Nepalese border, India sent a substantial consignment of arms and ammunition to Kathmandu. Meanwhile the Kashagh (Cabinet) at Lhassa had been imploring Nepal's aid to cast out the Chinese from their country.

In 1912 revolution broke out in China and put a stop to any further activities on the border. When the news reached the Chinese garrison of Lhassa, the troops at once cashiered their officers and set up a Republic of their own to terrorise the inhabitants. The Tibetans, at last united, rose and chased them out of their territory. Chandra intervened to prevent a bloody Tibetan revenge for all they had suffered at Chinese hands, Gurkhas escorting the demoralised Celestials through the Chumbi Valley into India to embark at Calcutta for their homeland, as it was impossible for the fugitives to return from Tibet to China by the northern land routes.

As far as Nepal's own relations with China are concerned, it may here be said that never has Nepal officially recognised herself as a vassal or tributary of China. For hundreds of years she had had intercourse with her great neighbour. As long ago as A.D. 1384 China had sent a seal to Nepal and Nepal had returned presents. In 1792 Nepal agreed to send a mission every five years to Peking. The mission took presents and it returned heavily laden with more from Peking, so it went out by the strait Kuti pass and returned with pack animals by the broad Kirong. The last of the missions went in 1908. Chinese Olympian pride and arrogance had always maintained that these friendly communications represented the tribute paid by a vassal to its lord. Nepal has always hotly refuted this.

It has of late years been brought home to the world at large that Chinese arrogance has not lessened and that her claims to suzerainty over lands that never were hers, or never had more than an exchange of courtesies with her, are still being pressed against all justice and against the wishes of their inhabitants. The leopard's spots are unchanged.

It may be regretted by some that Nepal did not take advantage of Tibetan follies during these years to re-occupy the regions at the head of the Kirong and Kuti passes, surrendered in 1792. Had she done so, this outpost area would have kept both Tibet and China, whichever was the sovereign power at Lhassa, at arm's length from the two main approaches to the heart of Nepal.

On 6th May 1910, one hundred and one guns roared across the Thundi Khel their farewell on the death of Chandra Shamsher's close friend, King Edward VII.

King George V announced his intention of visiting India in 1911 and sent a cordial acceptance of Nepal's invitation to one of their famous shoots in the Terai. As the batteries at Delhi saluted the King Emperor, the King of Nepal, Prithwi Bir Bikram Sah, passed away. Before he died this other friend of the Maharajah implored him on no account to postpone King George's visit and on no account to diminish in any way the reception and the sporting arrangements being made for him. So all went as planned and the British sovereign, one of the best shots of his day, accounted for twenty-one tigers, ten rhinoceroses and two bears. He took away with him for the Zoological Gardens of England a special present of rhinoceros, elephant, tiger, leopard, bear, snow leopard and the very rare Tibetan stag first noticed by Younghusband in the Chumbi Valley. There were also various deer, cattle and yak. General Kaiser, the Maharajah's son, had made this collection. King George invested the Maharajah with the Grand Cross of the Royal Victorian Order and presented him with a Coronation Durbar medal, two thousand modern rifles and five million rounds of small arms ammunition. The Maharajah's compliments were established at a salute of nineteen guns. The King Emperor's message of thanks concluded, 'Dear Maharajah, I can always count upon you and your people as my truest friends.'

On 6th August 1914, Kathmandu heard of war between Britain and Germany. Without question, without hesitation, King, Maharajah and people of the remote Himalayan kingdom, harnessed themselves for the struggle as though the quarrel were their own and theirs the task of ending it.

23

Nepal and World War

———————— ❊ ————————

THE story of the Gurkhas now flows along the channel familiar to a war-rior people, for it is one of war, and from time immemorial the profession of arms has been regarded in Nepal as the most honourable to which any man not of noble birth could aspire. Three days before he heard of the outbreak of hostilities and a day before war was in fact declared, the Maharajah had written to the Resident, 'I have come to request you to in-form His Excellency the Viceroy, and through him the King Emperor, that the whole military resources of Nepal are at His Majesty's disposal. We shall be proud if we can be of any service, however little that may be. Though far from the scene of actual conflict we yield to none in our devotion and friendship to His Majesty's person and Empire. We have spoken of our friendship on many occasions; should time allow, we speak in deeds. May I say I am speaking to you in double capacity: firstly as Marshal of the Gurkhas and secondly as Major-General in His Majesty's Army.' Thus the lists were set for the entry of Gorkha into the joust of the nations.

Since 1900 the British Gurkha regiments had had for them a very easy time. In the Abor country of Assam, or in China during the Boxer rising, they had seen little fighting, while the North West Frontier had provided them with only a few skirmishes in Waziristan and among the foothills. In China the Gurkha sentry who detected thieves taking his coal, to economise ammunition waited till two were in line, then took them both with one bullet. 'The people who were most voluble about the theft of their coal are now abusing the sentry who stopped it,' remarked the Adjutant with a sigh. Gurkha sentries had a busy time in these operations. There was one on duty outside the staff room at a railway station, with orders to let no one enter until the Staff Officer returned. A Russian

192

officer approached and demanded admittance, '*Hukm*, No, *Sahib*,'* said the sentry. The Russian struck him, whereupon the Gurkha split the Russian's ear with his swagger stick. Russia demanded the sentry's instant execution: Britain promoted him to Lance Naik.

By 1902 two Gurkha recruiting centres had been finally established in Indian territory at Gorakhpore and Ghoom. By 1908 the Gurkha Brigade had reached its permanent establishment of twenty battalions organised into ten rifle regiments numbered from one to ten. The increase had been in the main due to bringing the Assam Regiments, who had recruited Gurkhas ever since 1828, on to the cadre of the Gurkha Rifles, and to the raising of two regiments — four battalions — from the Kiranti country of Eastern Nepal. It had taken twenty years for Captain Mercer's recommendation to recruit from this area to be put into effect. The fact was, however, that the Assam Regiments and the Assam Military Police, soon to be called the Assam Rifles, and many other even more irregular corps, were all the time draining off a large number of eastern Gurkhas. The Assam Regiments had fought many a small campaign over the tangled hills of that country and out into the Chin hills of Burma, and had taken a leading part in the operations in Sikkim in 1865, where Bhakat Sing Rai captured an enemy standard, and in the third Burmese war. In 1904, now a Gurkha Rifle Regiment, a battalion of the old Assam Light Infantry scaled the almost impassable precipices and stormed the high-walled fort of Gyantse Jong. With Younghusband it marched into Lhassa.

In the war of 1914–18 the Gurkha soldier's ammunition boot clattered along the roads of France, crunched among the rocks of Gallipoli, Palestine, Baluchistan and the North West Frontier of India, padded the deserts of Suez, Egypt and Mesopotamia, and pounded the weary miles away from Khaniqin to the shores of the Caspian Sea, far from the villages sleeping peacefully on the sunny slopes of Gorkha, the Bara Mangranth, the Limbuana and the Panchthar, 'the land of the five tribes' as they call it. Two hundred thousand of them strolled in their careless way into the depots at Ghoom and Gorakhpore to follow the drum whose beat was a call not to be denied by the martial clans.

The renown of this small nation springs from its fighting capacity, from the Gurkha infantryman who in two world wars has fought from China to France and from the Black Sea to Indonesia. In this short account it is not possible to provide more than a few sketches of the Gurkha rifleman in battle over this huge area of war.

On the British request for immediate reinforcements, the Maharajah

* Forbidden, Sir!

sent his nephew, General Padma Shamsher,* with four Nepalese regiments to the North West Frontier of India, and General Tej Shamsher with two regiments to the United Provinces, following them up with a further four regiments under General Kaiser Shamsher, two of which joined Padma in the North West. Thus, over 16,000 men of Nepal's own army passed into the garrison of India. A constant and even flow of recruits went from Nepal to these regiments to repair wastage. Nepalese units, keeping the peace on the touchy and important frontier, thus relieved British and Indian battalions to join in the struggle overseas. The Nepalese had a little fighting on this border during the war itself, but, after the war was done and Afghanistan attempted an invasion of India and stirred up Wazir and Mahsud tribesmen against the British, then they had their fill. Nepalese help at that time was invaluable, for much of the Army in India, British and Indian, was demobilising and, even then, those units that were at strength were full of young and raw recruits. Chandra Shamsher, with the foresight he often displayed, had advised the British not to disband the wartime Gurkha battalions of the Indian Army as he knew there would be strife on the Frontier in 1919. Thus, India was able at a most critical time to throw in the weight of experienced Gurkha battalions to crush the widespread and, till then, successful and dangerous Mahsud rising, to capture their fortified strongholds and to punish their treachery, while defending herself against futile but irritating aggression from Afghanistan.

All through these years of war Gurkha regiments were writing their names on the scroll of honour among the armies of the world. Thrown into the winter trenches of France, ill-clad, ill-armed, lacking machine guns, without mortars, dependent on the worthless home-made jam-tin bomb, before a fully-equipped German enemy, they suffered fearful losses, nevertheless administering a smart beating to their opponents at Givenchy in 1914. When the clothing, the equipment and the weapons at last arrived, they dealt harshly with the Germans at Neuve Chapelle when, for the first time in the war, the enemy line was broken. Here, Gane Gurung, outstripping his comrades, assailed a German post on his own, taking seven prisoners: these he marched out — a small man with seven large ones, hands raised — to be greeted as he emerged with a loud cheer from the British Rifle Brigade advancing into the position.

In late April, Gurkhas attacked at Ypres, suffering severely but behaving with their usual courage. A young soldier, Bendhoj Rai, all his officers and N.C.O.s casualties, took command of two platoons and led

* In 1946, to become Prime Minister of Nepal.

them on, breaking through and capturing the German position. Motilal Thapa, his shattered arm hanging by a piece of skin, brought into safety by a British officer, holding his hat over the unconscious officer's eyes while he slept, and muttering that he must not groan in his pain for, 'I am a Gurkha' — dying in the ambulance a few hours later. Afterwards, at Festubert, Senbir Gurung was hit by a bomb which shattered his leg, but dragged himself on to direct his men in a most successful raid.

They took part in the costly assaults of September 1915 when Kulbir Thapa was the sole survivor of a party which had fought its way into a German trench. Kulbir was wounded, but he slipped through the wire and leapt across the enemy trench where he found a badly wounded man of the Leicestershire Regiment. This man begged Kulbir to leave him and save himself. The Gurkha stayed with him all that day and throughout the night. In the foggy morning he carried his wounded comrade back and laid him in a shell hole. He then returned and brought in a wounded Gurkha, and then another. Then he came back to the Leicester and, in broad daylight, carried him safely into the British trenches under fire most of the way. On another part of the front Subadar Sarabjit Gurung was bravely fighting it out against great odds, he and his party dying to the last man. Ratbaran Gurung, lying wounded in a field ambulance, still clutched to himself the remains of a German machine gun he had captured. Out of the five hundred and more who that day went into battle with his battalion, only one British officer and forty-nine Gurkhas answered the muster in the evening. At what a cost had Briton and Gurkha carried the German third line and covered their regiment with glory. 'The Regiment has acquired a magnificent reputation among those who know — at the expense of its existence,' wrote an observer from the front.

Late in 1915 the Regiments pulled out of France, some for Egypt, some for Gallipoli and some for Mesopotamia. Of them General Sir James Willcocks, commanding the Indian Corps, later wrote, '. . . I have now come to the conclusion that the best of my troops in France were the Gurkhas,' and, 'Taciturn by nature, brave and loyal to a degree, the Gurkhas ended, as I knew they would, second to none.'

We will follow them to Mesopotamia where some of their brethren have already been fighting hard and victoriously for some months.

The most romantic campaign of the whole war was Townshend's astonishing advance on Baghdad, leading a small and ill-found force hundreds of miles across desert and marsh, winning battle after battle, until, undaunted, he flung himself at a strong Turkish position near the arch of Ctesiphon, a few miles from Baghdad and five hundred miles from the sea. His intrepid brigades almost carried it but were in the end forced back. With him marched one of our battalions from the highlands of Himalaya. This battalion had already helped to defeat Djemal Pasha's attack on the Suez Canal and had then embarked on a destroyer and descended upon Tor in the Red Sea, snapping up the Turkish garrison of the place. In 1915 it was fighting under Townshend in the aquatic battle at Shaiba and played its full part in the battle for Nasiriyah. Thence the small force switched to the Tigris, captured Kurna, Amara and Kut and went on up into the fabulous regions of Baghdad. At Ctesiphon the climax was reached. The army's strength expended, it fell back. Outside Kut, with a famous Indian battalion, the Gurkhas held the whole of the Turkish 35th Division at a spot which came, from this fight, to be known as Gurkha Mound. Behind this stout defence, Townshend's weary force succeeded in dragging itself into safety inside Kut. There the garrison stood fast for many long months until food ran out and it had to surrender. As prisoners of war, an impartial witness said of the Gurkhas, 'I cannot speak too highly of this magnificent battalion.' Its coherence, self-respect and high state of discipline in adversity were a byword among the soldiers of this campaign. Padamdhoj Limbu, with six of his comrades, managed to escape and, after incredible privations, crossed the desert into Palestine where the Australian Light Horse picked them up just before the final surrender of the Turks. Outside the walls of Kut, beyond the besiegers' rings of works and counterworks, Gurkha soldiers gallantly strove, with heavy losses, to break through to the beleaguered army.

At Bait Aiessa they had surprised and overwhelmed the enemy and had killed and captured four hundred of them, with two guns and several machine guns. This was the first occasion, either in France or in Mesopotamia, on which they had come to hand-to-hand grips, and the value of the kukri as a close combat or trench weapon became patently manifest. It is strange that no others adopted it for this war and for the next great war: they were too wedded to the useless bayonet. Another battalion killed a hundred and fifty, took some prisoners and captured three machine guns. At the Khadairi bend, 'The Gurkhas saw red and translated the vision into fact: two hundred Turkish dead were found within a space of three hundred yards.' One Gurkha, a survivor from France, possessed himself of a bucket of bombs and, dashing through the Turkish counter-attack, 'laid a trail of dead Turks up to and beyond the fourth nullah,' his dead body being discovered a hundred yards ahead in the communication trench, badly mutilated by a bomb, but with six or seven dead or wounded Turks within bombing range in front of him. During

196

this time the struggle was on at Sanaiyat on the other bank of the river. The attack drove in and penetrated but a heavy counter-attack fell upon it before it could reorganise and 'a small party of Gurkhas on the extreme left held on, however, to their gains with the greatest gallantry and tenacity . . .', says the history.

Near the Liquorice Factory the leading platoons under Sarabjit Gurung and Dhanraj Gurung, and those following closely after them, took the first two lines of trenches, two more platoons passing on into the third line under Kharakbir Thapa, who fell badly wounded. The rest of the battalion carried the position and stubbornly held it against several counter-attacks. On 16th February 1917, in the Dahra bend, the 13th Division and 35th Brigade were to attack. The attack was cancelled because, the night before, Gurkhas pierced the position on their own and cleared it up to the banks of the Tigris where they flung bombs among the enemy attempting to escape in pontoons.

Finally, as the British clawed forward up the west bank of the Tigris, the chance of decisive battle offered itself in late February 1917. Rowed by men of a British regiment, two Gurkha battalions in pontoons crossed the Tigris one early morning, now swollen and running at five knots. Under a storm of bullets at point-blank range the survivors landed, closed with the Turks and in a bloody struggle overcame them. General Maude's despatch reads, 'By nightfall, as a result of this day's operations, our troops had by unconquerable valour and determination forced a passage across a river 340 yards wide in face of heavy opposition, and had secured a position 1,000 yards in depth, covering our bridgehead.' The strong fortifications of the Kut area were thus turned and the Turkish forces streamed off north, with the British in hot pursuit. At Tel Aswad, four miles south of Baghdad, they came up with their enemy. Jaman Sing's men got in with the bayonet, cleared the village, and then took up a position on the far side. . . . 'It was a fine bit of work . . . the splendid conduct of the Gurkha officers on this occasion was worthy of the highest praise. . . . I wanted him to stay, but, "No, Sahib, there's a battle on ahead," and off he rushed . . .' wrote a British officer.

And so on to Baghdad.

In the Palestine campaign, Gurkhas fought at Gaza and in the subsequent advance took Brown Hill with the steel after a costly failure by other troops. They fought steadily forward against Turk and German until the campaign was ended. During the fighting at El Kefr the leading companies were severely knocked about and finally held up in the open by a German machine gun which was playing havoc with them. Karna-bahadur collected a few friends, stalked the gun and knocked out the crew. He then set to work himself to silence the garrison and he kept them silenced until his comrades and his company could draw out to cover to reorganise. A short time before this a night patrol, unluckily spotted, fought its way into an enemy trench, there killed fifteen Turks and returned with what they wanted, a prisoner. Finding, when they got back, that two of their men were missing, into the enemy post once more, brought out their two comrades, beat off a heavy attack and came home. At Sharon, a Gurkha crawled round behind a machine gun post, jumped in, killed two men with his kukri and took the rest prisoner, while Kahar Sing Ale and Ramkishan Thapa worked their two platoons up to the enemy position, rushed it with the bayonet, slew a number of them and took prisoner six officers and one hundred and thirty men. And so on to the battle of Shirqat and the end in Palestine.

From Gaza, Jerusalem, and the Megiddo battles, we pass over the sea to Gallipoli where the Gurkhas fought alongside British, Australian and New Zealand forces, by their courage and skill in battle lending their name to the famous Gurkha Bluff. 'In order to mark the good work done by the Gurkha Rifles in capturing the Bluff on the coast west of Krithia, the General Officer Commanding has ordered that this Bluff will in future be known as "Gurkha Bluff!" ' On 4th June 1915 they took part in the bloody and fruitless attempts to seize Achi Baba, attacking again and again with numbers ever dwindling. Dhan Sing Gurung, in a party covering a withdrawal, was cut off and captured, so he jumped over the cliff and made off along the beach straight into the arms of more Turks. They marched him off, so he plunged into the sea and swam out with all his equipment on, under a shower of bullets. He escaped and landed in the British lines. From June onwards, without cessation, close fighting raged in the trench systems between Gurkha and Turk, where the Gurkha Brigade held its gains despite its lack of weapons. This was the struggle at Krithia and these were the men of the 29th Division of whose attack on 28th June General Sir Ian Hamilton spoke these words, 'Through the entanglements they swept northwards clearing our left of the enemy for a full thousand yards. Heavily counter-attacked at night, they killed or captured every Turk who had penetrated their incomplete defences, and today stand possessed of every yard they had so hardly gained.' Gurkhas had led off in the successful blow at the first Turkish position at J 11A and thrust a thousand yards deep into enemy positions. The 8th Army Commander sent them his congratulations on the mauling they had given to the Turkish counter-attack of 3rd July, but three days later they gave the Turk an even worse beating, two thousand enemy dead being left in No Man's Land.

In August they were fighting at Suvla, at Chanuk Bair, Sari Bair, Hill 60 and Kabak Kuyu. They climbed Sari Bair and there on the top of the crest raged for ten minutes a bloody hand-to-hand conflict — kukris, bayonets, clubbed rifles and even pistol butts and fists and rocks. Then the Turks broke and the weary victors looked down upon the Straits at their feet, the only men to force their way right across the peninsula and, what is more, to hold what they had gained despite every vigorous effort to throw them off. At last, reluctantly, they drew back under orders from above. The battle had been won and then given away.

Thence the tale travels to Kurdistan and Persia. In June 1918, Gurkhas moved in some three hundred Ford vans and in light lorries from Mesopotamia up over the Peitak Pass, heading for the Caspian Sea and Zinjan by way of Hamadan. After close fighting they drove the rebel Jangalis under Kuchik Khan out of Resht with heavy losses and thereby in the nick of time saved the British consular staff besieged in an already blazing consulate. From then until 1921 a Gurkha battalion was in almost constant touch with the Jangalis, then the Turks on the Tabriz-Mianeh route, and, after their defeat, with the Bolsheviks who landed at Enzeli on the Caspian. By this force, Norperforce, Persia was undoubtedly saved from serious civil war and from conquest either by Turks or Communists. Gurkhas opposed the Turks out by Tabriz and the Russians down by the Caspian. Throughout the winter of 1920–21 they held the forward posts against the Bolsheviks. It was a contest to gain and keep control of the strip of road between the two forces, and it did not take long for the battalion to exert its authority over the Russians. These were affairs of platoons. Kharak Sing drove the enemy piquets off the decisive Naglobar Ridge: Tilbir Thapa's platoon had a small fight and, on returning through the woods, lit on a Russian force of ninety men, of whom only thirty escaped: Mitralal Thapa and his men outflanked a strong forward outpost, killed forty and he, himself, single-handed dealt with the crew and captured their machine gun. A Bolshevik set foot on or near the road at peril of his life. When the day came to draw out in April 1921, the last man to go stood and looked northwards. As far as eye could see, there was no movement in the Valley of the Sefid Rud.

During this Persian interlude there were other Gurkha troops fighting in the so-called Arab Rebellion — in truth a bitter small war in the basting heat of an Iraq summer. Here they taught the Arab the meaning of 'closing with one's enemy' and found that he did not stand for the meeting after the first experience.

The spirit and achievement of the Gurkha Brigade of the old Indian Army are embodied in the distinguished personalities among its Gurkha officers. One of so many of these, the very ensample of all, was Lieutenant Bhim Sing Thapa whose father and grandfather served before him, in the Mutiny, Bhutan, Afghanistan and Burma, and whose son served after him — all in the same regiment. Bhim Sing himself fought in Waziristan, France, Sinai and Palestine winning the Military Cross, the Indian Order of Merit and four mentions in despatches. This is a record substantial enough to be noticed in a history of the Gurkhas of Nepal.

24

Nepal between the Wars

————————— ❈ —————————

In June 1921 the last Gurkha regiment returned to its cantonments from
overseas, coming in from distant North West Persia. The war was over
and Nepal, without pledge or contract, had bared herself to the bone to
send her men to Britain's aid. In the fields were only the women, the children and the old men: her youth had flowed out along the mountain ways
into depots in India and away over the wide seas. She was to act in this
manner again, but fatal advantage was to be taken of her exhaustion by
her powerful neighbour. The Allied cause, Britain, civilisation itself
owes a debt to the land of the Gurkhas which perhaps it can repay but
which it probably never will. It owed some debt, surely, to the Maharajah
Chandra Shamsher Jang Bahadur Rana and owed a debt to those of his
family who loyally supported him through these times and to those who
served Nepal and Britain in the next violent crisis of 1939–45.

Britain's thanks to the Maharajah himself were expressed by his promotion to full General in the British Army and his investiture with the
Grand Cross of St. Michael and St. George. He was further honoured by
being in future addressed as 'His Highness' by the Government of India.
To Nepal, Britain made a gift of one million rupees to be paid annually
in perpetuity.

In 1920 the Duke of Connaught and the Maharajah, who were old
friends, met in Calcutta, and in 1921 the Prince of Wales on his visit to
India shot with the Maharajah in the Terai. On 21st December 1923, to
cement the alliance of the two countries, a new treaty of perpetual peace
and friendship was signed at Kathmandu between Nepal and Great
Britain, Colonel O'Connor, the Resident, as British Envoy at the Court
of Nepal, signing on behalf of his Government and the Maharajah Chandra Shamsher, Prime Minister and Marshal of Nepal, signing on the part

of the Nepal Government. All previous treaties and agreements since the Treaty of Segouli were confirmed. Among the clauses were these: Nepal was to have the right to free and unrestricted import of goods and of arms and ammunition across India into her own country. Both parties were obliged to notify each other of any misunderstanding with neighbouring states likely to interfere with their friendly relations, and to remove the cause of friction. Neither party was to permit its territory to be used to the detriment of the other.

The free importation of consumer goods came near to ruining the cottage industries of the country.

Nevertheless, the last clause may possibly prove to be the most controversial in the light of history and in view of the activities of the Nepalese National Congress on Indian territory before and after August 1947.

In 1925 M. Daniel Lévi, the son of M. Sylvain Lévi whose name will ever be associated with Nepal for the scientific and historical research that he and his countrymen conducted during their missions to that country, came to Kathmandu to confer upon His Highness the dignity of a Grand Commander of the Legion of Honour. In his reply to M. Lévi's address the Maharajah spoke of the brilliant work of M. Sylvain Lévi in raising from obscurity the ancient and glorious history 'of this little kingdom'.

During these placid years the pressure of population on the land caused a wide diffusion of the surplus people of Nepal. The process had been going on for generations but was accelerating in these times so that by 1947 there were more than two million Nepalese living outside their country in Bhutan, Sikkim, Bengal and, particularly, in Assam, drawn thither by favourable employment in the tea gardens. In Bhutan some 50,000 occupied the lower hills into which the rarefied Bhotiya, like the yak, did not consider it tolerable for him to descend to live. Sikkim is almost wholly Gurkha, owing to its permeation from Nepal. The influence of the expatriates, some of them in enforced exile, others fugitive from Nepalese justice, but mostly those who could not gain a livelihood in their own land, was partially felt in 1950 and may be felt more acutely in years to come.

Four years later the illustrious Maharajah was gathered to his fathers, honoured by the whole of Nepal and by many in the western world. His had been a great reign, the reign of a benevolent despot, liberal in mind, steady in purpose, unhurrying and patient in pursuit of his aims, a wise and devoted patriot. As far afield as Imperial Japan, but not to democratic and exhilarating England, he had sent his younger relatives to study industry and modern ways. In India many of his young men had been encouraged to seek their education. Many were returning, charged with new wine in old bottles — young men in a hurry. An autocrat at the head of an oligarchy can in the end only maintain his and his colleagues' station by forthright, even harsh, methods against those who would encroach on their privileges or change the order of things. In the end there is no room for toleration. But the reforming Chandra Shamsher and his people's experiences in the wide world of the First World War had rendered harsh measures no longer a matter of practical politics. Without popular support at the seat of government and deprived by civilisation of the stern measures to assert their authority, the Rana family was moving inevitably to its end. The very sovereign independence of the country made it the more vulnerable for none had any right to advise, far less to interfere, with even the best of intentions. Both the Ranas and their well-wishers were therefore left at the mercy of those who had less scruples than they. The tenderness of the Nepalese about any sort of infringement of their country's sovereignty is by now familiar to those who have read these pages. In 1920, in order to allay any suspicion that Britain had designs on that sovereignty, the title of the British Resident was changed to that of Envoy.

Kathmandu was awkwardly balancing between two worlds.

After the great Maharajah came his brother, the Commander-in-Chief, Bhim Shamsher, now sixty years of age.

In Nepal, the duties of Commanders-in-Chief had come to be far less concerned with the armed forces than with purely civil administration. The system which the Maharajah Bhim Shamsher and his late chief had evolved in the provinces was somewhat akin to that of British India. The Maharajah was *de facto* ruler of the country, being the Marshal of the Gurkhas as well as head of the civil government. He was advised by a council of Bharadars, or Nobles, and by certain state officials whenever he saw fit to call for their advice. The King was known as the Panch Sarkar, his name being preceded by five *'sri's*; the Maharajah was the Tin Sarkar, his name preceded by three *'sri's*, an honour granted to him by the King for his services in the Mutiny and the Tibetan War.

The country was divided into administrative circles, each under a *Bada Hakim,* an officer corresponding with the Commissioner in India but with control over military as well as civil affairs. Within the circle were a number of *jillas* (districts) or *thums*, and at the headquarters of each of these were the collectors of revenue and the judiciary. Each village had its head-man, its *Mukhiya*, who collected the land revenue and paid it in to the *jilla*. The *Mukhiya* office was hereditary.

Although slavery had been abolished, there still remained a system of forced labour. It was divided into three classes, *Begari*, *Jhara* and *Beti*. *Begari* and *Jhara* were used in order to meet official requisitions and were applied by the village head-man under the orders of the local authority. *Begari* was solely for porters, usually to carry the baggage of a touring provincial governor or other high official: *Jhara* was for the building of bridges and roads and other constructional work, and might extend to a month's work. A head-man could demand a day's work every year from everyone in his village, to thatch his roof or work in his fields, or any other task of a private nature. This was *Beti*. On payment of four annas (four pence) an individual could obtain exemption from *Beti* for the year.

The Maharajah Bhim Shamsher survived his brother by only two short years, insufficient for him to make much impression on the task of national advancement to which his predecessor had set his hand. He will be remembered for the abolition of capital punishment for all crimes, other than for high treason and for certain breaches of military discipline. In 1930, his grandson, Basant Shamsher, was detected in a plot against his life and was arrested. Soon afterwards, he had to stamp out an attempted revolution when a small group of Nepalese in Kathmandu broke into and stole arms from the arsenal. At the end of 1931 he was succeeded by the fourth of the brothers, Judha Shamsher, who held the post of Prime Minister until his voluntary retirement late in 1945.

In 1934, in further recognition of Nepal as a sovereign power, the British Envoy became the British Minister, a minister plenipotentiary with full diplomatic status, at the Court of Kathmandu. From the days of Hodgson, the British representative was becoming more and more divorced from the affairs of the Gurkha régime. He could only advise as a friend would advise when advice was sought, and when personal friendship existed between himself and the Maharajah. To London Nepal appointed its Minister.

That same year, 1934, Nepal experienced her most devastating earthquake of modern times. Seven thousand dwellings were destroyed and severe damage done to many of her historic buildings. Lady Houston's expedition, led by the Marquess of Clydesdale, had flown over Everest. Within a few months Nepal was violently rocked and buildings fell in ruins, so that the people of the Valley were convinced that the gods who dwell and brood on the high mountains had shaken the earth in rage for the violation and desecration of their lonely holy of holies upon the tallest peak of all. The Maharajah thenceforward forbade the flying of aircraft over Nepal.

One outcome of this calamity was the setting up of the Banjya Bardhak Sanastha, or Development Board, under Bahadur Shamsher, the Maharajah Judha's eldest son.

One by one the shadows of coming events were falling across the Valley and over the palaces of the opulent Ranas, where they gave themselves to luxury and self-indulgence. In 1934 the Maharajah enlisted the help of his nephew Mohan Shamsher, Chandra Shamsher's son, to expel the C Class Ranas from the Valley, lest they became a nuisance in their aspirations for office and power, since the brother to brother succession forbade other sections of the Rana family from coming to the *Gaddi* after Judha's reign. There are various interpretations of the terms A, B, and C Class Ranas: probably the simplest and most easily understood is this. The A Class Ranas were the children of wives who were of equal caste with their husband: the B Class, of those wives entitled by caste to every form of association with the husband except the eating of rice together: the C Class, of those with whom no eating in common at all was permissible. The children of the Maharajah's first, or Bada, Maharani were A Class Ranas; those of the second or third — Kanchi or Maili — Maharani might be B Class: the C Class were children of his various mistresses. Chandra Shamsher had officially excluded the C Class from the succession, while the few B Class were becoming, generation by generation, further removed from the A Class line of succession of the Prime Minister. Both these categories were antagonistic to the privileged Ranas, and the C Class were in many cases bitterly hostile and resentful. A Class Ranas automatically became Major-Generals at the age of twenty-one and could rise to the highest rank: B Class became Lieutenant-Colonels at twenty-one and could rise to the rank of Commanding Colonel: C Class became 2nd Lieutenants but could rise no higher than Major. Previously, Judha's predecessor, Bhim Shamsher, had, contrary to custom, elevated his three C Class sons to the Governorships of Palpa, Birganj and Eastern Nepal, and to the rank of Commanding and Major-Generals. Of these, Rama was sent to Palpa, Hiranya Shamsher to Birganj and Prakash Shamsher to Eastern Nepal where he elected to live in and govern from the comfort of British Darjeeling. Hiranya's son was Major-General Subarna Rana and Prakash's son was Major-General Mahabir Rana, both of whom figure prominently in this story some fifteen years later. High though the ranks and appointments undoubtedly were, those who held them were thereby banished from the capital. These Governorships covered virtually the whole of the frontier with India from opposite Fyzabad to Darjeeling. To join these formidable exiles, Judha and Mohan now expelled a further band of even more justifiably disgruntled relatives. Many of them, including Subarna and Mahabir Shamsher, found their way into India where they consorted with any others who had designs on the over-lordship of the Rana family of the A Class.

One of the complications which had faced Judha was caused by his eldest brother, the late Maharajah Bir Shamsher. Bir had quite illegally inserted the name of the C Class Rana, Rudra Shamsher, his bastard son, into the roll of succession, thus making Rudra heir apparent to Judha and causing bitter ill-feeling in the family, especially among Chandra Shamsher's sons, Mohan and his brothers. Rudra had by now become the senior General on the active list and much respected in the Army. In this predicament Judha declared that the roll must be adhered to, thus gaining the loyalty of the C Class Ranas, while he awaited the opportunity to displace Rudra Shamsher. In 1934, the pretext offering itself, he arrested him along with the other competitors, removed him and four other of his illegitimate fellows from the roll of succession and sent him off to a military command in Western Nepal, as Bada Hakim of Palpa — a ready agent for any disaffected party that might come his way. The total of all these loppings from the tree amounted to seventeen branches.

Having eliminated the competition of the C Class Ranas, Judha applied himself to loosening the grip of Chandra Shamsher's family. The third brother, Kaiser (or Keshar), was Foreign Minister and, as such, was deputed to attend at the Coronation of King George VI. Advantage was taken of his absence to replace him. By 1938, Judha's own sons were installed in most of the responsible positions in the country, one son, Bahadur Shamsher, holding the portfolios of Foreign Affairs, Commerce and Industry and Law and Order. Thereupon arose a cleavage between the main branches of the A Class Ranas — jealousies which grated in time of crisis.

The relationship between the Prime Minister and the King, to all outward seeming, remained unruffled. King Tribhuvana had three sons, of whom Prince Mahindra, born in 1920, married the Maharajah Judha's granddaughter, and Prince Himalaya married his great-granddaughter. The King had three sisters. The eldest married Chandra Shamsher's son, General Kaiser; the second married another son, General Singha; the third married yet another, General Krishna. Since the days of Jang Bahadur the King had been consigned to the role of a purely spiritual ruler and around him had grown up the legend that he was the incarnation of Vishnu. His position was in some ways the same as that of the old Mikados or of the King-Gods of Egypt.

In 1938 a Bihar paper, *Janata*, was busy publishing articles inveighing against the Ranas and against Judha in particular, for holding the King as a prisoner in Kathmandu. It was significant that, as early as this, the traditional rift between King and Maharajah was being exploited from Indian soil. Doubtless, King Tribhuvana lived in a very fine palace standing in extensive grounds, in which were a millionaire's cottage with glass floors, a Japanese miniature garden and a private cinema, but all this could not compensate him for the loss of freedom to go where he willed when he willed and to exercise some authority in the land of which he was the King. Hodgson had, a hundred years before, remarked on the tightness of the rein on which Bhim Sen rode King Rajendra Bikram Sah. Times had not changed. Judha would barely acknowledge the King even on public occasions, in fact went out of his way to slight him, but he dared go no further for the Nepalese Sovereign was still the incarnation of Vishnu, and open oppression, violence or expulsion from the Kingdom would have been resented by the Nepalese Army and the Nepalese people.

The pinpricking of Judha and the Ranas went on. In 1940 there were strange and false rumours afloat in the Valley bazaars regarding Judha's health, that he had contracted leprosy and was likely to resign, and that he had by mistake shot a cow when on a tiger shoot. Generals Baber and Bahadur had had a violent quarrel in Durbar and Judha had ordered them out of the room. This real episode, magnified tenfold, followed the rest of the lies round and about the *tols* and *gallis* of Kathmandu. Bahadur Shamsher was overbearing and brusque, so any story against him at once found credence and a ready circulation. The atmosphere became nervy and feverish with anticipation.

A 'People's Committee', the Newar successors of Shukra Raj of 1937, distributed pamphlets both in India and Nepal setting themselves up as the intending liberators from Rana oppression and disapproving of the despatch of Gurkha soldiers to aid the British. Its secret policy was to subvert Gurkha regiments of the Indian Army and of the Nepalese Contingent recently lent to India, so as to use them on their return to Nepal for the massacre of the Ranas and the setting up of the King in their stead. It was noteworthy that these plotters in no way planned to use the disgruntled Ranas for the furtherance of their plans. The King, as might be expected, lent a sympathetic ear to the People's Committee. In 1940, at Kohat in India, a battalion of the Nepalese Contingent mutinied over a complaint about its ration money, the men pelting their officers with stones and abusing them whenever they approached. When the outbreak was quelled the battalion was disarmed and sent back to Nepal where twenty-two men were tried, one hanged, one sent to life imprisonment and the rest sentenced for periods from six to eighteen years. Much of the trouble had been due to the incompetence and ineffectiveness of the illegitimate Ranas, their officers. A few months later more disaffection was reported among men of the Nepalese Army, the chief conspirators being this time exiled Ranas and Indian money-lenders seeking for profit after the elimination of the A Class Ranas. The Newars were not deeply involved in this plot. The consequence was yet another banishment of Ranas from Kathmandu and Nepal.

Then suddenly the Maharajah's agents uncovered the plot to kill him and to wipe out the Rana family. So once more there prevailed the law of the jungle, reminiscent of the Rani Lakhshmi's plans to kill Jang Bahadur and his brothers. The story of the plot begins in 1936. In that year one Tanka Prasad, a Brahman, formed a secret political organisation of young men, by the name of the Nepal Praja Parishad. Their object was to put an end to the Rana domination and in its place to instal a more advanced form of Government. This party had its headquarters in Kathmandu and, in pursuance of the old dynastic quarrel between the Sah and the Rana families, King Tribhuvana patronised it and its leaders. By 1940 the plot matured. They would lay gunpowder beneath the King's private cinema and, when the Rana family was assembled to enjoy the latest production from Bombay, blow the place to smithereens. It is said that the bursting of a bag of gunpowder on its long aerial journey by the ropeway over the Chandragiri hills first led the police to enquire into the recent activities of the Praja Parishad. It is certain that in October 1940 one of its prominent members was induced to disclose all the secrets of the society. On learning of the conspiracy the Maharajah, a quick-tempered despot at any time, burst into a blaze of fury. He sent for the British Minister, Lieutenant-Colonel Geoffrey Betham. Meeting him at the door of the vast Singha Palace, he seized him by the hand and hurried him upstairs into a back room. There, in an access of rage, he told him of the whole plot and that he had arrested no less than fifty-seven members of the group. He then announced in lurid terms what he intended to do with his prisoners. Betham tried to calm him down but the Maharajah insisted that the conspirators at the Indian end be extradited to Nepal, there to face the inevitable consequences. At length Betham consented to approach the Indian Government advising it to adopt some less drastic line than that demanded by the incensed autocrat. The conspirators named by Judha were detained in India, only to be released within a few months for want of the evidence promised by the Nepalese Government. At the Kathmandu end two were hanged, two were shot and thirty-eight given sentences ranging from life to a year. Among the 'life' prisoners was Tanka Prasad, who, as a Brahman,* could not be executed. He and his fellow Brahmans were subjected in prison to the customary indignities and harsh treatment designed to render them outcaste.

It was widely and very naturally believed that the King was implicated in this projected revolution, so the Maharajah held an enquiry into his conduct in the affair. Despite many depositions as to Tribhuvana's guilt, Judha saw fit to set aside the charges and to declare the King's innocence, simply because there was no other feasible course to follow, the Crown Prince having stolidly refused to accept the Maharajah's offer of his father's throne. The monarch's next step was to seek for leave to pay a visit to India in order to consult physicians about his state of health, asserting that he was suffering much from a thrombosis. On this, Colonel Denham White, a well-known surgeon and physician, formerly of the Indian Medical Service, was called from Calcutta to examine him, only to report that his condition was in no way serious. However, the Maharajah decided that his Prince could visit India 'incognito'. So, late in 1944, King Tribhuvana, escorted by General Bahadur Shamsher, Judha's eldest son, arrived in Calcutta to stay in Alipore Road hard by the house of Colonel Denham White. General Kiran Shamsher, a C Class son of the Maharajah, came down from Kohima where he was ably commanding a contingent of the Nepalese forces, and daily the King and this officer might be seen about Chowringhee, the main shopping centre, often seated in Firpo's restaurant or in the lounge of the Great Eastern Hotel. From Calcutta he went on pilgrimage to holy Puri and visited the more worldly cities of Lucknow, Agra and Delhi. On return from his stay in Calcutta, the King asked to be allowed to abdicate but the Prime Minister persuaded him to wait until the Crown Prince was old enough to succeed to the throne.

The Maharajah Judha Shamsher was the last of the Rana Prime Ministers to exert absolute power in Nepal throughout his tenure of the office, from 1931 until he voluntarily retired in November 1945. His personality and his outlook are therefore of more than passing interest, living as he did in the past and but vaguely perceiving the future. Judha

---

* A practising Brahman who observes the ritual of his order, paradoxical in a politician of left and, supposedly, egalitarian views.

was a despot, albeit affable and with a ready, welcoming smile. He was
quick-tempered and liable to say and do unwise things in a fit of rage.
An active, fit man of over sixty years of age, he rose early and spent a long
day of incessant toil, interviewing petitioners and those who appealed
against the decisions of his officials and, in strict rotation, meeting the
heads of no less than thirty-six main offices. He read reports from the
provinces and discussed them with his advisers, ending up late at night
noting action to be taken on the day's business. A day and a half every
week he devoted to his own personal affairs and to a hard-earned leisure.

He insisted that there were rulers and ruled, and that the division between the two was clearly cut. He acknowledged the success and the wide
compass of the British parliamentary system but believed that it could
not be applied satisfactorily to such a country as India, for it had taken
Britain many hundreds of years to evolve a form of democracy which
suited itself though most unlikely to suit others. As far as Nepal was concerned it was ludicrous that anyone should attempt to democratise that
country and, in any case, it was impossible to do so without universal
education and adequate communications, and the latter were costly and
difficult to construct and probably unnecessary in hilly Nepal. The
British newspapers he did not like, for they were obviously written for
individuals or syndicates wishing to make 'big' money. Some of these
papers were so disloyal to the Government that not only did they damage
their own country but, since their example was copied in foreign lands,
they incited others to revolution, and revolution was a bad thing. Although it was aimed at the rulers, it usually led in the long run to greater
misery among the ruled. With all this in mind, the Maharajah regarded
the 'Cripps offer' of 1942, of self-government for India, as quite insincere
— Cripps had his tongue in his cheek, he said. It would be a bad day
when the British left India, not only for the subcontinent but also for the
whole of the East. He could not understand why the British in India
maintained their impartial attitude: they should stand firm for their
friends and deal with their enemies as they deserved.

Judha wished to develop Nepal's industries in order to bring some
sort of balance between her meagre exports and her comparatively lavish
imports. She lived by her export of manpower, by the remittances her
men sent back to their families and by the savings they brought with
them. At Birganj he built a match factory, producing a good and very
cheap article. At Biratnagar, in the Morang, close by the sources of raw
material and to the markets of India, he set up jute mills, powered by a
small hydro-electrical plant built by the British Electrical Engineer in

Nepal. At Jayanagar he built a sugar factory. All these industries were in the Terai and close to the Indian border. To them went the products of the Tribhuvana-Chandra College in Kathmandu. About them, therefore, grew up an urban industrial and partly literate population. From smaller factories were produced hair oil, umbrellas, petrol lamps, steel trunks and cigarettes. In 1937 was opened the first bank to be established in the country, the Nepal Bank Ltd. The Kingdom is a veritable mine of water-power but Judha was half-hearted about developing it on any grand scale. Perhaps, like Padma Shamsher after him, he was loath to extort the capital from his Rana supporters or to find it from his own not inconsiderable investments. He continued Chandra Shamsher's scheme of sending young educated men to Japan to study industrial and business methods. But his own inclinations were towards agriculture. Friesian and Ayrshire cattle he imported from England, Merino sheep from Australia. From Germany in 1939 he brought scientists, Filchner and Hermann, to make a geo-magnetic survey of Nepal. By Christmas 1940 the Germans had quarrelled with the Maharajah and sought internment in India, rather than to remain precariously at liberty in Nepal.

As far as linking Kathmandu with the outer world went, the Prime Minister considered that to cut a motor road through the mountains from Raxaul into the Valley and to maintain it against the landslides of every yearly monsoon would be less economical than to lift passengers and goods by air. On the Thundi Khel he had prepared an emergency landing strip, but in his time the scheme progressed no further and the restrictions remained on flying at will over Nepal. Thus, with no road and only an emergency air service, to the end of his days as Prime Minister it took a hundred and twenty porters eight days to carry a motor-car of reasonable size from roadhead at Bimphedi over the hills into the Valley. In Judha's time there were some four hundred such cars and rather less than two hundred lorries plying in Nepal.

With this introduction of the man to whom Britain and the Allies were to become so deeply indebted, we should turn our attention to the business of Nepal's prime export in its busiest season, the two hundred odd thousand men, each carrying his curved knife, whom she went out from her mountains between 1939 and 1945 to wander at large over half the world.

25

Nepal and the Second World War

———————— ❧ ————————

IT was fortunate that Britain had in Nepal during the crucial years of war
a Minister whose sympathy with its rulers was of great assistance in oiling
the wheels of diplomatic business. At the time of the Munich crisis the
Maharajah made a spontaneous offer of eight Nepalese battalions to assist
in the internal defence of India in the event of war. London thanked him
but said that the time was not ripe to accept. In 1939, immediately on the
outbreak of war, the Maharajah sent for the Minister, Lieutenant-Colonel
Geoffrey Betham, and renewed the offer. In due course the Commander-
in-Chief in India accepted it and, in 1940, the Nepalese Contingent arrived in India, the two brigades commanded by Brigadiers Nir and Kiran,
sons of the Maharajah Judha Shamsher. Kiran was later, in 1955, to be
Commander-in-Chief in Nepal. The whole contingent was commanded
by General Bahadur, Judha's eldest son. So, while India for a year dawdled
and made little or no preparation for war, Nepal had come into action.
Not until France capitulated in that lunatic summer of 1940 did India enquire from its Minister at Kathmandu whether the Maharajah would permit the Gurkha regiments of the Indian Army to go overseas. Without
this permission they could not go for, in Hindu fashion, the Maharajah
had to sweeten his priests before his Gurkhas crossed the 'Kala Pani',
the Black Water. France was knocked out of the war, so were Poland,
Belgium, Holland, Norway: Britain's army was shattered and she was in
imminent peril. All seemed lost.

That very morning the British Minister had been listening to the dole-
ful news flooding in from Europe. With a heavy heart he went to the
Palace to ask for an interview with the Prime Minister. He knew that not
all the Council were at one with Judha in his intention to fight to the last
at the side of the British. As he entered the room, he glanced about him,

to find himself confronted by the Bharadar of half-a-dozen Nepalese Generals with the Maharajah in their midst. Among them he noticed General Padma Shamsher, Judha's nephew, a man afflicted with a watery and chronic pessimism who never doubted that Britain would go down before the Axis onslaught. Betham conversed with Maharajah and Council about the capitulation of Belgium and France. They told him that the British Army in Europe would soon be captured with all its weapons and equipment and that Britain would then be invaded and conquered.

If Betham failed in the mission entrusted to him at this hour, then Britain in her extremity would at once be the poorer by twenty battalions and in the future by numbers not yet counted. The moment was historic, intense and grave. He readily admitted to the assembly that the capitulation was indeed a black business, a serious set-back, and that most of the equipment would be lost, but not, he insisted, by any means the whole army. He then said, 'We will never be beaten as there is no power on Earth that can beat us.' At this there was a momentary hush.

Judha then asked why he had come. He replied that the Commander-in-Chief in India had instructed him to obtain permission for Gurkha units to go overseas. Judha sharply enquired, 'Why have I not been asked this question before?' To which Betham answered that he had only just been approached himself. Without looking at any of the others about him, the Maharajah replied clearly for all to hear, 'Yes. Of course.'

Betham, unabashed by the occasion, then asked if his Highness would let the Indian Army recruit to increase its Gurkha battalions from twenty to thirty. Again looking only at Betham, the Maharajah repeated, 'Of course.'

On this the British Minister remarked with some emphasis that in view of the trend of their earlier conversation at that interview he found the Maharajah's immediate and unreserved agreement quite the most exhilarating he had ever heard. Judha retorted that Betham could never have read the Treaty of Segouli of 1816 or the revised Treaty of 1923, for if he had he would have remembered that in them were the words, 'of perpetual friendship.' Betham affirmed that he had of course read both Treaties.

'Do you', demanded Judha, 'let your friend down in a time of need?'

'No, Sir, but there is often a difference between countries and individuals.'

'There should not be. If you win, we will win with you. If you lose, we will lose with you.'

The Maharajah rose with a smile and conducted the British Minister to his car.

Betham, trundling back to the Legation, ran a finger round the inside of his collar.

He then telegraphed the Commander-in-Chief that the highly-skilled fighting men of the twenty battalions could be thrown into the maelstrom where others had disappeared. They could cross the Black Water wherever and whenever Britain needed. No Briton had ever doubted that the permission would be given, nor had any Gurkha soldier, but then they were not in Kathmandu in the summer of 1940.

Soon afterwards the Commander-in-Chief instructed Colonel Betham to ask that Nepal should permit India to recruit for another ten battalions. 'Of course', came the answer. And then for yet another ten battalions to form training centres for the forty now contemplated for the establishment. That was also granted. The next request was for a battalion of five hundred paratroops from volunteers in existing regiments. The Maharajah confessed to having no knowledge of this particular arm but gave his ready consent. In the event so many volunteers came forward that two of these battalions were formed. Next, Betham was authorised to send out for old soldiers to be recalled to furnish garrison battalions in India and battalions of armed police.

When news came in September 1940 that London was burning from horizon to horizon the Maharajah appeared unannounced at the Legation, in a state of great agitation. Betham went cold all over for here was another 'set-back'. He told Judha that London was the largest city in the world and was divided into three definite parts, the well-to-do western residential quarters, the busy commercial markets, and the poorer East End largely composed of docks from which most of the men had gone into the Navy and the Merchant Service. Judha asked which part was burning from horizon to horizon. 'The East End,' said Betham, 'where the poorer folk live.' 'That's dreadful,' observed the Maharajah, 'I will order the Nepalese Minister to give the equivalent of twenty-five thousand rupees in sterling to the Lord Mayor of London for the distressed area.' He was as good as his word and was soon proudly displaying a letter of thanks from the Lord Mayor.

Then, in early 1942, came the disgrace of Malaya and the consequent evacuation of Burma. In Burma and Assam were many domiciled Nepalese, some of whom had been there for generations and owned no sort of allegiance to Nepal. Betham once more approached his long-suffering friend, with the result that Nepal provided him with unlimited thatching, split bamboos and timber to build a transit camp for them on the borders of Nepal, together with 10,000 rupees to pay for the labour to build the camp. This camp held 1,200 refugees who passed through it to Nepal and India where permanent employment was found for them.

If money were needed, the Maharajah sent it, whether for charity or for war purposes. The British Minister asked if it were possible to organise in Nepal a silver trinket fund for Lady Linlithgow's charities. Judha Shamsher thought not, so he gave him Rs. 10,000 to make up for Nepal's inability to find silver trinkets.

The one occasion when the Maharajah hesitated was on the day when he sent for Betham and told him that Gurkhas were streaming out of the hills and getting themselves enlisted in every type of extraneous formation. 'This must stop,' he ordered.

'You're quite right, Sir, for I know of a man who has gone as a cook in a Sudanese Camel Corps, another as a water-carrier in the Dorsets, and of many others all over the place. If you don't want them to walk out and enlist of their own accord in odd units, you will have to deal with the matter, for many of our officers are new from England and don't understand conditions out here. They've learned who Gurkhas are and don't turn one away if he offers himself.'

'Perhaps not,' reflected Judha, 'but I think it would be a nasty thing for me to do to interfere.'

Soon after the Indian Congress Party had rejected the 'Cripps Offer' in 1942, it engineered a violent upheaval in the United Provinces and Bihar. It was making a bid to destroy the Government of India by disrupting all communications, rail and telegraph, over an extensive area athwart the life-line of the 14th Army in Burma, and bottling up Nepal so that her help in the prosecution of the war must cease. At this time the military situation in Burma and Assam was one of extreme peril for the British and their Allies. Judha was enraged that his country should thus be sealed away from the outside world but he would not send troops to intervene in India for he held that this was an internal quarrel of which he should take no notice. He sent for Betham who at once pointed out that if the Maharajah had not refused to permit aircraft to fly over Nepalese territory, then things would be very different. The Prime Minister retorted that he knew nothing about air transport. The outcome was that he asked Betham to lay out an airfield for him in the Terai. The Minister thereupon journeyed to Birganj and near there, at Simra, with the help of the local Nepalese Subha, he himself laid out a full-scale airfield complete with wind sock, on which the genial Flight Lieutenant Abdul Rashid of the Royal Indian Air Force landed and restored communications with Nepal. This success made the Maharajah more than ever disinclined to build the much talked-of mountain road from Bimphedi to Kathmandu. A few days later the hard beset British-Indian Government forced open the land routes by road and rail.

Fearing punishment, a number of the Indian Congress hooligans fled across the border into Nepal where they found a safe refuge, for demands for their surrender fell upon deaf ears or were met with calculated obstruction. Nepalese frontier officers were trimming their sails against the day when the British should release their control over India.

* * * * *

Down in India during the years leading up to the Second World War, there had been a great reformation in the Indian Army. It was no longer the army of frontier expeditions, small wars and 'imperial policing'. With an instinctive prescience it gradually trained itself up to the concert pitch of the world war to come. Starved of equipment though it was, its infantry was unsurpassed. The small wars it fought on the North West Frontier it used as a whetstone to keep the edge on its training. Prominent in these operations were the same twenty regular battalions of Gurkha riflemen. After the fighting of the 3rd Afghan War and its consequent operations in Wazir and Mahsud territory had died down, there were yet more expeditions into Waziristan to establish the new cantonment of Razmak in the heart of the mountains, together with its chain of posts connecting it with the plains about Bannu. There were fighting in the Mohmand country in 1935, and more, bigger and even more cumbersome operations in Waziristan in 1937–38 to settle the quarrel with the Faqir of Ipi. In affairs of ambush and night patrolling the Gurkha rifleman reigned supreme. 'Do you see that piquet of yours', said a Wazir leader after this affair was over. 'We could have captured it at night at any time. It was isolated.' 'Yes,' retorted the Gurkha, 'you could — very easily. We were never inside it. If you'd got in, you'd never have got out. We were outside waiting for you.'

26

Gurkha Riflemen

———— ❈ ————

AND so into the Second World War, with the twenty battalions eventually expanded to forty-five, and ten training centres. For a whole year India slept. 'This is H.M.G.'s private war,' said high officials to those who protested at the thoughtless inactivity. At last, with the débâcle of Dunkirk, there came the expected feverish appeals for help. The small men in the slouch hats landed with their divisions in Iraq and Malaya. In April 1941 they disembarked at Basra, some going north to Mosul and, later that year, with General Slim to Teheran to forestall the Russian armies, others moving from Basra to secure the oil region at Abadan and Ahwaz, where Persian forces, instigated by the Axis, were threatening the Anglo-Iranian installations. Then to Cyprus by road and sea in April 1942 where the regiment which landed was the same that had garrisoned the island in 1878. By June 1942 battalion after battalion of these highlanders were being heaped into the ill-devised, ill-conducted series of operations in the Western Desert from Gazala to Alamein where they, like all others, suffered heavily to no purpose whatsoever. In ill-fated Tobruk a Gurkha battalion held the wide eastern sector of the decrepit defences. Long after Tobruk had surrendered these men were fighting on. Of the battalion, Balbir's platoon was the last to give in, its ammunition expended and for twenty-four hours without water or food. The Battalion itself was the last of the garrison to give up and then only when no water and not a round was left and then many of them, on foot, tried to make their way over the desert back to the British lines. A few succeeded, as a few of this same battalion had succeeded in getting away from Kut after its surrender in 1916.

Gurkhas fought at the formal battle of Alamein and were called forward as the 8th Army crossed into Tunisia, to deal with Germans in the Matmata hills. In silence, by night, they scaled the slopes, located the German position and were in with the kukri. For five minutes the knives flashed and fell, then the German garrison fled screaming across the plateau. 'Our casualties were carried away and no trace was left of us except the bodies of German panzer grenadiers, many with their heads cut clean off by kukri slashes.'

Thence to Wadi Akarit and the silent gouging in one short night of a great gap in the Axis position, deemed unscalable and, by Rommel, impregnable. The tale of this night assault, a classic among battalion night operations, and of the subsequent German counter-attacks is full of incident. Lalbahadur Thapa carved the passage by which his battalion broke into the position that night, followed by the reinforcing brigade. Starting with a dozen men, only he and two others reached the crest having fought their way with pistol and kukri up the narrow rock funnel into which the enemy brought every weapon they could to bear.

There followed the relentless struggle on the bare rocks of Garci when the German counter-attacks from above were held for three days and nights. 'Scrambling over rocky ledges German and Gurkha met breast on amid the rip of Spandaus, the crash of grenades and the screams of the stricken. . . . The kukris were out and mortal grapples left clumps of sprawling dead. In the van Dhirbahadur brought down four enemies single-handed. Nirbahadur Mal, leaping over the body of his section commander, plunged into a mêlée that accounted for a dozen others. . . . Ranging across the hillside the Gurkhas plied knife and bomb until the enemy, shaken by the ferocity of their foes, broke and fled uphill. Forty-four German bodies were left behind' on D Company's front. So runs the tale of an impartial writer. Jaibahadur, on being told that it was doubtful if the battalion could hang on, replied, 'Now that we've taken the position, we certainly *shall* hold it.' Dewan Sing Basnet tells of his experiences one night: '. . . To make quite sure I crept up and found myself looking into the face of a German. I recognised him by his helmet. He was fumbling with his weapons, so I cut off his head with my kukri. Another appeared from a slit trench, so I cut him down also. I was able to do the same to two others, but one made a great deal of noise which raised the alarm. I had a cut at a fifth but I am afraid I only wounded him. Yet perhaps the wound was severe for I struck him between the neck and the shoulder. I was now involved in a struggle with a number of Germans and, eventually, after my hands had become cut and slippery with blood, they managed to wrest my kukri from me. One German beat me over the head with it, inflicting a number of wounds. He was not very skilful, however, sometimes striking me with the sharp edge but often with the blunt. . . . I pretended to be dead.' He lay there trying to plan how to deal with a machine gun post nearby. Later, his platoon came forward and set him on his legs. 'My hands being cut about and bloody, and having lost my kukri, I had to ask one of my platoon to take my pistol out of my holster and put it in my hand.' He wiped his face, took command of his platoon and went forward. His Company Commander ordered him back to the dressing station. Protesting and indignant, he went. To his chagrin, the doctor refused to let him return to his platoon for his wounds were so severe that he was invalided out of the Service.

The line held.

Nepalese mountaineers were in at the kill at the Medjerda on a dark night, when they and their British and Indian comrades broke the Axis centre, sent the 7th Armoured Division for Tunis town, attacked towards the Cap Bon peninsula and gathered up von Arnim and his headquarters.

From Tunis they went on to Italy and Greece, but it is time to turn eastwards to Malaya and Burma.

In Malaya the army was committed to a strategy of pious hopes and to an operational technique which was the plain opposite of what was demanded by a terrain which favoured movement, and movement again, away from the inhibiting roads, and movement, moreover, systematically operated on an area, and certainly not on a linear, plan. Malaya was lost by sheer bad soldiering at the very top. There is no excuse whatsoever that can be offered, and all the suffering and mental agony that the regimental officers and men underwent were in no way of their own making. Those who did not deserve this fate were these very men of the regiments, the brigades and divisions, among them the men from Nepal. There were enough troops to have taught the Japanese a smart lesson but there was no one at the summit in Malaya who had any idea how to train them or to handle them. In September 1941 a brigade of Gurkhas disembarked at Port Swettenham in Malaya. By the middle of February, the survivors were prisoners of war. The brigade had shown its usual gallantry whenever it was offered a chance but the constant order to withdraw and the failure to co-ordinate any sort of offensive from any sort of secure base gave no one in that army the opportunity to show his true mettle. At the last hoped-for stand on Singapore Island, the author of *Eastern Epic** writes of a Gurkha battalion that it '. . . still hoped to die fighting. That wonderful battalion had lost 11 British officers and 750 Other Ranks.' Another historian says, 'In so far as the Gurkha battalions are concerned, no apology for the Malayan débâcle is necessary.'

* Sir Compton Mackenzie.

Gorkha

In January 1942 the Japanese turned north and attacked Tavoy in Burma. Soon they were engaged by the 16th and 46th Indian Brigades, each with a Gurkha battalion, and before long by the 48th Brigade, a wholly Gurkha formation, and by the 63rd with another battalion. In the utter confusion of the early Burma fighting, it is hard to sort out one action from another. A bloody struggle early developed on the south bank of the Sittang, where British forces were striving to cover their retirement across the river. At Pegu, Prome and Kokogwa the Japanese thrust their heads into the Gurkhas and took a bad beating. The first clear-cut picture comes from Kyaukse thirty miles south of Mandalay, where the Brigade stood and counter-attacked. 'In the circumstances, the rearguard action at Kyaukse . . . must be saluted as an outstanding feat of arms by all those concerned,' says *Eastern Epic*. This was in late April after four months of that most wearing of all manoeuvres — retreat. How well, in their skilful and dashing counter-attacks, did the Kiranti justify Captain Mercer's faith in them.

With many who fought through those sad days, there remains one heartening memory — the cohesion and discipline of these Gurkha battalions and the astonishing manner in which their men, cut off in the forests, often wounded, always nearly famished, betrayed by the Burmese to their enemy, yet managed somehow to get back to their regiments, sometimes months later, carrying their arms and equipment and eager, despite their emaciated and lowered condition, to go into battle once more. Unlike most of the few men of other nationalities who escaped, they did not make for India and safety, but for their own battalions and to face once more the risks and rigours of the jungle war.

We will leave them now on the Chindwin River and in the Manipore Valley in the summer of 1942, preparing for the general advance of 1944 and glance at the 'first Arakan' and at Wingate's first Chindit Expedition, both somewhat futile operations. In early 1943 Gurkhas were sent in to the Arakan. After some desultory skirmishing, in which the battalion found its jungle legs, and after the now usual retirement of the force concerned, the rains broke. The Japanese went to ground during these drenching months: not so their opponent. Wrote a Gurkha officer: 'The initiative therefore lies with us and we can get as much or as little fighting as we choose. To the chagrin of the Japs, our choice is for all we can get.' It was this acceptance of adverse conditions as the most likely to yield the fruits of surprise which first put our forces in Burma on top of the Japanese.

A new Gurkha battalion was unlucky enough to accompany Wingate on his first operation in early 1943. Regardless of language differences, the unit was broken up, its organisation jettisoned, its sub-units mingled with British soldiers, complex tactical methods planted upon it and many of the men employed as mule drivers — an animal to which the young wartime Gurkha was little accustomed and, in any case, a noisy and vulnerable means of transport such as no experienced commander would ever have borne with for one minute in such operations in such country. The Gurkhas lost a lot of men and the whole clumsy expedition proved nothing that was not known before and achieved little, while the lessons, if any, that it taught were mainly what never again to do. For a hundred years enterprising officers of the old Assam Regiments and the new Assam Rifles had been operating all over these Assam hills and through their forests, away from the tracks, with porters for their transport when they took any; right in amongst their head-hunting enemy. In North Africa the Long Range Desert Groups, in open desert and without the friendly cover of the forests and the sustenance of the springs and rivers, had for many months been hammering away far into the enemy's rearward communications. Few have heard of Bagnold, the father of the deep desert patrols. 'Japanese officers interrogated after the war declared that no additional troops had been moved into North Burma to deal with the raiders,' writes one historian. But this expedition lost one-third of its men, to add to its waste and ineffectiveness. To some it may seem strange that life is held so cheaply by commanders.

Late in 1943 fighting again flared up in the Arakan. During the period from the spring of 1942 until early 1943 the Gurkha, who is a born jungle fighter, was beginning to grasp what it was all about, and from that time onwards he asserted his absolute superiority over the Japanese soldier, man for man, patrol for patrol and ambush for ambush. As on this front, so also on the main Imphal front. Deploying from Kantha village in the Arakan a company went in to the assault, the outflanking platoon fighting its way up the steep slope. Clambering on ahead Bhopal Ale, at first with a bren, and then hurling grenades and, lastly, rocks, managed to keep the Japanese at bay until ammunition and help arrived to enable him to drive the enemy off and secure the position. Later, at the Snowdon battle, a young rifleman distinguished himself, one Bhanbagta Gurung, when his section was stopped by heavy fire and a sniper took advantage of the situation to start picking the men off. Bhanbagta spotted him, jumped up in the open, took on the marksman at short range and shot him dead. On went the section, only to be once more brought to ground within twenty yards of its objective. He went in again, killed two

221

Japanese with a grenade, bayoneted a third and then flung himself on two more posts, destroying their defenders. Fast behind him came his comrades. He then raced off to a flank to destroy a machine gun post, sprang on the roof and dropped smoke grenades through the air slits. As the crew came out he felled them with his kukri, but the gun continued to fire, so he crawled in and despatched the last of them. Two of his section now came up with him just in time to meet head-on an enemy counter-attack. The undaunted three opened on it at point-blank range and it disintegrated. 'The capture of Snowdon was an outstanding feat of arms,' wrote the historian. Bhanbagta's was one part of it.

In these same operations a very young wartime battalion was ringed round by the Japanese 'March on Delhi' on the position known as Able and there besieged in the forests for thirty long days, sometimes fed by air but more often sallying out to sweep the way in for its mule convoys. Nothing the Japanese could do would budge it, not even the battering of its shallow defences by 150 mm. artillery. The Divisional counter-offensive relieved it when the enemy infantry, savagely mauled in its failures to break into the position, had had enough of the struggle.

On another part of the front a message from an Observation Post to the Commander of its artillery regiment ran, 'I am just witnessing one of the most glorious sights of the war, the Gurkhas attacking.' He was referring to a dashing and successful attack by another battalion. '. . . This note brings to you and your Battalion the congratulations of the whole of the Division . . .', wrote the Divisional Commander to this regiment when it carried Point 551, the hotly-contested key to the whole area, after repeated failures by other gallant troops.

Soon Gurkhas were airborne away up in the north on their way to Wingate's and Lentaigne's Chindit operations about Myiktyina. In early 1944 they were fighting for their airstrips. These were small affairs. Once a platoon surprised thirty-five of the enemy, closed with them and, in a vicious mêlée, slew nineteen with kukri and bayonet for the loss of two of their own. By patrol and ambush the tables were completely turned on the Japanese. The small affairs developed into the dire struggle about what came to be termed The White City where the Japanese were beaten into the ground. Mogaung was taken by the end of June, a formidable task for a lightly-equipped force. It was here that Tulbahadur Pun found himself the only survivor of his section, laid hands on a bren gun and went at it alone through the deep mud to do the job assigned to his section. Shooting from the hip he closed with his enemy, killed three of them, drove the crews off two machine guns, captured them and then, to finish his section's task, he lay down with his bren and covered his platoon up to reinforce himself. Probably the remark of a British officer after the storming of Hill 2171 in July typifies the conduct of these men in the fierce fighting of this time, 'I do not think anything could exceed the courage shown that morning. . . .'

There was an ambush on the Bhamo-Myiktyina road, 'The first lorry arrived at two o'clock, travelling steadily with its headlights. The plan was to let the convoy pass well into the killing area before we opened fire, but just then something very untoward occurred. The lorry fouled an overhanging branch and stopped to clear it. It drew up a few yards from a bren gun loaded with armour-piercing rounds; if the Japanese debussed they could scarcely avoid treading on it. Already there was movement in the lorry; a second lorry drove up and joined the first, and a third was approaching. The bren gunner, finger on trigger, was intently watching No. 1: he needed no indication what to do. The platoon commander, Thamabahadur Gurung, directed the Piat Gunner on to No. 2. There was a shattering explosion and the lorry burst into flames. Immediately the bren opened up on No. 1. The Piat then engaged the third lorry, destroyed it and turned to the fourth, but the range was too great and he missed it. However, the fourth was not allowed to escape.' Such Japanese as survived leapt into a hollow and were there killed with grenades. This action blocked the road so that the bombers caught a long convoy the next day, head to tail behind the wreckage, and destroyed it.

On the main battlefront about Imphal there was a lull while the Japanese were digesting Burma and sheltering from the monsoon. By the spring of 1943 the front was once more active. Patrol operations were the order of the day. On one occasion a handful of Gurkhas harrying a Jap post and making a show of strength with much noise of explosives, bombs and automatics, caused the Japs to launch a strong counter-attack from their main positions while their persecutors faded away. A two-man patrol, with ten days rations on its back, went off fifty miles through the hills to report on a large enemy force. It watched its quarry at close quarters for a few days and returned with a complete report of cardinal value. 'Commando' platoons harassed the Japanese rearward communications. By November 1943 the enemy was in strength on the Chindwin. At Khoriya Danre in the Chin hills, a Gurkha Company carried the vital Basha East feature, was mown down and thrown back: another Company, accepting the challenge, raised the warcry of old Gorkha, 'Ayo Gorkhali!',* carried it again and was hurled back: a second time these in-

* 'The Gurkhas are upon you!'

domitable men swarmed up the slope, and then a third time, with one irresistible charge, shouting their battlecry, they crashed into the enemy with their knives flashing, and destroyed him where he stood. At last Basha East was theirs. In this attack Gaje Ghale, early wounded in the arm, the chest and the leg, led his platoon in a bitter hand-to-hand struggle cutting their way from post to post, cheering them on with their warcry, until, covered with his own blood, he had the crest and he and his platoon there held fast. There was heavy fighting about Fort White, the Gurkhas drawing back and counter-attacking gallantly with varying success against superior forces. Remembering the ways of their old Kajis, they took one position by encircling it and cutting off its water supply. At Milestone 52, at great cost they burst into and seized the enemy position and, 'digging in' with their bayonets and bare hands, beat back all enemy counter-attacks for a whole night, standing fast till ordered to retire.

In the spring of 1944 the Japanese launched their much-vaunted attack on the Manipore Valley with three divisions. The outcome was a foregone conclusion with 4th Corps of equal strength and 33rd Corps assembling in reserve to attack up along the Dimapore-Imphal road, but the Japs were determined and heavy fighting developed along the Tiddim-Imphal route, and out towards Ukhrul to the north of it, and for the Bishanpore-Silchar track. On the Shenam position the Gurkhas held firm against far superior forces, nose to nose with their enemy, blunting the Japanese fighting spirit with cruel casualties at Scraggy and Gibraltar, then passed eastwards and attacked and carried the mountain positions about Tengnaupal. Eight miles north of Shenam, at Sita, there was fought on 15th April a terrific battle between Gurkha and Jap. At one hard-pressed post Minbahadur Rana fought a solitary contest with a Japanese platoon, thirty strong, trying to get a Bangalore torpedo in position. He stood out in the open between the forces and destroyed the platoon with grenades. At the end of the day, Malaun Post, the Gurkha position, was intact and more than three hundred Japanese lay dead about the exhausted defenders.

Cut off, their Division broke through road-block after road-block. An eyewitness of the fighting at the key position of Tuitum says: 'The hours of daylight were ours. We could do what we liked and gave the Jap much trouble. The whole of this period is characterised by the ferocity and determination with which the men dealt with the enemy whenever they met them, and this was particularly so when we would sortie out by day. One episode best illustrates what I mean. A patrol reported about eighty Japanese resting half a mile away. Lalbahadur Limbu took his platoon out to deal with them, stalked them, surprised them and killed at least forty. He put a section behind the Japs and was in among them with bayonet and kukri before they realised what was happening. They ran — into the arms of the waiting section. There was a great blooding of kukris on this occasion.' Sakaung was taken, the riflemen blazing their way forward with automatics at the hip; the Mhuabem position was cleared of enemy, terrible casualties being inflicted on the Japanese and at long last the hard-pressed Division came through to the Imphal defences.

There followed the struggle for control of the vital Bishanpore-Silchar track.

In April Wooded and Wireless Hills were attacked and carried. Light tanks struggled up two thousand feet of mountain side to the top of Wooded Hill in time to use their searchlights to help the battalion to beat off with devastating loss the repeated suicidal attacks of their enemy. The outcome of seven days of hard fighting was the seizure of the strong enemy positions about Potsangbam. There is a typical episode to be related here. A Gurkha platoon commander called for a volunteer to cross a ravine close against a heavily-defended Japanese position. Jagardhan Rai, smallest of small Gurkhas, stepped forward and waded across. Delving into his grenade pouch, he proceeded to extract bits of 4×2 (rifle flannelette), cigarettes and other unwarlike stores, whilst being roundly cursed by his platoon commander for disobedience of Battalion Orders. Eventually he found a grenade and, with exact aim, bounced it into an enemy post. He then crept on and eliminated half-a-dozen more. His platoon then established a much-needed bridgehead over the river. The positions gained at Potsangbam and, thence, at Topka Khul were held against the fiercest of assaults with heavy loss to their opponents. Here, on the exposed and isolated piquet of Mortar Bluff, vital to the defence, died Netrabahadur Thapa. For eight hours on a pitch black night he and his handful of men held the Bluff against overwhelming odds, often in hand-to-hand battle. Soon after dawn he died, kukri in hand, a dead Jap with a cleft skull lying before him.

In June the Gurkhas launched a counter-attack to throw the enemy out of a considerable footing he had obtained in their position. They were stopped dead by tanks, so Ganju Lama crawled forward with his anti-tank mortar and some grenades. Severely wounded in arms and legs he somehow managed to knock out the two leading tanks and killed their crews. He came back for more grenades and crawled forward again, with ebbing strength. He attacked a third tank and destroyed it. On surged his platoon, the attack went in and the Japanese were driven headlong from the position.

By July 1944 the army had defeated the Japanese invasion and was turning back to the final offensive, over the Chindwin, the Irrawaddy, Meiktila, to Mandalay and beyond, south to Rangoon and eastward to the banks of the Sittang River. In February 1945 the 20th Division forced the Irrawaddy, established a bridgehead at Myinmu and accepted the brunt of the whole savage counter-attack. Between 16th and 27th February Talingon was taken and held by a Gurkha battalion: the British battalion which relieved it found four hundred and fifty Japanese corpses at Talingon. For some days during the surging fight two riflemen sat in a tree on the enemy side of the conflict, observing for the guns. Dropping grenades on those who passed or sat below, they accounted for a number of Japanese, among them five officers, but were themselves somewhat cut about 'in their nether regions', as the record tells us, by the explosion of their own bombs. In March 1945 there floated down the dark slopes of Mandalay Hill the ancient warcry 'Ayo Gorkhali!' as Damar Sing's company swarmed up into the tight-knit fortifications and cut to pieces their defenders. Aiman's men, as dawn broke, echoed 'Ayo Gorkhali' with a great shout as they closed with the Japanese and the steel plied in the temple on the summit. The hill was won and the Gorkhalis, now the defenders, swept the slopes bare of the enemy's counter-attacks. At Tawma, near Meiktila, they killed 170 of them in their 'foxhole' positions, and at Pyawbwe, 250. Further south, on the banks of the Irrawaddy, the Japanese had another taste of the kukri in many small forays. One of the most bloody of these took place when a battalion cut in on the north-east of Myingyan and assaulted the place. For two days the fighting was close and stubborn, the Gurkhas systematically carving their way through the enemy's defended areas, consolidating and shooting away his counter-attacks. At Taungdaw in May the Jap attacked again, at one place piling two hundred men on a narrow front, the brunt of the attack falling on Lachhiman Gurung's section, heralded by a shower of grenades. Lachhiman hurled them back out of his trench but one exploded in his hand. His fingers were gone, his right arm shattered, face, body and legs lacerated. His two comrades fell badly wounded and helpless. With his left hand he loaded and fired his rifle, and there withstood attack after attack. Of the eighty-seven Japanese dead in front of the Company, thirty-one were counted close to this section's position.

The tide of war rolled on across the road from Rangoon to Mandalay. At Tambingon, near Tharrawaddy, one company met a strongly-entrenched enemy in head-high grass and were engaged from three sides, when a Japanese convoy drove up and, yelling and shouting, closed in on the fourth side. When all seemed lost a section commander, Kishan-bahadur, was mortally wounded in the head. To succour his comrades he rose to his feet to sell at a great price what was left to him of his life. With his tommy-gun in full spate he charged, emptied the magazine, threw it aside, hurled his grenades into the enemy, and then went in with the kukri. The next day his body was found with twelve dead Japs about him. Counter-attacking successively in three directions the Company broke through in the fourth and, leaving a trail of over a hundred enemy dead, drew itself steadily and deliberately out to fight again another day.

By the Sittang the 17th Division took condign revenge for their sufferings of 1942 on that same river. The 28th Japanese Army was penned in the Pegu Yomas: the 17th disposed itself between the Yomas and the Sittang and waited. The 28th Army came on with orders to do or die. In the drenching rice fields, their dead jostling each other as they bobbed their weird way down the channels and tributaries to the river and the sea, the 28th Army met its end. Here, near Penwegon, a young rifleman, Ujirsing Limbu, leading the remnants of his section, fell upon three machine gun posts, slew their crews and destroyed their weapons. Out of ammunition, they then cut their way back with the kukri.

There is much more to the tale of the Gorkhalese, as Kirkpatrick called them in 1793, in Burma but no space to tell it. All acknowledge that the Japanese was a brave fighter and a tough soldier. In Burma he met a man of equal courage and endurance but of a natural skill in battle, and particularly in the forests, that he could never match, and one whose aptitude with and love for the close combat weapon, the curved knife, came of centuries of understanding. The Jap will not forget the Nepalese highlander.

We will return to the Mediterranean. Italy, with its tightly-packed, lavishly-armed battlefront and sea flanks, did not offer the same scope for small enterprises as did the Desert and Burma. The fighting was not so picturesque.

The first engagement of importance was in February 1944, in the battle which never should have been fought, at Monte Cassino, where a gallant but costly attempt was made by a Gurkha battalion to seize by night the German positions near the Monastery. It all but succeeded. By mid-March another battalion had possessed itself of the lower slopes of Monte Cassino and there it clung on for sixteen days in a defensive battle on Hangman's Hill which will go down to history as one of the most stubborn ever fought. The defenders could only be reached by night and that at the cost of many casualties. Attempts, mostly abortive, were made to supply them by air. Hunger and thirst were added to the unceasing bombardment by a highly-equipped enemy. Of one night, a New Zealander wrote: '. . . among the barren rocks where our Indian [Gurkha] friends held grimly on under the hail of mortar and shell. . . . One wondered how men could live in such a place. On the night of the 18th they suffered a most ferocious bombardment. In the darkness shells and mortars crashed among the rocks, bursting and spraying red circles of flame on their flinty surfaces, and sent their echoes rolling down the hillside. . . . I thought I could see the occasional flash of grenades. As the storm subsided, through the comparative silence came the rip of an occasional spandau and by contrast — the slow rattle of a bren in reply. The Indians [Gurkhas] were still there!'

In May newly-arrived Gurkhas were successfully raiding on the Adriatic front. By August the same men fought the highly successful battle of Monte il Castello, taking the hill, being partly overcome by a smart counter-attack, then sealing the German attackers off within the position and 'the battlefield was littered with German bodies and abandoned equipment' — thirty-six machine guns, fifty-six prisoners and more than a hundred dead. It had been a bloody hand-to-hand fight.

Still on the Adriatic front Gurkhas were in the lead in pursuit, inclining left into Central Italy when the enemy drew out in June to retire on the Gothic Line. Near Torcillino ex-Mess Orderly Jitbahadur Rai, undergoing his first experience of battle, a smallish man even for a Gurkha, charged through the smoke of burning grass into a wood and cut down two Germans with his kukri. Unluckily, they collapsed on top of him. As he lay under 350 lb. of German, a third gunner came on. Freeing his sword arm, Jitbahadur slashed at the German as he bent down and almost severed the arm above the elbow. Later, the ex-Mess Orderly was seen walking beside the stretcher bearing his third victim, his reeking kukri in one hand, patting the German's shoulder with the other and explaining in fluent Khas-kura that he had no intention of completing the job.

'Tavoleto must be captured by dawn.' It was a narrow hill with only room for one Company to assail the position. 'A' Company had already suffered severely in the early stages of the attack but had a footing in the town. Its remaining platoon filtered forward into the main street, the bren gunners running up into the top floors. From room to room along the street, in and out of houses, there came the rip of spandaus, the answering chatter of tommy-guns and the rapping of the covering brens, with the shrieks of men dying under the knives, among the roar and smoke of grenades and the shouts of the attacking Gurkhas. Rifleman Jagatbahadur did magnificent work as a runner. He only made one mistake — when he passed a message to two Germans in a cellar. They acknowledged it in German so he passed them a grenade as well. Tavoleto fell before dawn.

By September the Army faced the Gothic Line. A Gurkha Brigade, losing its barrage up the steep slope in a pitch-black night, went in and took the Passano-San Savino position by sheer skill. The leading battalions, despite heavy machine gun fire, closed to hand-to-hand contact in which the Gurkha always excelled, two Gurkha officers alone accounting for eleven Germans between them.

'Auditore and San Giovanni were occupied against slight opposition', ran the Corps Intelligence Summary. Auditore and San Giovanni were hard nuts, the latter having defied other seasoned troops: they were well-organised and powerfully defended positions and they were both taken at night by the one battalion of Gurkhas in two swift and very skilful operations. They were cleverly reconnoitred by day by Bharti Gurung and his platoon, infiltrating man by man and drawing fire when he wished. That night two companies slipped through the enemy positions and into Auditore from the rear. In they went with the steel and the astonished German garrison fled.

The next night the battalion assailed the formidable San Giovanni. Silently, the men moved up: as they closed the position 'every spandau in Germany opened'. The Gurkhas raced uphill. Pahalman Sing Gurung's grim Company surged over the crest and destroyed the garrison of Point 151. They cleared the reverse slopes, cutting out machine gun posts and snipers' nests. When the German counter-attack had been dealt with, seventy German dead were counted in front of the one Company alone.

After further fighting, some severe, the Gothic Line was broken by 25th September. The whole Army roared forward and with it, Thaman Gurung. For cool bravery this young Gurkha has never been excelled. In November, he was with a small patrol at Monte San Bartelo, reconnoitring for the battalion attack. The patrol closed with the German positions by daylight and became engaged. Thaman succeeded in entering the positions and there he moved about killing wherever he could, sometimes stalking, sometimes rushing the enemy, until his patrol was to withdraw. Standing up he emptied two magazines of a bren gun into the German posts about him while his patrol got clear away with important information. Thaman died with a bullet through the throat.

The White House and Monte Chicco were taken with the cold steel and then held with the kukri after ammunition had run out. Of one German Grenadier company holding the position, only four men survived the onslaught.

Towards the close of 1944 Gurkhas found themselves in Greece, supporting the Government against the Communists; in 1945 in Indo-China clearing out Japanese and helping the French to restore order; in Java, Malaya and in Indonesia, 'mopping-up.'

R. N. W. Bishop in his book, *Unknown Nepal*, writes thus of the Gurkha way of fighting: 'As might be expected, a fighting man with such a love of order and discipline does not go wildly into battle. There is none of the excitement shown by some native troops in action. The Gurkha does not charge screaming texts from the Koran. He fights with a grim, quiet purposefulness which is the more terrifying as it is the more businesslike.... As soon as the enemy is within striking distance, he prefers to set aside his rifle and valuable cartridges and go in with the kukri or the bayonet, with which he is a first class performer, and make quite sure of his man, rather than to continue firing without being absolutely certain that the required objective is secured each time. His wiry, compact body, with centuries of hill-climbing ancestors to strengthen his physique; his absolute devotion to his officers; his perfect co-ordination to discipline and orders; and his personal fearlessness make him an opponent to be dreaded by the most experienced antagonist.'

At the end of September 1944 some young British officers of a veteran Gurkha regiment were standing at the door of an inn in Italy, when the Commander of the Eighth Army passed by. He hailed up the young officers and told them that in his opinion their battalion was the finest individual battalion in the Eighth Army.

* * * * *

In late 1945 the Indian Army started to demobilise. Most of the forty-five Gurkha battalions, however, remained in being.

The men of Gorkha and the Kiranti marched into their cantonments in India, modest, cheerful and careless, unaware that their name as a fighting race was now a household word in the western world and that they had placed Britain, the United States and the rest of the Allied nations deeply in debt to Nepal and indeed to the Rana family. With them the Gurkhas brought ten Victoria Crosses. Behind them they left a prodigious sum total of valour and achievement.

27

Nepal after the War

———————— ❈ ————————

AT the end of the Second World War in 1945 the position of Nepal on the Indian border had not changed. It had been the policy in British India to maintain Nepal as a true buffer state, that is to say, not only a state in close friendship and so in close consultation over all matters concerning their common foreign relations, but also a state enjoying complete sovereign independence. Thus situated Nepal and, since 1912, Tibet had served to keep on India's North East Frontier a state of unbroken peace. Any move by India to absorb Nepal or to infringe her independence might at any time have induced China to reassert her authority over Tibet and so to eliminate the outer buffer. The whole system would then be capsized. That the sub-continent of India, in possession of all Nepal's commercial routes to the western world, was in a position to strangle the Gurkha Kingdom or to enforce any demand whatsoever, had been recognised for many years. Britain, however, always abstained from using this particular compulsion against Nepal and so, perhaps, earned her gratitude, respect and trust and turned her away from her ancient associate, China. A reversal of British policy might be expected to have the opposite effect. It was accepted that Nepal's sovereign existence, as her economy became the more bound up with India, was at the mercy of the latter country.

Internally, like other belligerents, she had had little leisure to advance her institutions or to make any progress. The year 1945 found her as she was in 1939 except that her rulers were, like other belligerent rulers, a little war-worn and seeking for time and opportunity to recuperate, to look about them and to take stock.

In November 1945, at the age of sixty-two, the Maharajah Judha, taking with him his vast wealth and the strippings of the Treasury, had of

231

his own free will retired to Hardwar in India to live a life of contemplation in sacred surroundings. His nephew, Bhim Shamsher's son, Padma Shamsher, assumed his office. The new ruler declared that he would provide primary education for all, better medical services, more roads and more industries. His intentions were good but, against the opposition of the Chandra family, he effected nothing. The King soon became restive for the once-tasted flesh-pots of India and, despite Padma's protests, in 1946 paid another of his visits over the border, nominally for reasons of health, but more for mental and bodily refreshment.

Late in 1945 a British Parliamentary Mission arrived in India to examine the political situation and to feel the pulse of political thought and aspirations. As a result of their report a Cabinet Mission came out in early 1946 with the object of planning for the independence of the sub-continent. For a whole year, until May 1947, the illusion was general that the Indian sub-continent would continue to exist administratively and politically as one unit after independence had been granted. This illusion was no less prevalent in government circles in Nepal. The intoxicating haste in which, after May 1947, independence was thrust on India and Pakistan, afforded no time for the rulers of Nepal to adjust their ideas and plans to the new situation suddenly appearing beyond their borders. They never caught up with events: even now, though they themselves have changed, they are still labouring behind them. To the British Cabinet of the time and to their negotiators Nepal mattered little in the scheme of things, no more than Sikkim and Bhutan. It is the custom with the doctrinaire to be ruthless with all who might be irksome to his own principles and plans.

On page 202 it is recorded that one of the clauses of the 1923 Treaty with Nepal was that neither party was to permit its territory to be used to the detriment of the other. This was binding on British India up to 15th August 1947. In law, it may or may not have been binding on Britain's successor State, India: in equity, it certainly was.

Near Biratnagar, in the Nepal Terai, there lived a Nepali Brahman family of landowners, the Koiralas. The father was employed in Government Service under the Ranas in Kathmandu. The eldest son, Pandit Matrika Prasad Koirala, was born in Kathmandu some forty-three years ago and educated, as were his brothers, mainly in India. He was a very intelligent young man, well-educated and a brilliant linguist. In 1940 he obtained a post as Head Assistant to Mr. E. A. Smythies, the British Forestry Adviser in Nepal. As a consequence, the second brother, Matrika's half-brother, Bisheswar Prasad Koirala, was sent to Dehra

Doon in India where he qualified as a Forest Ranger and entered the Nepalese Forest Service. Disaster then suddenly fell upon the family. An article appeared in an Indian newspaper attacking the Ranas. This article was traced to yet another brother who was at the time studying at Patna University. On this, the father was at once arrested, dismissed from his post and, without trial, thrown into gaol. In 1943 he died in gaol. Matrika and Bisheswar were both deprived of their employment and exiled to the family estate at Biratnagar.

In 1946 there was formed in Calcutta, largely as the result of the work of the brilliant and temperamental B. P. Koirala, a body known as the Nepalese National Congress. B. P. Koirala was a friend of the Indian Socialist, Jai Prakash Narain. The object of the N.N.C. was to rid Nepal of its existing rulers, the Rana family, and to substitute for them the King, with a more advanced system of government. It was a left-wing party composed at that time of low-class domiciled and half-caste Nepalese, led by a *kami* (blacksmith), and permeated by Indians of extreme, sometimes Communist views.

Earlier still, in 1925, a number of domiciled Gurkhas founded in Dehra Doon a society known as the All-India Gurkha League. In the Doon there dwelt considerable numbers of pensioners and discharged soldiers and their descendants from the Gurkha regiments that had been stationed there for over a hundred years. The League was formed to foster education and employment among these people and to look after their welfare generally. In the early days it was certainly not a political organisation. In 1927, however, its President was Bahadur Shamsher, the son of the expelled Maharajah Deva Shamsher who had in 1901 been thrown out of Nepal to make way for his brother Chandra Shamsher. Thereafter the League linked itself politically with the fanatically Hindu party, the Hindu Mahasabha. A later President, Thakur Chandan Sing, had taken part in the anti-British non-co-operation campaign in India organised by the Indian National Congress. Later again, in 1942, one Rup Narain Sinha, a barrister, founded at Darjeeling near the Nepalese border, a branch of the All-India Gurkha League. His motives, and those of his followers at that time, were also non-political: it was a welfare league. Soon, however, the A.-I.G.L. fell into the hands of an adventurer, Dhambar Sing Gurung, a domiciled Nepalese who started to play politics with it for his own advancement, obtaining a seat in the Bengal Legislative Assembly on the Indian Congress ticket. Until late in 1946, Dhambar Sing was a democrat of a pink colour with no love for the rulers of his former fatherland. He was then requested to pay a visit to Kathmandu. He returned to India an upholder of the Rana régime, causing some speculation as to how this change of politics had come about. From then onwards the All-India Gurkha League faded out of the picture.

In the spring of 1947 Dr. R. M. Lohia of the Socialist Party of India managed to stir up trouble in Nepal. For his activities he chose its newest and best industrial plant, the jute mills at Biratnagar on the Bihar border. There he engineered a strike. The hands of the Nepalese Government were tied in putting down the resulting disorders because its slightest move to do so was sharply condemned by the only press in existence in those parts, the press of India. All sorts of rumours were put about, most of them nourished in the Darjeeling and Kalimpong bazaars close to the Kiranti country of Eastern Nepal. One widely believed was to the effect that the Ranas were casting agitators to the lions in their zoo to be torn up and devoured. Dr. Lohia, who was now meddling with the Nepalese National Congress, eventually sent an ultimatum to Nepal demanding the release of arrested strikers, among them being B. P. Koirala, on pain of country-wide agitation. He had already started the familiar *satyagraha*, or passive resistance, movement at Biratnagar. The Ranas gave in, directed that a Committee be set up to make recommendations for improvement in the constitution, released Koirala and deported him to India, and the strike ended. There was another reason why they held a weak hand in any quarrel of this sort and it was that, by that time, Pandit Nehru, whose socialist outlook was well known, was a power in the land in India. The Nepalese ruling family had vast investments in India: they could not afford to alienate Pandit Nehru who looked like being a force in the future government of that State. This commitment in their personal affairs throughout affected the resolution of the Ranas in all their dealings with India.

After the commotion caused by the Biratnagar episode had died down, the Nepalese National Congress and the Communist Party of India continued to stir the broth in the Valley of Nepal. They found the Newars, a capricious people as the old story of the Valley recounted in these pages will have shown, to be promising soil in which to sow nationalism, democracy, left-wing politics and communism. They and others sowed vigorously, but very secretly, buoyed up by the knowledge that stern measures on the part of the Ranas would raise a cry from India to split the firmament.

The river basins and their dividing ramparts, the high Himalaya and the fever-plagued forests of the Terai have in the past influenced the history of Nepal. They may do so in the future. The country which the Nepalese National Congress was assailing, strongly supported by the 'government party' of India, the Congress, and which the Ranas were defending, presented four distinct sectors. The Terai with its open frontier with India, where the inhabitants were in great part more Indian than Nepalese, through and among whom the Indian agitator could easily pass. The Valley of Nepal, peopled by the conquered tribe of Newars, an ancient folk with an ancient tradition, a bitter sense of being oppressed, and a hostility to the Gurkhas and the Ranas who held them in subjection. Then there were the Kiranti of Eastern Nepal to whom the Gurkha Kings had granted virtual autonomy, an independence respected by their successors. The Kiranti bordered on Tibet, later to be overrun by Chinese Communist armies, and they bordered on the very politically conscious areas of India, the lowlands of Assam and of Bengal. They were more aware than the Parbatiyas of the deficiencies of the Rana régime. West of the Valley of Nepal the Parbatiyas were careless and little interested one way or the other in happenings in the Valley and, while they were vaguely restless about the conditions in which they existed, they still respected '*Hamro* (Our) Maharajah Sahib', the Rana Prime Minister, under whose forbears they had conquered far into the east, the west and into Tibet, and professed a religious devotion to their King. Though the Kiranti and the Parbatiya get on well enough together, they prefer to go their own ways. With the Newars or the Taru of the Terai, neither will have much truck.

By May 1947 it had become palpable that affairs were marching towards a crisis in Nepal. The Government was so strongly influenced by its priests in every branch of public life that it might well be termed a theocracy. This spelt stagnation, and particularly in education as in every other priest-ridden country. Realising that he must take some sort of action to stop the mouths of his enemies, the Maharajah Padma Shamsher made public his intention to invite an eminent constitutional lawyer to advise on constitutional reforms for the State; to institute municipal and district boards; to extend education and introduce education for women; to publish an annual budget, to set up an independent judiciary, and to appoint consuls wherever necessary to look after the interests of Nepalese subjects. He also guaranteed to his people freedom of the press, of speech and of association and announced that about £250,000 had been sanctioned for improvement of roads, education and the lot of those in State employ. Two Rana members of his Council promptly resigned. They considered that the Maharajah was getting too democratic. By mid-June the Reforms Committee was in continuous session helped by three Indian constitutional advisers, and the elections to the Kathmandu Municipal Board had been announced. Implementation of the Committee's more important decisions was, however, constantly postponed. Opposition was obviously very stiff.

Out in the hills of the Parbatiya, life went on as usual as it does to this day. The peasants tilled their fields, entertained at nights by the *Tarunis* with their minstrelsy, the travelling *gaines* bringing the latest Tansing songs, and the nautch parties. The dugouts plied on the river ferries and the farmer built himself a new house when the priest condemned the old one as ill-omened. His new house was sturdily built of stone and either thatched or, preferably, given a slate roof of longer life. The war was done and over and the soldier happily returned to his little farm, but with a pang of regret and a little shame that his nation had not in the hills the fine things he had seen in the cities of India, the Middle East and Europe. But the hill villages were as leisurely busy and occupied as ever with their fields and their cottage industries, producing the simple needs of a simple folk, from paper to ploughshares, in one of the loveliest countries in the world, beneath the massive snows. There were signs of the pressure of population on the productive land. New terraced fields were being cut out of forests on the hillsides and here and there, through this and through the cutting of trees for firing and building, there were great scars where the land had slid away, taking fields and houses down into the torrents below. There was little use for money except for cigarettes and cloth, to buy land and to build a house. Still the grain went up through the passes and the salt came down from Tibet. Ex-soldiers clubbed together and started schools in most of the larger villages, rather better attended at first than latterly when parents found they needed their children's help on the land, but for all that a satisfactory advance. Fathers were bringing back the learning they had acquired in the Indian Army, back to the children they had left behind them through the war. Occasionally, they wheedled a small subsidy out of the Government, but usually they managed themselves. The little ones still started work about the place at an incredibly early age, carrying heavy loads from the water point up to the house and helping in the fields. But the villages were happy: they are still happy. Mostly they needed medical facilities in these hills: there were none then and very few indeed now even so long after the revolution.

In the Kiranti country conditions were similar to those among the Parbatiya except that there was a strong seepage of subversive political ideas coming through the mountains from Darjeeling, the exchange mart of the hills of Eastern Nepal and the plains of India. Limbus and Rais were, as ever, staunchly independent. Under the Red Seal of the King, Limbus held their lands for a song. Schools, roads and hospitals they demanded but, when reminded that for these benefits taxes on land and crops must be increased, they swore roundly that they would have none of such imposts — levies which would reduce them to the status of their brethren, the Rais on the other side of the Arun River. To this day the sturdy Limbu stands firm against taxation and he and the Rai resent as much as ever the superiority assumed by the high-caste Khas and Brahman officials from Kathmandu who seek to administer their country. Here, too, as in Western Nepal, the indiscriminate cutting down of the forests for fuel has brought misfortune, for whole hillsides of fertile soil are cascading down into the rivers below.

In the Valley things were different. In Kathmandu and among the students of the Tri-Chandra College, a liberal, even socialistic, tendency was rapidly developing, while graduates returning from study in India were still further on the Left. All were rebelling against restrictions on freedom of expression and on the inhibiting influence of the priesthood. There was no middle class to stabilise society. As in Russia until quite recently there was a topmost wealthy and leisured stratum and a hard-working, frugal, poorer class; nothing to link the two or to absorb the impact of a sudden emotion among the poor people, or to provide an ever-present opportunity for them to develop and to better their lot. It is possible that history was revenging itself on the Gurkha conquerors for destroying the craftsmanship of the Valley and for treading into the mud the cultured Newars who patronised and promoted that craftsmanship. Of late, leaflets urging social and political reform had appeared on the walls of the town and had been thrown into the aristocrats' cars — developments unheard of till then. Seldom were the agents caught and punished. Although every single important administrative post was in the hands of the Rana family, yet still the Government was too timid and too weak to crush the movement, so it spread.

Paradoxically, in the midst of this nervous flurry all about the Valley, the hoary religious taboo against the use of bullocks for work in the fields within sight of a temple still restricted the cultivators to their ancient ways of hand tillage.

The ruling family held all the higher posts in the Nepalese Army so the Army should have been dependable and it was a strong army of thirty-one battalions, many recently returned from India and from service on the North West Frontier and in Burma. In India their barracks had been reasonably good, their clothing and rations free and their pay regular and sufficient. The shops of Calcutta, Lahore, and other cities were a revelation to them and so were the cinemas, the canteens, the radio sets and the good uniforms and the equipment — and the efficiency of the officers. Things were not so satisfactory here in Nepal. For instance, General Padma Shamsher, the Commander-in-Chief, started his career in the army as a Major-General: he had not to work for his rank, it came to him. The officers on parade with the troops were sometimes unkempt, slovenly and unshaven. Of the 45,000 soldiers, nearly all were quartered in Kathmandu and its neighbourhood, partly in order that a governmental eye could be kept on its officers who might be tempted to become politically troublesome if on their own in a distant province.

The post-war malaise of armies had settled upon this one. Many of the men who had served abroad had taken their discharge and the officers were not of the calibre to train up the new intake. There were still virtually no barracks so the men had to find their own billets in or near Kathmandu and this meant that very often they had to leave their quarters at three in the morning and walk to the parade ground. There was no transport to take them, so that the soldier would have to sleep in the open near the parade ground because he could not get to his billet overnight and back in time for parade in the morning. The pay was bad. The best paid unit was the Kali Bahadur where the private soldier was paid fifteen rupees a month; from this he had to buy his food and keep up his uniform, of which he was given one free issue on enlistment. As local prices were at that time, it was not possible for a man to feed himself on fifteen rupees a month, so he perforce arranged for food to be sent down from his own village home to supplement his pay. However, this was only a part-time profession where most of the men could get away as they needed in order to farm their holdings, so their grievances would never become acute.

To have cut the army to about 15,000, to have eliminated all the needless ceremonials such as the firing of saluting guns for all and sundry among the bigwigs leaving or returning to Nepal, to have put its officers through a strenuous and full training starting them all on the bottom rung, and to have properly paid, equipped, clothed and accommodated the soldiers would have given Nepal a trustworthy army for the hour of need. All these innovations were at that time possible and reasonable. They were not brought in and the ill-clad, ill-trained travesty of an army remained concentrated about Kathmandu where the yeast of revolution was busily working in the dough of the State.

The rank and file of the army was well aware of the meanness of its treatment and some measure of discontent was spreading. The army was not likely to be actively disloyal, but would certainly be inefficient and spiritless.

The storm was piling up over Kathmandu and over its Prime Minister, His Highness the Maharajah Padma Shamsher Jang Bahadur Rana, and he was not a strong enough man to sail through it or astute enough to trim the rig of his ship to ride it out. He had too many fears and too few plans. He feared that when Britain left, India would fall into chaos and Communism, that she would quit the Commonwealth and so sever Nepal from her friends, and that she would treat his country with scant respect. At that time it was fondly believed that India would be handed over in June 1948 as one geographical and political unit. In fairness to the Maharajah, it must be admitted that the British Cabinet and its advisers gave him no cause for confidence. They seem even to have given him no advice. Confidently presuming on a hundred years of trust and friendship, they could have firmly impressed on him that he and his Rana relatives should right quickly make themselves worthy of this people they ruled, therewith explaining the manner in which this improvement could be accomplished. The sparkling, rather tawdry fairy story setting in which this begilded family lived was prophetically clear to anyone who visited that country in 1947.

The least that the Maharajah could have expected was that the British would on behalf of British India scrupulously respect the Treaty of 1923 to which they had put their signature, and in the interests of Nepal so bind the succession states that they could not break it. It is to Britain's discredit that she never repaid her debt of honour to Nepal and to her Maharajah, and, above all, that without protest she stood idly by as a witness of aggression against Nepal from the territory of India. Those who were her pliant instruments in this doubtful episode can in 1955, looking upon the confusion and corruption of the ensuing Nepalese administration, take the full blame upon themselves who have sold the British birthright for a mess of pottage.

On 15th August 1947 the British administration of India came to an end and two new States were born in painful labour — India and Pakistan.

* * * * *

Gorkha

All through the massacres of 1946 and 1947, through the carnage in the Punjab of that year, the Gurkha regiments of the Indian Army, regular and wartime, played the part that was expected of them, acting on behalf of law and order with complete impartiality between Muslim and Hindu. Some account of their experiences is given in another work.* It is no concern of this present record to narrate the squalid story of that time, the result of blundering on the part of British politicians determined to hand over according to a timed programme, as though this were a military operation. Yet there are those who pride themselves on a settlement which has left behind it quarrels in southern Asia that imperil the peace of the world.

* *While Memory Serves:* by the author.

28

Twilight of the Ranas

————————— ❖ —————————

IN Chapter 27 a brief sketch of conditions in Nepal in the months immediately following the war has been given, with a preliminary note of the forces rising up against the Ranas. In this chapter some further explanation is afforded of the nature of these forces, providing an opportunity for judging of their several responsibilities, and of assessing their sincerity or otherwise in the rebellion that was soon to spurt out over the Valley. In the summer of 1950 there were riots, and in November armed insurgents crossed the frontier from India. They entered Nepal from the Indian provinces of Uttar Pradesh (U.P.) and Bihar. The former Home Member of the U.P. Ministry was a Muslim, Rafi Ahmed Kidwai; it was he who permitted the 'invaders' to use Indian soil as a base for their preparations and for their military campaign.

It is now necessary to bring the story up to date, from 15th August 1947 to the riots in the Valley of the autumn of 1950, about two months before the invasion.

Up to that time Nepal had for ninety years been a tranquil and peaceful state with no agressive intentions towards anyone else, and was moreover an independent and stable country wherein the great majority of the people were happy, and where they held in respect both their King and his Prime Minister, the Maharajah, the descendants of distinguished Parbatiya Gurkha families. In 1947, in order to settle the political strike at his new jute mill at Biratnagar and to induce the Indian-based Nepalese National Congress to call off its highly provocative *satyagraha*, or civil disobedience, campaign, the Prime Minister, Padma Shamsher, had promised certain reforms in the country's administration to bring it more into line with modern democratic practice. When these reforms appeared in January 1948, they were not such as to recommend themselves to the progressives who had demanded them. On all important matters decisions were still to be left in the hands of the Maharajah and the rights of the ruling family to succession in the premiership were declared to be unalterable and inalienable for all time. There were, however, to be a National Chamber of sixty to seventy members, of whom twenty-eight were to be nominated by the Maharajah, and a Nobles' Chamber entirely so nominated. The Maharajah was to have power to veto any question or proposal made in the legislature which was in his opinion not in the public interest, while the legislature was forbidden to interfere with the rights, privileges or succession of either the King or the Maharajah or to discuss the civil lists of either of these dignitaries, or the expenditure on the armed forces or on foreign affairs, or the pay and pensions of the public services. The Maharajah would himself place before the Assembly the annual budget and would decide what expenditure would be a charge on the revenues. There would be an independent judiciary, village, town and district boards, compulsory primary education and increased higher education. The Act would guarantee freedom of speech, of the press, of association and of discussion, and equality before the law.

Whatever the all too palpable shortcomings of these proposed reforms, they were founded on a system which would have set Nepal's course of future progress and altogether obviated the turbulent methods introduced from India. They were probably quite as advanced as was healthy for the country at that time. Village *panchayats* (assemblies of elders) would elect district councils and these in turn would send members to the Advisory Assembly or Chamber in Kathmandu. It is a pity that these reforms were never fully implemented.

In April 1948 Padma Shamsher retired voluntarily, as a comparatively poor man. He was succeeded by his cousin, Chandra Shamsher's eldest son, the Maharajah Mohan Shamsher. In an attempt to resolve the impossible situation, Mohan Shamsher announced 'The Constitution Act', proclaiming a broadening of the Government and thereafter universal suffrage and the evolving of a new and democratic constitution which was to take about three years to come to fruition. The revolution anticipated by a year the new Constitution so it was never proved whether the Maharajah was sincere or not in his intentions. Those who knew him, trusted him. In fact, by September 1950, over five hundred village *Panchayats* had been established and the Maharajah had nominated the Advisory Assembly. At the time there was little chance of further testing his sincerity, for the political agitators of Kathmandu contrived to keep the Valley aboil so that, after the police had broken up a series of excited meetings, he was constrained to decree that prior notice of such gatherings, with lists of speakers and texts of speeches, must be afforded to the police, and that no association must be formed without official sanction. The Congress was banned and pre-censorship imposed on the press. These ordinances suited ill with the promised reforms. In November 1948 his police arrested some hundred *satyagrahis* staging a protest against the illiberality of the government. Thereupon the Congress met at Raxaul in India, near the border, to condemn the Nepalese authorities for detaining over two hundred prisoners without trial and to call upon the people to launch a non-violent campaign to secure political rights.

The forces which, both from within and from without, brought about the crisis of November 1950 were these. Some were actively opposed to the Rana régime: others merely antipathetic, and yet others apathetic.

In the very centre of trouble was the King, Tribhuvana, well-educated, well-read, inexperienced and hesitant, who had already at least patronised left-wing revolutionary parties plotting the life of the Maharajah. The relations between the King and the Prime Minister since 1772 have contributed a good deal of material to this book. For many years of that period there had been a struggle for power, overt or secret, between the two, and that contest had been one of life and death. With so many of the kings ascending the throne as minors, the Prime Minister had become habituated to wielding jealously the supreme authority and with it safeguarding not only his own life but also those of all his kindred and friends. Any faltering on his part would have brought disaster to all concerned with him. Jang Bahadur had settled the quarrel for many years when he put Rajendra Sah in virtual confinement and drastically clipped the authority of his evil son, King Surendra, so that he was impotent to influence state affairs in one way or the other. To provide him with a *raison d'être* and some façade of authority, Jang set the King at the head of the spiritual side of the State and saw to it that the venal Brahmans put it about that this feckless and degenerate monarch was the reincarnation of Vishnu. Before long it became accepted that the King should not risk his holiness outside the capital nor be absent from the palace for more than twelve hours. To say that the Prime Ministers kept him prisoner in the palace may not be strictly true, although doubtless they would not have allowed matters to be otherwise, having regard to the black records of so many of the ruthless chieftains who had been Kings and Princes of Nepal. None the less, this very enforced seclusion rendered the Kingship the more awe-inspiring and the more revered to its subjects.

King Prithwi Bir Bikram Sah, who was the personal friend of the Maharajah Chandra Shamsher, bore with the position without demur and lived on very good terms with the Prime Minister. In 1913 his son, a mere child, King Tribhuvana Bikram Sah Deva, was crowned king. Sixteen years later Chandra Shamsher died. It was not to be expected that the young Tribhuvana would assert himself against the supremacy of the great Maharajah, or even perhaps against the other two brothers, Bhim and Judha, successors in the first office of the State. In fact, Tribhuvana and Judha Shamsher managed to co-exist with some difficulty, although, as already related, Judha readily acceded to the King's wish to visit India despite what may be regarded as compelling reasons for keeping him under surveillance in Nepal. In Chapter 24 it has been told how closely Chandra Shamsher and his brothers had linked the Sah and the Rana families by marriage. The question to be answered soon after Judha's retirement in 1945 was whether these bonds would hold King Tribhuvana against the urge to burst asunder the other chains that kept him prisoner in his own palace. If he were to make the bid, then he would have to find allies to assist him, for he wielded no power in himself or his family comparable with that of the Minister. His forbears up to the time of Prithwi Bir Bikram Sah, with the possible exception of the first and only Prithwi Narain, were not the sort that he could expose for the uncritical admiration of his own people or of any foreign sympathiser. The inhabitants had suffered too much at their sovereigns' hands for him to feel any confidence that they would, unaided, rally to his cause if he raised the royal standard against the Maharajah. But he was a Gurkha and still the King of Gorkha. In other days Rajendra Bikram Sah had asserted himself against Bhim Sen and Bhim Sen had in the end been persuaded to take his own life. On the other hand, the life of a King had been held sacred, not excepting that of the monster Ranbahadur who died in open court under the sword of his half-brother. In conspiracy against the Maharajah, Tribhuvana risked exile but probably not death at the block. In 1943, when he was suspect of plotting against the Maharajah's life, he had asked Judha to permit him to abdicate and to retire to India. Owing to the extreme youth of the Crown Prince and to the boy's outright refusal to step into his father's shoes, the Maharajah would not agree to the proposal. Now, after a second visit to Calcutta, he made the same request to the Maharajah, Mohan Shamsher. To this Mohan replied that he could indeed relinquish the throne, but that he must either reside in Nepal or in any other country but India. The Prime Minister, looking back on Nepalese history, must have been well aware of the trouble that a hostile monarch sojourning in India could make, both for his Government and for the young Maharajadhiraj of Nepal.

In September 1950 there were riots in Kathmandu provoked by the Nepalese National Congress. From admissions made by witnesses it became apparent that the King had sponsored the revolt and that there was to be another attempt in the near future in the form of an 'invasion' from India. The Nepalese Government informed the Indian Ambassador at Kathmandu, Mr. C. P. N. Singh, requiring him to warn Delhi so that the 'invasion' could be aborted. It is not known if the Government at Delhi was ever fully aware of the extent of the impending incursion from its territory into Nepal, or of the military preparations being made by the Ranas, Mahabir and Subarna.

To exploit the ready-made quarrel between King and Prime Minister there was in India a sufficiency of eager and ambitious men. The most prominent of these men were the two Koirala brothers,* the younger of whom Bisheswar Prasad Koirala, has been shown as the virtual founder in Calcutta of the Nepalese National Congress and its first President. He was a member of the Indian Congress Party, the party of those who since 1947 have governed India, and had spent some time in prison as a political *détenu* during the Second World War. After the collapse of the Biratnagar strike in the spring of 1947 he was arrested in Nepal and sent to Kathmandu where he was imprisoned without trial as it was well known that the aim of the N.N.C. was revolution through violence. Six months later he was released and deported to India. In January 1949 he was again arrested while working secretly for the N.N.C. in Kathmandu, and he and twenty of his confederates were convicted of inciting hatred and violence against the Government. In prison he went on hunger strike. In June he was once more set free and expelled to India. His half-brother Matrika Prasad Koirala became President of the N.N.C. in 1949.

The history of Nepal from November 1950 until the regency of Prince Mahindra, King Tribhuvana's son, in February 1955 is in truth the outcome of the rivalry, ambitions and quarrels between the brothers M. P. and B. P. Koirala.

The next league which deserves attention is that known as the Nepal Democratic Congress. This was never a democratic party in any sense whatsoever. It was founded at Calcutta in 1948 by one Mahindra Bikram Sah with Soorya Prasad Upadhaya as General Secretary, and its members were mainly C Class Ranas. India was thickly salted with well-bred émigrés from Nepal and with the families and descendants of these

* See page 232.

people, men and women who had been expelled or had had to flee the country in the purges of Jang Bahadur, Dhir, Bir, and even of Chandra Shamsher, and of late in the milder expulsions of Bhim and Judha. The prime motive of this party was revenge against the despotic Ranas — that and nothing else that did not stem from that revenge. In March 1950 they, the N.D.P., joined with the N.N.C. as the 'National Congress'. The first President of the N.C. was M. P. Koirala. By its absorption of the N.D.P. the new N.C. gained the help of certain intellectuals and of some wealthy patrons. They also obtained some valuable collaborators and sympathisers both outside and inside Nepal, for some of these C Class Ranas held important posts, civil and military in the Provinces outside the Valley. The émigré Subarna Shamsher became Treasurer of the N.C. and Mahabir Shamsher, who had amassed a fortune in Calcutta, supported the party with his immense wealth. It is noteworthy that one of the prime objects of the N.C. was the expulsion of the Ranas from Nepal and the restoration of the authority of the King.

Then there was a splinter party from the original N.N.C. When B. P. Koirala was shut up in gaol, one D. R. Regmi* was elected President of the N.N.C. in his place. Regmi refused point-blank to yield the office to Koirala on his release. Thus, when the N.N.C. was transformed into the N.C., Regmi sheared off his piece, retained the title of N.N.C. and continued as its President. There is still in existence by virtue of this man's ambition a body called the N.N.C. which nominally pursues the same policies as the N.C., only differing in that it does not believe in violent methods. This splinter N.N.C. later divided again, one Shankar Prasad taking the leadership of the shaving off the splinter.

In September 1949 the Communist Party of Nepal was founded. The most prominent member of this party was later to be a Thakur, Dr. K. I. Singh, a distant relative of the King of Nepal.† This man was a Burmese citizen until 1942 when he came to India and later joined the Nepalese National Congress, whose policy up to 1951 was never to come to terms with the Rana régime but to seek its absolute annihilation. K. I. Singh fervently upheld this policy and eventually split with the Koirala brothers on that issue. His doctorate derives from his having set himself up as a homoeopathic physician at Nautunwa, near Gorakhpore, some years before the Nepalese revolution.

Imprisoned in Kathmandu there was still the unrepentant Tanka

* He is a Doctor of the Madras University.

† Dr. K. I. Singh's political colour is in some doubt. He is usually spoken of as a Communist, but his recent activities somewhat conflict with this assessment

Prasad of the Marxist-Leninist Praja Parishad, patronised by King Trib-huvana in the early 1940's.

Of the individuals mentioned above a special interest attaches to the Brahman, Soorya Prasad Upadhaya, the General Secretary of the N.D.C. because he was regarded as an associate of the former Home Member of the Indian provincial Government of Uttar Pradesh and this Minister, R. A. Kidwai, was thus connected with the N.C. by which the N.D.C., along with the influential Soorya Prasad, was absorbed.

The support of the Muslim, Kidwai, was so unexpected as to demand explanation. In 1936 an attempt had been made in India to stir Muslim feeling against the Ranas because of the law forbidding marriages between the small community of Muslims in Nepal and women of the Hindu faith. At that time, at any rate, little notice was taken of this agitation but it may perhaps have influenced a few Muslims of the Indian United Provinces who lived within hail of the Nepalese border.

Except for the party of the C Class Ranas, there was little that was truly Nepalese and less that was Gurkha about any of these organisations. They were at the best 'domiciled' Nepalese, many of them Indian sub-jects: at the worst they were the dregs of the Calcutta *basti* areas, the *goondas* or hooligans whose livelihood for ever depended on the pickings of riot and killings. These creatures and some of the homicidal agents who had before instigated fighting in Kashmir and the violent horrors of the Punjab in 1947 hooked themselves on to the N.C. as its armed force for action against Nepal.

In invoking the sympathies of any of these political parties in his quarrel, the King of Nepal was playing with fire. If he were ever to fall into their power, he would live to regret it. If he ever believed he could control them, he was doomed in the end to disappointment.

The press of India was consistently, and often violently, opposed to the Rana régime and as acutely in support of those Indian political parties, the Congress and the Nepalese National Congress, which displayed hostility to that family. Indeed, sections of the Indian press were so deeply involved in the preparations for the invasion of Nepal that one newspaper in Bombay, of the extreme left, published an article openly promising the support of the King and of the Indian Congress for the projected invasion. After the invasion the same newspaper detailed the whole tactical plan of the campaign.

It has been indicated that, however unaware the Government of India, a former Home Minister of the U.P. Government was associated with the party of the 'invaders'. The full extent of the assistance rendered is not yet known. It has been shown that the plans for the overthrow of the Nepalese Government and for its substitution by a government of individuals introduced from India, albeit acting under the King of Nepal, were initiated and matured by political parties in India who were in close association with the Indian Congress Party, this latter Party being the party of the Government of India from 1947 until the present time, 1956. Furthermore, the Indian press was openly hostile to the then Nepalese Government and certain sections of that press were fully aware of all that was going forward for its violent subversion. Whether the final result of the rebellion is fruitful of good or ill for Nepal, it is at least clear where and by whom it was begun, prepared and executed.

It is fair also to list the Government of India among those opposed to the Rana régime in Nepal.

Ever since the end of the eighteenth century the attitude of India had proved to be of immediate concern to the Government of Nepal and, indeed, to its King. The British at their departure had constituted a totally new State of India, with new boundaries and composed differently from any previous state on the sub-continent. It will long be argued whether, outside those boundaries, it had any hereditary rights whatsoever, for it was a new State, or whether, on the other hand, it inherited the rights and obligations of its predecessor until such time as these were repudiated.

The new State might treat with other rulers such as those of the Indian States or of foreign countries like Nepal and Bhutan in one of four ways. It could hold itself bound by the treaties and agreements of its British forerunner: it could refuse to recognise those contracts: it could continue those it wished to continue and refuse to recognise those it found disadvantageous to itself: it could take them on their merits and strive to act fairly and tolerantly. All states within its borders and on its landlocked north-eastern frontier lay at its mercy. By its forthright behaviour to the Indian States it had shown that it intended to pursue a line of its own, a completely independent policy to protect and to further the interests of the new India. It was therefore not to be fettered by old rules, agreements and precedents. Apart from the Indian States and their claims to a measure of sovereignty, there had been demands for independence put forward somewhat hesitantly by Nagas of Assam and Adibassis of Bihar. These demands were not conceded. Controversy will persist for many years over India's determined behaviour towards Junagadh, Kashmir, Hyderabad and, of late, Goa. Her attitude towards these several problems would be indicative of her attitude towards Nepal, a country which lay along her border and which her leaders regarded as not progressive, governed as it was by a hereditary ruling family holding absolute power. During 1946 and 1947, it was becoming clear that the British Socialist Cabinet and its representatives in India had little regard for the sovereignty of Nepal and Bhutan or for the semi-independence of Sikkim, deeming that, so long as they could 'hand India over to Indians', no one else's interests in those regions were of very much concern. The autocracy of Nepal was uncongenial to the young India. Nepal, as a sovereign state under autocratic rule, might serve as no good example to the huge democracy then in process of forming. The British Government, friendly to both states but still somewhat overwrought by its herculean exertions of the war and the turbulence of the post-war period, was in no mood 'to hold the ring'. So Nepal and India were left to their own devices. Nepal was a judicially independent state, ruled though she was by Chitoria Rajputs whose senior branch still reigned at Udaipur. She was not an 'Indian State'. If King Tribhuvana wanted assistance in hauling down the flag of the Ranas, then here was a willing auxiliary, a zealot for democracy very ready to extend its own territorial responsibilities. He was King in name: if he wanted to be king in fact, here was an ally to help him to that end. What would happen to the Royal Family after the Ranas had been deflated and the new Gurkha Dal party thus left free to form an opposition to the Throne — and, perhaps, to the Indian connection — would only later be apparent. In 1956 that time has not yet come.

Absorbed into India, or as her dependency or colony, Nepal would of course have certain useful assets to offer. She is the lucky possessor of gigantic resources of water-power. She has a great expanse of forest, valuable for timber and for pharmaceutical purposes; jute and indigo are indigenous, the former a welcome substitute for the jute areas lost to Pakistan at the time of partition; there are sulphur-bearing springs and traces of oil on some lakes and rivers north and north-west of Kathmandu: in the Naraini River are ancient gold washings. There may be other minerals also — cobalt, antimony, silver, manganese, nickel, and, possibly, precious stones. There may be more.

It is true that she possessed only three industrial concerns, the matchfactories and the mills in the Terai. Herein the banished C Class Ranas showed their foresight. Mahabir Rana, who was designated for command of the force to invade the area of Biratnagar, and others of his comrades, prepared for the campaign by buying up jute interests in Calcutta at well above market price, for at Biratnagar was the hydro-electric plant and the jute mills.

In view of all that has been recounted in Chapters 24 and 25, it seems strange to set Britain in the lists at that time opposed to the noble Gurkha family of Rana and to the established government of Nepal. The Maharajah Padma had in April 1947 remarked that when the British were gone, his friends, Britain, Australia and New Zealand would be 'very far away'. Distance, with wireless and aircraft, is almost eliminated, but he had made a miscalculation as regards his friends. Australia and New Zealand were indifferent to the fate of the little kingdom whose men had fought beside their men over half the world and whose blood was mingled with their own on the battlefields of Gallipoli, Palestine, Malaya, North Africa and Italy. Nor were they to be interested in the retention of buffer states on a Commonwealth boundary with Communist Asia — in fact, so obviously uninterested that Mao-Tse-tung saw fit to anticipate India's intervention on that frontier by invading defenceless Tibet at six different points on 7th October 1950, just a month before Nepal was invaded from India. The Chinese, of course, had further to march. As might be expected, India's advice to China to settle affairs peacefully with Tibet was ignored, the Chinese Government replying significantly that there might be foreign intrigue in the land of Bod. India's case was not a very good one. One of the buffers was then, with impunity, knocked away. After the declaration of Indian independence, British relations with Nepal had passed from the Indian to the British Foreign Office in London, and Britain appointed an Ambassador to Kathmandu, Nepal on her part appointing her Ambassador to London. Never since the critical days of Brian Hodgson, had Britain so needed at Kathmandu an envoy in the close confidence of the Prime Minister of Nepal.

Britain in these days was ruled by a Socialist Government. It had in 1946 sent its Cabinet Mission to India to arrange for the transfer to Indian hands of the government of that sub-continent. Until 15th August 1947, Independence Day, the relations between Nepal and India were in the hands of the Viceroy of India who was the representative of the Crown and of the Cabinet. Thus the British Government was directly responsible that the Treaty of 1923 was honoured from the British side, in particular that the clause was obeyed binding the British to ensure that Indian soil was never used by anyone working to the detriment of Nepal. Nepal had for her part scrupulously observed this clause at a time when she could, with India in political ferment, have made immense capital and a safe investment for her future by violating it. As has been related, in 1946 a party whose aim was the overthrow of the Nepalese Government took root in Calcutta and from there steadily spread into Nepal. Before the end of the year its mischievous activities were fully apparent, until, as already shown, in March 1947 they took shape in the political strike at Biratnagar in Nepal, seditious agitators from India entering Nepalese territory from Bihar, the U.P. and Western Bengal to manage and to ferment the movement.

While negotiations were proceeding in 1946–47 for the grant of independence to India, the British attitude was that nothing should be said or done that might alienate the Congress Party of India and so, perhaps, abort any sort of agreement. This attitude, for good or ill, was maintained long after Britain had left India. It seemed that, in any case, the autocratic Ranas could expect no support from Britain in any disagreement with the democratic, perhaps Socialist, Indian Congress which was by then the Government of India. For a hundred years the British Resident or Minister had always taken matters affecting their two countries to the Maharajah Prime Minister. No explanation has yet been afforded as to why, as Pandit Nehru stated in Parliament on 13th December 1950, '*In common with other countries* our Ambassador naturally went to the King as the head of the State.'* When passing judgment on the morality, as distinct from any legal consideration, of the behaviour of the British Government in the happenings soon to be related, the two things must be balanced against each other — Britain's debt to the Rana family and to the Gurkhas, against the benefits that might accrue to Nepal through violent interference from outside, the overthrow of her Government by political adventurers, and foreign intervention in her administration, together with the destruction of what was probably the only living example of the pristine Hindu way of life, despite all things in many ways admirable and not lacking in refinement and dignity.

Within Nepal were the rulers and the ruled and the two were fairly distinct, the distinction being most marked in the Valley. The rulers were the Gurkhas, among whom there came to be included the Kirantis, and the ruled were the Newars. The Newars, an old race though not a very proud one, resented the overlordship of Gorkha and resented being excluded from high office and from the Services. As long ago as 1937 one Shukra Raj had in Kathmandu stated that the original inhabitants of Nepal were the Newars; that Newars had perforce been ruled by Rajputs, but that these rulers had always employed them in important positions and that this should be so again; and, significantly, that the King should be restored to power. Shukra Raj was for peaceful reform but he went to prison for six years despite his mild temper. The Newars were intelligent, more so than the Parbatiyas or the Kirantis, and they were scorned.

* See page 256.

To them it was the Ranas, ever present in their great palaces in the Valley, who wielded the heavy stick of the conquerors.

The Parbatiyas were as usual careless but, if anything, likely to side with the descendant of their man, Prithwi Narain Sah. The Kirantis had an ante-chamber at Darjeeling which, though in Indian territory, was cram full of their own folk. Through this front door there entered the nationalism of India, the socialism of the Indian Congress and the revolutionary practices of Bengal and Assam. The Assam tea gardens proliferated Communism and many of the coolies working therein came from about Darjeeling. The Limbu and Rai corner boys of Darjeeling, well pickled in these vinegary ideas, spared no pains to sell them inland into the hills. In Darjeeling, too, was the headquarters of the All-India Gurkha League, the outward symbol of Eastern Nepalese political aspirations, Indian Congress Party in politics, but by no means innocent of self-seeking on the part of its leaders. In the autumn of 1950 there opened upon Eastern Nepal a back door from Communist Tibet into India; the bazaars of Kalimpong, close by Darjeeling, on the main road from India to Sikkim and Tibet soon filled with Chinese traders and political agents.

The Kiranti had always been well treated by the Nepalese Government and by the Ranas, so in fact had little cause to wish to cast off this easy yoke, but 'democratic' or socialist politics are mild or strong intoxicants for the inexperienced, according to the nature of the drinker. With the easily-roused Kiranti they were likely to be potent, more especially so in view of the long centuries of their absolute independence. Limbus and Rais now only awaited the opportunity to throw off the yoke of Gorkha, to break the Rana dominion and to see the last of the high-caste Khas and Brahman officials appointed to them by Kathmandu. Nevertheless, here, as in Western Nepal, the King was held in high respect and the feeling was general that, if a change of government ever came about, then at least the King would be at its head.

Although they were composed of the Gurkha Parbatiyas and the Kiranti, the outlook of the Gurkha regiments of the Indian Army has some bearing on the strength of the opposition to the Rana family. If these regiments had been likely to side with their Maharajah, there could have been no rebellion and no invasion. In the British-Indian Army in August 1947 there were the original ten regular regiments, that is to say, twenty battalions. In addition to these there were roughly the same number of wartime battalions forming the 3rd and 4th battalions of these ten regiments. There had always been a risk that if any of these ten regiments were handed over, lock, stock and barrel to the new India, then the latter would possess a means by which she could exert, if she so minded, a strong influence on affairs in Nepal, perhaps by using the economic lever since she paid these men, or by making play with any sympathies they might have for a particular faction or personality in their country. Of the forty or so Gurkha battalions, Great Britain, despite a desperate shortage of manpower which was certain to become more acute, asked only that she might be allowed to retain eight; India, with her huge excess of manpower, taking the rest.

While the men of these regiments respected the Maharajah, they felt a natural devotion for the King as the pope of their religion and as the descendant of the noted Gorkha chieftain, Prithwi Narain Sah. It was not for them to weigh in the balance the considerable achievements for their country of the Rana Maharajahs, against the backslidings of Prithwi Narain's successors on the throne of Nepal. There was, however, one fly in the ointment as far as the Maharajah and the Rana family were concerned. In Chapter 21 it has been mentioned as a matter of importance that Jang Bahadur insisted that from thenceforth the Ranas should marry none but those of pure Rajput blood. These brides were mostly got from India or the Valley and not from the villages of Western Nepal. Not only did this display an unwarranted disdain for the Parbatiya blood, some of the finest in the Himalayas, but it had the unfortunate effect of estranging this distinguished family from the true Gurkha people who, indeed, had thus of late inclined to regard the Ranas as foreigners and no longer as Gurkhas. Furthermore, the result was to dispose the family to become as careless alien rulers, to neglect the interests of their subjects, not to heed them and to exploit them. The soldiers, both serving and retired, were aware of this; many were ready to seek some other form of government which would care for their needs and raise their standard of living. Of recent years there had been blatant instances of selfishness among their rulers, one of them being the preposterous discount levied by the Nepalese Government on the exchange value of the Indian rupee and the Nepalese mohur, the effect of which was to deprive the devoted soldiers who had fought in the Second World War of no less than 40 per cent of their savings when they returned to their country, in addition to being still further fleeced by the money-changers at the border towns. The British Government of India protested and did all it could to persuade the Nepalese authorities to afford some relief to these men but they consistently refused to do so. As most of the revenues of the country found their way to Kathmandu and to this family, these impositions certainly embittered the men who suffered under them.

Though there was no proper system of taxation in the country, the Rana family managed to take £1,500,000 yearly in revenues, too much of which they devoted to themselves and too little to their country. It was in such circumstances, and when the British Government of India had in 1947 recently capitalised by a gift of £1,750,000 to the Maharajah the annuity that it paid to him, that he was complaining that he had not money enough to build a motor road to supplement the ropeway over the Chandragiri hills. It is not surprising that the Nepalese Congress of India had by 1947 fastened on to the Gurkha Regiments of India, assisted by Congressmen of the Indian Nationalist Party, first of all to impress upon them that British rule was on the point of ending and later to persuade them as to how much better off they would be under the aegis of India. After August 1947 there was no lack of agitators and others to 'brain-wash' the Gurkha soldier.

Anyone acquainted with Nepal and the Gurkhas of that time will find it hard to believe that a revolution and the introduction of jealous and inexperienced foreigners into the political life of Nepal was ever necessary in order to broaden the basis of the Government or to bring about ever-increasing measures of progress. For all to witness to the contrary was the recent example of the Maharajah Chandra Shamsher. There was no reason why a modern version of this Minister should not have been forthcoming. Doubtless the Rana family was wealthy and doubtless far too much of the revenue went into the upkeep of their establishments and to their own private investments. British friendship and firm persuasion, had both been forthcoming, might well have worked wonders in Kathmandu and spared Nepal the five years of confusion, suffering, quarrels between ambitious newcomers, the demoralisation, and the breakdown in law and order which have till now resulted from the invasion launched from India. Perhaps there has been no clear conception of the nature or extent of 'civilisation' that it is proposed to heap upon a Nepal which to many has appeared as Arcadia in the hurrying world about her. Edward Grey has said that civilised man should not progress on the material side beyond plumbing and electric light. In the Valley of Nepal this point had almost been reached: some extension of the two amenities, a more expeditious progress in education and the provision of medical facilities particularly in the hills, would have fulfilled the requirement. In the highlands the piped water was not so great a necessity with springs and streams and rivers in abundance, but some villages indeed had a piped supply and, after all, here in England there are still many rural areas at which the electric and water mains have not yet arrived and many more where earth privies are still the order of the day.

Did it really require a revolution to achieve the benefits of civilisation? Apparently not, for the revolution has not in its five brawling years achieved one tithe of them.* And the cheerful Gurkhas are now perturbed and likely to remain so until a strong personality with a greater love for his country and his people than for himself takes charge of their destinies.

* * * * *

The activities of the N.N.C. were intensified until, from March 1950, the concentrated vigour of the new Nepalese Congress was summoned to the task. Plans then began to crystallise. From Indian soil the N.N.C. had already introduced its fifth column into the Valley and into Eastern Nepal. While preparations for 'invasion' were in progress, the Indian Government concluded a Treaty of Peace and Friendship on 31st July 1950 at Kathmandu, the capital of Nepal. Those at the head of the Government of India in Delhi must have been unaware at that time of what was being forwarded close at hand in their neighbouring Provincial Government, a neglect, untimely and unfortunate.

The Indian Ambassador, Mr. C. P. N. Singh, signed the Treaty on behalf of the Government of India; the Prime Minister of Nepal, the Maharajah Mohan Shamsher, on behalf of his country.

The Treaty stipulated, *inter alia*, that there should be everlasting peace and friendship between the Governments of India and Nepal. The two Governments agreed mutually to acknowledge and respect the complete sovereignty, territorial integrity and independence of each other. The Government of Nepal was to be free to import from or through the territory of India, arms, ammunition or warlike material and equipment necessary for the security of Nepal. Each Government undertook in token of neighbourly friendship between India and Nepal to give to nationals of the other in its territory, national treatment with regard to participation in the industrial and economic development of such territory and the grant of concessions and contracts relating to such developments, Pandit Nehru then made a declaration that India would come to Nepal's aid if she were invaded from Tibet.

Thus while friendly negotiations were in full swing at Delhi, aggressive action was being prepared close by — a most unhappy accident liable to lead to a misunderstanding of the circumstances.

* Written in May 1956.

In October 1950 India signed with Nepal a Treaty of Trade and Commerce.

As Russia had always blocked her candidature for admission to the United Nations,* and as she was not a member of the British Commonwealth, the Government of Nepal had no court of appeal in any subsequent disagreement with India. In November and the months succeeding a situation was to be created in Nepal by agencies operating from India such as to invite and, in the view of some, to excuse the intervention of the Indian Government.

The Maharajah Mohan Shamsher in September 1950 warned India through her Ambassador at Kathmandu that an invasion of his country was being prepared in India. His information was well founded. The enemy was gathering in Bihar and in Uttar Pradesh. In October their bands were moving up by Indian State Railways to the borders of Nepal through those two provinces of India. With them and following them went their supplies and their reinforcements. Later, in early November, the tempo was speeded up, State lorries of the Bihar Government being employed to carry the insurgents to their points of concentration on the provincial border. On 9th November 1950, the Nepal border was crossed at nine points by the forces of the Nepal Congress. An unidentified aircraft, coming apparently from India, dropped leaflets over Kathmandu directing the people to obey the Congress and to use force if necessary. Until late in 1951, this latter organisation, firmly ensconced in the Government of Nepal, was directed from India.

On 13th December 1950, Pandit Jawaharlal Nehru, addressing the Indian Parliament, said of Nepal that he had 'fought not only to continue the old friendship with that country, but to put it on a firmer base',† and he said, 'Three years ago we assured Nepal of our desire that Nepal should be a strong and independent country, and we always added "progressive country". We added that because in the nature of things, we stood not only for progressive democracy in our own country and round about, but even in distant corners of the world.' Pandit Nehru then went on carefully to explain his Government's recognition of King Tribhuvana as the supreme authority in Nepal. 'In common with other countries our Ambassador naturally went to the King as the head of the State, although during the last hundred years or so the King has had no say in his Government. We continue to recognise the King. We see no

---

* Nepal has since been admitted as a member of the United Nations.

† The quotations from Pandit Nehru's speeches are taken from *India Record*, issued by the High Commissioner for India.

reason why we should do anything else. We propose to continue to recognise the King.'

A week later he returned to the subject, 'As the House is aware, we have observed the strictest neutrality in the internal struggle in Nepal.'

29

Nepal and Democracy

———————— ✦ ————————

Of one thing you may be sure, the British Government . . . does not forget those who have deserved well at its hands.

LORD LANSDOWNE, Viceroy of India,
speaking at Quetta, October 1889

THERE is confusion and perplexity in Nepal: there has been confusion and perplexity ever since November 1950. In May 1956 we are too close to the disarray of events and the mingled and uncertain motives to make a proper assessment of their relative importance. All, therefore, that will be attempted in this final chapter is to provide a concise summary of the most notable events running through the months of revolution which led to the downfall of the Ranas.

The rebel force, the Raksha Dal or Mukhti Sena, held in its ranks a number of Nepali watchmen and some of the riff-raff from Calcutta, who had received military training during the Second World War. It was therefore a fairly formidable force, armed as it partly was with modern weapons, S.M.L.E. rifles and automatics, smuggled to it from Assam and Burma during its long period of training and organisation on Indian soil, and lavishly backed by the wealth of the rich émigré, Mahabir Rana. It was commanded by Subarna Rana, its western wing being led by that interesting character, the quasi-Communist Dr. K. I. Singh. While the Doctor was leading his troops on the Gorakhpore front, another Communist and later associate of his, one Rampershad Rai, was commanding a column on the eastern sector.

The most notable successes of the rebels working from their bases in Uttar Pradesh and Bihar were the occupation of Birganj and of Biratnagar, towns of some importance. Birganj was attacked and taken by a force of two hundred to three hundred rebels under Mahindra Bikram Sah, but Biratnagar 'held out' for nearly a month until the Bada Hakim, its Governor, surrendered the place to the leaders, B. P. Koirala and his henchman, G. B. Yakhtumba formerly of the Burma Rifles. The insurgents attacked Bhairawa but failed to take it in the face of the firm defence organised by its Nepalese officials. Rebel columns penetrated deep into the Nepal Terai between these places, and advanced to the foothills near Palpa, having the marked advantage over their adversary of rail communications, both forward and lateral, as opposed to the mountain tracks on which his forces had to operate. Furthermore, as has already been noted, in Bihar the provincial government's own state lorries shifted some parts of the Raksha Dal and their equipment.

General Rudra Shamsher, the banished C Class Commander in the West, was removed from his Command and arrested by the Nepalese Government but promptly released by his soldiers, who had by now become his private army. He thereupon defected to the invaders.

In the Valley of Nepal there was no responsive uprising. Despite the assiduous efforts of the Congress to raise the western highlands by spreading the report that the Ranas were about to imprison the King, these areas also remained unruffled, but in the East, among the Kiranti, this provoking rumour had its effect and there were widespread outbreaks. Both Limbus and Rais rose against the Ranas. The government forces had little chance against disciplined, well-armed and experienced bands, many of them former British-Gurkha soldiers, veterans of many battles in many lands, led by skilled Gurkha officers. Bhojpur and Taplejung were occupied, the Rana garrison holding the strategic bridge over the Timur River on the road to Dhankuta was surprised and routed, and, finally, Dhankuta itself, the last Rana stronghold in the east, was taken. State forces sent to retake Bhojpur were tricked by a *ruse de geurre* by a small force of Rais, and surrendered. Okhaldunga then fell to the rebels.

By 28th November 1950 the Nepalese Army, though in great part com posed of reserves or militia, had reoccupied Birganj and, although the rebels remained in control of the much-coveted Biratnagar, the out break was to all appearances suppressed, though simmering away in pockets along the Terai, to break out again in December. The Nepalese government and its ill-trained units seem to have been gripped by a creeping paralysis. To retake Birganj, a force of a thousand soldiers had been sent from Kathmandu: arrived within five miles of the town, it sat down and demanded reinforcements. Three whole weeks were spent in sending yet another thousand. By this considerable force Birganj was finally reduced.

In the meanwhile there had been drama in high places in Kathmandu. The Maharajah Mohan Shamsher had in recent months at last raised his hand against the forces of violent revolution with whom the King and the rest of the royal family were in correspondence. In September he had uncovered another plot to assassinate himself and most of the leading Ranas. It was alleged that Subarna Shamsher, the Congress Treasurer, and Mahabir Shamsher, its financier, the C Class émigrés in Calcutta, were both implicated. They were alleged to have bribed assassins to shoot the Maharajah Mohan Shamsher as he rode through Kathmandu to the Indra-Jatra festival. King Tribhuvana, fearing that trouble might befall him, sought leave to travel to India for medical treatment. On the Maharajah refusing this request, he gathered up his three sons and the eldest of his grandsons and, on 6th November, on the pretence of going out for a picnic, took refuge in the Indian Embassy. While there, he declined to see the Prime Minister or any of his delegates. It thus came about that the Indian Ambassador offered his services to secure a peaceful settlement of the affair, provided that the King were allowed to go to India. The upshot was that India sent an aircraft to Kathmandu to remove the King and his royal party. At Delhi airport the deposed sovereign was met in person by the Prime Minister of India, Pandit Jawaharlal Nehru. Delhi now held the ace of trumps.

The Nepalese Government, in view of the King's complicity with the revolutionary Nepalese Congress and in view of his having fled his country, and regarding the succession as a domestic affair, announced the abdication of the King and that of the Crown Prince and proclaimed Gyannandra, the elder of the two remaining grandsons, whom they found hidden with his nurse in the cellars of the Palace, as King in Tribhuvana's place.

For many months there had been discussions between the Nepalese Government, who were seeking friendly advice, and the Indian Government on the subject of constitutional reforms in Nepal. As a result of these talks and of the new and untoward situation now developing, Delhi prevailed upon the Maharajah to agree to certain considerable advances in the system of government in his country. There would be an executive council with a popular majority and a Constitutional Assembly would be set up based on universal manhood suffrage. Additionally, Delhi pressed for the return to Nepal of King Tribhuvana. For many weeks the Maharajah would not prepare his own political suicide by agreeing to this last demand, that his mortal enemy, the man who had conspired against him, should return to his capital with the full physical and diplomatic weight behind him of the mighty India. In January he yielded and Tribhuvana came back to his palace in the Valley, accompanied by an Indian private secretary and an Indian administrative adviser. With the 'Delhi Pact' signed and sealed Pandit Nehru successfully appealed to the Nepalese to abstain from violence.

On page 256 there are extracts from Pandit Nehru's speech in December 1950 on the subject of the recognition of the King.

It is doubtful whether this monarch, who had frequently urged his desire to abdicate and to live in India, ever wished to be sent back to Nepal: it is also doubtful if there was among the people of Nepal any general desire for drastic change in their government. Britain could have supported the Maharajah by recognising the young King Gyannandra, but she, and the United States with her, chose to follow the lead of Delhi, to sponsor the deposed monarch and, with him, to foist on Nepal the chaotic and alien rule of the Nepalese Congress. The Government of Nepal, in view of its services to Britain, was deeply injured by this attitude. 'Do you,' Judha had demanded in 1940, 'let your friend down in a time of need?'

Though distressing to those who are unacquainted with diplomatic practice, the behaviour of the British authorities in this matter would not appear to be unusual or unprecedented. In April 1948, under dire threat of invasion by an Indian force, Sir Osman Ali Khan, G.C.S.I., G.B.E., Nizam of Hyderabad, 'Faithful Ally of the British Government', whose ancestor had hastened to Britain's aid in the desperate days of 1857, had written to the British Governor-General of India, 'To break faith with the weak causes perhaps less immediate disadvantage than to break faith with the strong, but assuredly it brings its retribution.'* Within six months Indian Army tanks were grinding the dust of Hyderabad's fields and roads and the Nizam's soldiers were falling before an onslaught ordered, directed and controlled by the Commander-in-Chief at Delhi and by the Army Commander at Poona.

It is relevant at this point to notice that Gurkha Regiments of the Indian Army took part in this invasion, or 'police action' and that, at the request of the Government of India, the Maharajah sent a contingent of about a Brigade of his Nepalese Army to garrison India in an Internal Security role while the bulk of the Indian Army was engaged either in Kashmir or in Hyderabad.

On 8th January 1951 Mohan Shamsher announced the legalising of

* *Fabulous Mogul* by D. F. Karaka.

political parties and a full amnesty for political prisoners not guilty of violence; he welcomed all political parties of Nepalese nationals functioning abroad and those persons in exile who abjured violence and desired to contribute to progress and good government in the country. Thereupon, Dr. D. R. Regmi, the Brahman leader of the splinter N.N.C., entered Nepal from exile in Benares, with a dozen of his staunch supporters. He had always professed his attachment to peaceful methods, and opposed the revolutionary violence of the Nepalese Congress. Tanka Prasad, the Brahman chief of the Praja Parishad, was released and at once started to re-form this Marxist-Leninist society, in due course appointing the Newar Communist, Gauri Bhatta Pradhan, as the Secretary of his new 'United Front' party. Mohan Shamsher also decreed the immediate setting up of a Cabinet of fourteen, half to be Ranas, a separate judiciary and the annual publication of a budget.

On 15th February 1951 King Tribhuvana made public the formation of an interim Cabinet based on the 'Delhi Pact', and a Council was set up consisting of an equal number of Rana members and members of the Nepalese Congress, with the Maharajah Mohan Shamsher as Prime Minister and his brother, Kaiser or Keshar, as Commander-in-Chief and Defence Minister. Just before this M. P. Koirala had been in conference with the leaders of the Congress and they and he had confirmed their determination to fight the war against the Ranas to the bitter end. Without referring the matter back to his colleagues he now accepted this new and most compromising arrangement. On this, Dr. K. I. Singh, who was throughout perfectly consistent, and who may have followed his conscience rather than his own ambitions, threw over the Congress and led his forces against Bhairawa, the headquarters of the Western Terai, just north of Gorakhpore, determined at all costs to throw down the feudal autocracy. This new upheaval was of a certain magnitude, so much so that India intervened and sent armed police into Nepal to arrest him. Because of his widespread popularity he was released, but the firebrand was soon on the warpath again, this time taking to dacoity on the pretext of robbing the rich to benefit the poor — an old game — but was re-arrested and sent up to Kathmandu as a prisoner in the Singha Durbar. At the same time another left-inspired rebellion broke out in the Eastern Terai and near the Tibetan border, hillmen raiding and looting villages in the plains.

Leading the Congress members of the new Cabinet or Council, was M. P. Koirala, with B. P. Koirala as Home Member. At the head of the rebelling C Class Ranas was a familiar figure, Mahabir Rana, who had

262

financed the revolution but who now refused to co-operate with the politicians in this Government. And so it was that Government succeeded Government while Mahabir, taking full advantage of the poor state of King Tribhuvana's health, made money and enjoyed himself among the intrigues of the Valley.

So, in February 1951, the century of Rana dominion came to an end — at any rate for a time. In June General Baber Shamsher, Defence Minister and next to his brother Mohan in the now obsolete Roll of Succession, was ousted from office.

In April the King proclaimed the termination of the hereditary premiership and the transfer of most of the Maharajah's powers to himself. The Maharajah's bodyguard was reduced and the King became Supreme Commander-in-Chief. With the Monarch's assumption of authority political parties cropped up like mushrooms, each with its own leader and his own personal ambitions. Among these was a new party, the Gurkha Dal, later named the Gurkha Parishad, a party of the A Class Ranas whose declared object was the restoration of individual liberty and true democracy, but whose object may also be the restoration of the Ranas by bringing the present Government into disrepute. It is strong financially. Its leader is one General Mrigendra Shamsher Rana, a son of General Baber Shamsher, the former Defence Minister: his assistant is a Limbu, Randhir Subha, a school teacher from Darjeeling and former Vice-President of the All-India Gurkha League. As might be expected it has won support in parts of rural Nepal.

Chaos persisted in the Valley. There was no progress. The new rulers had no conception of government, how to administer, how to plan, how to progress. The Rana and Congress Cabinet fell out, as they were bound to fall out, M. P. Koirala declaring that the Ranas obstructed all suggestions and plans for the betterment of the people, while the Maharajah was resolutely urging the rights of the people against the new despotism. The final break came late in 1951 but not through this quarrel in the Cabinet: it came because of the oppression of the people by the Congress Home Member, B. P. Koirala. The Government, like all revolutionary governments, ran true to form from the very start. It came as the champion of liberty: to survive, it abolished the very liberties it should have promoted. Early in 1951 it passed the 'Public Safety Act', by which it had absolute powers of arrest and detention and to prohibit political meetings. In April there were disturbances created by the new Gurkha Dal and B. P. Koirala's house was wrecked. He applied his Safety Act at once and ruthlessly, and within a few hours the leaders were cast into

263

gaol. But matters were different on 6th November, when students held a banned meeting in Kathmandu and the police marched in and opened fire. One man was killed. There was a riot and, to the relief of M. P. Koirala, his brother became so great an object of hatred that he was compelled to resign. By this time the King had come to realise that his Government was thoroughly detested throughout the Valley, not the least detestable part of it being its pampered and private but still unpaid army, the Raksha Dal, of whose impositions, cruelty and arrogance the inhabitants off whom it lived stood in daily terror. The King dismissed the Government, gladly ridding himself of the Maharajah Prime Minister, Mohan Shamsher.

B. P. Koirala went, firmly determined to sunder the Congress by creating a left wing. Before he quitted, he declared an amnesty and, to his brother's embarrassment, released among others the leaders of the Gurkha Dal.

Hearing from his Congress minister so many complaints of obstructions by the Ranas, the King now decided to form a Cabinet of twelve members, eight of whom were to be of the Nepalese Congress, with M. P. Koirala at its head as Prime Minister and Foreign Minister. Subarna Shamsher Rana was Finance Minister and Soorya Prashad Upadhaya Minister for Home Affairs, later succeeded by Tanka Prasad Acharya. Strangely enough, two A Class Ranas were summoned to this body, the one being the Maharajah's brother, the able and well-educated Kaiser, as Minister of Defence, and the other the Maharajah's son. But the Maharajah himself, who had been in the former Ministry, was not called upon for this one.

In December 1951 the Maharajah Mohan Shamsher, now over seventy years of age, disappointed at the trend of events in his country, shook the dust of Nepal from his feet and retired to live in India at Bangalore. In his farewell message he spoke rather naturally of the kindness shown and good advice given by the Indian Government in whose territory he was about to reside. The King, in somewhat totalitarian terms, praised the retiring Prime Minister of Nepal for 'accommodating himself to the new situation', or, in other and plainer words, for seeing the red light. This same proclamation went on to require the new Prime Minister, M. P. Koirala, to attend to those matters to which the former Government had obviously failed to attend, namely — to ensure that civil rights were properly defined and guaranteed, that an independent judiciary was established free from interference from the executive, that recruitment for the public services was made on the basis of merit, that arrangements were made for the holding of early elections for the Constituent Assembly, if possible by the end of 1952, and that the police and army were trained and organised.

Perhaps the departure of the Maharajah Mohan Shamsher Jang Bahadur Rana may mark the end of Gurkha supremacy in Nepal. History may allot to it the period from 1768 to 1951. From 1951 onwards the people of the Valley, the politicians — Brahman, Newars — are reasserting themselves against the soldiers, the men of Gorkha.

Very soon there were other happenings to dismay the Government. In April 1951, the Raksha Dal, now the nefarious armed police of Nepal, had risen to the occasion and come to their aid to suppress the Gurkha Dal eruption. Since then, because of its political instability, the Government had decided to disband the eastern wing of this, its private army, but the disbandment had gone no further than the intention. In January 1952 the enterprising Dr. K. I. Singh, set free by police rebels, staged a revolt to seize power for the Communists in Kathmandu. He and his supporters occupied part of the city and demanded that the King dissolve the Congress Party Cabinet, install an all-party government, including the Communists, and appoint him as Prime Minister. For a time, having seized the Singha Durbar, he held full authority except for the Royal Palace where the still loyal Mahindra Dal Regiment was stationed. The Raksha Dal mutinied and regular troops had to be called upon to bluff and then suppress the energetic Doctor. The defection of the Raksha Dal and the rotten administration enabled K. I. Singh and his confederate, Rampershad Rai, to escape over the border with an armed party, away into Tibet and later to China. His romantic escape and crossing barefooted, it was said, of the high passes in the depth of winter has created for him a reputation something like that of the dashing Budhuk robber leader of the 1840's, Mangal Sing, or our own Robin Hood. From Tibet Dr. K. I. Singh became a country member of the Marxist-Leninist party of Tanka Prasad, now known as the Left United Front. By the spring of the year Communist literature once more appeared in Kathmandu and before long a branch was set up at Dharan Bazaar, near Biratnagar, close by the future recruiting centre for British Gurkhas. That centre, owing to Indian objections to collecting Gurkhas on their territory for an imperialist power, is to be removed to Dharan in Nepal. Recruits are still collected in Gorakhpore and Ghoom for Indian Gurkhas whence many of them proceed *via* their depots to garrisons in Kashmir or on the borders of Pakistan.

In August 1952 M. P. Koirala resigned and an Advisory Council was set up, General Kaiser soon becoming Principal Adviser to the King. On 15th June 1953 Koirala was recalled as Prime Minister, Dr. D. R. Regmi taking over the Ministry of Foreign Affairs, with Major-General Mahabir Shamsher in charge of Planning, Industry, Commerce, Food and Civil Supplies, and General Kaiser back in his old post at the Ministry of Defence. Kiran Shamsher Jang Bahadur Rana was Commander-in-Chief.

Two years later, by 1955, very little of the King's programme had been fulfilled. In March of that year, King Tribhuvana died and his son, Mahindra Bir Bikram Sah, studious, conscientious and determined, but quiet and modest, who had acted as Regent during his father's absence in Europe for medical treatment, came to the throne. In February, looking upon the wretched conditions to which the country had been reduced by five years of political place-seeking, incompetence, corruption and mal-administration, he had dismissed the Prime Minister and Cabinet, assumed direct control and installed a Council of five. Sardar Ganj Man Sing became Principal Royal Adviser with Anand Shamsher Jang Bahadur Rana as his Deputy. Kiran Shamsher remained as Commander-in-Chief. The Koiralas passed out into political obscurity.

During all these years the meagre results accruing from meddling with Nepal's internal affairs were the breeding of new offices and positions and the introduction of new faces in old jobs. The administration itself showed little change. The Prime Minister came to be regarded in much the same manner as were the Prime Ministers of old, the personage in whom all authority was centred, to the exclusion of the King, with all the pomp and circumstance and the atmosphere of absolute power. He and his Ministers drove about in large cars in full state flying the Congress flag in place of the flag of Nepal. The Prime Minister's house and the Singha Durbar, now the Civil Secretariat, came to appear as small cantonments, so heavily were they guarded, while at each Minister's residence was a piquet armed with sten guns.

The rivalries are still lively. Congress, with the affluent Subarna Shamsher as President, faces National Congress: Gurkha Dal, led by A Class Mrigendra, Baber Shamsher's son, abhors them both: A, B and C Ranas have old differences to settle: sixty-odd more of political parties swarm in this small valley: the Left United Front, though itself somewhat disunited, would pull them all down. In Kathmandu among the students and the Newars, up in far Taplejung on the Kiranti border with Tibet, out in the Parbatiya country round Pokhara and Lamjung, and down near Biratnagar, the Communists are creeping in, but rather from India than from Tibet. Democracy is in disrepute in Kathmandu. And, into this kettle of fish, in September 1955, has been dropped Dr. K. I. Singh who has been granted a Royal pardon, together with his little band of faithfuls, on condition that they forswear violence and pledge loyalty to the Throne. The situation is full of opportunity for this politician if he is true to his red flag, but strange things happen in political Nepal where the King and Dr. Singh are both Thakurs.

In October 1955, after protracted negotiations with three of the main political parties, the Congress, the National Congress and the Nepal Praja Parishad, the King offered to form from these a coalition government with a Cabinet over which he himself would preside. There would be no Prime Minister. The Gurkha Dal declined to join this administration and the other parties insisted on the appointment of a Prime Minister. In January 1956 the King invited Tanka Prasad to form a ministry, the fifth government to be set up since the insurrection. Tanka Prasad's affiliations have already been examined in this and a previous chapter.

Communications are being improved. There is a five-days a week air service between Calcutta and the Valley and an all-weather airfield is being built near Kathmandu, with other airfields at Biratnagar, Pokhara, Simra, Dang Sallyan and Bhairawa. Indian sappers are making a lorry road, paid for under the Colombo Plan, from Bhainse Dobhan eighty-six miles to Thankote to link Kathmandu with railhead at Amlekhganj, thence to Raxaul in India. In 1954 the monsoon rains washed away the pioneer jeep road and its bridges, and caused serious landslides. From Pokhara Nepalese soldiers are cutting another road which has reached Deorali. In the provinces wireless has been installed but the sets are frequently out of order. And China has built a heavy motor road from her railhead at Chengtu to Lhassa, thence to extend it to the Nepalese border at Kuti; she has completed another highway from Lhassa to Phari Dzong near the Sikkim border on the Chumbi Valley road, thus syphoning off through Kalimpong commerce from the Nepalese routes. Eight years ago Mao's soldiers were 1,800 miles from Gangtok, capital of India's protectorate, Sikkim: today they garrison the Tibetan side of the Nathu-La Pass hard by Sikkim's border, on the Chumbi Valley road. Old quiet Gangtok is busy in the front line. Eight years ago the pack animals took trade and travellers from Darjeeling to Lhassa in three weeks to a month: today by car, with short interruptions on a bridle track, the traveller makes the journey in four days. In 1952 Tibet refused to pay to Nepal her annual tribute of 10,000 rupees, emphasising her independence of that Kingdom and referring the King of Nepal to Peking for an answer to his protests. The tribute is not paid.

The Nepalese rupee has lost half its value: those Ranas who have left the Valley have taken their capital with them, those who remain are still wealthy and still very influential. Compulsory labour has been abolished in the hills: at Pokhara there is a European mission hospital doing yeoman work in the region: outside Kathmandu, run by a Catholic Mission and providing a really good education, there is now the Godavari School. The United States Foreign Operations Mission is assisting in village development, in the exploitation of mineral and agricultural resources and in education. In the Valley law and order have deteriorated under the activities of a police who are mainly the riff-raff of Calcutta, only too often themselves responsible for the crimes they are there to prevent, few of which ever occurred in the days of the Ranas. With the more recent recruitment of old British Gurkha soldiers into the Nepal Armed Police,* the forces of law and order should improve. Bribery and corruption are rife over most of the country, deplored by the sufferers who would in all probability indulge themselves in the same way should opportunity offer. With the arrival of 'democracy' the authority of the village *mukhiya*, the head-man, has declined: there is no police to support him and no incentive for him to fulfil his responsible duties now that the one and only reward, that of forced, free labour, is denied him. The old system decays. There is no longer the old, prompt redress for grievances. In the Valley the hundred-year-old curfew is still enforced, but with more excuse than ever before. The cost of living is soaring, bearing hardest on the peasant, the least able to protect himself and the most honest and industrious.

Since 1948 British Gurkhas have been fighting Communist brigands in the forests of Malaya, and Indian Gurkhas have been facing in Kashmir their former friends now in the Pakistan Army.

British and Indian Officers may now visit the recruiting areas of the Parbatiya and Kiranti: there is an Indian Military Mission at work in the country: the army is reduced in size, is being organised as a light division, is more efficient, better housed, fed, equipped and paid, and it has been dispersed from Kathmandu to garrisons in the provinces, a stable element in the promotion of law and order throughout the land. There is also an Indian advisory mission helping the Government to re-organise, and India has assumed responsibility for Nepal's postal services. Away up on the Tibeto-Nepalese border about the 10,000 foot level, at such places as Namche Bazaar and in the upper Kali, are posts manned by Indian police in wireless touch with Kathmandu.

But all is not yet quite well between India and Nepal. The former

* Mainly composed of the old Raksha Dal.

Defence Minister has complained bitterly of Pandit Nehru's guarantee in 1950 of Nepal's outer frontiers, '. . . who is the Prime Minister of India to talk about borders without asking us first if we want to be protected? We have had for centuries excellent relations with China. We do not want to become involved.'* Chinese maps show Nepal as a part of China and Chinese present policy is to draw the northern areas of Nepal towards Tibet, emphasising the Mongoloid nature of these regions — and of Bhutan and Sikkim. Gurkha Hinduism is, however, an impediment to such an attraction. Mao Tse-tung has played his cards with some care in Tibet. His officers have been at pains to avoid interfering with the all-pervading religion, while they have found employment for a large body of unskilled labour. The impression deliberately created should be favourable to the Communist state. All should be placid, especially so because Lamaism has enervated the one-time martial Tibetans, but eastern Tibet still boasts a virile and turbulent few, resolute to cling to what they own.

In May 1956 a Hindu King of Indian Rajput descent, Mahindra Bir Bikram Sah, was crowned in Kathmandu. Soon after, under Chinese auspices, it is expected that the Buddhist Dalai Lama and the Panchin Lama of Tibet will pay a visit to do homage at the shrines of Nepal on the 2,500th anniversary of the enlightenment and the death of the Buddha, thus to emphasise the truly Buddhist character of Nepal. China uses Buddhism† as a magnet to draw Nepal towards Tibet; India, Hinduism to attach her southwards. 200,000 Nepalese settlers in Tibet are being taught to turn their eyes towards Peking, whence cometh their help. In Kathmandu India and China are grappling for the prize of Nepal and not even the sound of the heavy breathing of the contestants reaches the outer world. The outcome may depend on a quite unexpected development — the opening up of Nepal to wealthy tourists from the West, an innovation which will affect the whole of Nepal's economy and her main export, her fighting men.

At Kathmandu on 1st August 1955 Nepal signed an agreement with China to establish normal diplomatic relations. Nepal's Ambassador in Delhi and the Chinese Ambassador in India were to be accredited to China and Nepal respectively, the old treaty of 1792 having been abro-

* The *Manchester Guardian,* 31st March 1955.

† The Lamaic Buddhism of Tibet is in the main animistic. Unlike the religion of Burma and Ceylon, it bears virtually no relation to the teachings of Gaya in India, the priestly fountainhead of the Buddhist faith. The Lamas of Tibet use their religion as a means to shackle politically the peasantry of this vast upland. Mao Tse-tung can, through them, make of it the same use until he choses to replace the Lama hierarchy by a Communist oligarchy.

gated on the fall of the Manchu dynasty in 1912. Pakistan is at this interesting juncture preparing to send an Ambassador to Nepal.

The political ferment and demoralisation has till now been confined almost entirely to the Valley of Nepal. It is an old story, this one of power politics in the Valley. Out in the mountains life flows much as it has flowed for the centuries past, but change may yet come. Nepal of the Gurkhas, the Sahs and the Ranas, has existed for less than two hundred years: Nepal of the Newars and the Mallas is ages old: the Kirantis of Eastern Nepal are an ancient and independent people: the Terai is at least geographically separated, more a part of India than of the Nepalese mountains, whatever its strategic value to Nepal may be. There is much to split Nepal back again and not much at the present time for her to honour and to bind her, now that the Rana cement is being chipped away from the Valley and Western Nepal. There is not even a road to link the Kirantis with the men of the Bara Mangranth, away to the west of the dividing Valley. Furthermore, while the Parbatiyas of Gorkha followed in olden days a Rajput chieftain whose stock had been embedded in their villages for four hundred years, they have slowly inclined away from the same line of Kings and Chiefs since they dug up their roots and went to live in foreign parts and to take to themselves wives from another land.

A vital service that Britain can today render to the unity of this troubled land is to spread the net of recruitment across all the battalions in her service and thus gradually to mix the men of Eastern and Western Nepal in every platoon, every company and every battalion so that when they return to their homes they may speak with one voice, as Gurkhas and not as separate highland clans, nor even as Parbatiya and Kiranti. These two great sections of the mountain people must be brought together to safeguard the integrity, in fact the very future, of the State of Nepal. If they fall apart, their country tumbles into pieces. So decisively, then, can the British Gurkha influence the future of his mountain Kingdom.

* * * * *

No good, only harm, has yet come of the attempt to lather foreign democracy over feudal Nepal. Whatever its rulers in the Valley may deserve, it is a thousand pities that its careless, gallant highlanders of East and West should be required to share in their fate.

It is possible that, as history unfolds from today, this may be the last chapter to be written of the Gurkhas of Nepal.

Civilisation is poorer if democracy strips it of a generous and noble people.

A NOTE ON SOME OF THE
ABORIGINAL TRIBES OF NEPAL

In central Nepal, to the westward of the Valley in scant numbers and nearly in a state of nature, there were Chepang and Kusunda tribesmen, whom Hodgson in 1857 thought to be dwindling races and unlikely to last many years. These, he concluded, had been driven across in the dim past out of Bhutan. In the Nawakote valley, some twenty miles west of Kathmandu, there dwell Kuswar, Botia, Kumha, Bhamru, Denwar and Dari clans who do not belong to the Tartaric stock of the Magars and Gurungs, but rather to that of India, and who are probably immigrants from the plains countless generations ago. These are Awalias. They are termed the 'broken' tribes and were in the country before the 'unbroken' tribes came in from Tibet. The 'unbroken' tribes are the Khas, Magar, Gurung, Newar, Limbu, Rai, Murmi, Lepcha, Bodpa, etc. The Awalias appear to be related to the Hos and Santals, aboriginals of Bihar in India.

Outside the Valley of Nepal there dwell among the more mountainous and less desirable regions a tribe called the Murmis. They are of interest as indicating that, beside the Newars of the Valley, there were certainly other considerable primitive tribes in the country. They may have been an overspill from the highlands of Tibet and, judging by their language, may quite likely have been of the same race as the Newars, but one must confess that here probability may not necessarily be fact The Murmis are something of a mystery. In olden times there may well have been tribes of Tartar or Tibetan stock sprinkled over the mountains from whom Magar and Gurung as they are today have derived or developed under the gradual stress of Indian immigration. Many of the Lamas and all the Tamangs enlisted into the Gurkha Brigade are Murmis. The Tamangs, however, are closely akin to the Gurungs both in customs and language. The Tamangs have become so important as a source of military

271

recruitment that they are now recognised as a clan on their own, rather than merely as a sect of the Murmis. A favourite term today, and probably from centuries past, among Gurkhas is 'Bhotiya', referring to any Buddhist mountain barbarian of Tibetan type — a man from Bhot or Tibet. This rather vague term may often have been used by writers to describe what is in fact a type rather than a tribe. The 'Bhotiya' may have been the aboriginal of most of the Nepalese highlands. The Murmis are a case in point. They have come to be looked down upon, and the scornful title of Siyena Bhotiya, or plain Bhotiya, is given them to denote a carrion eater, as they were so fond of beef that, while they were not permitted by the Brahman priests to slaughter cattle, they would readily fall to on any oxen that died a natural death.

Little by little they have been elbowed into the fastnesses of the Himalaya as the rest of the inhabitants, imbibing the pure springs of Hinduism, have come to see this disreputable relative as less and less of a credit to them, better to be out of sight and forgotten.

In the Army officers will sometimes come across men from the highest altitudes, of Tibetan stock and dialects, Lamaic Buddhist by religion . . . Sherpas, Singsapus and Yolmas. The famous Sherpa mountaineers are from the Solu Kambu foothills of Mount Everest: the others from the north of the Valley. Little is yet known of the two last. Obscurity does not render them aboriginal: they are Tibetan immigrants of centuries ago, quite untouched by Hindu influence.

Over the term, or surname, Lama, there is some confusion. In Eastern Nepal and Darjeeling District it may cover any Buddhist of Tibetan stock as well as the Dhukpa from Bhutan. In turn all these may be spoken of as Bhotiyas.

From time to time other small peoples emerge as soldiers from the recruiting depots, such as Bhujel, who are slaves freed ages ago; Thami, Giri and Sunyesi, about whom very little is known. Majhe are professional boatmen, very useful in the Burma campaign; Kumel are potters. Both are of low caste and not usually enlisted. Among menials and low-caste men are Sonar (goldsmiths and silversmiths), not to be confused with the martial Sunwars: Kami or Lohar (blacksmiths): Sarki (leather workers): Damai (musicians and tailors). Humblest of the humble are the Poris, the sweepers. Some day experts will unearth the origin of these lesser folk.

THE GURKHA SYSTEM

———————— ❈ ————————

To understand the story of the Gurkha period in Nepal it is necessary to have some idea of the system of government that obtained in Nepal on Prithwi Narain's death. It may be classified as feudal both on the civil and the military side, the military predominating. Kirkpatrick in 1793 and Hamilton in 1892 made notes of the social, political and military systems of the country. Their personal observations were confined to the Valley of Nepal but they were both men of an enquiring turn of mind and much of what they have to say is borne out by those who came later. There is, however, a marked difference in character between the peoples of the Valley and of the Hills, particularly the western hills. The highlanders are more easy-going and more friendly and tolerant, like most other peasants.

At the head of the Government was the King, the Maharajah himself. Beneath him was a Bharadar or Council of State consisting of the following officials.

The Chauntriya. This was the Prime Minister, a near relative of the Ruler. In Prithwi's and Bahadur Sah's time there was usually only one of these, very occasionally two. As conquests added territory to the State, the number was increased to four and the duties put into commission. One of his first duties was to deal with inefficient or intractable officials, putting their cases to the King who could put them to the Panjni, or Court of Inspection. In any event, all offices were annually surrendered to the King who placed them before the Panjni to be filled. The Chauntri-yas as a body came to have a certain influence over the King's conduct of affairs but a strong Prime Minister such as Bhim Sen or Jang Bahadur could treat them lightly. The Prime Minister's emoluments came from fiefs granted by virtue of his office and from a commission on the rice-fields of the kingdom.

The Kajis. There were four of these. Their business was to super-

T

intend all civil and military affairs. Being a military Government, the rank was equivalent to that of a General or Commander-in-Chief. They managed the revenue and the Crown lands. The Senior Kaji was entrusted with the Red Seal of the King and ranked next to the Chauntriya.

The Sirdars commanded the armies and ruled the provinces. There were four Sirdars in the Council.

The two Khurdars were the King's secretaries who prepared all his despatches, both to his own officials and to foreign powers.

The Khazanchi or Treasurer, who not only regulated the transactions of the Treasury but also had charge of the public wardrobe from which dresses of honour were presented by the King.

The Kapradar, or Keeper of the private wardrobe and the King's jewels, and superintendent of the royal kitchen.

In addition to these important officials there were, at the centre of Government, the Tiksali or superintendent of the Mint; the Dharma-adhikar, chief criminal judge, whose sentences had to be approved by the King before they could be put into execution: four Bicharis whose business it was to investigate and report on all civil matters and to enquire into disputes over land and other property, sometimes presided over the Dharma-adhikar: the Dittha, or Chief Constable, at the head of the police, who also supervised the Bicharis: the Jaitha-Burra (meaning 'The Elder') whose business was to discharge offices of a complimentary nature, bear despatches to Governors and to proceed on embassy.

Then there were the Subahs who were Governors of districts, often 'farmers' of taxes and tax-collectors of all sorts, working under military officers, Sirdars; and the Umaras who commanded military stations and fortresses, also under the Sirdars.

Out in the provinces the Lord of the Manor (*gang*) was an Umara-Muqaddem. Over anything from ten to twenty of these *gangs*, presided a Chaudhri, assisted by a Majumdar, or accountant. In cases of dispute or petty crime, one or other of these officers summoned a Panchaiyat, a court of elders, from whose sentence appeal could be made to the King's Court. Here the Bichari would adjudicate, referring the matter if he thought it sufficiently serious, or in case of appeal from his finding, to the Karyi, the King's Minister. The King would then order the Bichari to summon a Panchaiyat and the case would be heard again, the King himself now deciding upon the punishment after consulting the Dharma-adhikar on points of law. There was yet another court of appeal if the criminal did not accept the royal decision — to the Bharadar, or Council of State.

The Law was based on the Hindu *Shastras*.

Evidence was seldom taken on oath, though there was provision for this to be done by placing in the hand of the witness the Haribansa, a part of the holy scripture, the Mahabharat. The Gorkha dynasty was the first to introduce trial by ordeal, the most familiar of which, the ordeal of water, was well known in India at the time. After a great deal of religious ceremony, two men, strangers to the contestants, submerged themselves. Depending upon which man surfaced first, the verdict was given. As this was a lottery in which the first man up would in ignorance be casting his vote either way, the result might bear no relation to the rights of the case. The ordeal was, however, undertaken voluntarily by both litigants, so they had no complaint at the outcome.

The recognised punishments for serious offences were confiscation of the whole estate, banishment of the whole family, degradation of the whole family by delivering the members to the lowest tribes, maiming the limbs, and death by cutting the throat. The Gorkha Kings introduced other capital punishment such as hanging and flaying alive. In accordance with Hindu custom women were never put to death but they might be, and were, subjected to terrible punishments, the most common being to cut off the nose, while for torture they would be smoked in a small chamber with the suffocating fumes of capsicum. Rank and birth made no difference to the nature of the punishment. Brahmans were, however, also exempt from capital punishment.

Fines could be either *Prayaschit* for religious backsliding, or for crimes, the fines for the latter being paid to the King and the former being split into eight shares of which the King took one, two other officials one each, and the remaining five went to the Brahman families, among whom were the Pandes.

The Subahs of districts could not inflict any of the severe punishments, so seldom had with them any legal adviser. Sirdars had powers of capital punishment. As a military Government, crimes and punishments, civil and military, became inextricably mingled.

The Chaudhris collected the land revenue and passed it on to the Subah who, as often as not, 'farmed' the taxes, guaranteeing a certain annual sum to the State and taking for himself whatever else he could exact without driving the people to forcible resistance. This was not the last of the taxation, for if ever the King at any time found himself short of funds he would send a special royal collector to gather in the Rajangka.

The establishment of the army was essentially feudal. In some parts of the country the Company Commanders were assigned land and in return had to maintain a properly armed Company of regular soldiers. In other parts the system was more complicated. Some soldiers received their pay from the Treasury, some were paid from the Granary, some partly in land and partly in money, but the most usual method was to give them land where they could settle their families. On the whole, as was consistent with a military régime, the soldier was treated fairly and generously so that he had no anxiety as to the well-being of his family and his relations.

The Pati, or squad of twenty to twenty-five fusiliers, was the smallest sub-unit, commanded by a Jemadar, with one Havildar and one Amaldar as N.C.O.s. It is interesting that the term 'Amaldar' was quite common among the men in British Gurkha units to denote a Naik or Corporal. The Jemadar received seven to twelve *khets*, or fields, of land and two hundred rupees in money. Over him was the Subahdar or Company Commander whose Company might be five or six Patis, and always had a band of ten musicians if it were of six Patis. The Company was the military unit, containing the necessary tradesmen and artificers. The Subadar's pay was fifteen to twenty-four *khets* of land and four hundred to five hundred rupees a year. For arms the men had firelocks or bows and arrows, *khoras* and *kukris*. They did not use the bayonet but seem to have had some means of fixing the *kukri* to the muzzle of the fire-weapon.

Hamilton, in 1802, made these observations on slavery in the kingdom.

'In Nepal most of the domestic servants are slaves. A male slave is called a *keta*, and costs about thirty Mohurs. A female is called *keti*, and costs about the same price; but if young and handsome she will bring ten Mohurs additional. There are some Brahmans who are slaves even to Rajputs: but they are not degraded by the name *keta*, and are employed in great families, either as cooks or in the service of the private chapels. All other ranks are sold for common slaves: and persons of the best families have often been degraded by the Rajas, and given to the Damais or Tailors, by which they lose not only their liberty, but their caste, which is of more importance to a Hindu. In general, however, among the higher tribes, the caste of the slave is respected, and no duty is imposed on him, by which that would be injured. It is reckoned very disgraceful for any persons but those of the lowest rank, to sell their children to any person of impure birth, or who is an infidel. Still, however, this is occasionally done by persons of high birth, who happen to be in necessitous circumstances; nor do the parents on this account lose caste. They would however, inevitably become outcasts, should they ever afterwards admit their child into their house, even were he to be set at liberty by his master. Most of the slaves, it must be observed, have been born free.

A few have been degraded and sold by the Raja on account of crimes alleged against them: but by far the greater part have been sold by necessitous parents. All the *ketis*, even those belonging to the Queen, are prostitutes, and therefore seldom have children. . . . The *ketis* of the Court, indeed, are allowed some privileges, and have a considerable influence among the young men of the family. In the daytime they attend the Maharani or Queen; and when she goes out, some of them armed with swords, follow her on horseback, and form her bodyguard. They are well dressed, and ride astride like men. . . .'

He describes the ill-treatment meted out to the slaves in Nepal. Later writers show that much of this had certainly changed and that on the whole the slaves were well treated and that some were not at all wishful to change their circumstances, instancing cases of male slaves who had become wealthy but still remained with their masters and maintained them out of their earnings.

'The masters in general do not give their slave girls any other allowance than a small quantity of rice; and a great many of them are so obdurate, that even this allowance is stopped, when sickness prevents the slave from working. The poor creatures are therefore forced to sacrifice their chastity, in order to procure clothing; and beggary is the usual resource of those who are old and infirm!'

AN ACCOUNT OF AN EMBASSY TO THE COURT OF THE TESHOO LAMA IN TIBET; IN 1783

———————————❋———————————

by Captain Samuel Turner
(Messrs G. & W. Nicol, Pall Mall. 1806)

'THE affairs of Tibet continued in a flourishing and prosperous state till the year 1792, when intelligence was received that a race of people who inhabit the mountains of Nipal, which are situated to the south of Tibet, to the west of Bootan, and border on the northern frontier of Bengal, had commenced hostilities against the states of Tibet. A numerous body were reported to be then in motion, and actually engaged in open invasion of the possessions of Teshoo Lama, to whose superior power, a nation without soldiers and without arms, was quickly found to be an easy prey.

'The progress of the Nipalese then was rapid in the extreme; and though, roused by the alarm, multitudes assembled in the way, they could oppose no effectual resistance against the rude incursion of an impetuous enemy, naturally daring, and now animated with the hope of plunder. Their advance, therefore, against a panic-stricken and unarmed multitude, was but very slightly impeded. No sooner had the alarm been given, than they appeared before Teshoo Loomboo [Digarchi], and with great difficulty the Lama, himself, and all the Gylongs of the monastery, found means to escape in time across the Berhampooter. Here, choosing a station remote from the river, the party remained awhile free from annoyance or pursuit; till at length the Lama, when it was perfectly ascertained that his capital had become a prey to the rapacity of plunderers, was conducted by slow marches towards Lassa.

'In the mean time the Nipalese, eager to possess the spoils, which

278

the fortune of war had placed within their reach, abandoned themselves entirely to plunder. The valuable booty, which had for ages been accumulating at Teshoo Loomboo, appears to have been the chief, if not the sole, object of their inroad; for no sooner had they stripped the monastery of its treasures, and robbed the mausolea of the Lamas of all their most valuable ornaments, than they withdrew themselves towards the frontier, in order that they might effectually secure the spoils they had acquired.

'In the mean time intelligence was conveyed, with the utmost expedition, to the court of China, of this daring and unprovoked aggression, from a people who had commenced hostilities upon the sacred territory. This information was no sooner received in China, than an edict was issued for the instant formation of an army, to protect and avenge the Lama.

'The borders of Tartary, immediately contiguous to China, afforded a force amply sufficient for the occasion; and troops were summoned to assemble, and directed to proceed without delay, to Teshoo Loomboo. The Nipalese, however, had already decamped from thence, with a view immediately to lodge in safety, the treasures of which they had stripped the monastery. This purpose having been completely accomplished, they then reassembled in full force upon Tingri Meidan, an extensive plain, lying about midway between Nipal and Teshoo Loomboo, where they determined to wait, and try their strength, in case the Tibetians should choose to give them battle.

'The Chinese general, with the Tartar troops under his command, advanced without hesitation, and with a fixed determination to attack the enemy, having first directed the Tibetians, whom he came to succour, to keep aloof during the contest, that he might have only, under his command, men who had been disciplined and trained to arms. Thus adopting every necessary and prudent precaution, he marched to attack the enemy, and a severe contest is said to have been obstinately maintained, which at length terminated in the complete defeat of the Nipalese.

'The general being determined to pursue his success with all convenient speed, came up with the enemy again immediately, upon the frontier: here he engaged them a second time with the same good fortune as at first. The Nipalese were now forced to abandon the confines of Tibet, and hastened to enter their own territories. The pass, upon the borders of Nipal, was protected by a military post called Coti, and this they took especial care to strengthen with a powerful detachment, sufficient to keep the Chinese force in check, for a considerable time. From the advantage of position, these troops were enabled at first to maintain themselves against all assaults; but at length worn out by repeated attacks, the Nipalese were ultimately compelled to abandon this place also, and retire within the fastnesses of their mountains: yet this step was not determined on, without the most prudent circumspection. All the roads upon the hills were broken up, the bridges were removed from across the torrents, and every possible object was thrown in the way of the enemy.

'Thus closely pressed by a victorious army, and destitute of any immediate resource, the Nipalese were induced to solicit the interference of the British Government.

'Captain Kirkpatrick, an officer in our service, was at this time appointed ambassador to Nipal, and he was the first of our nation who ever obtained admission into that country. The object of his embassy was considered in different points of view, by the parties that were either directly, or remotely, engaged in the present contest. The Chinese commander is said to have made no very favourable report of the English, at his court, for he viewed our connection with the Nipalese in a most inauspicious light. These representations from him, and our declining to afford effectual assistance to the Lama's cause had considerable weight at the Chinese court; the similarity of dress and discipline between the Nipal soldiers and the battalions in the British service, is said, also, to have been most forcibly stated, and not without considerable effect, since the suspicious character of the Chinese could hardly be persuaded to believe that we had not given assistance to their enemies.

'The Chinese troops, however, pursued their fortune with uniform success; and, daunted by their superior conduct and courage, the Nipalese now began to look upon all further resistance as vain, and immediately had recourse to the most abject and most submissive entreaty.

'The Chinese general at length listened to their overtures, and granted them a peace, upon the conditions of an annual tribute to the empire, and the full restitution of all the spoils which they had carried away from the monastery of Teshoo Loomboo. Hostages were delivered for the due execution of these engagements; the stipulations of the treaty were performed, and the army under the Chinese general withdrew, but not without establishing several military posts along the southern frontier. So careful, indeed, were the Chinese to avail themselves of every possible advantage within their reach, that they occupied an intermediate country between Bootan and Nipal, the territory of a petty chief, denominated Raja of Segwin or Seccum, [Sikkim], who had been sometimes vexed by the hostile interference, and long obnoxious to the caprice and rapacity of the Nipalese, on his offering to become subject to China, and accepting protection from the victorious general. A station was then established, of which a guard was left in charge; and thus the Chinese were put into actual possession of a military post, immediately adjoining the territory of the East India Company in Bengal.

'The Chinese commander attempted to extend his frontier over the country of the Deeb Raja, which bounds the possessions of the Company on the north, by a long continued line; but he was not permitted to lead his forces over the intermediate mountains of Bootan; and, in consequence of the opposition made by the Deeb Raja to his design, he was necessarily obliged to become content with establishing a station on their northern boundary, at Phari, which is a post of strength, upon the frontier of Tibet.'

Turner then goes on to say that this turn of events put a complete stop to the intercourse between the Company and Sikkim and Tibet. An Iron Curtain of jealous Chinese power had been let fall across the frontiers of these lands so that even the Hindu Gosains, the holy men, were evicted from Tibet and forbidden to return.

He, himself, had entered Tibet through Bhutan, following the Tehin-Tchieu River, the Pa-tchieu River to Phari, thence across by the Rham-tchieu Lake, where he and his party skated in December 1783, down the Pynom-Tchieu River to Teshoo Loomboo, near the banks of the Brahmaputra.

This Nepalese excursion into Tibet produced a situation in which China and Britain might easily have come into conflict in the eighteenth century for the possession of Eastern India, Bengal and Assam.

EXTRACTS FROM
'PAPERS REGARDING THE ADMINISTRATION
OF THE MARQUIS OF HASTINGS IN INDIA'

———————— ❈ ————————

Translations of intercepted Letters, April 12th 1815.
From Ummer Sing, and his sons Ram Doss and Urjun Thappa,
to the Rajah of Nepaul, dated Raj Gurh, 2nd March 1815.

A COPY of your letter of the 23rd December, addressed to Runjore Sing, under the red seal, was sent by the latter to me, who have received it with every token of respect. It was to the following purport: 'The capture of Nala Panee by the enemy has been communicated to me from Gurhwall and Kamaon, as also the intelligence of his having assembled his force and marched to Nahun. He now occupies the whole country from Barra Pursa to Subtura Muhotree. My army is also secretly posted in various places in the jungles of the mountains. An army under a General has arrived in Goruckpore from Palpa; and another detachment has reached the borders of Beejapore. I have further heard, that a General Officer has set out from Calcutta to create more disturbance. For the sake of a few trifling objects, some intermediate agents have destroyed the mutual harmony and war is waging far and wide. All this you know. You ought to send an Embassy to conciliate the English otherwise the cause is lost. The enemy, after making immense preparations, have begun the war, and unless great concessions are made, they will not listen to terms. To restore the relations of amity by concession is good and proper. For this purpose, it is fit, in the first place, to cede to the enemy the departments of Bootwul, Palpa, and Sheoraj, already settled by the Commissioners, and the disputed tracts towards Barra. If this be insufficient to re-establish harmony, we ought to abandon the whole of the Terraie, the Dhoon, and the Lowlands; and if the English are still dissatisfied, on

282

account of not obtaining possession of a portion of the mountains, you are herewith authorized to give up along with the Dhoon, the country as far as the Sutleje. Do whatever may be practicable to restore the relations of peace and amity and be assured of my approbation and assent. If these means be unsuccessful, it will be very difficult to preserve the integrity of my dominions from Khunka Irishta to the Sutleje. If the enemy once obtain a footing in the centre of our territory, both extremities will be thrown into disorder. If you can retire with your army and military stores, so as to pursue any other plan of operations that may afterwards appear eligible, it will be advisable. On this account, you ought immediately to effect a junction with all the other officers in the western service, and retire to that part of our territory which (including all in your rear as far as Nepaul) you may think yourself capable of retaining.' These are your orders. In the first place, after the immense preparations of the enemy, he will not be satisfied with these concessions; or if he should accept of our terms, he would serve us as he did Tippoo, from whom he first accepted of an indemnification of six crores of rupees in money and territory, and afterwards wrested from him his whole country. If we were to cede to him so much country, he would excite another disturbance at a future opportunity, and seek to wrest from us other provinces. Having lost so much territory, we should be unable to maintain our army on its present footing; and our military force being once reduced, what means should we have left to defend our eastern possessions. While we retain Beshehur, Gurhwall is secure; if the former be abandoned, the Bahateras of Rewanee will certainly betray us. The English having thus acquired the Dhoon and Rewanee, it will be impossible for us to maintain Gurhwall; and being deprived of the latter, Kamaon and Dootee will also be lost to us. After the seizure of these provinces, Acham, Joomba, Dooloo, Duelekh, will be wrested from us in succession. You say, 'That a proclamation has been issued to the inhabitants of the eastern "Kurats".' If they have joined the enemy, the other Kurats will do so likewise and then the country from Dood Koosi on the east, to Bheri on the west, cannot long be retained. Having lost our dominions, what is to become of our great military establishment? When our power is once reduced, we shall have another Knox's Mission, under pretence of concluding a treaty of alliance and friendship, and founding commercial establishments. If we decline receiving their mission, they will insist; and if we are unable to oppose force, and desire them to come unaccompanied with troops, they will not comply. They will begin by introducing a company, a battalion will soon after follow, and at length an Army will be assembled for the subjugation of Nepaul. Thus you think, that if, for the present, the Lowlands, the Dhoon, and the country to the Sutleje were ceded to them, they would cease to entertain designs upon the other Provinces of Nepaul. Do not trust them. They who counselled you to receive the mission of Knox, and permit the establishment of a commercial factory, will usurp the Government of Nepaul. With regard to the concessions now proposed, if you had, in the first instance, determined upon a pacific line of conduct, and agreed to restore the departments of Butwool and Sheoraj, as adjusted by the Commissioners, the present contest might have been avoided. But you could not suppress your avarice and desire to retain these places and having murdered the Revenue Officer, a commotion arose, and War was waged for trifles. At Jytuck we have gained a victory over the enemy. If I succeed against Ochterlony, and Runjore Sing with Juspoo Thappa and his officers prevail at Jytuck, Runjeet Sing will rise against the enemy. In conjunction with the Seikhs, my Army will make a descent into the plains, and our forces crossing the Jumna from two different quarters, will recover possession of the Dhoon. When we reach Hurdwar, the Nawaub of Lucknow may be expected to take a part in the cause; and on his accession to the general coalition, we may consider ourselves secure, as far as Khunka. Relying on your fortune, I trust that Bulbudder Koon and Rewunt Kajee will soon reinforce the garrison of Jytuck; and I hope ere long to send Punt Kajee with eight companies, when the forces there will be very strong. The troops sent by you are arriving every day; and when they all come up, I hope we shall succeed both here and at Jytuck.

Formerly, when the English endeavoured to penetrate to Sindoolee they continued for two years in possession of Barra Pursa and Mahatree; but when you conquered Nepal, they were either destroyed by your force, or fell victims to the climate, with the exception of a few only who abandoned the place. Orders should now be given to all your officers to defend Choundinde and Chounund in Beejapore, the two Kurats, and the ridge of Mahabharut. Suffer the enemy to retain the lowlands for a couple of years: measures can afterwards be taken to expel them. Lands transferred under a written agreement cannot again be resumed; but if they have been taken by force, force may be employed to recover them. Fear nothing, even though the Seikhs should not join us. Should you succeed now in bringing our differences to an amicable termination by the cession of territory, the enemy in the course of a few years would take possession of Nepal, as he did the country of Tippoo. The present is, therefore, not the time for treaty and conciliation. These expedients should have been adopted before the murder of the revenue officer, or must be postponed till victory shall crown our efforts. If they will then accede to the terms which I shall propose, it is well: if not, it will be my business, with the favour of God and your fortune and country, to preserve the integrity of my country from Khunka to the Sutleje. Let me entreat you, therefore, never to make peace. Formerly, when some individuals urged the adoption of a treaty of peace and commerce, I refused my assent to that measure; and I will not now suffer the honour of my Prince to be sullied by concession and submission. If you are determined on this step, bestow the humiliating office on him who first advised it; but for me, call me to your presence. I am old, and only desire once more to kiss your feet. I can recollect the time when the Goorkha Army did not exceed twelve thousand men. Through the favour of Heaven and the renown of your forefathers, your territory was extended to the confines of Khunka on the east. Under the auspices of your father we subjugated Kamaon, and through your fortune we have pushed our conquests to the Sutleje. Four generations have been employed in the acquisition of all this dignity and dominion. At Nala Panee, Bulbudder cut up three or four thousand of the enemy: at Jytuck, Runjore Sing with his officers overthrew three battalions. In this place I am surrounded, and daily fighting with the enemy, and look forward with confidence to victory. All the inhabitants and Chiefs of the country have joined the enemy. I must gain two or three victories before I can accomplish the object I have in view of attaching Runjeet Sing to our cause. On his accession, and after the advance of the Seikhs and Goorkas towards the Jumna, the Chiefs of the Deccan may be expected to join the coalition, as also the Newaub of Lucknow and the Salih Ramee Saudh. Then will be the time for us to drive out the enemy and recover possession of the low countries of Palpa as far as Beejapore. If we succeed in regaining these, we can attempt further conquests in the plains. There has been no fighting in your quarter yet. The Choundinde and Choundund of Beejapore, as far as the ridge of Mahabharut and Selleanah, should be well defended. Countries acquired in four generations, under the administration of the Thappahs, should not be abandoned, for the purpose of bringing matters to an amicable adjustment without deep and serious reflection. If we are victorious in the War, we can easily adjust our differences; and if we are defeated, death is preferable to reconciliation on humiliating terms. When the Chinese Army invaded Nepaul, we implored the mercy of Heaven, by offerings to the Brahmins and the performance of religious ceremonies; and through the favour of one and the intercession of the other, we succeeded in repulsing the enemy. Ever since you confiscated the jageers of the Brahmins, thousands have been in distress and poverty. Promises were given that they should be restored on the capture of Kangra, and orders to this effect, under the red seal, were addressed to me and Nya Sing Thappa. We failed, however, in that object, and now there is an universal commotion; you ought, therefore, to assemble the Brahmins, and promise to restore to them their lands and property in the event of your conquering and expelling the English. By these means, many thousand respectable Brahmins will put up their prayers for your protection, and the enemy will be driven forth. By the practice of charity, the territory acquired in four generations may be preserved, and through the favour of God, our power and dominion may be still further extended. By the extension of territory, our military establishment may be maintained on its present footing, and even increased. The numerous countries which you propose to cede to the enemy yielded a revenue equal to the maintenance of an army of four thousand men, and Kangra might have been captured. By the cession of these provinces, the fear of your name and the splendour of your Court will no longer remain. By the capture of Kangra your name would have been rendered formidable; but though that has not happened, a powerful impression has nevertheless been made on the people of the plains, by the extension of our conquests to the Sutleje. The effect a reconciliation by the cession of the country to the west of the Jumna, would give rise to the idea that the Goorkas were unable to oppose the English, would lower the dignity of your name in the plains, and cause a reduction in your Army to the extent of four thousand men. The enemy will, therefore, acquire possession of Beshehur, and after that the conquest of Gurhwall will be easy: nor will it be possible, in that case, for us to retain Kamaon; and with it we must lose Dootee, Acham, and Joomba. He may be expected to penetrate even to Bhoree. If the English once establish themselves firmly in possession of a part of the hills, we shall be unable to drive them out. The countries towards the Sutleje should be obstinately defended: the abandonment of the disputed tracts in the plains is a lesser evil. The possession of the former preserves to us a road to further conquests. You ought, therefore, to direct Gooroo Rungnath Pundit and Dulb-hunjur Paudre to give up the disputed lands of Bootwul, Sheoraj, and the twenty-two villages in the vicinity of Barra, and if possible, bring our differences to a termination. To this step I have no objections, and shall feel no animosity to those who may perform the service. I must, however, declare a decided enmity to such as, in bringing about a reconciliation with the English, consult only their own interests and forget their duty to you.

If they will not accept the terms, what have we to fear? The English attempted to take Bhurtpore by storm; but the Rajah Runjeet Sing destroyed a European regiment and a battalion of Sepoys. To the present day they have not ventured to meddle with Bhurtpore, and one fort has sufficed to check their progress. In the low country of Dhurma (perhaps Bhurma) they established their authority; but the Rajah overthrew their Army and captured all their artillery and stores, and now continues in the quiet possession of his dominions. Our proffers of peace and reconciliation will be interpreted as the result of fear, and it would be absurd to expect that the enemy will respect a treaty concluded under such circumstances. Therefore, let us confide our fortunes to our swords, and by boldly opposing the enemy, compel him to remain within his own territory; or if he should continue to advance, stung with shame at the idea of retreating after his immense preparations, we can then give up the lands in dispute and adjust our differences. Such, however, is the fame and terror of our swords, that Bulbudder, with a nominal force of six hundred men, but scarcely amounting to five hundred, destroyed an Army of three or four thousand English. His force consisted of the old Gorukh and Burukh companies (which were only partly composed of the inhabitants of our ancient Kingdom) and of the people of the countries from Bheri to Gurhwall, and with these he destroyed one battalion and crippled and repulsed another. My Army is similarly composed; nevertheless, all descriptions are eager to meet the enemy. In your quarter, you are surrounded by the veterans of our Army, and therefore cannot apprehend desertions among them: you have also an immense militia, and many Jageerdars who will fight for their own honour and interests. Assembling the militia of the low lands and fighting in the plains is impolitic: call them into the hills, and cut them up by detail. [A passage here, the sense of which cannot be discovered.] The enemy is proud and flushed with success, and has reduced under his subjection all the western Zemindars, the Ranas and Rajahs of Kurnoul and the Takhoorae, and will keep peace with no one. However, my advice is nothing. I will direct Ram Doss to propose to General Ochterlony the abandonment on our part of the disputed lands, and will forward to you the answer which he may receive. All the Rajahs, Ranas, and Takhoorae, have joined the enemy, and I am surrounded. Nevertheless, we shall fight and conquer; and all my officers have taken the same resolution. The Pundits have pronounced the month of Bysack as particularly auspicious for the Goorkas, and by selecting a fortunate day we shall surely conquer. I am desirous of engaging the enemy slowly and with caution, but cannot manage it, the English being always in a desperate hurry to fight. I hope, however, to be able to delay the battle till Bysack, when I will choose a favourable opportunity to fight them. When we shall have driven the enemy from hence, either Runjore Sing or myself, according to your wishes, will repair to your presence. In the present crisis it is very advisable to write to the Emperor of China, to the Lama of Lassa, and to the other Lamas; and for this purpose I beg to submit the enclosed draft of a letter to their address; any errors in it will, I trust, be forgiven by you; and I earnestly recommend that you lose no time in sending a petition to the Emperor of China and a letter to the Lama.

* * * * *

Translation of a Draft of a Petition to be addressed to the Emperor of China by the Rajah of Nepaul, enclosed in Ummer Sing's Letter from Rajgurh, dated 2d March 1815.

I yield obedience to the Emperor of China, and no one dare invade my dominions; or if any power has ventured to encroach on my territory, through your favour and protection I have been able to discomfit and expel them. Now, however, a powerful and inveterate enemy has attacked me, and as I owe allegiance to you, I rely on obtaining your assistance and support. From Khunka to the Sutleje, for a thousand coss, war is waging between us. Entertaining designs upon Bhote, the enemy endeavours to get possession of Nepaul, and for these objects he has fomented a quarrel and declared war. Five or six great actions have already been fought; but through the fortune and glory of your Imperial Majesty, I have succeeded in destroying about twenty thousand of the enemy. But his wealth and military resources are great, and he sustains the loss without receding a step. On the contrary, numerous reinforcements continue to arrive, and my country is invaded at all points. Though I might obtain a hundred thousand soldiers from the hills and plains, yet without pay they cannot be maintained; and though I have every desire to pay them, I have not the means. Without soldiers I cannot repel the enemy. Consider the Goorkas as your tributaries: reflect that the English come to conquer Nepaul and Bhote, and for these reasons be graciously pleased to assist us with a sum of money, that we may levy an army and drive forth the invaders. Or, if you are unwilling to assist us with subsidies, and prefer sending an army to our aid, 'tis well. The climate of

288

Dhurma is temperate, and you may easily send an army of two or three hundred thousand men by the route of Dhurma into Bengal, spreading alarm and consternation among the Europeans as far as Calcutta. The enemy has subjugated all the Rajahs of the plains, and usurped the throne of the King of Delhi, and therefore it is to be expected, that these would all unite in expelling the Europeans from Hindostan. By such an event your name will be renowned throughout Jumboodweep, and wherever you may command, the whole of its inhabitants will be forward in your service. Should you think that the conquest of Nepaul, and the forcible separation of the Goorkas from their dependence on the Emperor of China, cannot materially affect your Majesty's interests, I beseech you to reflect that, without your aid, I cannot repulse the English; that these are the people who have already subdued all India, and usurped the throne of Delhi; that, with my Army and resources I am quite unable to make head against them; and that the world will henceforth say, that the Emperor of China abandoned to their fate his tributaries and dependants. I acknowledge the supremacy of the Emperor of China above all other Potentates on earth. The English, after obtaining possession of Nepaul, will advance by the routes of Budrenauth and Maunsurwar, and also by that of Deggurcheh, for the purpose of conquering Lassa; I beg, therefore, that you will write an order to the English, directing them to withdraw their forces from the territory of the Goorka State, which is tributary and dependant upon you, otherwise that you will send an Army to our aid. I beseech you, however, to lose no time in sending assistance whether in men or money, that I may drive forth the enemy and maintain possession of the mountains, otherwise in a few years he will be master of Lassa.

*   *   *   *   *

From Ummer Sing, Ram Doss Urjun, and Bhopaul Thappa, to General Beem Sing and Kajee Rundoz, dated Raj Gurh, 1st March 1815.

I have sent this letter enclosed in a bamboo (Nepalee hill-bamboo) in consequence of which I have not room to say much, but refer you for particulars to my address to the Rajah. When the Emperor of China invaded our country, we succeeded in repulsing him by the prayers of the Brahmins and the favour of heaven. (The remainder is nearly verbatim of what is stated in the letter to the Rajah on this subject.)

u

APPENDIX V

CAPTAIN THOMAS SMITH'S ELEPHANT

———————— ❀ ————————

CAPTAIN Thomas Smith of the 15th Bengal Native Infantry was commanding the Resident's escort at Kathmandu from 1841 to 1845 during the time of Brian Hodgson and Henry Lawrence. In his book published in 1852, *Residence at Nepaul*, he tells the story of one of his elephant hunts. It must be remembered that Captain Smith challenged this mad elephant with muzzle-loading 'rifles' charged with black powder, and that he 'fought it out' on foot.

'The elephant whose death I am about to describe was eleven feet four inches in stature. His head and tusks were in the possession of the late Earl of Derby, at Knowsley Park, near Liverpool; and, as his lordship's splendid collection there was open to the public, any one wishing to satisfy himself of the battering required by an Indian elephant before he bites the dust could inspect the specimen to which I refer. I can well remember that he fought me for two hours before I killed him. . . .

'. . . the Rajah asked me at an audience if I thought I should be able to kill a wild elephant. I answered in the affirmative, when he added; "But I wish you to understand that the elephant I allude to is a fearful shaitan (devil): he has been musth for many years!". . . . His Highness added that his elephant-catching had been entirely put a stop to by the animal in question, and that no one dared to go into that part of the forest in which he took up his quarters. I replied that in elephant shooting I had acquired but little experience, having at that time killed but one, an unfortunate wretch, about fifteen years old, who, either from stupidity or fright, would not get out of my way, and that I had brought him down with the third shot. The Rajah then said that as he had given me permission (which was the first that had been granted to an English officer) to sport in his forests, I ought to endeavour to render an important service to Nepaul, and that I certainly should do so if I succeeded in destroying this elephant.

290

'I immediately undertook the trial, and promised to do my best; but, upon taking leave, the Rajah said: "I am not quite in earnest about that elephant, and would rather you should not go near him; for two years ago, I sent down a couple of guns, six-pounders, to destroy him, but the party, after firing two shots at, and missing him, had to run for their lives, leaving the two six-pounders, which the elephant amused himself by upsetting." I told His Highness that, as the elephant had already destroyed so many human beings (native reports had stated upwards of one hundred, though I considered the number to have been greatly overrated), I had made up my mind to encounter this animal. The Rajah thereupon appointed two native chiefs, named Sirdar Bowanee Sing and Sirdar Delhi Sing, the reputed Nimrods of Nepaul, to accompany me. . . . We took our departure the following day. I had my own usual battery of two double-barrelled rifles, one single rifle carrying a three-ounce ball, and three first-rate double guns. . . . On the day following this last event, whether out of revenge or from an anxious desire to stand well with their sovereign, the two chiefs courageously proposed that we should go at once to destroy the Shikar Bassa, or famous wild elephant. They both promised faithfully to support me, vowing to stand by, even to their toe-nails (a favourite Indian expression), alleging that their honour was at stake, and without some such finale, they dare not shew their faces at Court again. . . .

'The morning dawned splendidly; we were all in excellent spirits. While we were examining our guns and carefully arranging our ammunition the savage Shikar Bassa elephant was marked down, having been discovered in his usual retreat. In order if possible to render the deity Goruck more wrathful, he had only the day before destroyed a Brahmin for firing a matchlock ball into the elephant's side; the Brahmin having been provoked to do so by the elephant destroying and eating up two fields of rice for his own private amusement. I saw the poor priest's mangled remains close to his hut; not a vestige of humanity remained, so frightfully had the brute trampled on and kneaded his body that not a bone escaped uncrushed; legs, arms and carcass could only be compared to some disgusting, indescribable mass, well pounded and furnished with a skin covering. This exhibition excited my anger, and I vowed the destruction of the destroyer.

'I had in my establishment some old and well-tried Shikarees, (beaters), who had witnessed some startling occurrences during our intercourse with the animal kingdom. One of them, dubbed Jack, was a low caste fellow, but when under the influence of arrack, he was very courageous

291

and a firm believer in the transmigration of souls. I sent for Jack, who appeared as usual well impregnated, though his nervous system was somewhat influenced by the sudden epidemic of alarm, which had already attacked the natives of the higher caste. Jack could sport a little English, and after being duly informed as to what would be required of him, he said, "By Gar captino dis dam job; dis elerfant de divil; kill captin sure enuf." Upon my asking him if he was prepared to stand by me, he vowed he would, simply remarking that by that time tomorrow he should be a grazing bullock, and hoped he should have a good master.

'At daylight the next morning, I was up, and found some two hundred Taroos had come in during the night. . . . Accustomed to almost daily encounters with wild elephants, the Taroos have little to fear, but they all expressed the utmost dread of this Shikar Bassa elephant, declaring their conviction of its being neither possible to take nor to destroy him. After a long consultation it was decided that the operations should be commenced by the two famous tame male elephants employed in the taking expeditions. They were the finest animals of the kind I have ever seen, both being ten feet and a half at the shoulder and in the highest condition. Their respective names were Arang Bahadoor and Motee Persaud, the latter with only one tusk and noted for his courage.

'At eight o'clock in the morning of the 7th of March 1844, we started from the tents, and at the expiration of an hour we arrived at the place where this monster was to be found. Never shall I forget the scene! Upon our coming within a few yards of his position, Motee Persaud was leading, when out rushed the wild elephant with a terrific whistle, and immediately commenced a furious attack upon Motee. The meeting of these two mountains of flesh was really grand. Motee stood the shock well, but in ten minutes it was quite evident the wild one was master; they crossed their tusks and pushed at each other like infuriated rams. Upon Motee giving way a general shout was raised by about three hundred voices. I immediately got off my elephant, followed by my five gun carriers, and fired a three ounce ball into the wild one's flank; he gave a hideous roar, eased his purchase on Motee Persaud, and retired to his quarters. A general scamper now took place. Away went the chiefs and Taroos (the former had never dismounted) with Motee Persaud at their heels, and after going about two miles at a rattling pace, Motee was secured with some difficulty and fastened to a tree.

'I now determined upon attacking the brute on foot, Jack and my other attendants standing by me, though much disappointed that I had not joined in the general flight. The enemy soon showed symptoms of

292

the humour he was in by tearing down branches of the trees, and dashing them in all directions; many of them were thicker than my body. Shortly afterwards about twenty tame buffaloes which were grazing in the neighbourhood, and probably disturbed by the Taroos' elephants, came galloping across the plain near the monster's position. I saw him issuing from the forest and in an instant he trampled one of the buffaloes to death, crushing every bone in his body; he then lifted another off the ground with the greatest ease, driving his tusks through and through him, and throwing the carcase to some distance, quite dead. He once more retreated to his cover, and in a few minutes I advanced to the attack; when within a hundred yards of him, out he came with that peculiarly shrill whistle, which must be heard from a wild elephant to be appreciated. He made his appearance with an enormous branch of a tree in his trunk, holding it well up over his head. His rush was splendid, and stopping at about sixty yards from me, he hesitated what to do; whisking the branch about and kicking up the ground with his fore and hind feet with astonishing force. I certainly did not like his appearance but it was now too late, so hostilities commenced. I first gave him the benefit of my old well-tried double rifle, and discharged the right barrel as true as the branch he was holding to the centre of his forehead would allow me to direct it. The ball stung him sharply; he dropt the branch as if it had been a red-hot poker; shook his enormous head and roared violently. I now had a clear look at him; the hole made in his forehead by the ball annoyed him exceedingly; he turned up his trunk to examine the wound, sucked out the blood, and throwing it over his head and shoulders, appeared to experience considerable astonishment. I was not at all disposed to allow him much reflection, for fear he might prove troublesome, and as he was standing still, I favoured him with the left barrel, this time well planted just into the bump of his trunk, where it rises out of the head. As there was nothing to intercept my sight, this shot brought him upon his knees, in which position he remained just long enough to enable me to reload. On getting up he turned wildly about, looking for me, and upon discovering my position, came down towards me at an awful pace. Anticipating this movement, I had my three ounce rifle prepared for his reception, and allowed him to come within twenty yards, when I sent the ball again into his forehead which stopped him short; he began to stagger and roll about as if drunk, turned round three or four times, again felt over his bleeding forehead, sucking out pints of blood with his trunk, and showering it over his head and body which, originally black, had now been changed to a deep scarlet.

'The fight up to this time had been carried on in the dry bed of the Raptee River, without a bush between us, and with a dense jungle on either side, so finding him a much thicker-headed and more disagreeable antagonist than I had inwardly bargained for, I considered it prudent to retreat into the jungle on my right, taking up my position behind a large tree. Not many minutes had elapsed ere he missed me and rushing down to the spot where he had last seen me, he began to hunt me out. Elephants possess a very keen sense of smell through the proboscis, but the blood was now streaming through the interior of that organ, which sadly perplexed his endeavours to sniff me out. By hard blowing he partially cleared the trunk, and discovering a clue to his opponent, came straight to the tree behind which I was concealed. I had no time to lose, I therefore treated him to a salute from the right and left barrels in quick succession; the last shot, from his shaking head at the first, glanced off the bone and scooped out his right eye, the pain of which drove him nearly mad. He spun himself round in intense agony; his roars were appalling and he dug up the ground with his feet to an extent that, if described, would appear an exaggeration to those who have not seen an elephant, particularly an enraged one, in the act of performing that operation. His small eye hung from the socket, I therefore determined to manoeuvre on his blind side and ply him well with lead.

'I had fought him for an hour and a half. Now, a scorching sun and a fast, are *rather* trying; indeed, I had almost had enough of it, and began devoutly to wish that the beast would either take to his heels or allow me to take to mine. The brute, unfortunately, was in no such humour. It is a notorious fact that when two wild elephants meet in a musth state, they never separate till one or the other is destroyed. Their fight sometimes lasts for a week, when the one who possesses the greatest physical capacity for fasting will destroy the other. Large male carcasses are thus frequently discovered by the elephant catchers, and their tusks are turned to a profitable account.

'I was now greatly exhausted and blown, retreating after every shot to a fresh tree, the elephant invariably following me up. In a hurry I took up a position behind a tree which I should not have selected had I not been so fatigued. My opponent being from his wounds slow in pursuit enabled me to recover my wind, and while so it struck me I had occupied a bad position, the tree not being much thicker than my body. I immediately retreated to another tree a few yards off, affording much better cover, and fortunate it was I did so, for I had barely taken up my new ground when the elephant again commenced hunting me up, and when within four yards of the tree I had just quitted, he stopped, and putting his trunk out after clearing it and scenting for some minutes, made a terrific rush. But this was fortunately nearly his last. On coming up to the tree he made sure I was behind it, and encircling it with his trunk he endeavoured to break it down. Failing in this, he half leaned, but in a very exhausted state, against the tree, and after two more efforts tore it up by the roots and cast it down. Evidently making sure that I was under it, he now knelt down and commenced driving his tusks into both sides of the tree, flattering himself that he was probing my carcass. I was only a few yards from him during this operation. Having considerably revived, I determined upon acknowledging his good intentions. Stepping from behind the tree I had occupied while he was employed in his humane undertaking, I fired four shots successively into his forehead, which, however, stunned him. On reviving he stuck his tusks heavily into the ground, and remained motionless for some minutes. I began to hope he was dead, and retreated to another position to reload.

'My mouth was in a fearful state from thirst, my lips and tongue so cracked and parched, that they were bleeding profusely. The monster to my disgust, again got up, but now very weak and rolling about as if he had been indulging, *ad libitum*, in gin and leaden bitters. He staggered back with some difficulty, reached a tree, which he leant against. Jack, now, for the first time during the encounter, spoke, or rather, shouted, "By Gar, Captin, him going." I began to think so, and stepped out to within three yards of him. He made two very drunken attempts to come at me, and I plied him well with lead, so that he again reeled up against the tree. I retreated to re-load and had barely done so, when, to my great annoyance, I saw him moving again towards me, but now very feebly. He could hardly walk. I fired another shot at him, when he stopped, staggered, quietly drew his hind legs under him, then his fore, dropped his head heavily, and drove his tusks up to the roots in the ground, and then remained motionless. After waiting a quarter of an hour at least, during which time he never moved, we all agreed he was dead, and I proposed that Jack should go and ascertain the fact. To this Jack strongly objected. I then moved up and fired at the monster. The shot did not disturb him.

'I again proposed that Jack should go and pull his tail to ascertain if he was dead or merely feigning; Jack demurred, however, at this. I promised to stand by him and protect him. He then declared that he, Jack, had been dead himself at least six times during the encounter; and that if I wanted to kill him outright, I had better shoot him at once. . . .

'Thus died the savage Shikar Bassa elephant, for ten years the terror of that part of the Nepaul forest. . . . For killing this elephant I was presented in open Durbar, by the Rajah and heir apparent, with a handsome Khillut, or dress of honour, which was of great value, but which, of course, I was obliged, after wearing a few hours, to make over to the British Treasury in Nepaul, where all presents, according to the invariable custom at every British Residency, are annually sold, and the proceeds placed to the credit of the Treasury.'

APPENDIX VI

THE GURKHA BRIGADE

———————— ❋ ————————

THIS famous 'Brigade' in the British-Indian service consisted of ten Rifle Regiments, each of two Battalions. The first three Regiments were raised in 1815 during the British war with Nepal. The last of these regiments, the 10th Gurkha Rifles, was finally established in 1908, its first battalion having been raised in 1890 from the Kubo Valley Police Battalion in Burma. One regiment, the 2nd, became a rifle regiment in 1858; the remainder, either in 1891 or as they were brought into the Gurkha Brigade.

Until 1947, the officer cadre, ... 2nd Lieutenant and upwards, ... was British. These officers, like the Gurkhas who served them, often followed, generation by generation, from father to son on the father's or the mother's side. The Brigade was thus to some extent a family affair and to a great extent, like so many other regiments of that magnificent Service, the Indian Army, a collection of officers whose family traditions were those of the Indian services, civil and military, stretching back for close on two hundred years.

During the two World Wars all twenty regular battalions saw much active service and their war-time battalions, the third and fourth battalions, had their fair share of fighting, particularly in the Second World War in Burma. In 1947, at the time of the grant to India of independence, the old Gurkha Brigade was unfortunately broken up; four of its regiments, the 2nd, 6th, 7th, and 10th, passing to the British Army and the other six Regiments, the 1st, 3rd, 4th, 5th, 8th and 9th, to the Indian Army. Those which passed to the British Army are known as 'The Gurkha Brigade'. These Regiments have been the mainstay of British operations against the Communist rebels in Malaya. Those that passed to the Indian Army have in many cases been serving on the Pakistan 'frontier' in Kashmir.

The full list of the Regiments of the old British-Indian Gurkha Brigade which existed up to August 1947 is as follows:

1st King George V Own Gurkha Rifles (The Malaun Regiment). Raised at Sabatthu, near Simla, by Lieut. R. Ross in early 1815, from hillmen, mainly Kumaonis and Garhwalis, who had fought under the Gurkha Kaji (General) Amar Sing Thapa against Sir David Ochterlony in the operations ending with Amar Sing's surrender of the fortress of Malaun. The home cantonment of this Regiment was later sited at Dharmsala in the Himalayas.

2nd King Edward VII Own Gurkha Rifles (The Sirmoor Rifles). Raised at Nahan, Sirmoor, in early 1815, by Lieut. F. Young, from men of the same races as in the 1st Gurkha Rifles, who were captured by the British during the war with Nepal and held in the camps in Sirmoor and Dehra Doon. This Regiment's 'home' was at Dehra Doon, at the foot of the Himalayas.

3rd Queen Alexandra's Own Gurkha Rifles. Raised at Almora, Kumaon, in early 1815 by Lieut. Sir R. Colquhoun, Bt., from hillmen who took service with the British after the conquest of Kumaon by Colonel Jasper Nicolls during the Nepal War. This Regiment may well claim to be in fact the oldest of the Gurkha Brigade by a month or two, for its beginnings were in late 1814 when Colonel Gardner was assailing Almora. However, officially it was raised by Colquhoun a few days after the 1st and 2nd. Its 'home' was at Almora.

4th Prince of Wales' Own Gurkha Rifles. Raised at Pithoragarh, Kumaon, ten miles from the Nepal border, in 1857, by Lieut. D. Macintyre as the Extra Gurkha Regiment, renamed the 4th Gurkha Regiment in the same year. Its 'home' was at Bakloh in the Himalaya, close to the hill station of Dalhousie.

5th Royal Gurkha Rifles. Raised in 1857 at Abbottabad in the North West Frontier Province, on the borders of Hazara, by Captain H. W. F. Boisragon as the Hazara Gurkha Battalion. This Regiment was the only one of the Gurkha Brigade to belong to the old Punjab Frontier Force, sometimes known as 'The Piffers'. Its 'home' was at Abbottabad.

6th Gurkha Rifles. This is one of the old Assam Regiments. Raised by Captain S. Fraser at Chaubiaganj in Cuttack, Orissa, in 1817 as the Cuttack Legion. In 1828 it became the Assam Local Light Infantry and in 1886, the 42nd Gurkha Light Infantry. Its 'home' was later at Abbottabad alongside the 5th.

298

7th Gurkha Rifles. One of the Burma Battalions. Raised in 1902 at Thayetmyo in Burma by Major E. Vansittart as the 8th Gurkha Rifles. Its 'home' was eventually in Quetta, Baluchistan.

8th Gurkha Rifles. Another of the old Assam Regiments. Raised at Sylhet in Assam in 1824 by Captain P. Dudgeon as the Sylhet Local Battalion. In 1886 it became the 44th Gurkha Light Infantry. The 2nd Battalion was raised in 1835 by Captain W. Simonds as the Assam Sebundy Corps, later to become the 43rd Gurkha Light Infantry. This is the oldest of the 2nd Battalions of the Gurkha Brigade. Its 'home' was at Shillong.

9th Gurkha Rifles. One of the old Bengal Battalions. Raised at Fatehgarh in the United Provinces in 1817 by Major C. S. Fagan as the Fatehgarh Levy. Became the 9th Gurkha Rifles in 1901. Its 'home' was later established at Dehra Doon alongside the 2nd.

10th Princess Mary's Own Gurkha Rifles. One of the Burma battalions. Raised in 1890 by Lt.-Colonel C. R. Macgregor as the 1st Burma Infantry. In 1895 became the 1st Burma Gurkha Rifles. Its 'home' was at first at Maymyo in Burma, later at Quetta.

The 7th and 10th Gurkhas recruited from Eastern Nepal, among the Kiranti tribes, mainly Limbus and Rais; the 9th, from Khas Gurkhas of Western and Central Nepal. The other seven Regiments drew their men from the Magar and Gurung clans of Western Nepal.

In giving a list of the Victoria Crosses won by men of the Gurkha Regiments, it would be invidious to mention the units to which they belonged. The honour of their achievements goes to the Gurkha Brigade in which they were all proud to serve.

It was in 1911 that the Gurkha Ranks of the Gurkha Brigade first became eligible for the grant of the Victoria Cross. The occasion was the visit of King George V to India. In 1915 they won their first V.C. Here is a list of the recipients of that decoration, probably the most coveted award for bravery in the whole world.

1915.	France.	Rifleman Kulbir Thapa.
1918.	Palestine.	Rifleman Karanbahadur Rana.
1943.	Tunisia.	Subadar Lalbahadur Thapa.
1943.	Burma.	Havildar Gaje Ghale.
1943.	Burma.	Rifleman Ganju Lama.
1944.	Burma.	Rifleman Tulbahadur Pun.
1944.	Burma.	Subadar Netrabahadur Thapa.

1944.	Burma.	Naik Agan Sing Rai.
1944.	Italy.	Rifleman Sherbahadur Thapa.
1944.	Italy.	Rifleman Thaman Gurung.	2/10ᵗʰ
1945.	Burma.	Rifleman Bhanbagta Gurung.
1945.	Burma.	Rifleman Lachhiman Gurung.

BIBLIOGRAPHY

Buchanan, F., *An Account of the Kingdom of Nepal and of the Territories Annexed to this Dominion by the House of Gorkha*, 1819.

Kirkpatrick, W. J., *Account of the Kingdom of Nepal*, 1811.

Fraser, J. B., *Journal of a Tour through Part of the Snowy Range of the Himalaya Mountains*, 1820.

Hodgson, B. H., 'On the Administration of Justice in Nepal', *Asiatic Researches*, Vol. XX, Part I, 1836.

'Comparative Vocabulary of the Languages of the Tribes of Nepal', *Miscellaneous Essays on Indian Subjects*.

Essays on the Languages of Nepal and Tibet, 1874.

Egerton, F., *Journal of a Winter's Tour in India with a Visit to the Court of Nepal*, 1852, 2 vols.

'Nepal' in *Blackwood's Magazine*, Vol. LXXII (1852).

Wheeler, J. T., *Short History of India and of the Other Frontier States of Afghanestan, Nepal and Burma*, 1880.

Oldfield, H. A., *Sketches from Nipal Historical and Descriptive, with Anecdotes of Court Life, and Wild Sports of the Country . . . to which is added an Essay on Nipalese Buddhism*, 1880, 2 vols.

Bendall, C., *Journey of Research in Nepal*, 1886.

Temple, Sir R., *Journals Kept in Hyderabad and Nepal*, 1887, 2 vols.

Hunter, Sir W. W., *Life of B. H. Hodgson, British Resident at the Court of Nepal*, 1896.

Quin, E. W., 'Sport in Nepal', *Nineteenth Century*, 1899, Vol. XXVI, p. 60.

Ballantine, H., *On India's Frontier or Nepal, The Gurkhas' Mysterious Land*, 1896.

Uddhava Simha, *The Gurkha Conquest of Arki*. (Punjab Printing Works, Lahore, 1903.)

Lévi, S., *Le Népal, Étude Historique*, 1905. (Paris, Musée Guimet Annales. Bibliothèque d'Études.)

Landor, A. H. S., *Tibet and Nepal Painted and Described*, 1905.

Vansittart, E., *Gurkhas*. (Government Printing Office, 1906.)

Brown, P., *Picturesque Nepal*, 1912.

Massieu, I., *Nepal et Pays himalayens*, 1914.

Gorkha

Cavanagh, Sir O., *Rough Notes on the State of Nepal: its Government, Army and Resources.* (Calcutta, 1851.)

Gimlette, G. H. D., *Nepal and the Nepalese*, 1928.

Wright, D., *Sketch of the Country of Nepal open to Europeans.* (Calcutta, 1872.)

Landon, P., *Nepal*, 1928, 2 vols.
    Lhasa, 1906, 2 vols.

Northey, W. B., *The Land of the Gurkhas or the Himalayan Kingdom of Nepal*, 1937.

Northey, W. B. and Morris, C. J., *The Gurkhas: Their Manners, Customs and Country*, 1928.

Shah, I. A., *Sirdar Saiyad*, 'Nepal: The Home of the Gods', 1938.

Smith, T. *Captain.* 'Narrative of a Five years' residence at Nepaul', 1852, 2 vols.

Bishop, R. N. W., *Unknown Nepal*, 1952.

Boeck, K., *Aux Indes et eu Nepal.* (Paris, 1907.)
    Durch Indien ins verschlossene Land Nepal. (Leipzig, 1903.)
    In Banne des Everest. (Leipzig, 1922.)

David-Neil, A., *Au coeur des Himalayas. Le Nepal.* (Paris, 1949.)
    Im Schatten des Himalayas. (Wiesbaden, 1953.)

Davis. H., *Nepal, Land of Mystery*, 1942.

Filchner, W., *In der Fieberhölle Nepals.* (Wiesbaden, 1951.)

Formichi, C., *Il Nepal.* (Roma, 1934.)

Lobsiger-Dellenbach, M. and others, *Himalaya du Nepal: mission scientifique genevoise.* (Geneva, 1952.)

Oliphant, L., *A Journey to Kathmandu, the Capital of Nepal*, 1852.

Petech, L., *ed., I missionari italiani nel Tibet e nel Nepal*, Pte. 1–5, 5 vols. (In progress.) (Roma, 1952–.)

Adam, L. *The Social Organisation and Customary Laws of the Nepalese Tribes.* (Menasha, 1936.)

Gibbs, H. R. K., *The Gurkha Soldier.* (Calcutta, 1944.)

Prinsep, H., *History of the Political and Military Transactions in India*, 1813–1823.

Papers Regarding the Administration of The Marquis of Hastings in India. (East India Company Publication, 1824.)

The Regimental Histories of the 1st to the 10th Gurkha Rifles.

In addition there are many papers written by B. H. Hodgson on the Mammals and Birds of Nepal. A list of these is given in Appendix XII of Landon's *Nepal.*

Recent publications from Kathmandu:

Regmi, D. R., *Whither Nepal*, 1952.
Purnabahadur, *Nepal Behind the Curtain*, 1953.
Ramraj Poudyal, *Introducing Nepal*, 1955.
Rishikesh Shah, *Nepal and the World*, 1955.

By the Department of Publicity:

Nepal, Marching towards Progress.
One Year of Democracy.
An Introduction to Nepal, 1953.
Nepal at a Glance, 1954.

ENVOY

'As I write these last words my thoughts return to you who were my comrades, the stubborn and indomitable peasants of Nepal. Once more I hear the laughter with which you greeted every hardship. Once more I see you in your bivouac or about your fires, on forced march or in the trenches, now shivering with wet and cold, now scorched by a pitiless and burning sun. Uncomplaining you endure hunger and thirst and wounds, and at last your unwavering lines disappear into the smoke and wrath of battle. Bravest of the brave, most generous of the generous, never had country more faithful friends than you.'

PROFESSOR R. L. TURNER in the Preface to his
Dictionary of the Nepali Language

INDEX

Index

Index

Index

India
  Nepal, relations with (*contd.*):
    trade route and market for, 100; failure
    to agree on commercial treaty, 101;
    Nepalese invasion of India conspiracy
    (1840), 106; efforts to renew friendship,
    107; Jang Bahadur visits (1850), 139;
    (1874–5), 160; Rana Udip visits (1880),
    163; close friendship, 164; position of
    Maharajah *vis-à-vis* the Viceroy, 169;
    Bir Shamsher visits, 169; relations based
    on Nepalese loan of her men, 175; trade
    treaty (1923), 179; India pledges sup-
    port for Nepal against China, 190;
    Nepalese regiments in garrison (1914–
    1918), 194; Nepalese battalions offered
    for Indian defence (1938–39), 212; con-
    tingent arrives in India (1940), 212;
    contingent mutinies, 207–8, 212; com-
    munication re-established with India
    (1942), 215–16; border position in 1945,
    231; Indian attitude to Nepal after in-
    dependence, 232, 239, 248–50, 256;
    invasion of Nepal from India (1950),
    245–50, 254–7, 258; value of resources
    to India, 249; recognises King of Nepal
    as supreme authority (1950), 251, 256–7;
    treaties with Nepal, 255; King of Nepal
    removed to India, 260–1; King returns
    to Nepal (1951), 261; armed police sent
    to Nepal, 262; missions in Nepal, 268;
    present relations with Nepal, 268–9
  Russian invasion, rumoured (1838), 99
  Tibet, relations with, 18; invasion of
    India, 18; direct communication, 187
Indian Army, Gurkha regiments in: *see*
  Gurkha Regiments
Indian Congress Party, 215, 216, 233, 235,
  245–8, 251, 252
Indian Mutiny, 94, 100, 107, 151–8
Indian Nationalist Party, 254
Indian Political Service, 96
Indian States, 248–9, 261
Indo-China, Gurkhas in, 230
Indonesia, Gurkhas in, 230
Indra-Jatra festival, 52, 260
Industrial development, 168, 184, 210–11
Ipi, Faqir of, 216
Iraq, Gurkhas in, 217
Irregulars, raising authorised, 86
Italy, Chandra Shamsher visits, 189; Gurkhas
  in, 219, 227–30

Jagardhan Rai, 225
Jagat Jang, 162–7, 174
Jagat Jaya Malla, 24
Jagat Shamsher, 112, 138–40, 142, 148
Jagatbahadur, 229
Jaibahadur, 218
Jaitha-Burra, 274
Jaithak, 83, 85, 86, 88, 128
Jalap-La pass, 5, 6, 172
Jaman Sing, 197
Janata, 207
Jang Bahadur Konwar, 111
Jang Bahadur Rana, parentage, 70, 112; early
  life and character, 112–18; kills 'must'
  elephant, 114; plot against, 116; shoots
  Mathbar Sing, 118; carries on administration, 123; relations with the Maharani, 123–33; and Kot massacre, 126–30;
  appointed Prime Minister, 128–9;
  further plots against, 130–3, 135, 142–3,
  146; reign as Prime Minister, 133–6;
  visits England (1850), 137–41; returns
  to Nepal (1851), 141–2; Oliphant's
  assessment of, 143–7; marriages, 145,
  147, leniency, 147; and Tibet, 148;
  resigns as Prime Minister, 149; offered
  the Crown, 149; accepts title of Maharajah, 149–50; resumes as Prime Minister,
  150; and Indian Mutiny (1857), 151–2,
  156–8; tributes to his rule, 157; supreme
  authority in Nepal, 158–9; receives
  British and Chinese honours (1860),
  159, 188; withdraws into isolation, 159;
  sets out for second trip to England
  (1874), 159–60; passes through India;
  accident at Bombay postpones trip to
  England, 160; returns to Kathmandu,
  160; entertains Prince of Wales (1876),
  160; death (1877), 160–2; ten sons, 162,
  163, 166; loyalty to Britain, 173; and
  marriage of Ranas, 177, 253; and *suttee*,
  179–80; and slavery, 180, 181
Jaunpore, 155, 156
Java, Gurkhas in, 230
Jaya Prakash Malla, 24, 46–53
Jaya Singh Rama, King, 22
Jayanagar, 211
Jhanga, 148
Jil Rais, 39–40
Jit Jang, 165–6
Jit Shamsher, 166
Jitbahadur Rai, 228

Index

Index

Manik, 40, 42
Manipore, 172
Manjusri, 10, 13
Manmath Ranaji Rava, 29
Mao Tse-tung, 250, 269
Marley, General, 74, 75, 80, 83, 88
Marsiangdi river, 6, 43
Martindell, General, 82-3
Mathbar Sing Thapa, 95, 98, 101-3, 110-18, 123-5, 134, 144, 162
Maude, General, 197
Maurya kings, 11, 14
Maya, 14-15, 49
Medical services, 232, 236, 254
Meerut, 74, 151, 152
Mercer, Captain C. A., 174, 175, 220
Mesopotamia, Gurkhas in, 195-7
Michael Angelo, Father, 51, 52
Minabahadur Rana, 224
Mincha, 30, 34
Mithila, Kingdom of, 11
Mitralal Thapa, 199
Mohan Shamsher, Maharajah, 177, 205-6, 242-4, 255-6, 260-5
Mohindra Rai, 53
Moira, Lord: see Hastings, Marquis of
Monte Cassino, 227-8
Morang, 22, 40, 57, 58, 79, 210
Morley, Lord, 177
Motilal Thapa, 195
Motor-cars in Nepal, 211
Mrigendra Shamsher Rana, General, 263, 266
Muhammed bin Tughlak, 21-2
Mukhti Sena: see Raksha Dal
Muktinath, 6, 147
Municipal boards, 235, 236, 242
Murder, Nepalese attitude to, 124, 146, 163
Murmis, 271-2
Muslims, 21-2, 39, 246
Mussoorie, 74, 170

Naga Vasa Lake, 10
Nagas, 248
Nahan, 64, 74, 78, 83
Nairs, 11, 102
Nalapani, 74, 82
Namr Srong Btsan, 17
Nanda Deva, King, 11, 19, 22
Nanda Devi, 1
Nanga La, 5
Narain, Jai Prakash, 233
Narain Hatti, 166, 169, 170

Naraini river, 249
Narbhupal, King, 24, 42, 44
Narendra Deva, King, 18
Nasiri Battalion, 86, 87, 120, 151, 155
Naskatipore, 52
National Congress (amalgamation of N.C.C. and N.D.C.), 246-7, 255-6, 259-67
Nawakote, 7, 19-20, 23-4, 44-9, 99, 179, 271
Ne Muni, 10, 11, 13
Nehru, Pandit Jawaharlal, 234, 251, 255-7, 260, 261, 269
Nepal, Kingdom of (see also names of subjects and persons throughout index), expansion since 1768 and present area, 1; borders, 1, 4, 5; original inhabitants, 10; origin of name, 10, 11; early history, 11-15, 16-25, 27; divided into three kingdoms, 22-3, 50; Prithwi founder of modern Nepal, 55, 56; hereditary Prime Minister with authority over the King, 149-50; parts of the Terai returned to after the Indian Mutiny, 157, 159; influx of mutineers from India, 158; Jang Bahadur's reforms, 158-9; death of Jang Bahadur (1877), 160; reforms under Rana Udip, 168; Bir Shamsher's administration, 169; foreign relations based on loan of her men, 175; Chandra Shamsher's achievements, 177-9; maintained as buffer state, 231; political strike at jute mills (1947), 234, 241, 245, 251; agitation fostered from within and without, 234, 237, 242-3, 250-1; proposed reforms, 235-6; riots (1950), 241, 245; invasion from India (1950), 245, 247-7, 250, 254-8; value of resources to India, 249; King recognised as head of the State (1950), 251, 256-7, 261; revolution leading to downfall of the Ranas, 254, 258-65; administration since the revolution, 254-5, 258, 265-70; hereditary premiership terminated (1951), 263
Nepal Valley, extent, 1, 7; travel restricted within, 2; difficulty of access, 8-9; anciently a lake, 10; religion, 12, 19; history, 13-15, 19-20, 42, 44; tribes, 31, 36, 38; Gurkha invasion, 48-54; united under one king, 54; hostility to Ranas and Gurkhas, 235; position in 1950, 259; political ferment, 270
Nepalese Army: see Army

Index